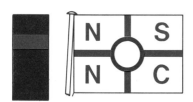

Neptune S.N. Co. Ltd

Metcalfe Shipping Co. Ltd.

Prince Line Ltd.
Rio Cape Line Ltd.

Houlder Line Ltd.
British Empire S.N. Co. Ltd.
Empire Transport Co. Ltd.
Ore Carriers Ltd.

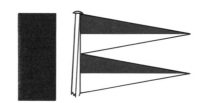

British & Argentine S.N. Co. Ltd.

Furness-Houlder Argentine
Lines Ltd.

Alexander Shipping Co. Ltd.

Warwick Tanker Co. Ltd.

Dee Navigation Ltd.

Ocean Gas Transport Ltd.

'K' Shipping Co. Ltd.

Shaw, Savill & Albion Co. Ltd.

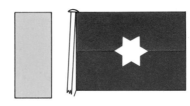

Aberdeen & Commonwealth Line Ltd.

Crusader Shipping Co.

Royal Mail Lines Ltd.

Pacific S.N. Co.

Cairn Line of Steamships Ltd.

FURNESS WITHY

1891 — 1991

The Furness Withy Coat of Arms
(see page 137)

FURNESS WITHY

The centenary history of
Furness, Withy and Company, Ltd
1891 - 1991

David Burrell

WORLD SHIP SOCIETY
KENDAL

Endpapers: Houseflags and Funnel markings of some of the Furness Withy Group companies.

Published in Great Britain by The World Ship Society, 28 Natland Road, Kendal, LA9 7LT.

ISBN 0 905617 70 3

Printed by William Gibbons & Sons Ltd, Wolverhampton WV10 0JA

CONTENTS

ERRATA

page 129, line 5: Insert cross reference page 141.

page 147:   The photograph of Frank Charlton actually depicts C. W. Warwick.

page 152:   The picture caption date should be 1981. This vessel, previously Dart America, was owned in Hong Kong and managed by Furness Withy (Shipping) Ltd.

FOREWORD

Royal Mail, Pacific Steam Navigation Company, Houlder Brothers and Shaw Savill, all founded between 1830 and 1860, each had their history written on attaining their 100th birthday. We could not therefore let this landmark pass for Furness, Withy and Company, Ltd without similarly going into print, since it was for almost all of its first 100 years the ultimate parent of the Group.

The History of Furness Withy is essentially a story of many individual companies. In 1972 the then Chairman, Lord Beeching, described the Group as "a loose collection of warring tribes". He was right of course, and I do not suppose Furness Withy was very different from many other shipping groups at that time. Rationalisation has been the name of the game since then both within and outside the Company, and many household names have gone from the Shipping scene.

Containerisation has led to the age of cooperation within "consortia" and this has enabled numerous operators to remain within various trades. This era is now showing signs of ending, from which only those who can truly benefit from economy of scale will survive in the fiercely competitive world of moving boxes around the world. We look forward to the future as part of Hamburg-Sud and the Oetker Group.

I am sure that shipping in every facet of the activity, will continue to be one of the most fascinating and fulfilling careers open to young men and women. The industry will, as it always has done, have room for the entrepreneur. To judge the future, it helps to understand the past, so I trust those embarking on their careers, as well as all other readers, will find this history of interest.

J E Keville
Chairman and Managing Director
Furness, Withy and Company, Ltd

INTRODUCTION

In 1891 Furness, Withy and Company, Ltd was registered to amalgamate the shipowning and shipbuilding interests of Christopher Furness. In the century since, the company has passed through many transformations in meeting the challenge of the time.

When steamers were first built for Furness, in 1876, they were ancillary to the provision business, and remained so until 1882 when Christopher Furness assumed control of them, leaving the provision side to his brother.

Shortly afterwards, Furness purchased control of the Withy shipyard and, until the merger in 1891, shipping remained a relatively small operation. The number of new and second-hand ships passing through the fleet gives a misleading impression of size, in fact shipping was probably well overshadowed by shipbuilding. After the merger in 1891, shipping grew in importance with increasing interest in the North Atlantic liner trade. Manchester Liners and British Maritime Trust were part of this, but shipbuilding and marine engineering probably retained a premier role.

Had not the International Mercantile Marine been formed in 1902, it is likely Furness Withy would have become a major passenger line. Instead, they withdrew and concentrated on bulk trades, with some liner routes such as those of Manchester Liners. During this period efforts to develop new liner trades largely came to nothing.

With the purchase of Houlder Brothers (1911), Johnston Line (1914) and Prince Line (1916) came a dramatic change. These companies added extensive liner interests, although bulk trades were still important.

During World War I, the shipyards were sold. The 1919 management buyout broke the links not only with the Furness family, but also the new shipyard and the coal, steel and engineering undertakings which Furness had controlled. Post-war efforts went to developing liner trades, rather than bulk. The Depression saw many tramp ships sold; the Group assumed the cargo liner character of the next forty years.

After 1960, trade patterns changed, container ships and bulk carriers became the norm. Like similar companies (P & O, Cunard, British and Commonwealth) Furness Withy started to look for a new identity and role. These included partnerships in Overseas Containers Ltd, offshore oil, gas, travel, hotels, cruising and industrial investment. Whilst Overseas Containers and bulk carriers were successful, offshore oil fluctuated with the industry after initial success. In retrospect travel, cruising and leisure give an appearance of piecemeal development rather than a co-ordinated venture.

After 1970 the asset rich Group attracted take-over and fought off predators as it sought a suitable partner. Unlike P & O and Cunard, Furness Withy did not succeed in finding such a marriage partner, and in 1980 an attractive Tung purchase offer was accepted. Initially Furness Withy was unchanged, until the 1985 Tung financial collapse. The rescue operation recognised Furness Withy as a major asset. Reorganisation followed, with compatible areas of Furness Withy being absorbed into Tung's Orient Overseas Container Line. Other sectors, such as offshore and insurance, were sold.

At this stage Furness Withy was much leaner, and encompassed interests outside the main thrust of the Tung empire. Royal Mail Lines, Houlder Brothers and Pacific Steam services to South America, Caribbean services, Prince Line and Manchester Liners' Mediterranean services, Gazocean, the gas carriers of Ocean Gas Transport, the Ecuadorian Gas venture, Furness-Houlder Shipbroking and Furness Withy Australia, plus a small travel organisation remained. These formed the Furness Withy Group when it was sold by Tung to Hamburg-Sud in 1990.

This history of Furness, Withy and Company, Ltd over its first hundred years includes short biographies of the many subsidiary companies who have a role in the history, and also includes some notes on the shipping conditions in which Furness Withy had to operate. The constraint of a volume of this size obviously precludes the inclusion of much more material, hence the interested reader is referred to other published works on Group companies.

ACKNOWLEDGEMENTS

Having commenced my working life in the offices of Royal Mail Lines, I have for long been interested in the history of the Furness Withy Group, although the complexity of their story had a deterrent effect. Hence I greatly appreciate the opportunity afforded me by the Chairman and Directors of Furness, Withy and Company to prepare this Centenary History.

The full story of the Group companies would fill many volumes, hence this work can only outline the history, leaving much for future consideration in works dedicated to individual companies.

At this point I would express my appreciation to the many people, past and present staff and others, who have willingly helped in the preparation. It is an invidious task to decide the value of individual contributions, so most are listed alphabetically below. But several must first be noted, John E Keville as Chairman for his continued interest and encouragement and Sir Brian Shaw, a past chairman. Richard Alexander, Centenary Consultant (formerly Public Relations officer), editor of The Log and my principal contact, and his wife Lesley for her charm and kindness as a hostess. Needless to say The Log and other Group magazines were a goldmine.

Alec Henderson, whose lifelong career in Furness Withy commenced with colleagues who recalled the early days, has always taken a great interest in the Company history, and his name has been associated with articles in Sea Breezes and other publications. He willingly made available to me his unpublished manuscripts which provided both a valued source and base on which to build and, after trying several alternatives, the style of presentation best suited to the complex story of the Group. Dennis Johnzon opened his encyclopaedic data files on Houlder Brothers and Gordon Boyce's unpublished thesis "The Growth and Dissolution of a Large-Scale Business Enterprise; The Furness Interest, 1892-1919" provided a wealth of material. I am also grateful to Edgar Collard and Canada Steamship Lines for access to the unedited manuscript of "Passage to the Sea" (since published). Needless to say published works have been consulted, also such rare material as "Missed Opportunities" by T H Darlington, the 1943 story of the Pacific Steam Navigation Company which was so vigorously suppressed.

D Attenborough; Sir Charles Alexander; R Ayling; C J M Carter; the late T B Casey; N Castelli; L Dunn; I J Farquhar; J A Fisher; R Fuller; J Gawne; J Hill; J M Houlder; M W Hulbert; M Jones; J Lingwood; J S Lingwood; J L Loughran; D McBrien; C Maguire; G N A Murrant; K O'Donoghue; G Penny; J D Pitcairn; T R Pulley; L Sawyer; W A Schell; B R Seton-Winton; B E Spaldin; R Stoker; A J Tennent; P J Warwick. If your name is missing the omission is mine and not intentional, and I tender my apologies.

In addition to individuals, invaluable help has been received from Lloyd's Register of Shipping (Mrs B Jones), Lloyd's of London and Lloyd's of London Press Ltd, the Guildhall Library (Miss J Wraight) — keepers of the Lloyd's Maritime Collection — the Public Record Office, Merseyside Maritime Museum Maritime Records Centre, Gray Art Gallery and Museum, Hartlepool and Hartlepool Library (Miss M E Hoban). The holders of Furness Withy Group archives, the National Maritime Museum (Miss C MacLeod) and City of Southampton Museum (A Forsyth) were most helpful in making material available.

Illustrations are acknowledged where sources are known. Where no acknowledgement is given they are from the Furness Withy Collection with, in many cases, the original sources not now known. As with the list of people whose aid is noted above I would apologise for any omitted or incorrect references: those made are believed to be accurate.

Although preparation of this volume has now been completed, I welcome further material on the Group and member companies which future opportunity may allow to be used.

Finally, and far from least, to my wife, Rosemary, for her forebearance as the files of paperwork multiplied.

Cumnock,
Ayrshire KA18 2QY

July, 1992

1. Small Beginnings—the years to 1891

As Napoleon watched his beloved France slip below the horizon for the last time from the quarterdeck of HMS *Bellerophon*, Hartlepool, a fishing village of some thousand people, nestled sleepily on its narrow peninsula beside a dilapidated harbour. To the south lay the small village of Stranton behind an open beach sweeping away to the horizon and the River Tees. Thirty years later the sand dunes and marshes backing this beach were to become the site of a Victorian industrial New Town which, by the end of the Queen's reign, was to rank as the fifth port of the kingdom. The population of 300 in 1845 had risen to 40,000 in 1888 when the Prince of Wales paid a Royal Visit shortly after the town had achieved borough status. Such was the birth and meteoric rise of West Hartlepool, home to Christopher Furness. He, too, was to develop his business interests on the same scale until he controlled, in 1910, the largest fleet under the Red Ensign, over 300 ships of 1.4 million tons.

Cleveland and Tees-side in the early nineteenth century was largely a rural agricultural district, although, in hind-sight, the Durham coalfield gave a hint of the future. Lack of cheap transport prevented Durham giving serious competition to the coal trade of Tyne and Wear to the north. The catalyst to remedy this appeared with the opening of the Stockton and Darlington Railway in September 1825.

The demand for Durham coal rapidly developed. The first year of the railway saw 18,588 tons loaded into ships at Stockton, and in the second year this grew to 52,290 tons. Naturally, such growth drew the attention of estate owners and industrial developers of pits, railways and ports. Hartlepool soon became the focus of alternative routes avoiding the problems of navigating the lower Tees and coal staithes (loading berths) controlled by competitors. Within a few years the Hartlepool Dock and Railway Company was carrying, and shipping, coal to such good effect that by 1841 it handled twenty seven per cent of the tonnage shipped from north east coast ports.

Other promoters of railway lines sought to use Hartlepool. The Dock and Railway Company were happy to provide facilities for them but, by judicious setting of charges, ensured these new lines could not capture traffic already being carried by the Dock and Railway Company. Such action soon led to alternative facilities being sought and planned by the newcomers.

In May 1844, an Act of Parliament was obtained to promote the Hartlepool West Harbour and Dock Company. So was West Hartlepool born, to absorb and replace the little village of Stranton. The first dock opened on 1 June 1847. Rapidly the new town grew round it, encouraged by Ralph Ward Jackson, chairman of the Harbour and Dock Company. Shiprepairing and shipbuilding soon followed, the first vessel launched being the full-rigged ship *Mirage* in December 1854. Within a decade, West Hartlepool came to rank alongside the old established ports on the coast.

The Furness Family

Amongst those attracted to Hartlepool in 1834 was John Furness, a young bachelor born at Myton-on-Swale in September 1808. Family tradition recalls that the family had left the Furness district of Cumbria rather hurriedly due to Jacobite involvement, selling horses to Bonnie Prince Charlie. The first record we have, however, is of John's grandfather Thomas Furnis (or Furnace) at Middleton Tyas, near Scotch Corner, about 1770. The family were farm labourers, a job abandoned by John Furness when attracted by opportunities in the new industrial Hartlepool. He took up work as a coal trimmer, a profession responsible for the proper and safe stowage of cargo on board ship. Earning the princely wage of fourteen shillings (70p) a week he courted Averill Wilson, the teenage daughter of John Wilson, tenant farmer at Naisbet Hall some four miles north-west of Hartlepool. They were married in February 1835, and had two sons, Thomas (born 1836) and John (1838), before moving south to Haverton Hill-on-Tees where the family continued to grow, Mary Jane (1839), Eliza Wilson (1841), Robert Wilson (1843), Wilson (1845), Stephen (1848) and Alfred (1850).

John Furness prospered and late in 1850 returned north to the booming new town of West Hartlepool, still a coal trimmer by trade. Averill was to present him with the last members of their family in the new home in Lynn Street, Christopher (born 1852) and Eliza Ann (1855). At the same time a little corn merchants business was established in 1854, to which provisions were subsequently added. In this venture he was aided by his teenage sons Thomas and John.

Provision Merchants

Christopher Furness, born on 23 April 1852, grew up with the town burgeoning round him. The tradition that he was the seventh son of the seventh son seems a half truth. He was a seventh son but his father is unlikely to have been. Completing his education at Anderson's Tower Street Academy, he joined the family business as a clerk. Two years later, aged only nineteen, he was dispatched on a task destined to develop into the first stage of a career to fame and fortune. Most of the grain and provisions imported into North East England, to feed the growing industrial population, were purchased from Hamburg. In 1870 Christopher was dispatched to Denmark and Sweden to ascertain if cheaper supplies might be purchased direct. He was in Gothenburg when news reached him of the outbreak of war between France and Germany on 19 June 1870.

War had been brewing in Europe for some time. In Spain the troubled reign of Isabel II had ended in the autumn of 1868, when she was driven from her throne by the dynastic Carlist Civil Wars that had racked the country since 1833. A contender for the vacant throne was Prince Leopold of Hohenzollern-Sigmaringen, a branch of the Prussian royal house. Threat of a future Prussian-Spanish combination against France was enough to cause dismay and opposition in Paris. At the same time in Prussia, Bismarck, the Iron Chancellor, was busy moulding the independent German states into a Prussian dominated German Empire. The Iron Chancellor perceived an opportunity to bring the South German states into the North German Confederation and provoked Napoleon III of France by releasing an edited text of the Ems telegram. Clamour for war grew in both countries and five days later France declared war. It brought disaster after disaster to France, Napoleon surrendered to German forces in early September, the Second Empire fell and the Third Republic was born in a Paris threatened by advancing enemy forces. Shortly after, the siege of Paris commenced, lasting for four months until surrender on 28 January 1871. The armistice that day led to the Treaty of Frankfurt on 10 May 1871, and ended French leadership in Europe. Bismarck achieved his goal of uniting Germany, with Wilhelm I of Prussia proclaimed German Emperor at Versailles on 18 January 1871.

In Gothenburg the immediate effect of the outbreak of war was a glut of grain and produce, while ports filled with unemployed ships diverted from their destinations by the war and a French fleet blockading the Elbe. The trade route from Scandinavia to Hamburg and thence across the North Sea to England was disrupted, bringing with it the real risk of famine.

Christopher Furness quickly realised the opportunity and risk. Unable to communicate with the family at home, he took an important decision on the spot. Purchasing samples of flour he persuaded a local baker to stay up all night and test bake them. Finding the quality suitable, Christopher immediately commenced buying at favourable prices on the glutted market and chartered many of the unemployed ships to load direct for Hartlepool. Famine was avoided at home and, by the time he was able to return to England after the war, a profit of some £55,000 had accrued (probably worth £1.5 million today).

Made a partner in 1872, Christopher was destined to be responsible for the development of a completely new facet to the business. The industrial revolution had developed to the stage that an increasing volume of both foodstuffs and raw materials were required from abroad. From 1867 to 1877 the value of British imports rose from £275 million to £394 million, with foodstuffs taking a large share of the increase. A growing empire of colonies looked to the mother country for support and capital goods to help them develop to the stage of commencing to industrialise themselves. Increasingly the British industrial society was forced to look abroad for foodstuffs. The American midwest prairies were one source and, as the Furness business grew in West Hartlepool, it was natural for the partners to turn their eyes across the Atlantic.

A representative was first sent to America in 1870 and during the years that followed supplies were shipped east. In 1873 a resident agent and office was established at Brantford, Ontario, introducing a name with long Furness Withy associations, as the company telegraphic address, a ship's name and a company title.

Into Shipowning

From being shippers only, it was a logical step to chartering on occasions when the volume of cargo warranted. That this grew and developed into liner service was a logical step, reported on by the South Durham Herald of 17 June 1876:

"Direct Communication between West Hartlepool and Boston, U.S.—Messrs Thomas Furness & Co, wholesale provision dealers, West Hartlepool, have recently commenced to run a line of sailing vessels between West Hartlepool and Boston, U.S. The first ship arrived about three weeks ago, and on Saturday last, the clipper barque Ladnoi (which had made the passage across the Atlantic, a distance of 3,200 miles, in 24 days), reached West Hartlepool, with a miscellaneous cargo of provisions, comprising bacon and hams, maize, lard, and peas, and beans, making the third vessel chartered to Messrs Furness & Co direct from the American city. These vessels will arrive about every three weeks, and, should it be found to answer, the trade will be further developed, and a line of steamers put on as soon as the new docks, now in course of construction at West Hartlepool, are completed, and a sufficient depth of water can be obtained for the accommodation of steamers of a large draught."

These first ships were North American built softwood ships chartered from American owners. The identity of the two earlier arrivals is difficult to confirm, the only arrivals in the Hartlepools in the weeks preceding *Landnoi* (note correct spelling) were *Gratia* (Captain Fredrikson) which arrived at West Hartlepool on 27 May 1876, followed by *Agra* (Captain Steen) on 3 June. Both these ships had timber cargoes from Pensacola whereas *Landnoi* (Captain Aske) arrived from Boston on 10 June with a cargo of foodstuffs.

From the beginning the advantages of steam were appreciated to ensure regular dispatch and arrival of ships and cargo, so the following year the sailing vessels were superseded by chartered steamers, typical of which were the locally built *Hecla* (built 1874, 1,175gt), *Valetta* (1875, 1,327gt) and *Melita* (1877, 1,390gt). *Hecla* was owned by F Herskind, *Valetta* and *Melita* by the shipbuilder William Gray.

By this time Christopher Furness, along with his father and brother, had taken the common path of many businessmen and invested in ships. Whilst no complete record exists of the extent of this family investment, it has been possible to identify four ships concerned, two of which had Christopher and his brother appointed as managing owners.

The first transaction traced was on 23 April 1868 when John Furness, Senior, and John Furness, Junior, each purchased sixteen shares in the brig *Astley* (1839, 206gt). John, Senior, added another eight shares in May 1871 and Christopher sixteen on 30 September 1875. The following month Christopher was appointed managing owner, with 56 of the 64 shares held in the family. The next investment was in the barque *Penelope* (1849, 303gt). John Furness, Junior, took eight shares in May 1867, and Christopher another eight on 28 July 1875—the first identified purchase by Christopher. The following year John, Junior, was registered as the owner of 28 shares in the snow *Williams* (1812, 184gt). He added another four two years later and after Christopher purchased 32 in September 1875 from the estate of Robert Hutchison (giving the brothers full ownership) John was appointed managing owner. The fourth purchase was in early April 1875 when John purchased 24 shares in the brig *Solon* (1849, 164gt), followed by Christopher taking sixteen in September.

These elderly ships, *Williams* was over sixty years old, were unlikely to have been purchased to serve the growing grocery trade of the family. They fit with the pattern of investment in shipping common to a wide range of businessmen. However, it did bring Christopher Furness closer to the shipowning profession and was to lead into the trade with which his name has become inseparably linked.

Now a successful businessman, Christopher decided to set up home and in 1876 married Jane Annette Suggett from the village of Brierton, four miles south of Hartlepool. They were to have only one child, a son Marmaduke who showed little interest in the business until after his father's death, although he had been appointed a director of Furness, Withy and Company, Ltd in 1906. The relationship between Christopher and Marmaduke is said to have been taken by Rudyard Kipling as the basis for his poem "The Mary Gloster".

Solon had only a brief association with John and Christopher Furness, being wrecked at Saltfleet on 13 April 1876. *Penelope* traded until damaged in collision with the steamer *Celeste* off Tynemouth on 31 October 1878. Laid up at Hartlepool until the end of July 1881, she was then taken to Middlesbrough and subsequently sunk in the Tees as a breakwater. *Williams* was reported broken up in December 1882.

Late in October 1880, the country was swept by a violent storm, likened in violence to the storm which had destroyed the Tay Bridge less than a year previously. The East Coast was exposed to the full fury of the gale from the north and east. Friday, 29 October, found wreckage strewn from end to end. Marine losses were estimated at over three hundred lives and £4 million in ships and cargo, over 160 ships having gone to pieces on the British coast. Lifeboats saved 113 lives but sadly the Wells lifeboat capsized, eleven of the crew drowned and only two survived. In the long list of ships lost is *Astley*. On ballast passage from Germany for West Hartlepool, she was driven ashore at Cullercoats. Fortunately Captain Bryson and his crew of six were saved.

First Venture into Steam

The Northern Daily Mail for 20 October 1877, reported:

"Messrs Furness of West Hartlepool have advanced another step in the conduct of their extensive business. Some time ago I mentioned they were chartering sailing ships to bring over the produce purchased by their resident agents in Canada and US and then, that finding the irregularity of this mode of transit unsatisfactory, they had substituted steamers. The *Hecla*, belonging to Messrs Herskind, is due in November and the *Valetta* of Wm Gray in December.

"But Messrs Furness have now resolved to run steamers of their own. They have ordered one of Messrs Gray and Co to be ready for launching in April and contemplate giving her three companions, one immediately and the others by and by. They will thus secure a fortnightly arrival at West Hartlepool and the firm is making arrangements by which it expects to secure a regular cargo outwards.

"Boston is the port on the other side of the Atlantic from which Messrs Furness bring their goods, which are conveyed thither from Chicago and Canada. The American railway companies have given highly favourable terms, their object being to encourage trade between Boston and the North of England, and our own North Eastern might well take a leaf out of their book. Messrs Furness have been led into this enterprise by its saving effects. The entire cost of bringing over a cargo from Boston and delivering

Brantford City, outward bound for the United States flying the Thomas Furness and Company houseflag. *(A Henderson)*

it at their warehouses in West Hartlepool is no more than the landing charges at Liverpool and the carriage to West Hartlepool. Some idea of the vast scale on which the provision trade is conducted in Chicago may be formed upon the fact that 5,000,000 pigs were killed there last year."

From the ownership pattern of the early fleet and the dissolution of the Furness partnership in the summer of 1882, it is evident that Christopher Furness was at this early age exhibiting more of the entrepreneurial spirit, as seen earlier in Gothenburg. Although Lloyd's Registers list the early steamers under the management of Thomas Furness and Company, the name of Thomas Furness does not appear in the lists of shareholders in the ships. All the early fleet were owned on the legal 64 share basis by individuals, rather than by the company. William Gray, the local shipbuilder, was a major financial backer in the venture, retaining large holdings in the ships he built which were sold to Christopher Furness over a number of years. In the meantime Christopher was marketing shares to the local community and most holdings consisted of only one or two 64ths. At initial registration the shares registered in the names of Furness and Gray were:

Vessel	Furness	Gray	Vessel	Furness	Gray
CHICAGO	18	44	BOSTON CITY	42	22
AVERILL	25	39	DURHAM CITY	33	31
BRANTFORD CITY	20	44	RIPON CITY	34	30
YORK CITY	52	12	WETHERBY	32	32

The complete fleet of steamers, all built in the Gray shipyard, before the brothers ceased trading together as Thomas Furness and Company was:

Name	Built	GRT
CHICAGO	1878	1384
AVERILL	1878	1690
BRANTFORD CITY	1880	2371
YORK CITY	1881	2325
BOSTON CITY	1882	2334
DURHAM CITY	1882	3092

The volume of cargo generated by Thomas Furness and Company was such that they were importing 1,300 tons of oatmeal monthly from America. They had obtained several large provisioning contracts including those for the prisons in Durham, Yorkshire, Northumberland and Lancashire. These absorbed large quantities of cereals, lard and bacon imported from North America and Europe— the prison contracts alone absorbed twenty five tons of grain a week. Lard was shipped from Boston in the rough to be rendered and refined ready for market in Furness's own West Hartlepool refinery. A typical cargo was that carried by the chartered *Melita* in July 1877 which included, amongst other goods, three hundred tons of lard and four hundred tons of bacon.

The career of the first steamer, *Chicago,* gave an inauspicious start to the venture. Registered at West Hartlepool on 3 May 1878, she sailed for Boston only to be wrecked within twenty four hours, going ashore on Haisboro' Sands off the Norfolk Coast on 8 May.

Chicago and the other early steamers were locally built, eight of the first ten by William Gray and Company, the other two by Edward Withy and Company. Their iron hulls and compound engines, from various North Eastern engine works, were the latest state of the art of the shipbuilder and marine engineer. The 240 feet length of *Chicago* was surpassed by the 260 feet *Averill* delivered six months later. They were followed by a trio of 2,300gt sisters in 1880-82, *Brantford City, York City* and *Boston City.* Gray delivered the much larger *Durham City* in the Spring of 1882, at 3,092gt and 314 feet the largest vessel to be owned for the next decade.

An examination of the careers of these first ten ships serves to remind us of the risks inherent at sea a century ago, before the invention of radio, radar and other navigational aids. Only two of them were sold for further trading, *Boston City* and *Ripon City* in 1897. Another, *Durham City*, was broken up the same year. The other seven were all lost, mainly wrecked on, or close to, the North American coast.

The trade of Thomas Furness and Company was one way only, the import of foodstuffs to feed the growing industrial population of Britain. Christopher Furness sought any possible cargo for the return passage, in 1881 obtaining a contract to ship cement from the West Hartlepool works of Casebourne and Lucas to New York. Another regular cargo would have been rails and other material for the network of railroads rapidly expanding to cover the continent in the years following the American Civil War.

Thomas Furness remained aloof from direct involvement in these developments. Reluctant to undertake the risky ventures which kept Christopher happy, and probably aware that his younger brother had even more ideas to develop, the partnership was terminated by mutual consent in the summer of 1882. Seventy five years later Walter C Warwick wrote of Christopher Furness "speculation seemed to have an irresistible attraction and he frequently spent not only a good deal of time but often a great deal of money in a variety of speculative operations in various parts of the world," a view which had been earlier reflected by the biographer in the Dictionary of National Biography writing in 1912 (see page 21).

Thomas retained the grocery business and henceforth Christopher concentrated on shipowning, although he would soon take the first steps to becoming an industrialist with interests including iron and steel, coal, shipbuilding and engineering. Interestingly the split in 1882 was not to last forever as in 1895 Christopher purchased his older brother's company, now Thomas Furness and Company Ltd, and brought it into the fold of his fast growing, but looseknit, group.

Independence

Christopher Furness found himself, with capital said to be £100,000, manager of a modern fleet of five steamers, *Averill*, *Brantford City*, *York City*, *Boston City* and *Durham City*, with *Newcastle City* building and the snow *Williams* (a two masted sailing ship similar to a brig) which was shortly broken up. The most obvious evidence of change was the new houseflag. The brothers had adopted a blue flag with the white letters "T F & Co". Christopher chose to hoist a Union Jack defaced by a blue edged white central square containing a blue letter "F". This only lasted a short time until spotted by a naval officer at Halifax, Nova Scotia. He ordered it hauled down, objecting to the defacing of the national flag without official authority. Christopher then reverted to the original plain blue flag with the lettering simplified to a white "F", a flag which was to last until after World War II.

Within a matter of months, a new service was added to that already operating from West Hartlepool. For several years the London firm of Adamson and Ronaldson had operated a service from London to Boston with owned and chartered ships. Crop failures in America in 1881 led this undercapitalised venture to suspend the service and sell the ships. Adamson and Ronaldson's manager, Robert E Burnett, saw *Brantford City* discharging on the Thames at Deptford cattle market and proposed to Furness that he place ships in the London to Boston trade with his firm acting as loading brokers. *Newcastle City* took the first sailing on this route when she left London on 23 December 1882, followed in the New Year by *York City*, *Brantford City*, *Newcastle City* again and *Boston City*. The ships initially loaded cargo for both Boston and Canadian ports, but trade developed so fast that, within a year, ships were loading for either Boston or Halifax. Two years later, in 1884, Robert Burnett left Adamson and Ronaldson to join Furness. He was immediately dispatched to Boston to open an office dedicated to handling the growing company trade. Burnett was to remain with Furness until his death in 1945, having been appointed a director of Furness, Withy and Company, Ltd in 1905.

Burnett's sighting of *Brantford City* at Deptford cattle market is a reminder of the important trade in live cattle. Refrigeration was in its infancy and the only method of carrying meat any distance was "on the hoof" as live animals. As restrictions were placed on the movement of cattle from abroad, slaughterhouses and processing plants were erected alongside the discharge berths. Even after refrigeration had become accepted the trade continued, down to the start of World War II, as it attracted the label "home killed meat", a tag of value to the retail butcher in suggesting freshness.

Early Employees

Meanwhile, in West Hartlepool, Furness had been building a small team to run his growing fleet. His early employees included George Woolley, Robert Stoker, Frederick Lewis and Robert Burnett, all destined to become leaders of the business.

Typical was twenty four year old Robert Burdon Stoker. Born at South Shields, he had been educated in Liverpool. In 1876, aged 17, he joined a firm managing sailing ships in the Canadian timber trade. Moving to J T Bowden and Company in 1879 he became manager during 1881 until offered a position by Furness the following year. Two months after joining Furness in the West Hartlepool office, Stoker was sent north to open the first branch office, in Newcastle, to canvass for cargo and serve the ships calling there to load on passage from West Hartlepool for Boston.

Not all the early staff remained with Furness, T D Davis, for example, left to join Robert Ropner, retiring as Ropner's London office manager in 1920 after thirty three years' service. At that time he was noted as the last survivor in business of Christopher Furness's original staff.

Newcastle City, built in 1882, foundered in December 1887 after five years service. *(WSPL)*

New Fields

Names chosen for two ships commissioned in 1884, and also reports on their launch, show Christopher Furness venturing into new fields. The North Eastern Daily Gazette for 31 March 1884 reported *Gothenburg City*, and her sisters *Stockholm City* and *Lincoln City*, as building for the Direct Scandinavian & American Steamship Company. They were fitted for twenty 1st and thirty 2nd class passengers, plus 700 steerage for emigrants. The steerage accommodation, in the 'tween decks, was spartan and used on the eastward passage for cattle. Many launch reports of the period note the suitability of vessels for the carriage of emigrants, troops or cattle. The first sailing from Stockholm was to be taken by *Gothenburg City* in early May 1884, but she stranded on the ballast passage from England and had to return for repairs. The new service was a disappointment, although all three vessels took a sailing from Stockholm during the summer of 1884. Thereafter they were placed on the London berth for Halifax or Boston. In 1885 *Gothenburg City* was ten days out on passage from London for Boston when she lost her propeller, not an uncommon occurrence in those days. Steamers were fitted with sail not for economy but because of the known limitations in reliability of their machinery. Turning east, it took her 33 days to reach Falmouth under sail, running short of stores and being helped in this regard by a passing ship.

Edward Withy and Company—Shipbuilders

As he stepped into the 10.17 am train to London on Wednesday, 3 September 1884, Christopher Furness could contemplate his new role of shipbuilder. With Henry Withy and I J Robinson he was accompanying Edward Withy and his family on the first stage of their journey, to take ship to a new life in New Zealand.

Having made a small investment in the shipbuilding firm of Edward Withy and Company during the previous year, Furness seized the opportunity afforded by Edward Withy's desire to seek a new life, to become the major shareholder in the Middleton shipyard of Edward Withy and Company, holding a controlling interest, with Henry Withy and Richard Vick as junior partners. Withy headed the shipyard with Vick in charge of finance and naval architect G W Sivewright, a shipbuilder of long experience, as yard manager.

The Withy shipyard, across the Old Harbour from Hartlepool, was well established with over 120 ships built since Edward Withy and Edward Alexander had commenced business in 1869. Shipbuilding on the site dated from 1838 when Joseph Parkin and Thomas Richardson launched the snow *Thomas Wood* and schooner *Independence* before selling to J P Denton the following year. Becoming Denton, Gray and Company in 1863, growth of business led to space problems, so in the summer of 1868 a lease was taken on the Pile, Spence and Company yard at West Hartlepool, vacant since Pile, Spence and Company had collapsed as one of the casualties resulting from the 1866 failure of bankers Overend, Gurney and Company. Without delay Withy, Alexander and Company opened for business as Denton, Gray and Company moved out.

Edward Withy had been employed by Richardson, Duck and Company, South Stockton whilst Edward Alexander had worked for Denton, Gray and Company as head cashier. Both came of Quaker families: the Withy roots lay in Bristol, the Alexander in Kent and London. They were soon joined by Henry Withy who travelled from Bristol to learn shipbuilding from his older brother. Henry's training continued; six months experience with Napier and Sons during 1873 was followed by a voyage from Hamburg to South America aboard a Kosmos Line ship. Then back to the Clyde for two years in the yard of John Elder and Company before returning to Hartlepool where he was soon appointed manager by his brother.

Edward Alexander *(R Alexander)*.

In the summer of 1874, Edward Alexander sold his interest and moved to Cardiff to join his cousin, Captain E H Capper, in a new shipbroking and owning business. Edward Alexander's place in the shipbuilding firm, now Edward Withy and Company, was taken by Richard Vick. The Alexander family rejoin our story many years later when, after World War II, Capper, Alexander and Company and Alexander Shipping Company Ltd became members of the Houlder Brothers Group.

Along with other Hartlepool builders and owners, the yard were early proponents of the well deck steamer. Flush deck steamers suffered from a design defect: the shaft tunnel reduced the capacity of the after holds and they accordingly trimmed by the bow. To overcome this the well deck, or raised quarter deck, ship was evolved, although initial reaction by Lloyd's Register of Shipping and other bodies could only be termed hostile. It is claimed that Denton, Gray and Company built the first welldeckers in 1868/9 (*Lizzie English* and *Sandsend*). Edward Withy was also one of the promoters of the Well-deck Insurance Society.

Shipbuilding Initiatives

Patents registered by the Withy yard, partners and staff related to stockless anchors, cellular double bottoms and the longitudinal bracket system of hull construction. The yard was among the first to adopt cellular double bottoms in steamships and was also a pioneer in the employment of steel wire ropes for launching purposes. For strength, and to speed construction, the yard was the first to employ steel hull shell plates measuring up to 70ft long and over 5ft wide. Later, as Furness, Withy and Company, Ltd, the yard was the first to recognise the value of the "turret" design developed by William Doxford and Sons Ltd on the Wear. In July 1894 they negotiated a licence to build to the patent, although in fact it was never implemented.

On 10 September 1885, the yard launched *Washington City* for Furness, noteworthy as one of the first steel hulled, triple expansion engined steamers on the North Atlantic and the first in his fleet. The yard also commenced building to standard designs which both speeded construction and minimised costs, thus enabling them to offer competitive prices. In 1887 the single deck *Amphitrite* of 2350gt with dimensions of 290ft x 38ft x 19ft was the first of a group of four which was developed into a slightly larger 2400gt type measuring 300ft x 38.5ft x 20ft of which seven were built, led by *Oswestry* of 1888.

Another design commenced in 1890 with the launch of *Zanzibar*, a 2900gt welldeck steamer with raised quarterdeck and dimensions of 314ft x 40ft x 21ft. Two years later the same hull design had an awning deck added, the first of this variation being launched as *Birdoswald*. The forward well was plated in to produce a more versatile vessel with a better cubic capacity when employed in the carriage of light cargo to England. Twenty one of these ships were built, twelve with awning decks. The spar deck design was also in favour during the period, later strengthened into the shelter decker. At the end of 1896 the 3750gt *Apollo* was launched, the first of eighteen ships to enter the water over the next decade with standard dimensions of 340ft x 47ft x 20ft (27ft to spar deck).

Shipbuilding Finance

Shipbuilders were closely involved in the finance of shipowning, rather than bankers. Many ships were built for managers who, after signing the contract, raised finance by establishing an owning company and selling shares to friends, business associates and the general public. Many shipbuilders took up blocks of shares in such companies as part of the agreement to build the ship, in the same way as William Gray had done with Furness's own early ships.

If the shipowner was unable to raise the full sum an alternative source of finance was to give the builder post dated bills of exchange which, when due, would be paid from the earnings of the ship. The builder could discount the bills with his bank to meet his cash needs. No details of the financial arrangements of the Withy yard have survived, but along the coast at Sunderland the records of William Doxford and Sons Ltd reveal the extent to which this arrangement operated. For example, early in 1906 Doxfords had "bills running", discounted at the bank, worth £939,951 13s 1d and others valued at £131,063 17s 10d in the safe. Over £1 million, the equivalent of some 25 ships or 15 months output from the yard. Other builders would have had a similar involvement in the financing of shipping.

The Middleton yard was solely concerned with the building of hulls, and had no engine works. Machinery and boilers were purchased, mainly from Thomas Richardson and Sons Ltd whose works lay alongside the shipyard. Small numbers came from Blair and Company, Stockton, and the Central Marine Engine Works of William Gray and Company situated on the other side of the North Basin.

Although a shipbuilder as well as a shipowner, Furness did not limit orders to his own yard. Always ready to order if a good price was to be obtained, whether speculatively or for specific employment on his routes, he was a good customer to many builders, both along the North East Coast and on the Clyde.

The Furness Fleet—1882-1891

The five ship fleet of 1882 was added to over the years that followed. Many ships stayed for only a matter of months before sale to other owners as Furness developed his speculative building programme with orders placed both with the Withy yard and elsewhere. The fleet of newbuildings retained in service eventually consisted of some sixteen ships whilst another fifteen can be identified as sold prior to completion or after only a short period in service. The sixteen permanent fleet members were

Name	Built	GRT	Name	Built	GRT
AVERILL	1878	1690	STOCKHOLM CITY	1884	2686
BRANTFORD CITY	1880	2371	GOTHENBURG CITY	1884	2529
YORK CITY	1881	2325	WASHINGTON CITY	1885	2296
BOSTON CITY	1882	2334	BALTIMORE CITY	1888	2334
DURHAM CITY	1882	3092	NEW BOROUGH	1888	1795
NEWCASTLE CITY	1882	2129	TYNEDALE	1889	2217
WETHERBY	1883	2129	TYNEHEAD	1890	2258
RIPON CITY	1883	2141	OTTAWA	1891	1719

In 1886, the nearly new *Damara* and *Ulunda* were purchased from the Clyde builders Alexander Stephen and Sons. They had been completed the previous year for the Halifax Steam Navigation Company Ltd to operate a fortnightly service from London, Havre and Swansea to Baltimore, Halifax and Quebec, and St Pierre and Miquelon should passengers and freight be available. Supported by a Canadian Government subsidy, both the Canadian and French Governments anticipated benefits to accrue from the service. *Damara* had taken the first sailing, followed by *Olympia*, *Stanmore* and *Ulunda*, all new vessels. The company having fallen behind in payments to the builders, the ships were repossessed and sold to Furness who continued to run them using the name of the Halifax company, doubtless to protect the subsidy payments. After the loss of *Ulunda*, in 1890, she was replaced by the newbuilding *Ottawa* which was herself lost the following year. *Damara* and *Ulunda* were the only two second-hand ships added to the fleet and retained in the years prior to 1891, although a long list of vessels passed briefly through Furness's hands.

Edward Withy

Born to Quaker parents in Bristol on 22 December 1844, Edward Withy moved to Stockton on Tees in 1859 and was apprenticed to the shipbuilders Richardson, Duck and Company. Completing his training during December 1865, he remained with the shipyard until resigning as yard manager in February 1869, the year after his marriage. Whilst with Richardson, Duck and Company Withy had made a trip round the Cape to Bombay in 1867 in connection with work being undertaken for P&O, returning via Suez, where the Canal was nearing completion. Then in 1868 he oversaw the building of the steamer *Deccan* at Dumbarton for P&O.

On resigning from the service of Richardson, Duck and Company, he entered a partnership with Edward Alexander as Withy, Alexander and Company, shipbuilders at Hartlepool. Their first contract was the iron barquentine *Maria Ysabel* for Spanish owners, after which the shipyard concentrated on steamships. Consequent on the stress of business Withy was ordered, by his doctor, to take a rest, and consequently spent half of 1873 with his wife on a voyage to Melbourne, again returning via Suez where the Canal was now open. In 1874 Edward Alexander withdrew and the firm became Edward Withy and Company.

In 1884 Edward Withy decided to make a new life for himself and, having selected New Zealand, sold his interest in the shipyard to Christopher Furness for £80,000 and sailed for Auckland on the *Waitemata*. Here, as in England, he took a prominent role in local government and education, being elected to the New Zealand House of Representatives between 1887 and 1890.

Returning to England in 1912 Edward Withy settled in Jersey where he died in 1927. Many of his family of six sons and seven daughters remained in New Zealand.

Stockholm City. Note the artist has portrayed sails full of wind but smoke and flags blowing out against the wind. This anomaly was often ignored by artists of the period. *(A Henderson)*

Name	Built	Acquired	GRT
DAMARA	1885	1886	1779
ULUNDA	1885	1886	1789

In 1887, *York City* suffered a fire in her cargo of cotton four days after sailing from Portland, Maine. On 10 August, also four days out from New York, the Inman liner *City of Montreal* caught fire and was destroyed in mid-Atlantic. All 135 passengers and 110 crew were taken off by the German barque *Trabant,* to be shortly afterwards transferred to *York City.* Landing the survivors at Queenstown she proceeded on passage to Tallinn where the fire damaged cotton was discharged. Having loaded a cargo of oats at Reval, she sailed for London, only to meet stormy weather during which she went ashore on a reef off Faro Island on 22 December. Despite the efforts of the Neptune Salvage Co, she broke up within three weeks and only realised Kr 1,100 when auctioned.

The day after *York City* was wrecked, *Newcastle City* was also lost on the other side of the Atlantic. Having sailed from Newcastle on 29 November 1887 with general cargo for New York, she experienced stormy weather and it was 23 December before the Nantucket light was sighted. Night came on with a near gale blowing from the North West. *Newcastle City* struck a rock, sliding off half an hour later. Water came in faster than the pumps could handle it, the boiler fires were soon extinguished by the inrush and waves commenced to break over her. The crew, and one passenger, took to the boats as she foundered, and pulled against the storm to reach shelter on the South Shoals lightship. When the weather abated they were landed at Hyannis, Massachusetts, and proceeded to New York and passage home in the *Durham City* which arrived in the Tyne on 31 January.

The year 1888 saw continued developments. In January, Christopher Furness announced the opening of a coastal service between Hartlepool and London, both to serve local needs and to connect with his deep sea services from London to Boston, St John's NB, Halifax and Baltimore. The summer saw the completion of a new office block, Baltic Chambers, on the corner of Surtees Road and George Street, West Hartlepool, to accommodate the growing needs of the firm. The first floor consisted of a suite of offices for Furness, two private rooms, a cashier's office, general office and a telephone office. On the second floor were offices for George Pyman and Company and C Nielsen and Company, both shipowners, whilst the third floor was Furness's sail loft.

Fleet losses—1882 to 1891

AVERILL. 21 June 1883—wrecked at Green Cove, Ingonish, CB. Barrow for Montreal, steel rails.
BRANTFORD CITY. 10 August 1883—wrecked on Arnolds Point, near Little Harbour, Lockport, NS. London for Halifax and Boston, general cargo and five passengers.
YORK CITY. 22 December 1887—wrecked on Salvor Reef, Faro Island, Sweden. Reval for London, oats.
NEWCASTLE CITY. 23 December 1887—wrecked off Nantucket Island, Mass. Newcastle for New York, general cargo and one passenger.
SULTAN. 1 March 1889—abandoned in 42.51N 57.7W. New Orleans for Bremen, cotton and general cargo.
ULUNDA. 26 August 1890—ashore on Cow Ledge, Briar Island, NS. St John NB for London, general cargo. Later refloated and sold.
GOTHENBURG CITY. 27 June 1891—wrecked on St Mary's Island, five miles south of Blyth. Montreal for Tyne, cattle & deals.
OTTAWA. 1 November 1891—wrecked on Blonde Rock, near Seal Island, Bay of Fundy. London and Halifax for St John NB, general cargo.

Shipping Services

The main routes of the period were from London and the North East Coast ports to Canadian and United States North Atlantic ports. When cargo was available, ships were also dispatched from other ports, such as Leith, Dundee and Barrow. Ships were chartered to other owners, like the *Wetherby* and *Gothenburg City*

Lynn Street, West Hartlepool. John Furness was at number 18, Thomas Furness at 31. The Thomas Furness premises were this side of Prinsky, seen in the distance right side at 29.
(G Colley)

which, in 1888, sailed from Antwerp on charter to the Puritan Line. The previous year, Furness had taken the steamers *British Crown* and *British Queen* on charter for the London to Boston service. As well as looking for official backing and finance, as when buying *Ulunda* and *Damara* in 1886, Furness also looked for co-operation with other owners to their mutual benefit. This was apparent by 1887 at the latest when advertisements for the Wilson and Furness Line confirmed the co-ordination of the two services from Newcastle to New York. In the coming decades this co-operation with the Wilson Line was to be developed further.

Chignecto Ship Railway

A major contract, obtained early in 1889, was to ship all the materials, machinery and rails for the building of the Chignecto Ship Railway, scheduled for completion in September 1890.

The heavy maritime traffic from the St Lawrence to Saint John and other Atlantic ports had to transit the Canso Straits and brave the open Atlantic. All that stood in their way to a shorter and safer passage was a narrow isthmus of land between the Gulf of St Lawrence and the Bay of Fundy. If this could be opened to ships it was estimated they would save a week or more in time and the crossing of up to 500 miles of open sea.

The genius behind the project was H G C Ketchum (1839-1896). The idea of transiting the isthmus was not new, for proposals had been made as far back as 1686. Ketchum became interested in the 1870s and proposed a railway as cheaper and better suited than a canal. His plan was for a double line to run from Tidnish on the Gulf to Fort Lawrence on the Bay, over practically flat country.

At Fort Lawrence a wet dock able to hold six 1,000 ton ships, included a gridiron to lower a cradle into the basin. 230ft by 40ft, this cradle ran on 192 wheels. Once a ship was secured, the gridiron was raised hydraulically and the cradle hauled by locomotives across the isthmus at ten miles per hour. On arrival at Tidnish, on Baie Verte, the procedure was reversed and the ship refloated.

Estimates calculated that if 7% of the trade used the Railway an income of about $500,000 a year would result. With a survey carried out in 1881, Ketchum submitted proposals to the Government of Canada and an annual subsidy was voted. In 1888 the first finance was raised in London and construction commenced. Bogs were dug out and filled, the terminals built and machinery installed. Twelve of the seventeen miles of track, the heaviest laid in the world, were in position. Then, in July 1891, work was suspended. In the middle of a depression it proved impossible to raise the $1.5 million needed for completion.

The railway lay incomplete for years. Material was salvaged and sold, much of the rail going to the Intercolonial Railway. Today few remains can be seen, only overgrown ditches and buildings converted to other uses. The dream of cutting the isthmus was never realised and, in due course, improved rail and road systems made such plans redundant.

Christopher Furness—Industrialist

Christopher Furness was not only a shipowner and builder, he was also interested in other business opportunities that presented themselves. Although the development of his steel and coal interests was to take place in the late 1890's, he had much earlier on invested in a number of enterprises, although it is not possible now with any degree of certainty to list them all. During the 1880's he participated in the development

London office staff, 1893. Standing: C Tomkins, T Winspear, R H Wheeler, E Hull, A Houlton, A C Kenway, E Pull and E Bulgian. Sitting: T Gibbon, J H Hugill, R B Stoker, S W Furness, F W Lewis and P J Hutt. Front: H Poole and C Spencer. *(Courtesy M Jones)*

of West Hartlepool, buying tracts of land and building houses for sale.

In the 1880's we can identify three named businesses, all situated in County Durham, in which Furness invested. In 1883 The Hartlepools Steam Tramway Company Ltd was formed to connect the two towns of Hartlepool and West Hartlepool with a tramway authorised under "The Hartlepools Tramway Order 1883" at a contract price of £48,455. The promoters promised extensions of the line to serve other destinations, although they never fulfilled their promise as financial difficulties led to the appointment of a Receiver in 1888. Furness had taken a small block of fifty £5 shares at an early stage and in 1892 he purchased the undertaking from the Receiver for £2,400 and sold it to the Town Council for the same figure.

During March 1889 Thomas Jones and Matthew Gray purchased the British and European patents of J F Golding covering the use of expanded metal in a wide range of applications. To produce and market the product British Metal Expansion Company Ltd was floated in August 1889. The capital of 2,500 £10 shares was placed almost entirely with three shareholders, Matthew Gray 1,246 shares, Christopher Furness and Robert Irvine, Jr, 625 shares each. The business was only kept for a few years as in 1892 a new firm, Expanded Metal Company Ltd, was formed to acquire "as a going concern the business of working certain patents relating to metal, trellice or lattice work now carried on by the British Metal Expansion Company Ltd at West Hartlepool". The patents, purchased in 1889 for £8,500 were sold back to Golding for £13,000 and passed to the new company controlled by him. Gray, Furness and Irvine took no further interest in the business after the completion of the sale in December 1894.

The third business was The Greatham Salt Company, formed to extract and market rock salt from the northern edge of the Middlesbrough salt field. Boreholes enabled water to be injected and then pumped to the surface as brine. Furness, one of four original partners in the venture, bought out the other interests and retained sole control until selling the business in December 1903. Later the salt business became better known as part of the Cerebos Salt Works.

These interests had little in common with the shipbuilding and owning ventures and were therefore never integrated, even with the formation of Furness, Withy and Company, Ltd in 1891.

London Office

The third branch office was opened in 1890 when Robert Stoker was dispatched to London. The new office at 5 and 6 Billiter Avenue, operating as Christopher Furness and Company, not only acted as agents for the

Furness Line sailing card of 1885 depicting the houseflag objected to by the Admiralty.

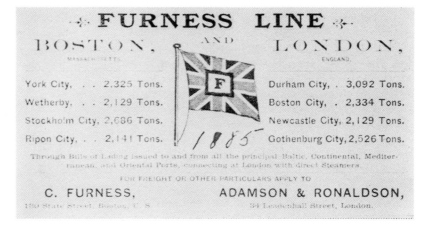

services, transferred over a number of years from the previous agents, but also commenced ship management with the steamers *Tynedale* and *Tynehead*. The office also advertised as brokers for the sale, purchase and chartering of steamships.

The primary reason for opening an office in London was the appointment, by shareholders, of Christopher Furness to be manager of the British Maritime Mortgage Trust Ltd. Incorporated in 1888 as the Trustee, Debenture, Assets Purchase, & Mortgage Guarantee Company Ltd, and renamed in 1889, it had been formed "to assist approved shipowners to build tonnage on the security of sound mortgages on ships". Bad management in the initial months had accumulated heavy losses, resulting in the change of management in 1890.

It was to be 1896 before "the unfortunate losses of the original management ... were entirely wiped out". Over the same period Furness steadily purchased shares in the Trust until, in 1896, this interest reached a controlling level.

The office in London was to grow in importance over the years until, in 1916, the head office moved there from West Hartlepool after a brief period in Liverpool.

Speculative Shipbuilding

In view of the relatively short interval between gaining control of the shipyard and the application of his ideas, it is likely Furness already had a clear vision of the relationship he intended to develop between his shipbuilding and shipowning interests. Shipping has always been cyclical in nature and within a normal decade owners expected two or three years of good freight rates and financial returns to offset the poor, break-even or loss situation of the other years. This fluctuation in owners' fortunes was reflected in the shipyards with only a relatively short time lag. During good years orders were plentiful, and at times more than could be accepted for delivery in the required time. When shipowning profits were poor this was reflected in a fall off of orders, and often within a year the appearance of empty slipways and temporarily closed yards. Hardship resulted for the workforce, who were laid off without pay.

Probably within months, or at most a couple of years, Furness commenced laying down ships on vacant berths in the Withy yard, even though there was no firm order for them. These ships were built to designs for which a known market existed and enabled early, or even immediate, delivery to be offered to prospective buyers. An early return on this investment came in 1887, when the freight market showed a good recovery after several years of recession. As a result, it is recorded, Furness made a profit of £250,000 on ships sold during this period, a sum that doubtless played a large role in the development of his business interests during the last decade of the century.

The ship management office became involved when ships were ready but nobody had signed a contract to buy. The ships would be placed under the Furness flag and employed on company routes or tramping until a market was found. An incomplete list of these ships includes the following vessels, in which identification problems can be seen because of the repeated use of the same name for newbuildings—for example the launch of four as *Calcutta City* in 1890/1. All were sold prior to completion, becoming *Langoe*, *Ashlands*, *Daybreak* and *Melbridge*.

Name*	Built	GRT		Name*	Built	GRT	
LINCOLN CITY	1884	2729		HALIFAX CITY	1890	2289	
CARLISLE	1889	1035		PAKEHA	1890	4331	
TRURO CITY	1889	1006		GUERNSEY	1891	2856	
ALBOIN	1889	1047		Calcutta City	1891	2922	DAYBREAK
WITTEKIND	1889	1047		Calcutta City	1891	2868	MELBRIDGE
BUSHMILLS	1890	2466		Cundall	1891	4637	CHANCELLOR
Calcutta City	1890	2306	LANGOE	Welldeck	1891	2907	INCHDUNE
Calcutta City	1890	2303	ASHLANDS				

At the same time, a number of old vessels were accepted in part exchange for newbuildings and these entered the fleet for varying periods, either trading or laid up, until sold or broken up. Typical of the old tonnage thus obtained was *Baron Hambro* built in 1861 and owned from 1888 to 1889, then sold. Another was the geriatric *Blanche* dating from 1863, with a two cylinder single expansion engine and a boiler pressure of only 27 lb/sq in. She was kept from 1889 until sold in 1892 (to survive until wrecked in July 1901). Others included *Fire Queen, Scandinavia, Medina, Orion* and *Pleiades*. When *Cundall* was sold to Thomas and James Harrison of Liverpool prior to completion in 1891 and renamed *Chancellor*, the elderly *Statesman* and *Historian* dating from 1869/70 were taken, probably in part exchange, only to be sold within a matter of months to Portuguese owners.

*Note.- Names in lower case type (for example, Calcutta City) indicate the ship was sold prior to entering service and was not registered under that name.

Durham City, built in 1882 and broken up 1897. Note the flags, as in the *Stockholm City* picture, flying against the wind *(A Henderson)*

The full list of the second-hand ships registered as managed by Christopher Furness in the years prior to 1891 is informative.

Name	Built	Acquired	GRT	Name	Built	Acquired	GRT
KATIE	1880	1886	2796	MICHIGAN	1881	1889	2949
DHU HEARTACH	1868	1887	149	JAMES SPEIR	1890	1890	535
SAINT LOUIS	1870	1887	1862	VEGA	1879	1890	3064
MADURA	1873	1887	2324	MANDALAY	1872	1890	1915
BARON HAMBRO	1861	1888	579	TAYMOUTH CASTLE	1877	1890	1827
FIRE QUEEN	1864	1888	1220	CENISIO	1867	1891	1431
SCANDINAVIA	1876	1888	851	DUART CASTLE	1878	1891	1839
MEDINA	1867	1888	286	INCHBORVA	1881	1891	2301
ORION	1873	1888	2297	INCHGARVIE	1882	1891	2614
PLEIADES	1874	1888	2297	INCHULVA	1881	1891	2229
SULTAN	1873	1888	2525	MADRID	1873	1891	2439
BLANCHE	1863	1889	246	HISTORIAN	1870	1891	1830
CHANTICLEER	1853	1889	539	STATESMAN	1869	1891	1865

Christopher Furness

Now, in 1891, in his late thirties, Christopher Furness could look back on a business career many would have considered sufficient. However, his outlook, attitude and character were such that development would not cease but grow even faster on the foundation laid. His definition of a partner indicated this; years later he characterised a partner as being

"a man who is concerned constantly for the success of the business with whose welfare his own welfare is so closely inter-woven—a man who is as unbending as granite against waste, whether in material or time, a man who watches keenly for every avenue for the adoption of economies—a man who is ever zealous in the performance of his part and ever alert to secure to the firm the utmost advantage out of every factor with which he may come in contact."

Such a description fitted the men who early rose to positions of responsibility, such as Stoker, Lewis, Warwick and others. The difficulty of finding such men would, in the years to come, see Furness turning to his nephews and introducing them to positions of trust and responsibility, coupling the loyalty of blood ties to ability.

An autocratic Victorian entrepreneur, he nevertheless enjoyed the loyalty of his staff, as witness the number who remained and rose to lead the business over the years. In later years his staff recalled Furness variously as arrogant, brusque and bumptious but his confidence and ability, intuition and perception led to success. Henry Davies, in completing the entry for the Dictionary of National Biography was led to write —

"Furness was a man of remarkable character, and possessed extraordinary powers of organisation, which were always displayed at their best in times of stress and difficulty.

"He was extremely energetic and never spared himself. He was not popular in his own neighbourhood, or among business competitors; and his business methods were severely criticised. But to friends and associates he was singularly loyal. The outstanding feature of his career is the ability with which he applied the policy of integration and combination to the characteristic industries of the North-East coast."

2. The Expanding Empire—1891 to 1902

The shipyard and shipowning businesses were merged with the formation of Furness, Withy and Company, Ltd on 16 September 1891.

The desire to amalgamate his interests and delegate managerial responsibility had been in Christopher Furness's mind for some time and was noted in his correspondence with Robert Burnett, manager of the Boston office, as early as 1889. With a team of able and experienced lieutenants heading the offices at Boston (R E Burnett), Baltimore (C Rowley), London (F W Lewis) and Newcastle (Captain T King), Henry Withy and Richard Vick in the shipyard plus others like George Woolley and Robert Stoker, he led an organisation many shipowners would have coveted.

The financial situation had also changed with accumulated capital. This enabled Furness both to consolidate his interests and to assume control of the company, rather than rely on the investments of many others as had been necessary a decade earlier, with himself as part owner and manager. During the first year, the new company purchased the various ships previously managed, paying cash rather than issuing shares in the new company. The company organisation also enabled him to raise finance using new methods, such as the issue of debentures which carried no voting rights. Typical of the use of such debentures was the issue of £36,400 to A Stephen and Sons in 1896 as part payment for *Megantic,* followed by £51,700 to William Gray and Company in respect of *Cambrian.*

The other business interests, such as British Metal Expansion Company and Greatham Salt Company, were in no way related to shipping and so remained outside the amalgamation. The full industrial empire that was to be constructed was, in the main, still in the future. The continued growth of Furness, Withy and Company, Ltd was to enable Furness to finance his developments which, to a large degree, involved the amalgamation and reorganisation of undertakings in need of finance and new management.

The authorised capital of Furness, Withy and Company, Ltd in 1891 was £700,000, of which £695,000 was issued in £100 shares, 5,894 to Christopher Furness, 523 to Henry Withy and 533 to Richard Vick; a decade was to pass before any were made available on the open market. The first directors were Christopher Furness, Richard W Vick and Henry Withy, soon joined by Captain Thomas King, George L Woolley and Robert B Stoker.

The first thirty years of the company fall into three periods, each of approximately a decade. First, until 1902 and the formation of the International Mercantile Marine, was a period of steady development, albeit overshadowed to a degree for Furness's attention was concentrated on the growing industrial empire. During this period the North Atlantic services were both upgraded and moved increasingly into the passenger field. Following this, the period from 1902 to 1912 was influenced by Morgan's International Mercantile Marine. Furness chose to withdraw from the passenger arena, and concentrate on cargo routes and the development of the coal and tramp trades. Lastly, from 1912 to 1919 came the rapid expansion into liner trades with the purchase of businesses such as Johnston and Prince Lines with their large fleets and extensive route networks.

Furness Lines Fleet

The complete fleet, a total of fifteen vessels, was transferred to the new undertaking, three in 1891 and the balance during 1892, totalling 34,603 tons gross. Furness also held interests in seven other shipping firms and owned shares in twenty one ships under other management. Between 1891 and 1900 the fleet registered in the name of Furness Withy, can be split into groups, vessels employed long term and others retained only for short periods.

The relatively small number of ships in continual service through the decade was concealed by the long list of second-hand vessels, few only of which were to fly the Furness flag for any length of time. In the main they were to have only brief lives under Furness Withy management, in some cases they were never actively employed. One important purchase, in 1898, strengthened the service to Canada when the two ships, service and goodwill of Canada & Newfoundland Steamship Company Ltd (a company controlled by C T

Bowring and Company) was acquired. Included in the package was the Canadian Government subsidy for the route. The ships were the elderly *Barcelona,* scrapped the following year, and *Ulunda* which remained in service until sold foreign in 1910.

Name	Built	Acquired	GRT	Name	Built	Acquired	GRT
a. Ships previously managed, transferred to the new company:							
BALTIMORE CITY	1888	1891	2334	MADURA	1873	1892	2324
DAMARA	1885	1891	1779	NEW BOROUGH	1888	1892	1795
INCHULVA	1881	1891	2229	RIPON CITY	1883	1892	2141
BOSTON CITY	1882	1892	2334	STOCKHOLM CITY	1884	1892	2686
DURHAM CITY	1882	1892	3092	TYNEDALE	1889	1892	2217
INCHBORVA	1881	1892	2301	TYNEHEAD	1890	1892	2258
INCHGARVIE	1882	1892	2614	WETHERBY	1883	1892	2129
MADRID	1873	1892	2439				
b. New tonnage added to the fleet 1891 to 1900:							
ANTWERP CITY	1894	--	3229	SYLVIANA	1898	--	4187
CARLISLE CITY	1894	--	3002	LIZZIE	1900	--	631
HALIFAX CITY	1894	--	2141	EVANGELINE	1900	--	3901
SAINT JOHN CITY	1895	--	2153	LOYALIST	1901	--	3909
c. Second-hand tonnage bought and sold or broken up:							
AUSTRALIA	1870	1892	2252	GODWIT	1891	1896	1682
STRAITS OF BELLE ISLE	1870	1892	2484	HEATHER BELL	1896	1897	1253
BAVARIAN	1869	1894	3030	MONARCH	1897	1897	7296
BULGARIAN	1870	1894	3118	BARCELONA	1878	1898	1802
ISTRIAN	1867	1894	2963	DAHOME	1891	1891	2470
SAINT RONANS	1881	1894	4457	LONDON CITY	1891	1898	2487
ZEBRA	1858	1894	551	RAPIDAN	1898	1898	7359
SORRENTO	1878	1895	2208	ULUNDA	1885	1898	1717
ALBERT	1856	1895	525	SPRITE	1870	1898	826
COVENTRY	1883	1895	1702	DALTONHALL	1899	1900	3538
EDITH	1864	1895	609	BUCCANEER	1890	1902	925
OREGON	1882	1895	3714	FLORENCE	1889	1902	2492
PLATO	1857	1895	793	LOYALIST	1891	1902	2294
SARNIA	1882	1895	3728	EVANGELINE	1891	1902	2266
FRANCE	1867	1896	4281	LONDON CITY	1882	1902	2461
MANNINGHAM	1880	1896	1924	ST JOHN CITY	1891	1903	2265
OPORTO	1870	1896	570				

Saint John City, as fitted when new in 1891 with auxiliary sail.

Member of Parliament

Christopher Furness's interest in public affairs doubtless influenced his plans for the merger and devolvement of responsibilities to others. He had been one of the first council members of the new Borough of West Hartlepool when it was incorporated in November 1887, and in 1891 he defeated William Gray, the Tory candidate, by 293 votes to become Liberal Member of Parliament for the Hartlepools. Holding the seat at the 1892 election, this time by only 76 votes, against Thomas Richardson, Jnr, he was unable to repeat the victory in 1895 when Richardson took the seat by 81 votes. On all three occasions the total number of votes cast was 9,000 to 9,500. In 1900 the rivals, both now knighted, again met and Sir Christopher Furness defeated Sir Thomas Richardson by nearly 2,000 votes in a poll of 11,000. Returned unopposed in 1906 the next opposition came from Howard Gritten, a professional London politician, who was defeated by 800 votes in 1910. The result was disputed and Furness unseated.

Joint Services

Whereas the 1880s had been a time of largely independent operations, the decade that followed was one of increasing co-operation with other parties for mutual benefit.

In 1891 there was a short lived co-operation with the Allan Line on the Canadian service. This was followed in 1894 by a westbound cargo sharing agreement with Johnston Line for the London to Boston trade and, in 1897, an association with Elder, Dempster and Company on the Canadian route. In 1902 this association with Elder Dempster developed further when the Canadian Government, wishing to increase trade with South Africa, awarded a contract and subsidy for a Canada-Cape Line jointly to Elder Dempster, Allan Line and Furness Withy. The first sailing took place on 18 October 1902. Trade failed to develop sufficiently to warrant continuation so, after two years, the line was abandoned.

F Leyland and Company Ltd

Following the death of Frederick Leyland in 1892, Furness was at the centre of bids to take over Leyland's Atlantic and Mediterranean services. At the time he was also negotiating the formation of the Chesapeake & Ohio Steamship Company and proposed a similar arrangement with the directors of the Fitchburg Railroad. The Fitchburg proposal came to nothing but the other two soon came to fruition.

Furness was largely instrumental in forming a syndicate consisting of himself, Walter Glynn, John Ellerman and H O O'Hagan to purchase the Leyland assets and form Frederick Leyland and Company Ltd to assume control of them. The capital of the new company was set at £800,000, the syndicate members taking the £200,000 of ordinary shares, and with it control, whilst placing £250,000 preference shares and £350,000 of debentures with the public. Christopher Furness was elected chairman. Logical co-ordination between the Furness and Leyland services to Boston followed and, in 1896, developed into the Wilson's and Furness-Leyland Line Ltd.

Although, in 1896, Furness sold his shares in Leyland to John Ellerman, this in no way prevented or stopped continued co- operation in Wilson's and Furness-Leyland Line which took over the London to New York and Boston services. Further south Chesapeake and Ohio Steamship Company was operating in the Virginian trade.

Chesapeake and Ohio Steamship Company Ltd

Eager to develop their traffic, the Chesapeake & Ohio Railroad looked eastward for a transatlantic service from their Newport News railhead. Negotiations with Furness resulted in the formation of the Chesapeake and Ohio Steamship Company Ltd with a ten year agreement giving the company exclusive access to railroad controlled traffic and the Railroad sales organisation, plus a guarantee to meet any operating losses.

Incorporated in November 1892, the new company had a share capital of £200,000, 60% held by the Railroad and associates (56% alone in the name of J N Wallace, c/o Central Trust Company, New York) whilst the balance was held by Furness and his friends. Extra capital to finance the six ships ordered was raised by an issue of £150,000 first mortgage 5% debentures, privately distributed to the Railroad (£100,000) and Furness (£50,000). For future use an unlimited amount of second mortgage debentures was agreed, of which only £45,282 was issued (all to the Railroad).

With the new fleet ordered and building, the first services were undertaken by chartered tonnage. The purpose built fleet of six ships came from two yards; Alexander Stephen and Sons on the Clyde delivering three shelter deckers of 3885gt, named *Rappahannock*, *Shenandoah* and *Kanawha* when they entered service from Liverpool to Newport News between August and December 1893. Three 2875gt spar deckers, *Appomatox*, *Chickahominy* and *Greenbrier*, came from the Furness Withy yard at West Hartlepool between September and December the same year for the London to Newport News route.

First launched was *Appomatox* on 12 July 1893. Designed to carry general cargo, cattle, emigrants and troops, she had two decks plus a shade, or spar, deck above. Portable hinged fittings in the 'tween decks enabled cattle to be carried from America to Britain and for the space to be available on the return passage for either cargo or emigrants. Piped water supplies for the cattle, ventilation and fittings were in excess of the regulations. Designed for 12 knots, on trials in September 13.5 knots was recorded.

Two weeks later, on 27 July, the first of the Stephen's ships was named *Rappahannock* by Mrs Mackenzie, wife of a company director. Larger than the Furness Withy trio, the Clyde built ships differed in basic design, being part shelter deckers. The shade, or spar deck, of the Hartlepool built ships was of lighter construction than the rest of the hull and could not be included for freeboard calculations. The shelter deck design of the Stephen's ships gave scantlings above the main deck of full hull strength, enabling the upper deck to be included. Fitted for the carriage of 760 cattle, the fittings were similarly portable.

Without change of name, the Hartlepool built trio were sold in 1902 to become the pioneer ships in the fleet of Elders and Fyffes Ltd. Fitted as insulated banana carriers, they gave good service until sold in 1910. *Chickahominy* was broken up, *Appomatox* became the Turkish *Seyer* until sunk on 13 March 1916 in the Black Sea by the Russian destroyers *Bromkij* and *Bystryj*, whilst *Greenbrier* passed to the Tropical Fruit Company until mined off Amrum on 2 April 1915, under the American flag. The Stephen's built sisters stayed with the company until transferred to Furness Withy in 1907. *Shenandoah* and *Rappahannock* were both war losses, being respectively mined on 14 April 1916 and torpedoed on 26 October 1916 by U69, sadly with the loss of all 37 crew. *Kanawha* survived the war to be broken up in 1922.

The 7359gt shelter decker *Rapidan* joined the fleet in 1898, one of the speculative products of the Furness Withy shipyard. Chesapeake and Ohio ownership was brief as her capacity, double that of the earlier steamers, probably made her too big for the trade. The same year she was transferred to Furness Withy and sold to Houlder Brothers in 1902. As their *Haversham Grange*, she traded until abandoned on fire in the South Atlantic.

Although intended for the Chesapeake and Ohio trade, the next two additions were not registered as owned by the company until 1902. *Powhatan* and *Alleghany* were products of the Furness Withy yard. *Powhatan* was launched on 27 August 1900 as *Austriana* (and completed in December as *Powhatan*) for the British Maritime Trust. Joining Chesapeake and Ohio in 1902, she was transferred to Furness Withy in 1909 and sold out of the Group in 1913. *Alleghany* had a similar career and ownership pattern until she became *Saigon Maru* in 1912. These two replaced the three ships sold to Elders and Fyffes, leaving a fleet of five ships plus chartered tonnage when required.

In 1905 Furness Withy purchased the Railroad shareholding for £75,000. The Railroad also wrote off their debenture holding and had made guarantee payments totalling $698,000 covering deficits incurred in the operation of the services. Two years later, in 1907, new traffic agreements were concluded between the shipping company and the Railroad, and also with the Norfolk and Western Railroad and the Southern Railroad, to carry all the import/export traffic between Newport News/Norfolk and London/Liverpool. To handle this, two ships were transferred to the company and orders placed for a further six vessels.

The two ships transferred had been completed late in 1905 and registered as owned by Sir Christopher Furness, although designed for the Chesapeake and Ohio trade. *Albiana* was a three-island steamer of 4224gt built by Northumberland Shipbuilding Company Ltd, Newcastle. Slower than the ships of 1893—her designed speed was 10 knots and she made 11 knots on trials—her maiden voyage was to Newport News to load cattle. The 4204gt spar deck *Mariana* came from A Rodger and Company, Port Glasgow. *Albiana* was soon sold, to Lloyd and Company, London, and renamed *Evesham*. *Mariana* was sold in 1908 and as the Belgian *Gouverneur de Lantsheere* was broken up in 1934.

To finance the newbuilding programme, the outstanding debentures of £65,282, owing in February 1907, were redeemed and a new issue of £300,000 5% first mortgage debentures registered, to be redeemed at £105 commencing January 1909 at an annual cost of £15,750. These funds were required to meet the costs of the six new ships, the price of which totalled £254,750. Not all of these ships were liner tonnage suitable for the Newport News route, several being single deck tramps.

Shenandoah, built on the Clyde for the Liverpool to Newport News service.

From the Furness Withy yard came the sisters *Rapidan* and *Roanoke* early in 1907. Later in the year, they were chartered to Clan Line and renamed *Clan Maciver* and *Clan Macinnes*. Both returned to Furness Withy and their old names in 1914, *Roanoke* to be sunk by *U48* on 12 August 1917. *Rapidan* remained in the fleet until sold and renamed *Dovenby Hall* in 1923. Northumberland Shipbuilding Company delivered *Norfolk* in March 1907, a single deck tramp. She passed to Furness Withy in 1908 and was sold to Greek buyers in 1914. Finally, Irvine's Shipbuilding and Engineering Company, West Hartlepool, delivered three vessels between April and September. *Richmond* was a shelter decker whilst *Washington* and *Newport News* were single deck sisters. All passed to Furness Withy, *Richmond* in 1908, the other two in 1907.

In October 1907, it was decided to absorb the ships of British Maritime Trust and Chesapeake & Ohio Steamship Company into the main Furness Withy fleet. The price for the Chesapeake and Ohio ships, £489,000, was the valuation given by T W Tamplin and Company. Transfer took place between 1907 and 1909. Chesapeake

Name	Built	Acquired	GRT		Name	Built	Acquired	GRT
APPOMATOX	1893	--	2875		RAPIDAN	1907	--	3760
CHICKAHOMINY	1893	--	2875		NORFOLK	1907	--	3836
GREENBRIER	1893	--	2875		RICHMOND	1907	--	2921
RAPPAHANNOCK	1893	--	3884		WASHINGTON	1907	--	3031
SHENANDOAH	1893	--	3886		NEWPORT NEWS	1907	--	3031
KANAWHA	1893	--	3884		ALBIANA	1905	1907	4224
RAPIDAN	1898	--	7359		MARIANA	1905	1907	4204
POWHATAN	1900	1902	4262		GRACIANA	1903	1912	3536
ALLEGHANY	1901	1902	4262		ALBIANA	1898	1912	3607
ROANOKE	1907	--	3755					

and Ohio lay dormant until, between June 1912 and November 1913, they again appeared as registered owners of two ships.

The first of the two, transferred from Furness Withy, was *Graciana*. Built in 1903 as *Sierra Morena* for Liverpool owners, she had stranded off the Florida coast on 12 October 1910, been refloated and sold to H & C Grayson, the Liverpool ship repairers. After repairs, she was sold to Furness Withy in November 1911 and renamed *Graciana*. Retained by Chesapeake and Ohio until November 1913, she then reverted to Furness Withy until sold to Greek owners in 1924. The second ship came from Glasgow owners; *Braemount*. Dating from 1898 she had been completed as *Corby Castle*. Renamed *Albiana* she was sold in August 1913 to Sale and Company, London.

With the Chesapeake and Ohio routes incorporated into the Furness Withy network, the need for a separate company no longer remained. The decision was taken on 16 October 1913 to go into voluntary liquidation and distribute assets to shareholders. At that time, Furness Withy held 12,860 and British Maritime Trust 5,250 of the 20,000 shares issued.

Having owned nineteen ships between 1893 and 1913, Chesapeake and Ohio had an enviable record, not having lost a single ship at sea from any cause.

Wilson's and Furness-Leyland Line Ltd

The National Line of 1863 was, by 1895, in poor financial state due to losses sustained in 1889-90: the burning of their New York piers and the loss of *Erin* (missing) and *Egypt* (burnt). The Line then gave up the passenger trade, restricting itself to the carriage of cattle and freight. In this situation an offer to buy the company and its London to New York service came from the group that was to become Wilson's and Furness-Leyland Line. Rejection of the offer, and competition from the new Line finally brought National Line to its knees. Finally a lower bid was accepted in 1896 from Atlantic Transport Line.

Furness had operated a London to Boston service since 1882 and, with Leylands, now operated a joint London to Boston service as Furness-Leyland Line. Thomas Wilson, Sons and Company Ltd had opened a Hull to New York run in 1875 and ten years later commenced calling at London. In 1887 Wilsons purchased the Monarch Line fleet, and their service from London to New York, from the liquidator and since 1891 had operated as the Wilson- Hill Line. Furness and Wilson had also been operating a joint service from Newcastle to New York (Wilson-Furness Line) since 1887, if not earlier.

With these associations it was logical that the various partners should co-ordinate their interests. The Furness-Leyland Line Ltd had been incorporated in March 1896 to consolidate the interests of these two partners and planned to take over Furness's *Carlisle City* and Leyland's *Bostonian*. Before these plans could be implemented however, grander designs developed with Wilsons. In August, Wilson's and Furness-Leyland Line Ltd was established to bring together the parties' London, New York and Boston interests. Weekly services were to operate between London and New York, also London and Boston, plus a ten to fourteen day service from Newcastle to New York.

At the outset ships chartered from the partners were employed. *Carlisle City* was not taken over as intended, although *Bostonian* and the larger *Georgian* were transferred from Leyland. Three new cargo ships were added at the same time, sisters from William Gray and Company Ltd (one) and A Stephen and Sons (two); all ordered by Furness Withy, one was launched as *London City* but sold to Wilsons and completed as *Idaho*. The second Stephen's ship, intended to be *Chicago City*, was completed for Furness Withy as *Megantic*. In October 1896 both, plus the third building at Gray's as *Cambrian*, were transferred to Wilson's and Furness-Leyland Line and placed on the London to New York service.

Plans were immediately formulated to upgrade the service and introduce ships with passenger accommodation. Orders were placed for four 14 knot near sisters fitted for 120 1st class passengers (*Victoria* had accommodation for 150) and 800 cattle, able to make the crossing in ten days. A fifth member of the group was completed by Harland and Wolff, Belfast, as *Winifreda* for Leylands. Stephens completed *Alexandra* and *Boadicea*, Furness Withy *Victoria* and Earle's *Cleopatra*. As they came into service, *Alexandra* being the first in October 1897, the earlier ships were transferred to the Boston run and released some of the chartered

Cambrian, typical of the Intermediate liners operated by Wilson's and Furness-Leyland Line.   *(WSPL)*

tonnage. The Wilson's and Furness-Leyland Line now operated the largest and finest ships regularly to connect London with New York.

These four new ships were members of a numerous class of large cargo carriers being built by Furness in various yards, some without passenger accommodation. Included in the group were *Rapidan,* employed on the Chesapeake and Ohio route to Hampton Roads, and the sisters *Bengalia* and *Bethania* sold on the stocks to Hamburg America Line. From an examination of photographic and other material it would appear that a skeleton specification was given to the various builders to develop, hence the variation in length and tonnage, number of hatches, etc. Whilst no evidence has so far come to light it is possible that other similar ships, such as the rest of the Hamburg America Line group, originated as speculative orders placed by Furness.

The full service was never to be implemented as, prior to the sailing of the last ship to be delivered, *Cleopatra,* due to leave London on 28 July 1898, the London to New York service and all five ships were sold to Atlantic Transport Line.

Dating from 1882, when established by B N Baker of the Baltimore Storage and Lighterage Company with the financial backing of the Pennsylvania Railroad, Atlantic Transport prospered with its fleet of British registered ships. By 1898, twelve ships were in service and, with an eye to expansion, Baker made an offer for the London to New York service of Wilson's and Furness-Leyland Line. In the middle of these negotiations, the Spanish-American War erupted on 21 April 1898.

The culmination of rising tension between Spain and America, the war only lasted until 12 August. Spanish colonial misrule had led to revolt in Cuba and the Philippines. American sympathy lay with the colonists, her own freedom from colonial rule little more than a century earlier being still fresh in the mind. The loss of the USS *Maine,* blown up in Havana harbour on 15 February, led to claims of treachery and demands for vengeance. An ultimatum demanding Spanish withdrawal from the colonies brought a declaration of war from Madrid. Naval reverses for Spain resulted in the arrival of American troops to support the revolutionary movements in both Cuba and the Philippines. America was rapidly faced with a shortage of suitable troop transports and turned to commercial companies to fill the urgent need. Although the Atlantic Transport Line ships were registered under the Red Ensign, the company was very much American owned and rapidly agreed to sell the seven latest ships to the Government and donated an eighth as a hospital ship. Left with the four oldest ships, and not wishing to withdraw from the North Atlantic trade, Baker successfully increased the offer for Wilson's and Furness-Leyland's ships and service to £968,000 plus additional sums for the West End offices and New York berth. The sellers undertook not to return to the route for seven years.

The ships sold all had long careers with their new owners, apart from *Cleopatra.* Renamed *Mohegan* after her first voyage, she sailed for the second, and last, time from London and was sighted off the Cornish coast in the early evening of 14 November 1898. Instead of being 10 miles off Falmouth she was way off course, heading for the Manacles which, despite warning rockets from Coverack Coastguards, she hit. Her starboard side torn open, she sank in ten minutes taking with her 106 passengers and crew. Captain Griffiths and all his officers died and no explanation of how she came to be on that dangerous course was ever established.

The day after *Mohegan* was lost, *Idaho* which had been renamed *Londonian* in 1897, and was still in Wilson's and Furness-Leyland service, sailed from Boston, bound for London with general cargo and cattle. A week out, bad weather developed into a gale, the steering gear jammed and she broached to. On her beam ends and with the engine room flooded, she was sighted on 25 November by Johnston's *Vedamore* which, over the next four days, saved 45 of the crew despite horrific odds. Sadly one boat capsized and 17 men from *Londonian* were drowned. At dawn on 28 November there was no sign of *Londonian* so *Vedamore* proceeded for Baltimore with the survivors. However, Captain Lee and seven others were still on board *Londonian* which continued drifting helpless before the gale until she was sighted by the German steamer *Maria Rickmers*, a lifeboat from which managed to reach the derelict and take them off.

To replace *Londonian*, Wilsons transferred their *Chicago* early in February 1899. She was the last ship to join the Line prior to sale, the full fleet to 1901 being —

Name	Built	Acquired	GRT	Name	Built	Acquired	GRT
BOSTONIAN	1888	1896	4668	BOADICEA	1897	--	7057
CAMBRIAN	1896	--	5626	ALEXANDRA	1897	--	6919
GEORGIAN	1890	1896	5088	VICTORIA	1898	--	6849
IDAHO	1896	1896	5532	WINIFREDA	1898	--	6833
1897 LONDONIAN				CLEOPATRA	1898	--	6889
MEGANTIC	1896	1896	5532	CHICAGO	1898	--	6408
1898 ANGLIAN				1903 ETONIAN			

In 1901, an offer for the company, fleet and the Boston service was received from the International Navigation Company (later International Mercantile Marine) and accepted, the company becoming a subsidiary of F Leyland and Company (1900) Ltd. No outward change was noticeable and in 1902 an order was placed with Harland and Wolff for two 18,000 ton liners to be named *Servian* and *Scotian*. Development of the International Mercantile Marine combine and rationalisation of services saw the order cancelled after the hulls had been launched. Left on the builder's hands, they were purchased in 1906 by Hamburg America Line and entered service the following year as *President Lincoln* and *President Grant*. During 1908/9, Harland and Wolff delivered two other large cargo ships to Wilson's and Furness-Leyland, *Mercian* and *Meltonian*.

Early in 1915, the decision was made to integrate the service and ships into the Leyland Line. Wilson's and Furness-Leyland Line Ltd was placed in voluntary liquidation on 21 February and, on 5 March, the ships were transferred and the Line became history.

The North Atlantic Passenger Trade

The movement of Furness's interests into the passenger trade will have been noted from the descriptions of the Wilson's and Furness-Leyland Line ships. The accommodation differed from that available on earlier ships which could carry emigrant passengers in spartan conditions: these ships could classify their passengers as travelling 1st-class. Reporting on the launch of *Victoria* by Lady Furness at the Furness Withy yard on 31 July 1897, the magazine "Marine Engineer" wrote —

"Accommodation for about 120 1st-class passengers is to be fitted in the bridge and large deckhouse. This accommodation is of the most elaborate description, the materials and workmanship being of the very highest character. The main saloon, which is approached by a grand double staircase, is handsomely finished in polished oak and walnut, a large amount of massive carved work having been tastefully worked into the panelling. The state-rooms are effectively finished in walnut and mahogany and the smoke-room is finished in polished oak richly carved. Everything will be done to make this accommodation up to date and luxurious in the extreme. The music-room, which is in the fore part of the deck-house above the main saloon, is tastefully enamelled in white and pink, and an upright grand piano by Brinsmead, having a special case to match the rest of the framing, is to be supplied. Bath-rooms, lavatories, electric bells, awnings, etc, will be fitted complete to ensure the comfort of the passengers at sea, and spacious promenades extend the whole length of the bridge and deck-house. The wants of the passengers will be attended to by an efficient staff of stewards, stewardesses and cooks."

This luxury was again reflected in the two smaller ships, *Loyalist* and *Evangeline*, completed in 1900 by Alexander Stephen and Sons for the Furness Withy Canadian service from London to St John's, Newfoundland, Halifax and St John, N B. Whereas the earlier ships had been rather ugly, angular and severe four masted vessels with little beauty, these two were at the other extreme. Beautifully proportioned and yacht-like, with clipper stem and short bowsprit, finely carved figurehead (*Loyalist's* being a Canadian volunteer in khaki uniform) and tall, raking masts they presented a handsome appearance. *Evangeline* was reported to be fitted for 70 1st-class and an unknown number of 2nd class, *Loyalist* could carry 100 1st-class and 70 2nd-class. "Marine Engineer" reported in early 1901 that *Evangeline* —

"… has the most luxurious passenger accommodation for 70 1st-class passengers arranged amidships under the bridge, and also in large deckhouses on top of the bridge, with a very handsome and commodious dining saloon, the full width of the vessel at the fore end of same. On top of the bridge deck there are spacious deckhouses for a large music saloon and smoke rooms, etc. Abaft the music saloon in the deckhouse there are a number of large special state-rooms. The bridge deck, being extra long, affords a very fine promenade for the passengers, and is considerably more spacious than is usual in passenger steamers.

"The 2nd-class passenger accommodation is fitted under the poop aft, which is fitted up in first class style almost equal to the first-class accommodation. There is a special companion entrance to the 'tween decks, where it is intended to have accommodation for carrying emigrants or troops."

The beautiful yacht-like *Evangeline* completed for the service from London to Canada.

"Steamship" later commented on *Loyalist* —

"She has handsome and luxurious cabin accommodation and is replete with everything for the comfort of passengers, with handsome dining saloons, staircases, music-room, halls, and smoke-rooms, each saloon being fitted up in hardwoods and Tynecastle tapestry of harmonious design."

British Maritime Trust Ltd

During 1896, the interest held by Furness Withy in British Maritime Mortgage Trust Ltd was increased to bring full control and, in October 1897, the name was simplified to British Maritime Trust Ltd. At the same time, the trust commenced a building programme of ships suitable for sale and charter to others or use by Group companies. This was, in fact, a continuation of the London based fleet which from 1891 to 1900 had Robert Stoker listed as managing owner. The fleet in Stoker's name was:

Name	Built	Acquired	GRT
ADRIA	1864	1891	844
SYDENHAM	1891	--	2377
CYNTHIANA	1891	1892	2864
FELICIANA	1891	1892	2922
MANDALAY	1872	1892	1915
MAY	1890	1892	1178
DELHI	1864	1893	2009
STRAITS OF MENAI	1894	1896	2870
SRAITS OF SUNDA	1895	1896	2992
LADY FURNESS	1895	1897	3158

Under British Maritime Trust management, *Cynthiana* was sold in 1900 and renamed *Saxon King*, *Straits of Menai* was sold in 1899 and *Lady Furness* went missing in November 1897 on passage from Japan for Singapore with coal.

The fleet ordered and commissioned by British Maritime Trust can be conveniently divided into two categories, the ships retained in ownership and those transferred, before or soon after completion, to other owners or within the Furness Withy Group. An examination of the fleet is interesting for the manner in which it indicates the close connection between the various enterprises in the loose knit empire. Although Sir Christopher Furness was never one to turn down a good opportunity to build in other yards, a large

Boliviana, built for charter by British Maritime Trust Ltd.

percentage of the ships were products of those yards under his control and were fitted with machinery provided by the engine builders Sir Christopher Furness, Westgarth and Company Ltd and, later, Richardsons, Westgarth and Company Ltd.

Name	Built	GRT		Name	Built	GRT	
MEDIANA	1897	2440		PERSIANA	1902	4015	
Gloriana	1898	3379	POLARSTJERNAN	SANDOWN	1905	3790	
Gloriana	1898	2768	BETTY	CYNTHIANA*	1905	3185	
ITALIANA	1898	2663		PERUVIANA*	1905	3153	
CEBRIANA	1899	4221		ALMERIANA	1905	1603	
Adriana	1900	2931	WHANGAPE	CROXDALE	1906	1283	
POWHATAN	1900	4262		MALINCHE	1906	1868	
BOLIVIANA	1900	4573		TUDHOE	1906	1298	
WYANDOTTE	1900	4204		GUARDIANA	1907	6852	
BIRMINGHAM	1901	4027		Adriana	1906	4169	MIDGARD
ALLEGHANY	1901	4262		WESTHAMPTON	1907	1860	
AUSTRIANA	1901	4025		TUNSTALL	1907	3825	
Gloriana	1902	6060	SEMINOLE	BRAZILIANA	1907	3827	
COMO	1902	5137		ROTTERDAM	1907	4859	
INDIANA	1902	3869		THORNLEY	1907	1327	
POTOMAC	1902	3618		Adriana	1907	5420	MEINAM
RAPALLO	1902	5166		Graciana	1907	5520	PEI-HO
ATHENIANA	1902	2300		Adriana	1907	4200	FLODDEN
Gloriana	1903	3926	FRANK COVERDALE	GRACIANA	1907	4266	
Gloriana	1904	4240	AGINCOURT	ARABIANA	1907	3001	
ORIANA	1902	4419					

*In 1905 both CYNTHIANA and PERUVIANA were registered as owned by Sir Christopher Furness, transferred to British Maritime Trust 1906.

Sir Christopher Furness, Westgarth and Company Ltd and Richardsons, Westgarth and Company Ltd

In 1896, the opportunity arose to purchase two old established Middlesbrough engineering firms, Westgarth, English and Company Ltd and Tees-Side Bridge and Engine Works Ltd for £32,821 3s 4d and £28,236 9s 9d respectively. They were reorganised and a new company promoted, in which the public were invited to invest: Sir Christopher Furness, Westgarth and Company Ltd. This public involvement in the newly floated company differed from Furness, Withy and Company, Ltd, where Sir Christopher Furness retained most of the issued capital and with it control.

Rather than having to buy machinery on the open market, Furness now had some control over supplies for his shipyard. Four years later, in 1900, control of these supplies of machinery was strengthened when he was instrumental in organising the amalgamation of three firms to form a new combine, Richardsons, Westgarth and Company Ltd. These were Thomas Richardson and Sons Ltd, Hartlepool, Furness's own Sir Christopher Furness, Westgarth and Company Ltd, Middlesbrough, and William Allan and Company Ltd, Sunderland. Henceforth, a large percentage of the ships built in the associated shipyards would be engined by one or other of the works controlled by Richardsons, Westgarth and Company.

Thomas Richardson and Sons had been established at Castle Eden in 1837 and had moved to Hartlepool during 1847, acquiring the works built in 1839 for the Hartlepool Iron Company. Originally builders of locomotive and stationery engines, they commenced erecting marine engines about 1854. William Allan, a Dundee born Scot, had taken over management of Carr, Fowles and Company at the request of the shareholders in 1877 and reformed the business as William Allan and Company operating from the extended and renamed Scotia Engine Works.

Irvine's Shipbuilding and Dry Docks Company Ltd

In 1896, the Furness Withy Middleton shipyard was extensively modernised. The yard was now re-equipped with three extended building berths of 450ft, 550ft and 700ft. A 380ft graving dock was constructed, electric power provided and the fitting out quay refurbished. It was the first shipbuilding yard in the world to be wholly lit by electricity.

Negotiations commenced early in 1897, and were completed during July, to buy Irvine's Harbour Dockyard. Robert Irvine had commenced shipbuilding at West Hartlepool in 1864 as Irvine, Currie and Company on a site situated on reclaimed land inside the south pier of the harbour entrance. By the mid-1890s the dockyard, now known as Irvine and Company, was becoming outdated and after launching *Jacob Bright* in December 1896, it was run-down and modernisation commenced. A new company was formed, Irvine's Shipbuilding and Dry Docks Company Ltd, with all the capital of £75,000 held by Furness, Withy and Company, Ltd. Robert Irvine's son David remained as Managing Director, assisted by A S Purdon, whilst Henry Withy, Richard Vick and Stephen Furness joined the Board. In the coming years the yard was to benefit from the business methods employed by Furness, with joint speculative ventures filling gaps in the order book.

Irvine's Harbour yard.
(Hartlepool Reference Library)

When it reopened for business, the Harbour Dockyard had three building berths able to build ships of up to 500ft in length and 10,000 tons deadweight, whilst the dry dock, built in 1866, had been lengthened from the original 315ft to 380ft. New cranes had also been installed, including a travelling steam crane to lift 20 tons.

Irvine's were builders of tramp tonnage; typical of the standard designs they marketed being a 4000gt spar decker of 345ft x 48ft x 19ft (27ft to spar deck). Twelve such ships were built between 1900 and 1902, led by *Lindenhall*. A smaller edition followed with *Vera* in 1903. Of 2975gt, their dimensions were 325ft x 47ft x 14ft (22ft to spar deck). Fourteen of this type were launched between 1903 and 1908, plus a further three strengthened as shelter deckers and three completed as single deckers. A single deck collier or tramp was introduced with *Minister Delbeke* in 1909, 1800gt and measuring 280ft x 40ft x 18ft, with twelve being built before the outbreak of war in 1914.

Northumberland Shipbuilding Company Ltd

An important addition to Furness's loose knit shipbuilding empire soon followed in the shape of the Northumberland Shipbuilding Company Ltd with their yard at Howden-on-Tyne. Dating from 1883, the yard had previously been Edwards' Shipbuilding Company. Harry Edwards had died in 1898 and the yard, which had only been in partial use for some years, was acquired by Rowland Hodge, previously yard manager for C S Swan and Hunter, Wallsend. He transferred it to the new company for £6,000 in shares whilst Furness took a controlling holding.

Like the other two yards, Northumberland with modernised facilities able to build up to 600ft ships, commenced to construct standardised designs alongside individual orders. The first of these standard designs was a spar decker of 4,300gt on dimensions of 360ft x 48ft x 20ft (28ft to spar deck). Three island ships, they had a deadweight of 7,300 tons. *Rosalie*, launched in December 1899 for Cardiff owners, was the first of the design. Within a period of nine years, forty five were built, most being laid down for Furness as speculative ventures. Another two were built with heavier scantlings as two deckers and four spar deckers to the design were built at Furness Withy's Middleton shipyard to take the total to over fifty.

In 1907, a revised design was introduced with *Graciana*. Having a smaller gross tonnage of 4,200, she could load 7,500 tons on a reduced draught, an added advantage. Dimensions had changed to 380ft x 49ft x 18ft (26ft to spar deck). Five ships were built as spar deckers and fifteen were strengthened as two deckers.

The third standard design came to life with *Rotterdam* of 1907. A shelter decker of 4,800gt, 9,700dwt and dimensions of 400ft x 52ft x 27ft, eleven were built in the years up to the outbreak of war in 1914.

Coal, Iron and Steel

Between 1898 and 1900, Sir Christopher Furness was heavily involved in the promotion and organisation of various coal, iron and steel interests.

In late 1898, South Durham Steel and Iron Company Ltd was formed by William Gray and Sir Christopher Furness following their purchase of three local steelworks, Moor Steel and Iron Works and the Stockton Malleable Iron Works, both of Stockton-on-Tees and West Hartlepool Steel and Iron Works, West Hartlepool. With a capital of £650,000 divided into £350,000 ordinary shares and the balance as cumulative preference shares, the company owned three works covering 166 acres and employing about 5,000 men.

The amalgamation was intended to avoid undue competition for both supplies of raw material and in the sale of finished steel. The output of finished material in 1899 was recorded at 284,568 tons and included more than half the North East Coast output of plates for the shipbuilding industry. Gray and Furness each intended to retain some £50,000 in ordinary shares. In addition to these two (Furness was Chairman), other directors included E L Pease of Weardale Steel, Coal and Coke Company, J Stothart, chairman of engine builders Blair and Company Ltd and C J Bagley, managing director of the South Durham Steel and Iron Company. This board therefore interlinked with at least four shipyards and two firms of engine builders.

Within a year, Sir Christopher Furness featured as the promoter and chairman of another company, Weardale Steel, Coal and Coke Company Ltd with E L Pease again a fellow director. Furness had purchased all the shares in Weardale Iron and Coal Company Ltd of Spennymoor for £1,025,000 and promoted the new company to continue the business. With a share capital of £900,000, the new company took over a business dating from 1845 and now one of the most important producers of coal, coke and Siemens-Martin steel in the North of England. Average output for the three years prior to the reorganisation had been 1,350,000 tons of coal, 380,000 tons of coke, 68,200 tons of steel ingots, 47,300 tons of finished steel and iron and 4-5 million bricks.

The steel and iron works of the company were situated at Spennymoor. To these was added the Cargo Fleet Iron Company Ltd which was purchased in 1900 to became a wholly owned subsidiary. Collieries owned by the new company were situated at Tudhoe, Croxdale, Black Prince, West Thornley, Hedley Hill, Middridge, Thornley, Ludworth and Wheatley Hill. Brickworks were owned at Tudhoe and Wheatley Hill. A controlling interest was held in the Tudhoe and Sunderland Bridge Gas Company. With some 30 miles of railway owned, a large fleet of locomotives and wagons was serviced by extensive wagon, engineering and other facilities. Finally, at the time of formation, a total of 2,128 dwellings were owned for the use of employees.

Hardly had the dust settled on the South Durham and Weardale undertakings than news of another venture was received. In November 1900, Broomhill Collieries Ltd was registered to bring together, at a price of £650,000, Broomhill Shipping Company Ltd, Radcliffe Coal Company Ltd and Chevington Coal Company Ltd. Collieries were situated at Broomhill and Chevington, the Broomhill Shipping Company operated in the coastal collier trade, and Warkworth Harbour was controlled as the company held all the debentures issued by the Harbour Commissioners.

Other coal companies in which Furness played a part included Easington Coal Company Ltd, formed to develop the largest coal mine in the country with a planned output of two million tons a year, Wingate Coal Company Ltd and the South Wales undertaking of John Lancaster and Company Ltd at Blaina, Monmouth.

This period of activity by Sir Christopher Furness in the coal and steel industries took place against the background of a massive wave of investment and mergers in British industry, a time of economic growth. Whilst all fitted into the jigsaw of trades which supplied his shipbuilding and shipowning interests with raw materials and cargo, they were also in need of capital injection to enable them to keep pace with technology. This was especially true of the steel works which were modernised with the introduction of Talbot's continuous process. At Cargo Fleet, the old obsolete works were replaced by a modern steelworks.

In 1903, the Furness connection between South Durham, Weardale and Cargo Fleet enabled the companies to co-ordinate their production in the face of competition from other manufacturers and foreign imports, whilst at the same time continuing a process of plant modernisation.

The largest single export commodity of Britain was coal, and both the Broomhill and Weardale collieries exported a large part of their output. Furness, with his Newcastle coal office, was able to take advantage of this trade as is witnessed by the steady growth in the fleet of colliers owned by Furness Withy during the first decade of the 20th century.

In this industrial enterprise Furness did not develop a unified group, rather it was a collection of loosely associated companies with himself as the main link. When formulating policy and directing firms to co-operate to their, and his, mutual benefit, he at times encountered opposition to the consequent limitations placed on local management. An example of this was the co-ordinating of coal supplies through the Newcastle office, whereas the steel works managers would have preferred to retain freedom of supply in their own hands. The result of this loose knit organisation was to be seen after Furness's death, in 1912, when the various companies tended to go their own way.

Manchester Ship Canal

Thirty miles inland from Liverpool lies the metropolis of Manchester. Both cities were major centres in the industrial heart of Lancashire with textile and heavy industries. During the dramatic growth of the Victorian era both prospered, yet the thirty mile gap resulted in a growing bone of contention, and resulted in one of the major industrial memorials of the age, the Manchester Ship Canal.

Raw materials from abroad had to be carried overland to Manchester. The natural port of entry was Liverpool, but the port charges, when added to on-carriage, gave resultant costs as if the goods had been landed at Hull, nearly three times the distance away on the east coast, over the Pennines. Many approaches were made to reduce the financial burden imposed at Liverpool, but to no avail.

As early as 1721, the need for a canal to Manchester had been recognised. In 1825, a company was formed and sought suggestions. One envisaged a fifty one mile cut from the River Dee at Dawpool. Sir John Rennie favoured a link from Runcorn in 1838 and two years later Henry Palmer prepared proposals to upgrade the Mersey and Irwell Navigation into a ship canal.

Finally, on 27 June 1882, Daniel Adamson (1820-1890), a local engineer, boilermaker and iron founder, invited seventy six prominent people to a meeting at his home, The Towers, Didsbury. At this meeting a provisional committee was formed and consultant engineers commissioned. The committee resolved to act on the report received and the Manchester Ship Canal Company was formed, with Adamson as chairman, to obtain powers to construct a canal to connect Manchester with the sea.

Despite strong opposition, the Manchester Ship Canal Bill became law in 1885, authorising the construction of a waterway some thirty five miles long with dimensions to take ocean going ships. Fierce battles still lay ahead despite the Act. Next was to raise capital, an uphill struggle with public criticism from opposers, and the sheer size of the undertaking. Between 1887 and 1893, twenty thousand navvies excavated fifty four million cubic yards (eighty two million tons) of spoil, half as much as from the Suez Canal two decades earlier. Serious flooding caused delays and building embankments on mud foundations brought both delay and expense. The extra expenditure placed the undertaking in jeopardy. With finances running out, the Corporation of Manchester, with foresight and courage, intervened and advanced £5 million, nearly a third of the final cost of over £17 million.

Commercial traffic commenced on 1 January 1894, although the official opening ceremony by Queen Victoria did not take place until 21 May when she sailed up the canal on the yacht *Enchantress*. Manchester was immediately constituted a customs port. The response from shipowners was, however, an anticlimax. The country was at the time in a period of commercial depression and Liverpool shipowners saw no reason to come up to Manchester. They also prophesied dire problems for vessels navigating the new waterway. It was to be mainly North East Coast interests who responded and established many of the shipping related industries of the new port. From West Hartlepool came Sivewright, Bacon and Company who, within a few years, were to transfer all their shipowning interests from the Hartlepools to Manchester. Christopher Furness played a major role in the formation of Manchester Liners. Additionally, moving south from Glasgow, Herbert Watson established a line of fruit carriers from Spain and the Mediterranean to Manchester. Ashore, the Furness, Bacon and Stoker families were also concerned with Manchester Dry Docks and Morrell, Mills and Company, both ship repair undertakings. The Sivewright, Furness and Bacon families were related: Christopher Furness's older brother John and Captain Bacon had both married into the Sivewright family.

Manchester Liners Ltd

The first Furness Withy proposal, in 1894, had been to promote a service between Manchester and Bombay (Manchester, Bombay and General Navigation Company Ltd) to carry cotton goods from mills in and around Manchester. Such potential incursion and competition for the conference lines brought opposition and an early compromise. The conference lines paid £11,000 to buy out Furness and, as a result, both Anchor and Clan Lines became regular customers of Manchester docks.

Defeated at this first step, Christopher Furness explored further avenues, services from Manchester to the Levant, Channel Islands and Montreal being considered. Frustrated in the purchase of ships for a Montreal line in 1895, a service was operated with a few sailings during the summer of 1897. The following year success was achieved with the formation of Manchester Liners Ltd. Furness had realised the need for local support and expressed his willingness to take a major holding in the new company if Manchester interests were

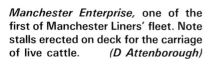

Manchester Enterprise, one of the first of Manchester Liners' fleet. Note stalls erected on deck for the carriage of live cattle. *(D Attenborough)*

Manchester Merchant, serving as a Boer War transport. *(D Attenborough)*

prepared to invest. Representatives of the Canal company also visited Canada and received promises of a subsidy of £8,000 a year from the Canadian Government, plus declared support from the Canadian Pacific Railway and Mr Swift, the Chicago meat packer.

With a share capital of £500,000, split half preference and half ordinary shares, Sir Christopher Furness took up £150,000 to make him the largest shareholder. He also undertook to manage the new venture from West Hartlepool until the necessary organisation had been established in Manchester. Within a fortnight of the first directors' meeting, Robert Burdon Stoker, one of Furness's able lieutenants, was appointed Managing Director, a position he was to hold until his death in 1919. The senior of all Furness's managers, this move opened the way for Furness to introduce his nephews to senior positions in Furness Withy. Moving to Manchester, Stoker resigned as a director of Furness Withy but retained his seat on the board of British Maritime Trust.

Immediate attention was given to the tonnage needs for the service to Canada. The second-hand market provided two vessels, purchased from Elder, Dempster and Company for £60,000. Both built in 1890 as the Johnston Line *Queensmore* and *Parkmore,* they were immediately renamed, introducing the distinctive nomenclature of the fleet, *Manchester Enterprise* and *Manchester Trader.* Not the best of ships for the service, *Manchester Enterprise,* with a reputation for rolling, only lasted eighteen months until 15 November 1899 when she foundered on passage to Montreal. *Manchester Trader* lasted longer, until sold to Norwegian interests in 1912. Additional chartered tonnage was drawn from Furness Withy, including *Cynthiana* and *Straits of Menai.*

Sir Christopher Furness, who had been elected chairman, was keen to provide tonnage for the company from his shipyards and the early minute books contain many references to his offers of ships available for early delivery. In view of his conflict of interests at such times, he withdrew from meetings whilst his fellow directors discussed the matter. Their reluctance to take up the proffered vessels can be gauged from the number of times they deferred a decision until a future date. Often this led to a later minute noting the ships were no longer available, having been sold. Most of the speculative tonnage offered by Furness was of the single deck tramp type whereas spar or shelter deck designs were more suitable for the wide range of general cargo to be carried and, at the same time, able to handle bulk grain to Manchester.

Manchester Liners' fleet was, nevertheless, rapidly expanded. Three shelter deckers on order for Furness Withy were taken over whilst still under construction by Sir Raylton Dixon and Company (*Manchester City*) and Palmers' Shipbuilding and Iron Company (*Manchester Port* and *Manchester Merchant*). Orders were placed for four further vessels, two each with the Furness Withy (*Manchester Corporation* and *Manchester Commerce*) and Irvine's yards (*Manchester Importer* and *Manchester Shipper*). Despite the loss of *Manchester Enterprise* in November 1899, the new century saw a fleet of eight ships, plus chartered tonnage.

Name	Built	Acquired	GRT	Name	Built	Acquired	GRT
MANCHESTER ENTERPRISE	1890	1898	3878	MANCHESTER EXCHANGE	1901	--	4091
MANCHESTER TRADER	1890	1898	3318	MANCHESTER ENGINEER	1902	--	4302
MANCHESTER CITY	1898	--	7696	MANCHESTER INVENTOR	1902	--	4247
MANCHESTER PORT	1899	--	5658	MANCHESTER MARKET	1902	--	4901
MANCHESTER MERCHANT	1900	--	5657	MANCHESTER SPINNER	1903	--	4227
MANCHESTER CORPORATION	1899	--	5397	MANCHESTER MILLER	1903	--	4234
MANCHESTER COMMERCE	1899	--	5363	MANCHESTER PORT	1904	--	4093
MANCHESTER IMPORTER	1899	--	4028	MANCHESTER MERCHANT	1904	--	4152
MANCHESTER SHIPPER	1900	--	4076	MANCHESTER MARINER	1904	--	4106

The Directors did not limit their attention to ships: they were also considering further services. Within a year, they were dispatching ships to southern ports like New Orleans and Galveston to load cotton, thirteen ships arriving at Manchester during the first season. In 1904, this became a joint service with Frederick Leyland and Company. Earlier, a joint Boston service with Leyland had commenced with chartered Furness Withy ships and, in 1900, both had commenced running to Philadelphia, supported by a £300 subsidy per voyage from the Pennsylvania and Reading Railroad. Between 1901 and 1904, a joint weekly service was operated from Avonmouth to Philadelphia with R W Leyland and Company, the first sailings being taken by *Manchester Corporation* and *Planet Neptune.*

Despite the loss of *Manchester Enterprise* and the sale of *Manchester Port* in 1900, fleet replacement and expansion continued. From 1901 to 1904, nine ships were delivered from the associated yards of Furness Withy (four) and Northumberland Shipbuilding Company (five). Close sisters, they were to form the backbone of the fleet for the next decade, apart from the nearly new *Manchester Market* which was wrecked in fog on Tuskar Rock on passage to Philadelphia. Earlier, on 15 January 1903, *Manchester Merchant*, nearing the end of her first voyage for the company (she had been on continuous charter for the Boer War since completion), was scuttled on fire in Dingle Bay with a cargo of cotton from New Orleans.

Sylviana ashore at Skinningrove between 14 December 1901 and 8 June 1902.

Marine Losses

The seven ships lost during the decade reflect the pattern of services and tramping of the period. The small *Edith* was broken up following collision damage in the Thames, *Baltimore City* and *Manchester Enterprise* were casualties on the Canadian service whilst *Wetherby, New Borough* and *Manningham* were carrying bulk cargo, the first two phosphates from America and the third Swedish iron ore. All were in the North Atlantic or European waters.

Fleet losses—1892 to 1902
WETHERBY—2 December 1893 wrecked on Diamond Shoal, off Cape Hatteras. Fernandina for Rotterdam, phosphate.
NEW BOROUGH—17 April 1895 ashore off Washwood, North Carolina. Tampa for Stettin, phosphate. Refloated, sold foreign 1895 as PENSACOLA.
MADURA—28 November 1895 foundered in 43N 32W. Hamburg for Norfolk and Port Royal, salt & general.
EDITH—25 November 1895 sunk in collision with R W BOYD in Thames. Ghent for London, general. Raised, broken up.
MANNINGHAM —28 May 1896 ashore at Medelkallen, between Snipan and Walsoarne. Lulea for Amsterdam, ore. Refloated and sold foreign 1896.
BALTIMORE CITY—17 July 1897 wrecked on Flat Island, entrance to Straits of Belle Isle. Montreal for Manchester, cattle, corn, deals, etc.
MANCHESTER ENTERPRISE—14 November 1899 foundered in 50N 42W. Manchester for Montreal, general.

The Boer War

As the new century dawned, events were to see the development of the Furness interests take a new direction. The shipping trade was to go into recession, having had rates boosted by wars between China and Japan, then the United States and Spain, the Boer War in South Africa and the Boxer Rising in China. Peaking in 1901, the freight market fell sharply the next year and a decade was to pass before reasonable levels were to return. One of the causes was the optimistic building of new tonnage, in which Sir Christopher Furness took a lead. The Boer War undoubtedly benefited the Furness Withy Group indirectly by taking competing tonnage off the market and keeping rates high.

Whilst some companies were heavily involved in chartering their ships as troop transports or supply ships, Furness Withy only had *Rapidan* taken up for one voyage with troops from Liverpool to Cape Town in November 1899, hire of £24,736 being received. Wilson's and Furness-Leyland Line's *Chicago* was trooping for a much longer period, October 1899 to August 1901 for which hire of £123,172 was paid. Manchester Liners had four of their ships taken over for varying periods, *Manchester Merchant* for thirty months from February 1900 to October 1902, *Manchester Port* for three trips between October 1899 and November 1902 whilst both *Manchester City* and *Manchester Corporation* made single trips. A Government offer to purchase *Manchester Port* and *Manchester Merchant* was declined.

West Hartlepool Steam Navigation Company Ltd

In 1899 the West Hartlepool Steam Navigation Company Ltd was established in West Hartlepool to bring together the fleets of a previous company of the same name and that managed by J E Guthe. The older company dated back to 1856 when it had been formed under the control of the West Hartlepool Harbour and Railway Company and R W Jackson. Sir Christopher Furness became a minority shareholder in the new company and was elected first chairman. This interest was sold to J E Guthe in 1904, at which time Furness also resigned as chairman.

The management of this fleet never impinged on the Furness Withy offices, although ships such as *Whitehall* of 1897 and *Daltonhall* of 1900, both members of the Furness Withy fleet, reflected the nomenclature of this company, which in addition to tramping operated liner trades from West Hartlepool to Gothenburg and Hamburg and from Stockton and Middlesbrough to Hamburg. During 1902, a joint service was opened from Manchester, Cardiff and London to the Persian Gulf, in partnership with Bucknall Line and Frank C Strick and Company.

3. Change of Direction—1902 to 1914

The appearance of the International Mercantile Marine in 1902 was the major factor affecting the direction in which Furness Withy were to develop in the coming decade.

The North Atlantic was the scene of intense competition with large volumes of traffic flowing between the Old and New Worlds. Migrants flooded westward and the produce of the growing North American economy, grain, timber, cotton and oil, moved east to Europe. For several years, William Pirrie of Harland & Wolff and Albert Ballin of Hamburg America Line had been working to get agreement between North Atlantic operators for a cartel covering services and fares. Others sought amalgamation, such as J R Ellerman who, in 1898, proposed a merger of Cunard with his own interests.

Nothing came of these endeavours until the American financier and railroad baron, John Pierpont Morgan, engineered the formation of the International Mercantile Marine. Undoubtedly influenced by the knowledge that most of this trade was in European hands and fresh from a series of reorganisations and mergers, he turned his thoughts to shipping. In May 1901, "Fairplay" reported the rumour that he "is busily engaged in forming an enormous American Atlantic Shipping Trust".

The Morgan fortune, built up by his grandfather, Joseph Morgan, came from farming, stage coaches, hotels and fire- insurance companies. His father, Junius Spencer Morgan, was a drygoods merchant when John was born, who became, in 1854, partner to George Peabody, an American merchant and London banker.

J P Morgan entered the London banking house in 1856 and from 1860 to 1864 was New York agent. After the American Civil War he prospered as a financier by obtaining control of the Albany and Susquehanna Railroad from Jay Gould and James Fisk and breaking the monopoly of Jay Cooke in Government refunding operations.

During the last decades of the 19th century, he reorganised various Railroads including Philadelphia and Reading (twice), Chesapeake and Ohio, Southern, Erie and Northern Pacific. In rehabilitating them he employed "voting trusts", small groups of trustees selected by himself. The Morgan railroads were one of the six major American railroad "empires"—only two of which were completely outside Morgan influence.

Morgan then turned to industrial reorganisation starting with Federal Steel Company in 1898, National Tube Company and American Bridge Company. In 1901, he created the largest corporation in the world in United States Steel Corporation, a merger of Morgan, Carnegie, Moore, Gates and Rockefeller interests. In 1902 came International Harvester Company and International Mercantile Marine.

Many of these combines were grossly over capitalised, the consequences of which were only avoided by careful centralised control and the existence of prosperity with growing markets absorbing output. When recession set in, the future of such undertakings was in question.

The International Navigation Company (also known as the Red Star Line), dating from 1871 when it was founded by Peter Wright and Sons, Philadelphia, and the Pennsylvania Railroad, was the vehicle to be developed into Morgan's planned Shipping Trust or combine. Renamed, the capital was increased from $15 million to $120 million to finance acquisitions. It already owned the American Line (purchased in 1884) and had just purchased Atlantic Transport Line. In 1901-1902 Leyland Line was added to the assets, followed by Dominion Line and White Star. Public acknowledgement of the existence of the new combine had to wait until April 1902, even though the provisional agreement had been signed in February.

At the same time as the above purchases took place, a 51% holding in Holland America Line was obtained (bought back in 1915-1917) whilst Norddeutscher Lloyd and Hamburg America Line entered into association although no shareholdings were involved. The services of the various lines were rationalised and covered by pooling agreements, with White Star the prestige operator.

Some lines remained aloof from the combine including Cunard, Allan Line, Elder Dempster's Beaver Line and Compagnie Generale Transatlantique (French Line). Rather than compete, John Ellerman sold his Atlantic interests to the new combine. At the Admiralty concern was felt as they paid a subsidy to White Star for ships earmarked as auxiliary cruisers in time of war, and now these were passing into foreign ownership and control.

Lord Inverclyde at Cunard commenced discussions with the Admiralty and other affected parties in an effort to protect the interests of those who were not members of the new combine. They might find it difficult to survive should a price war develop with a competitor apparently having such extensive financial resources. Sir Christopher Furness was one who was likely to suffer competition from the new giant as his interests had exhibited a steady upward progression from cargo to intermediate passenger-cargo vessels and a logical development to first class passenger status could be anticipated.

Furness's reaction was to propose the formation of a British based Combine under his control, Navigation Shipping Syndicate, consisting of companies who were not members of the International Mercantile Marine, such as Cunard Line, Elder Dempster's Beaver Line and his own Furness Withy interests. It was suggested that the Admiralty would exercise their right to buy the eight White Star ships receiving subsidy payments and sell them to the British Combine. Further help from the Government would include assistance in building eight new ships and increased operating subsidies.

For months negotiations continued without result. Morgan's Combine consolidated its position and the British Government tempered its initial enthusiasm for the proposed British Combine. By August 1902, the proposals were effectively dead and with them Furness's ideas to extend beyond the North Atlantic. Individual lines developed their own futures: Beaver Line, since 1899 under Elder Dempster management, was sold in 1903 to the Canadian Pacific Railway, thus introducing another railroad to the North Atlantic. Cunard announced in September 1902 agreement with the Government for a subsidy to build two new steamers, *Lusitania* and *Mauretania,* and compete with the Combine. Furness, Withy and Company effectively withdrew from the North Atlantic passenger trade and concentrated on their few remaining North Atlantic cargo routes and the coal and tramp trades.

The subsequent history of International Mercantile Marine can be told quite briefly. The shipping slump which started in 1901 and continued for much of the decade, plus overcapitalisation, led to deterioration in their financial position and the appointment of P A S Franklin as receiver in April 1915. With a book value of $172 million, the company was only worth some $26.5 million. The war shipping boom saved the combine and within a year market values had risen to $165 million.

Post-war recession and changed United States immigration laws led to the disappearance or sale of many of the lines owned, the outstanding disposal being of White Star to Lord Kylsant's Royal Mail Group in 1927. Continuity for the International Mercantile Marine was achieved by investment of funds in United States Lines which had been formed in 1921. During the summer of 1934 the shareholding was increased, resulting in International Mercantile Marine obtaining a controlling interest. Finally the two merged in 1943 and International Mercantile Marine, a New Jersey company, was renamed United States Lines. Sadly, United States Lines filed for bankruptcy in 1986.

Royal Mail Steam Packet Company

Furness's thoughts extended beyond the North Atlantic, although the failure of the proposals for the Navigation Shipping Syndicate at an early stage meant that many details of how the Combine would be established and operate were never considered.

The Syndicate would have included the Royal Mail Steam Packet Company, which was one of the early Royal Chartered companies and had been established to carry passengers and mail to the West Indies, later extending its network of services down the South American coast. By 1902 the company was in financial difficulties. The fleet was ageing fast and for the first time no dividend was paid to shareholders. The need was for new management and for finance to renew the fleet to meet the challenge of competitors with modern tonnage. By June 1902, negotiations between Sir Christopher Furness and the Royal Mail Board had reached the stage of the Packet Company being prepared to sell to the "amalgamated companies", subject to approval by Government and shareholders. Invited to become a director, Furness declined unless he was appointed chairman and submitted his views on the management changes needed.

Soon after, the Combine proposals foundered and with them went the Royal Mail negotiations. As a last resort, Furness offered to buy shares from any Proprietor at the average price over the previous two years if he were appointed chairman, but nothing transpired and the following year Owen Philipps (later Lord Kylsant) was appointed to that post. During the years that followed, the careers of these two outstanding shipping entrepreneurs were repeatedly to cross as they vied for control of companies and fleets. Ultimately the companies were to come closer and closer together until, in 1965, complete union was achieved.

Furness Withy Fleets

The changes in Furness Withy shipping interests following the appearance of International Mercantile Marine is illustrated by the sale of Wilson's & Furness-Leyland Line and the charter out, and then sale, of the two year old *Evangeline* and *Loyalist* as Furness Withy withdrew from passenger trades. Both passed to Lamport and Holt and served as their *Tennyson* and *Byron* for twenty years until sold to Chilean interests. Their place on the North Atlantic was taken by two smaller ten year old Clan Line cargo ships, *Clan Mackinnon* and *Clan Macalister* which assumed the names *Evangeline* and *Loyalist*. Two other Clan Line ships were also bought at the time and given the Furness names *London City* and *St John City*. All four continued to operate the cargo service from London to Canada.

Potomac seen loading china clay at Fowey, was typical of the Furness Withy tramp fleet during the early 20th century.

It is instructive to review the fleet as Sir Christopher Furness completed his adjustments to meet the new conditions on the North Atlantic. At the end of 1902, 26 ships of 87,561gt were owned and operated by the three companies: Furness Withy itself had eleven of 28,112gt, British Maritime Trust ten of 39,271gt and Chesapeake and Ohio five of 20,178gt.

Furness, Withy and Company Ltd					British Maritime Trust Ltd			
Name	Built	Acquired	GRT		Name	Built	Acquired	GRT
DAMARA	1885	1885	1779		CEBRIANA	1899	--	4221
SYLVIANA	1898	--	4189		BOLIVIANA	1900	--	4573
BYRON	1901	--	3909		WYANDOTTE	1900	1900	4204
ex Loyalist					BIRMINGHAM	1901	--	4027
DAHOME	1890	1898	2470		AUSTRIANA	1901	--	4025
ULUNDA	1886	1898	1789		INDIANA	1902	--	3869
DALTONHALL	1899	1900	3538		POTOMAC	1902	--	3618
BUCCANEER	1890	1902	925		ATHENIANA	1902	--	2300
FLORENCE	1889	1902	2492		ORIANA	1902	--	4419
LOYALIST	1891	1902	2294		PERSIANA	1902	--	4032
EVANGELINE	1891	1902	2266					
LONDON CITY	1882	1902	2461					

Chesapeake and Ohio Steamship Company Ltd			
Name	Built	Acquired	GRT
RAPPAHANNOCK	1893	--	3884
SHENANDOAH	1893	--	3886
KANAWHA	1893	--	3884
POWHATAN	1901	1902	4262
ALLEGHANY	1901	1902	4262

The decade to follow was to see the fleet grow with newbuilding and purchased tonnage until in the years prior to the outbreak of war in 1914 it became the largest fleet under the Red Ensign. Between 1905 and 1909 a total of 58 new ships would be added to the fleets, 24 of these in 1907 alone.

In addition to building new tonnage, many opportunities were taken by Furness, Withy and Company to purchase companies and fleets that became available for a variety of reasons. The two major purchases were, of course, Houlder Brothers and Johnston Line, which with Prince Line were largely instrumental in changing the character of the company. The move was also made from private company status owned by Sir Christopher Furness and a few close colleagues, to public status with a growing number of shares held by outside investors.

When, in 1907, an extraordinary general meeting was convened to approve the increase of capital from £2 million to £3.5 million, in order to finance the amalgamation of the British Maritime Trust and Chesapeake and Ohio fleets into Furness, Withy and Company, Sir Christopher Furness, as chairman, was able to report that with newbuildings the fleet consisted of 86 steamers. Controlling interests were also held in 35 other ships, plus under 50% ownership of a further 55 and investment in various shipping companies. The "Shipping Gazette" was able to write of the —

"large number of screw colliers which he has lately had built and still is building on the North-East Coast, and which are presumably controlled at present by the British Maritime Trust. The number of these colliers is much larger than most people imagine, and as they are all new boats, well employed, they constitute a big factor in the coal trade of the East Coast and on the North Sea.

"Under the new regime, Messrs Furness, Withy and Company (Limited) will not only rank amongst the largest owners of British steamers, but they will also have a larger interest in the coal carrying trade than any other individual firm." ("Shipping Gazette Weekly Summary", 8 November 1907)

Coastal Services

In January 1888, Christopher Furness had announced the opening of a line from Hartlepool to London, connecting with the services already operating from London to Boston, St John's N B, Halifax and Baltimore. In due course this became a weekly service.

By 1903 a network of routes from the North East was transferred to Tyne-Tees Shipping Company Ltd, formed from the interests of Furness, Withy and Company, Ltd, Tyne Steam Shipping Company Ltd, Tees Union Shipping Company Ltd and Free Trade Wharf Company Ltd. The Furness holding was a seventh of the capital and two ships were transferred —

Name	Built	Acquired	GRT
BUCCANEER	1890	1902	925
NEW OPORTO	1903	--	502

These services were now outside Furness, Withy and Company control although the interest in Tyne-Tees Shipping was retained for some considerable time. Newcastle shipowner B J Sutherland gained control of Tyne-Tees in 1919; in 1943 Tyne-Tees again changed ownership when it passed to Coast Lines and, with Coast Lines, ultimately became a subsidiary of P & O.

In 1909, Furness Withy took a 50% holding in George V Turnbull and Company, Leith and a new company, George V Turnbull and Company Ltd was formed. The other shares remained with A V Turnbull until 1914 when they were also purchased, and the company was merged into Furness, Withy and Company during 1916. In those years, three coasters were registered in the name of the company —

Name	Built	Acquired	GRT
PETER PAN	1909	1912	938
TOGSTON	1909	1913	1057
WENDY	1913	--	958

Harlingen, later *Peter Pan,* arriving at Bristol City Docks.

The following year the related interests of Stocks, Turnbull and Company Ltd were acquired. As the London and Kirkcaldy Shipping Company they operated *Abbotshall* and *Kirkcaldy* between Kirkcaldy and London, with linoleum a major portion of the cargo carried. The line was renamed Kirkcaldy, Fife and London Steam Shipping Company, whilst Stocks, Turnbull and Company Ltd became H L Stocks and Company Ltd in 1914 on the withdrawal of A V Turnbull. Following the death of Stocks in 1917, Furness Withy gained total ownership and the following year sold the business and fleet to Coast Lines Ltd.

Name	Built	Acquired	GRT
KIRKCALDY	1903	--	525
ABBOTSHALL	1890	--	421
NEW ABBOTSHALL	1911	--	783

Centred on Cardiff, a pattern of Furness Withy services ran to ports such as Antwerp and Rotterdam with tinplate and coal as important outward cargo, and rails and manufactured goods on the return trip. This sphere was developed in 1911 with the purchase of London Welsh Steamship Company Ltd and their London route. The old ships employed on this route were replaced by four new ships, two of which passed with the company to Coast Lines in 1924.

Name	Built	Acquired	GRT	Name	Built	Acquired	GRT
CARDIFF TRADER	1878	1908	562	LONDON TRADER	1913	--	684
SWANSEA TRADER	1883	1908	480	CHANNEL TRADER	1913	--	684
WELSH TRADER	1891	1908	786	TEES TRADER	1913	--	701
LLANELLY TRADER	1913	--	702	1914 LADY OLIVE			

Emerald

Furness confirmed his interest in technology when ordering a new yacht from Alexander Stephen and Sons Ltd. He specified Parsons steam turbine power.

Launched by a daughter of Stephen Furness on 21 October 1902, *Emerald* was of 797 tons Thames measurement on a length of 236ft. A forced draught boiler fed steam to three turbines driving five screws on three shafts. Luxuriously fitted, the owner's suite had four staterooms and the guests' suite, a further six.

Given a builder's preliminary spin on 2 December, full trials were deferred as Furness was not due back in the country from the Delhi Durbar until the end of January 1903. On 10 April four runs over the Skelmorlie Mile averaged 15 knots. Like most early turbine installations, she suffered cavitation and required changes in propeller design.

Chartered by George Gould, she arrived at New York on 6 May 1903, the first turbine powered vessel to cross the Atlantic. Gould used her to follow the America's Cup races in August/September when *Reliance* defended. The 1903 challenge, the twelfth since the schooner *America* had lifted the "hundred guinea" cup in 1851, was the third attempt by Sir Thomas Lipton with *Shamrock III*. Lipton, like so many others, failed in his five attempts between 1899 and 1930 to "lift that ould mug".

In 1908, the "Combination" system, reciprocating engines exhausting to turbines, was being promoted for economy. So at Cowes J Samuel White and Company removed *Emerald's* centre turbine and fitted triple expansion machinery exhausting to the two wing turbines.

Sir Christopher Furness used *Emerald* for many business trips, such as in 1909 after his appointment to the Board of the new Port of London Authority. With fellow members, he toured many European ports, including Antwerp, Kiel and Copenhagen, to study their methods.

Following her owner's death, *Emerald* became Lord Inverclyde's *Beryl* in 1913. Moored for the winter in the Gareloch, fire was discovered on 21 December 1913. Despite all efforts she burnt out and in January was sold for £1,510, for use as a coal hulk by Ardrossan Shipbuilding Company. The loss was blamed on militant suffragettes, but was never proven and seems unlikely.

Gulf Line Ltd

Whilst ready to sell some shipping assets, Sir Christopher Furness was equally interested in purchase and in January 1903 concluded the first development in the second period of the company when control was taken of Gulf Line Ltd.

Gulf Line was an 1899 amalgamation of Greenock Steamship Company Ltd and Gulf Line Association Ltd. Formed in Scotland during 1879 to build and operate a fleet of modern steamers, the Greenock Steamship Company's first ship was *Gulf of Suez* which entered service in May 1880. A regular charter, until 1892, was to Thames and Mersey Line for their service from London to Adelaide, Melbourne and Sydney. In 1890, they had also commenced to place steamers on the Glasgow berth of Loch Line, loading alongside the sailing ships for Melbourne and Sydney, whilst in their own name they operated a service which dated back to 1866 from the United Kingdom to the West Coast of South America.

To raise extra capital for fleet expansion an associate company, Gulf Line Association Ltd, was formed in 1891. *Gulf of Guinea* and *Gulf of Lions* were transferred from the older company to this new Association. Thereafter all new tonnage was built for the Association. In 1899, an arrangement started with F and W Ritson to place their Nautilus Steamship Company Ltd Branch Line ships on the monthly Gulf Line Conference berth to South America, Gulf Line then concentrating on the non-conference run to Australia. The same year another new company, Gulf Line Ltd, was formed to take over the assets of both Greenock Steamship Company and Gulf Line Association which were in poor financial shape and only had assets to match a third of their capital. In 1900, when Holt's Blue Funnel Line started to load from Glasgow for Australia, Gulf Line withdrew as they were in no condition to undertake a rate war, concentrating, in agreement with Blue Funnel Line, their ships on the Liverpool berth for Australia.

The youngest Gulf Line ship, *Gulf of Taranto*, dated from 1892 so, in 1902, the capital was increased from £120,000 to £250,000 to finance modernisation. Sir Christopher Furness took up most of the new shares (£116,364) in January 1903 which, with a previous small holding, gave him 65% and control. The company offices thereafter moved from Greenock to London. At this date, the fleet was reduced to six ships and the four most modern of these, *Gulf of Genoa*, *Gulf of Bothnia*, *Gulf of Siam* and *Gulf of Taranto* dating from 1891/2, were sold to Hamburg America Line (Hapag). Gulf Line took from Hapag in part exchange four older ships dating from 1879/81, *Athos*, *Rhenania*, *Allemania* and *Polynesia*. Only *Rhenania*, renamed *Sicily*, was to remain in the fleet any length of time.

Name	Built	GRT	Name	Built	GRT
GULF OF VENICE	1883	3022	GULF OF BOTHNIA	1891	3452
GULF OF ANCUD	1890	2716	GULF OF SIAM	1892	3433
GULF OF GENOA	1891	3448	GULF OF TARANTO	1892	3431

Gulf of Ancud, purchased with Gulf Line in 1903, was one of two ships retained in service.

Gulf Line's *Appenine* of 1909 loading timber.

Under Furness's control, two ships were transferred to Gulf Line; thereafter it was to be 1908 before further additions were made. Control of Gulf Line had formed part of Sir Christopher Furness's wider plans for a shipping group to balance against International Mercantile Marine but his plans to upgrade the Australian service were frustrated by poor conditions in Australia, and also the recession in finance and shipping. The Gulf Line fleet was henceforth employed in general trading alongside those of Furness, Withy and Company and British Maritime Trust.

Name	Built	Acquired	GRT
RAPALLO	1902	1902	5166
SICILY	1881	1904	1818
Gulf of Carpentaria	1904	--	5804

The most interesting action taken by Sir Christopher Furness in connection with his new acquisition was to demand admission to the Australian Conference in line with the service and cargo carried for many years. The Conference members promptly replied that this in no way entitled Gulf Line to membership of their body. Not to be outflanked, Furness's next move was to advise the Conference of his intention to place on the route four large new ships then being built, if necessary competing with the Conference members to secure fair treatment for Gulf Line.

The outcome of the negotiations was agreement in 1904 for the Australian Conference to pay a lump sum to Gulf Line and purchase one of the new ships, Gulf Line for its part withdrawing all claim to rights. The ship, which was building on the Tees as *Gulf of Carpentaria,* was launched for British India Steam Navigation Company on 13 August 1904 as *Carpentaria* and served that company for two decades before passing to Italian interests.

At the same time, Ritsons had approached Gulf Line with the claim that by usage their Branch Line had become entitled to the Conference rights on the West Coast of South America. Sir Christopher Furness immediately reversed his argument from the Australian case and maintained that Ritson's had earned no such rights. Many years later W C Warwick recalled in his memoirs the lesson he learnt in handling negotiations as he watched Furness switch his negotiating stance in these two concurrent situations. Ultimately, in 1906 the South American situation was concluded with the sale of Gulf Line rights to Ritsons who, until they ultimately withdrew from the service, continued to advertise it as the Gulf Line.

Gulf Line's subsequent history is tied in closely with Furness, Withy and Company. During and after 1908 the company became the vehicle for owning many of the general cargo tramps which were being built so rapidly for the Group in the years up to World War I, ships employed in various company trades' and for charter. The end came in 1929 when the decision was taken to liquidate the company. All the ships were employed on Group companies' routes and there were no tax or other advantages in maintaining Gulf Line

Ltd as a separate entity. *Pacific Exporter* and *Pacific Pioneer* were transferred to Norfolk and North American Steamship Company and Gulf Line Ltd became history. The full fleet list of Gulf Line ships from 1908 until winding up in 1929 is —

Name	Built	Acquired	GRT	Name	Built	Acquired	GRT
TUSCANY	1908	--	3001	SALERNO	1909	1916	3667
FELICIANA	1909	--	4277	TURINO	1914	1916	4241
CROSSBY	1907	1910	3893	ORTONA	1916	1916	5524
ORISTANO	1911	1911	4220	LUGANO	1917	--	3810
APPENINE	1909	1913	3684	RAPALLO	1917	--	3811
CATERINO	1909	1913	3729	MODESTA	1917	--	3832
MESSINA	1911	1913	4271	ARIANO	1917	1919	5155
ROSSANO	1909	1913	3729	CASTELLANO	1918	1919	5227
BOLDWELL	1901	1914	3118	COMINO	1918	1919	4618
FLORENTINO	1900	1914	3411	LONDON MARINER	1922	1922	7896
SANTERAMO	1914	--	4670	PACIFIC PIONEER	1928	--	6723
SANTERAMO	1904	1916	3045	PACIFIC EXPORTER	1928	--	6723

Liner Services, The Direct Clay Line and Bulk Shipping

With the sale of Wilson's and Furness-Leyland Line, the company had effectively withdrawn from the important routes to Boston and New York. There remained the other routes, such as the Furness service to Newfoundland and Nova Scotia purchased in 1898, Manchester Liners with their independent operation to Canada and the Southern States from Manchester, and Chesapeake and Ohio's Newport News service.

By purchase and development, attempts were made to enter a number of trades. Gulf Line's South American and Australian routes did not endure, but an attempt was made to enter the Persian Gulf trade and, using tonnage available following closure of the joint Furness Withy and Elder Dempster service between Canada and South Africa, an entry was made into the River Plate frozen meat trade. In 1908, the Plate Conference paid Furness Withy and Manchester Liners to withdraw, after which the ships which had been employed on the route were chartered to Anglo-Argentine Shipping Company Ltd, a non-conference operator. This company built further ships but defaulted on mortgage payments in 1908. Thereafter the company was purchased by Furness, Withy and Company through the medium of the British and South American Steam Navigation Company.

The bulk cargo trades were strengthened during 1905 with the establishment of the Direct Clay Line in partnership with the Grand Trunk Railway, to carry exports of china clay from Fowey in Cornwall to Boston and Portland, Maine.

Coal and bulk cargo trades were the order of the day, keeping many of the fleet busy. Britain supplied over half the world's energy requirements in the form of coal, which in turn comprised 75% of the country's export trade. With the London and Newcastle coal offices co-ordinating the marketing of coal from companies under Furness's influence, cargo was assured. The Newcastle office for example shipped 500,000 tons a year to London. South Wales was another major loading area for Furness Withy colliers.

One triangular pattern worked was the Pomaron Ore trade to United States Gulf ports. Today Pomarao is a sleepy Portuguese village thirty miles up the Guadiana River on the southern border with Spain, the only reminder of this past trade being the trackbed of the dismantled railway and a rusting loading chute. Having loaded coal to Iberian or Mediterranean destinations, the ships then proceeded in ballast upriver to Pomarao to load copper ore for America. The third leg was a cargo of pitch pine, phosphate, resin, turpentine, etc for Europe. Many ships then moved to the coal loading berth for a repeat voyage. A variation on this trade was to load iron ore in Spain, produced by Soria Mining Company, a subsidiary of Palmer's Shipbuilding and Iron Company. This was discharged on the Tyne and the vessel was ready for another outward cargo of coal.

Gloriana loading china clay at Fowey.

Neptune Steam Navigation Company Ltd

The next acquisition came in 1906 when the Sunderland based Neptune Steam Navigation Company Ltd was in difficulties. Established in 1891 and managed by the Pinkney family, they had suffered heavy financial loss through building the big 6,317gt *Moreno* in 1902. The intended employment of *Moreno* is not known, but they sold her to Austrian interests soon after. In 1905, financial conditions forced them to reduce the capital from £350,000 to £232,227 by writing off £117,773 not represented by assets. The decline continued and the following year Furness, Withy and Company purchased seven of the fleet (see below) and the liner service from Baltimore to Rotterdam. The rest of the fleet, along with the owning company, passed to the management of Bolam and Swinhoe, Newcastle, until 1910 when it was purchased by Furness, Withy and Company.

Name	Built	GRT	Name	Built	GRT
VENANGO	1891	2938	QUEEN WILHELMINA	1898	3590
TAMPICO	1895	2968	OHIO	1899	4006
DURANGO	1895	3008	RUNO	1900	4016
TABASCO	1895	2987			

In 1909, Holland America Line attacked the Rotterdam to Baltimore service, commencing to load their own steamers in opposition to Furness Withy. Competition from a company of the size and standing of Holland America Line, with its association with International Mercantile Marine, and also the fact that Furness Withy was a cross trader and not a Dutch company, did not augur well for a satisfactory outcome of a freight war on the route. So in February 1909, Furness offered to sell the service with five ships *Brantford*, *Rotterdam*, *Como*, *Ohio* and *Runo* to the Dutch company for £222,650. The deal was finally agreed with a sixth ship, *Rapallo*, also included.

Furness and Nephews, Rotterdam

With the purchase of the Neptune Line service from Rotterdam to Baltimore in 1906 the decision was taken to open a branch office in Rotterdam to care for that interest, so in that year Furness and Nephews Ltd opened for business—the nephews in the title being Stephen, Walter and Ethelbert. With a share capital of £1,000, soon raised to £5,000, the venture was soon to expand into a healthy undertaking.

The ships agency business soon developed into stevedoring and, in 1912, was converted from a British to a Dutch registered company, NV Furness' Scheepvaart- & Agentuur Maatschappij. By this time they were also owning and managing ships under the Dutch flag, ships registered in their name and also the names of Stoomvaart Maatschappij Hollandia, Stoomvaart Maatschappij Indische Lloyd and Rotterdamsche Scheepvaart Maatschappij. Many of these ships were purchased from Furness Withy in England, either new or second-hand.

The association with the Rotterdam business continued until NV Furness' Scheepvaart- & Agentuur Maatschappij was sold in 1916. Although no longer a member of the Furness Withy Group the Dutch concern continued to expand to become a major force in the transport scene in Holland, and to this day still operates under the Furness name.

Turrets, Monitors and Arch Decks

During 1907 two unusual ships, for Furness, Withy and Company, joined the fleet. Six "turret" ships had been ordered from William Doxford and Sons by London based J Sunley and Company at a price of £40,500 each. Due to breach of contract by the buyers, they were left on Doxford's hands and two were sold to Furness Withy at £42,000 each. *Billiter* had already been launched and was completed as *Tunstall* whilst *Billiter Avenue* was launched as *Braziliana*. Only one other "turret" was owned in the Group; this was bought second-hand in 1910, to become Neptune Steamship Company's *Cleveland Range*.

The decades to 1914 were marked by efforts to perfect better hull form, both for seaworthiness and economy. In 1891, the Great Lakes whaleback steamer *Charles W Wetmore* had called at Liverpool, arousing considerable interest. Johnston Line responded by commissioning Doxford to build *Sagamore*, the only British built whaleback.

Doxford also gave serious consideration to the design of the whaleback and from this they developed the "turret" ship, launching 176 examples into the Wear between 1892 and 1911. Another eight came from other yards, mainly licence built. In 1894, Furness Withy were the first to take a licence from Doxford, although they never built or ordered one.

The "turret" concept produced a ship in which a trunk ran the length of the hull. The ship sides turned in above the waterline to meet this trunk. A number of advantages included better longitudinal strength, seas tended to be turned back rather than wash over the hull, the trunk created a "feeder" advantageous when carrying bulk cargo and under the tonnage rules then current a "turret" ship had a lower tonnage than conventional ships which reduced Suez Canal transit fees.

Johnston's *Sagamore,* the only British built "whaleback", and *Cleveland Range,* one of the few "turret" ships owned by the Furness Withy Group.

After leaving Doxfords, A H Havers, the naval architect closely involved with the "turret", developed the "Monitor", intended to have the same hull form plus corrugated sides said to further strengthen the vessel, increase deadweight and improve fuel economy. No "Monitors" were, however, built with the "turret" hull form; all took a normal hull and added corrugations. After experience with the first two on charter, *Monitoria* and *Hyltonia,* compared with four non-"Monitor" sister ships, Furness Withy ordered *Wingate,* delivered in 1914 and sold out of the fleet in 1926.

Soon after the "Monitor" hull form was introduced, Maxwell Ballard, a young naval architect with Swan, Hunter and Wigham Richardson, patented the "arch deck". This introduced a reverse sheer and designed the hull as an inverted girder. Furness Withy again gave the design a trial by ordering two ships for their coal trade. Unfortunately *Bedale* became a war loss in 1917 but her sister *Pensacola* traded until sold in 1923.

Although not yet part of the Furness Withy group, Johnston Line followed up their *Sagamore* with three "turrets" from Doxford, *Ashmore, Noranmore* and *Beechmore,* between 1896 and 1899. As the "turret" did not receive favourable treatment from the British authorities, they were registered under the Belgian flag and owned by an Antwerp based subsidiary in which Doxfords held a 50% interest. In 1904, Cairn Line of Steamships Ltd, a company later to join the Furness Withy Group, ordered a single "turret", *Cairntorr.*

Shipbuilding

The three shipyards owned, Furness Withy's Middleton yard, Irvine's Harbour Dockyard and Northumberland's Howden-on-Tyne facility, continued in full production throughout the decade.

Examination of figures for the period between 1900 and the acceptance of Admiralty wartime orders, confirms the importance of the relationship between the shipbuilding and shipowning interests. Ships built for group companies, or known to have been laid down as speculative ventures, account for nearly 40%, over 140 out of 353 ships launched. It is certain that this figure was higher as it is not possible to identify many of the speculative ships. Irvine's had the highest percentage of the identifiable ships, 46.5% for 47 out of 101 launches, followed by the Withy yard at 40%, 42 out of 104, and Northumberland was lowest with 34%, 51 out of 148 ships.

The "Shipping Gazette" in April 1909 was able to write of Sir Christopher Furness "He could claim in the last 20 years to have built more steamers than any firm in the world in the same period, ...". No wonder Albert Ballin of the Hamburg America Line had been able to write in his diary for 5 June 1902, when considering the recession into which shipping was moving:

"In England, in consequence of the national excitement, a very awkward situation has arisen. Sir Alfred Jones and Sir Christopher Furness know how to make use of this excitement as an opportunity for shouldering the British nation with the burden which the excessive tonnage owned by their companies represents to them in these days of depression."

Whilst the three shipyards continued to concentrate mainly on simple cargo vessels, many to standard designs, they were fully equipped and capable of building a wide range of vessels, including passenger carrying vessels such as *Digby* and refrigerated ships like *El Paraguayo* and *La Correntina*.

Palmers' Shipbuilding and Iron Company Ltd is often listed as being owned in these years by Furness. Sir Christopher Furness was appointed a director in 1903, and chairman during 1910, as he was the largest single shareholder in the company. However, this holding never exceeded about 6% of the capital invested and that had all been sold by 1916.

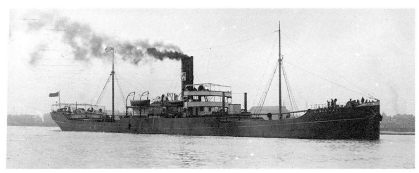

Linda Fell, a unit of the Hessler Shipping Company fleet from 1906 to 1915.

Hessler Shipping Company Ltd

In March 1907, Furness, Withy and Company acquired control of this company, purchasing the shares previously held by J K M Hessler to bring their holding to over 90%. The company, managed from West Hartlepool and, later, Liverpool continued as shipowners and lasted until wound up in 1923. The Hessler Shipping Company had been formed in 1901 by Jacob Hessler and Company Ltd, West Hartlepool, to purchase a speculative cargo vessel ordered by Furness from Grangemouth and Greenock Dockyard Company, Greenock. Yard number 220, she cost £32,500 and was launched as *Jupiter*, entering service in September 1901.

Furness Withy took an interest in the new company, subscribing for £4,000 of the £70,000 capital, plus a mortgage on monies owing. This interest was increased when, in 1903, the Swedish company Rederi A/B Norman—owned 100% by Furness Withy and owners of the steamer *Norman* - was transferred at a price of £24,000, paid in shares. In 1913 *Norman* was transferred to the British flag and renamed *Saltburn*. Then in 1906/7 two Irvine built sisters joined the fleet as *Linda Fell* and *Myra Fell*.

In addition, Hessler managed several ships under the Norwegian flag owned by companies controlled by Blohm and Ohlsen, Frederikshavn.

Name	Built	Acquired	GRT	Name	Built	Acquired	GRT
JUPITER	1901	--	2124	MYRA FELL	1907	--	3024
LINDA FELL	1906	--	3025	SALTBURN	1901	1913	1840

Laing Steamship Company Ltd

The fleet of three ships owned by Laing Steamship Company Ltd was purchased in 1909. This company had been established in 1903 by Sir James Laing and Sons to take over the French owned *Ile de la Reunion* which they had built for Compagnie Havraise Peninsulaire de Navigation in 1897. She was probably taken in part exchange for the new *Havraise* launched on 29 January 1903. Renamed *Swaledale*, she was soon joined by two newbuildings from the yard, *Wensleydale* and *Langdale*.

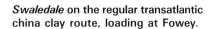

Swaledale on the regular transatlantic china clay route, loading at Fowey.

Purchased for £73,000, the three ships were integrated into the fleet of Furness, Withy and Company without change of name and were all sold late in 1911. J J van Meel of the Rotterdam office of Furness and Nephews was promoting a service to the Far East and had earlier approached Furness Withy to buy suitable tonnage. Various ships were offered and the deal was finalised as the three Laing ships plus *Acara*, of Wood's fleet, for £120,000.

Name	Built	Acquired	GRT
SWALEDALE	1897	1909	3658
WENSLEYDALE	1903	1909	3964
LANGDALE	1903	1909	3930

Agincourt Steamship Company Ltd

Lloyd and Company, London shipbrokers, formed this company in March 1904, Tom Lloyd having agreed to buy Northumberland Shipbuilding Company's yard number 111, laid down speculatively by Sir Christopher Furness. Named *Agincourt* when completed, she had been launched in December 1903 as *Gloriana* for British Maritime Trust. *Agincourt*, which was wrecked in March 1906, was followed by five further ships, all products of various Furness yards.

Lloyd financed the ships by heavy use of mortgages granted by the builders and, after he died, Furness, Withy and Company acquired the company and fleet as mortgagees in 1910. They wound up the company in November 1913 as it "cannot by reason of its liabilities continue its business". By that time three ships had been sold, the two left (*Balaclava* and *Dettingen*) being transferred to Furness Withy.

Name	Built	Acquired	GRT	Name	Built	Acquired	GRT
BALACLAVA	1906	--	4220	EVESHAM	1905	1907	4224
CORUNNA	1906	--	3810	FLODDEN	1907	1907	4226
DETTINGEN	1899	1907	4221				

Anapa, was one of the fleet of J M Wood, Liverpool.

James Marke Wood, Liverpool

Following the death of J M Wood, whose fleet had been employed in trade to the Far East, Furness Withy purchased the fleet at the executors' sale in 1909 for £105,000. This added seven ships to the fleet, all of which had left the Furness Withy fleet within four years.

Name	Built	Acquired	GRT	Name	Built	Acquired	GRT
AVALA	1890	1909	3751	ASAMA	1897	1910	4217
ABANA	1894	1909	4189	ADANA	1897	1910	3448
AMANA	1895	1910	3412	ACARA	1904	1909	4982
ANAPA	1896	1910	3524				

Neptune Steam Navigation Company Ltd

When the liner trade interests had been purchased by Furness, Withy and Company in 1906, the balance of the fleet, and the company, passed to the management of Bolam and Swinhoe, Newcastle, who proceeded to add several new ships to the fleet. However, the shipping climate saw the company still returning poor results and consequently an offer from Furness Withy in the summer of 1910 saw the company acquired for £148,341.

In the years leading up to the war in 1914, a number of typical tramps were added to the fleet. All except one were newbuildings from Group yards. The exception was *Cleveland Range*, one of the few "turret" ships in any Furness fleet. Completed in 1898 as *Heathdene*, she was purchased as *Forest Dale* and renamed to fit the Neptune fleet nomenclature. Retained for only a short period, she was sold to Italian owners in 1913 and became *Giuseppe G.*

The fleet consisted of—

Name	Built	GRT		Name	Built	GRT
a. Ships purchased with the company in 1910:						
PENNINE RANGE	1903	3397		LOWTHER RANGE	1906	3792
CHEVIOT RANGE	1903	3458		MALVERN RANGE	1906	3573
GRAMPIAN RANGE	1905	3148		SNOWDON RANGE	1906	3060
NORFOLK RANGE	1905	3054				
b. New tonnage added 1910-1915:						
BRANTFORD	1910	4113		HAMBLETON RANGE	1914	3682
CHILTERN RANGE	1911	4220		CHEVIOT RANGE	1914	3691
COTSWOLD RANGE	1912	4248		MALVERN RANGE	1915	4524
Hambleton Range	1913	3655		Pentland Range	1915	5812
MENDIP RANGE	1914	4495				

Pennine Range wearing Furness Withy funnel colours shortly before World War I. *(WSPL)*

Management Structure

The "Syren & Shipping" photograph of the board of directors, taken in 1910, gives a revealing insight into the policy followed by Furness during the first two decades as, of the twelve directors, six were members of the Furness family.

Whilst the first generation of managers recruited to fill the need for competent personnel proved, in the main, to be well chosen, Christopher Furness found several not to be dependable. As these had been posted to offices abroad, for example to Montreal, New York and Rotterdam, distance enhanced the problem.

A similar problem arose in regard to the latitude given to senior managers to undertake private ship management. In the case of J F Lund, Furness considered that he spent too much of his time on this private interest at the expense of Furness, Withy and Company, and also chose to place chartering and insurance business through outside firms rather than through Furness Withy channels. Ultimately Lund decided to resign and devote himself to the continued development of his own business.

Sir Christopher Furness' son Marmaduke evinced little interest in business, preferring the life of a gentleman, so Christopher recruited the six sons of his brother Stephen, all born in Sweden. The oldest nephew, Stephen Wilson Furness, became a director in 1894 and over the years became the recognised heir to his uncle as head of the shipowning and shipbuilding interests. His five other brothers also joined the company and all were appointed directors between 1905 and 1915, Harry C, John E, Walter H, Carl E and Ethelbert.

There was a tendency to send these nephews to take charge of overseas branches and in all cases the personal blood bond was a success in avoiding problems and achieving dependable operations. For example John Furness went to Halifax, Walter and Ethelbert Furness to Rotterdam.

It has been suggested that with these nephews coming up through the managerial chain, Furness moved some of his senior staff sideways in order to make room for them, such as R B Stoker to Manchester Liners in 1898. At the time Stoker was his senior employee, so it is open to debate whether this was paternalism or a case of placing his most trusted aide in an important post at Manchester where he could be relied upon. The transfer of W C Warwick to Houlder Brothers in 1911 also comes to mind in this context.

The Remarkable Epic of *Snowdon Range*

Under the command of Ernest Dickinson, *Snowdon Range* sailed from Philadelphia on 22 November 1912, bound for Leith with 4,000 tons of grain. She was met by severe and continuous gales, which were to cause heavy losses to shipping on the North Atlantic. Two days before her the steamer *Whittingham* had sailed from Baltimore for Rotterdam. In December *Armstor* passed Port Eads on Christmas Eve, bound from New Orleans for Aalborg whilst *Therese Horn* left Port Arthur on 26 December, like *Whittingham* bound for Rotterdam. All three were never seen again, posted missing at Lloyd's and probably victims of the storm conditions. Another vessel, *Birchtor*, was so overdue her reinsurance rate was being quoted at 75 guineas per cent before she belatedly arrived. *Snowdon Range*, Dickinson's first command, was also long overdue when she arrived

THE BOARD OF DIRECTORS OF FURNESS, WITHY AND CO. LIMITED

The names reading from left to right are—Mr. F. W. LEWIS, Mr. S. W. FURNESS, M.P., Mr. R. E. BURNETT, Mr. A. S. PURDON, J.P., Mr. R. W. VICK, J.P.,
the Hon. MARMADUKE FURNESS, J.P., Mr. R. J. THOMPSON, the Rt. Hon. LORD FURNESS (Chairman), Mr. JOHN E. FURNESS, Mr. WALTER
FURNESS, Mr. W. H. BECKINGHAM and Mr. C. E. FURNESS

at Queenstown 52 days after sailing from Philadelphia. Before she was safe in harbour her reinsurance rate had reached 94 guineas per cent.

On 5 December hurricane force conditions had broken the rudder and left it swinging uselessly. In continued bad weather, the crew secured the rudder with steel wire. With it secure, the next task was to rig a jury rudder and bring the ship under control. Three days later, the damaged rudder was torn completely off the ship. Using whatever materials were available, spars, canvas, chains, engine-room floor plates and a small anchor, a total of thirteen jury rudders were made and fitted, only to be torn away and destroyed.

On 19 December, the Swedish ship *Vesterland* was sighted 700 miles West of Scotland. Due to the weather she was unable to take *Snowdon Range* in tow, so offered to take off the crew. This offer was declined and Captain Dickinson continued slowly to work his disabled ship eastwards with bunkers, food and water running low. At last, on 1 January 1913, the Dominion Line *Welshman* was sighted and three days later a tow line was passed. On 11 January the line broke, but they were able to reconnect. At this time the trawler *Salome* agreed to take a line from the stern of *Snowdon Range* and help in steering.

Three days later, after a 500 mile tow, *Welshman* was able to hand over to the tug *Flying Fish* off Old Head of Kinsale. But *Snowdon Range* was far from safe. Approaching Cork, a violent gale forced the tug to let go the tow and *Snowdon Range* found herself anchored in an exposed position outside the harbour. In the dark and with anchors dragging, *Snowdon Range* began driving down toward the rocks at the harbour entrance. Helped by searchlights from Camden Fort, Captain Dickinson used his engine to obtain some control of his ship as she dragged into the harbour and eventually grounded on a sand bank.

For their services, *Welshman* was awarded £9,550 in salvage and *Salome* £450. Amongst the many awards made was Lloyd's Silver Medal for Meritorious Services to Captain Dickinson and five of his crew.

Neptune Steam Navigation Company steamer *Lowther Range*.

Lowther Range Salvage

Lowther Range sailed from Cardiff for Bombay with a cargo of coal on 27 May 1910. In the Indian Ocean, she sighted the drifting Lloyd Austriaco steamer *Trieste* which had sailed from Trieste on 3 June with passengers, cargo and bullion. Disabled, with her tail shaft broken and propeller lost, *Trieste* was taken in tow by *Lowther Range* and arrived in port seven days later. As well as the normal salvage award, Captain Matthews was awarded Lloyd's Silver Medal for Meritorious Services, as were also Chief Officer Hedley, 2nd Officer Baker, Chief Engineer Aiken, 2nd Engineer Ramshaw and 3rd Engineer Craig. Captain Matthews also received a gold watch from the Austrian Emperor.

Industrial Relations and the Co-Partnery Scheme

Throughout his life Christopher Furness took a keen interest in labour relations, considering the reconciliation of employer and employee to be to their mutual advantage.

The oustanding application he made in this field came in 1908 when he introduced the Co-Partnery Scheme into the shipyards. At an address made on 7 October 1908 in West Hartlepool, entitled "Industrial Peace and Industrial Efficiency", he made two offers to promote workers interests, the first being to sell his shipyards to the Labour Unions at valuation, the second to make employees limited co-partners.

In return for a no-strike undertaking Sir Christopher Furness made shares available for sale to the workers. 5% of their wages would be used to buy these shares, which were guaranteed to return 4% dividend. They were also to receive a share of the profits remaining after 5% had been paid to shareholders. The first year of operation gave employees a return of 9%.

As might be expected, the Trade Unions were bitterly opposed to the Co-Partnery Scheme, as it removed much of their power base in the shipyards. Their pressure and anti-Scheme publicity led to a ballot in April 1910 at which Co-Partnery was rejected by 598 votes to 492. This ended one of the most interesting experiments in labour relations prior to World War I, although in due course such ideas would come to be more commonly accepted as both practical and beneficial.

South Point sailing from Philadelphia with a cargo of flour for the Belgium Relief Commission.

Norfolk and North American Steam Navigation Company Ltd

A useful purchase in 1910 was the Norfolk and North American Steam Navigation Company Ltd with its Philadelphia Trans-Atlantic Line from Philadelphia to London. Dating from 1893 when it was established under the management of Simpson, Spence and Young to operate in the trade from Virginia to the United Kingdom, the company had suffered during the depressed years of the 1900s and when Furness, Withy and Company paid £51,000 for control, they had a fleet of five ageing ships, the youngest completed in 1901.

Name	Built	GRT	Name	Built	GRT
MONTAUK POINT	1899	4822	NORTH POINT	1900	5216
CROWN POINT	1900	5218	EAST POINT	1901	5234
EAGLE POINT	1900	5222			

Immediate steps were taken by adding three new ships to the fleet in 1912, which were followed by three larger cargo liners, one of which (*Dominion Miller*) was transferred while building to the newly established Furness-Houlder Argentine Lines as their *Abadesa*.

Name	Built	GRT	Name	Built	GRT
SOUTH POINT	1912	3837	SOUTHWESTERN MILLER	1915	6514
WEST POINT	1912	3847	NORTHWESTERN MILLER	1915	5046
START POINT	1912	3840	Dominion Miller	1916	6572

John Bull: "Thanks! An enormous improvement. That's the future form of association between Labour and Capital."

(Daily Dispatch)

Houlder Brothers Joins Furness Withy

When the directors of Houlder Brothers and Company agreed to sell a 50% interest in their business to Furness, Withy and Company in July 1911 it was the first of three acquisitions that changed the character of the Furness Withy Group, the others being the purchase of Johnston Line and Prince Line. From being a largely tramp operation with some limited liner trades, the enlarged Group now became one of the major liner and refrigerated meat carrying companies under the Red Ensign.

Like so many of the companies coming into the Furness Withy fold, Houlder Brothers had financial and managerial problems which threatened the future well-being of the venture. Although the shareholders, led by J A Linley and W A Starling (respectively the former local director and secretary of Houlder Brothers in Australia) had been defeated on a vote at the Annual General Meeting on 29 July 1901 when the founder, Edwin Houlder, had collapsed and died, their criticism of management and results might well have carried the day if presented a few years later.

HOULDER BROTHERS
& Co., Ltd.

Regular Steamship Services
from the United Kingdom
to

River Plate & South Africa.

Passengers booked, freight engagements made, and
insurances effected to all parts of the world

HEAD OFFICE:
146, Leadenhall Street, London, E.C.

BRANCH OFFICES AT
Liverpool, Glasgow, Newport (Mon.), Manchester, Bristol,
Swansea, Port Talbot, Birmingham, Sheffield, Leeds,
Immingham, Buenos Aires, La Plat, Sydney (N.S.W.)·
and Cape Town.

During 1901 shipping started to slip into a period of recession which was to affect Houlders badly. There were also differences of opinion between directors on policy matters. After 1902 no ordinary dividend was declared. Worse, preference dividends went into arrears in July 1904 and depreciation provisions required by the Debenture Trust Deed were not made after 1905. The fleet aged, and no new ship was commissioned for the refrigerated trade after *Oswestry Grange* in March 1902. Only the scope and fleet of the subsidiary Empire Transport Company was extended in 1910 with new capital and a debenture issue to finance ten new general cargo ships.

The younger Houlder family directors, Edwin's sons Frank and Maurice, were not happy with the conduct of business by their older cousins. Frank Houlder accordingly resigned in 1907 and only returned the following year when elected chairman. A further cause of conflict was the influence of Alan Hughes of Birt, Potter and Hughes Ltd, managers of the Federal Line, and with Houlders members of the joint Federal-Houlder-Shire service to Australia.

Matters came to a head in 1910 when it was proposed to re-organise Houlder Line finances, issue £500,000 of new shares to Federal Line, A H Houlder and H Houlder. The resulting dispute between the two groups of directors went to court with Frank and Maurice Houlder questioning the legality of the share issue and charging fraud and collusion. A settlement was reached, and the fraud and collusion accusations were withdrawn, as was the share issue which would have resulted in a take-over by Federal Line.

However, action was getting increasingly urgent, as effectively all the ordinary and half the preference capital of Houlder Line Ltd had been lost, there being no assets left to match the capital. Various parties made bids for control, including Owen Philipps (later Lord Kylsant). Philipps and Furness had competed for other companies in the past and every time Philipps had won, the latest occasion being in the autumn of 1910 for Glen Line. Philipps was so certain of success with Houlders that he openly spoke of his new acquisition. But, unknown to both Philipps and Sir Christopher Furness, Frederick Lewis, a director of Furness, Withy and Company, Ltd since 1899, had seized the initiative and, uninvited, walked into a Houlder directors' meeting to conclude a deal on the spot.

The fleet controlled by Houlder Brothers in July 1911 consisted of nineteen ships —

Name	Built	GRT	Name	Built	GRT
Houlder Line Ltd			Empire Transport Company Ltd		
HORNBY GRANGE	1890	2356	EVERTON GRANGE	1903	7144
URMSTON GRANGE	1894	3423	EMPIRE TRANSPORT	1909	6291
ELSTREE GRANGE	1892	3930	BRITISH TRANSPORT	1909	4143
ROYSTON GRANGE	1897	4213	CANADIAN TRANSPORT	1910	4139
BEACON GRANGE	1898	4237	CAPE TRANSPORT	1910	4109
RIPPINGHAM GRANGE	1898	6827	INDIAN TRANSPORT	1910	4111
THORPE GRANGE	1889	4188	NATAL TRANSPORT	1910	4114
DRAYTON GRANGE	1901	6592	AMERICAN TRANSPORT	1911	4767
SUTHERLAND GRANGE	1907	6852	ARGENTINE TRANSPORT	1911	4763
Oswestry Grange Steamship Company Ltd					
OSWESTRY GRANGE	1902	7381			

As neither debenture nor preference shareholders were favourably disposed towards a capital reorganisation following the Furness Withy take-over, it was decided to review the business. W C Warwick was seconded from Furness Withy as Managing Director and it was quickly decided to sell the Australian shipping interests which had, for some time, shown disappointing results. Henceforth the company was to concentrate on the River Plate trade where contracts signed in 1910 had given Houlder Brothers and Company, Furness, Withy and Company and the Royal Mail Steam Packet Company a near monopoly of the frozen meat trade to the United Kingdom, their only competition being from the Nelson Line which formed part of a conglomerate incorporating everything from meat packing plant, through shipping to a retail chain of butchers shops. By 1912 Nelson Line were to control the world's largest fleet of refrigerated meat ships. A fleet of nine fully refrigerated ships owned by Houlders, Furness Withy and Royal Mail would operate a weekly service and carry a major portion of the frozen meat exported from South America to Britain.

Natal Transport, built in 1910 for Empire Transport Company.   **(WSPL)**

Another factor considered in the sale of the Australian routes was the strained relationship with Federal Line following the take-over bid. Early in 1912 Federal itself was purchased by New Zealand Shipping Company Ltd, so in April these routes and the four ships involved, *Drayton Grange, Rippingham Grange, Oswestry Grange* and *Everton Grange* passed to New Zealand Shipping.

A further decision taken was to recover the fleet depreciation lost since 1905 before commencing to pay off accumulated preference dividends. A sum of £332,631 10s 5d was written into the accounts for this purpose. In 1915 capital re- organisation was finally undertaken, ordinary shares were halved in value, from £5 to £2 10s each, and the outstanding preference dividend funded by the issue of £115,063 19s 9d of funding certificates. These were to be redeemed after 5% depreciation had been set aside on the fleet, and payment had been made of the debenture interest, the preference dividend and 5% on ordinary shares. With better returns following re- organisation of company interests, and higher freights resulting from World War I, these funding certificates were all redeemed by the end of 1916. Finally, in 1919, the accretion of reserves allowed a distribution of assets and ordinary shares reverted to a value of £5 each.

With the sale of the four ships to the New Zealand Shipping Company the fleet was reduced to seven ''Grange'' ships. Orders were placed for another seven, two (*El Paraguayo* and *La Correntina*) fully refrigerated for the weekly Royal Mail, Furness Withy and Houlder service from the River Plate to Liverpool and five general cargo ships (*Lynton Grange, Denby Grange, Oaklands Grange, Rounton Grange* and *Oldfield Grange*) for the service from Antwerp, London and South Wales to the Plate which for many years had been operated with chartered tonnage.

The Houlder Story

Edwin Savory Houlder was, like Christopher Furness, a younger son of the family. They had much else in common, their business ventures starting from nothing and developing during their lifetimes into major undertakings. However, Houlder was from an earlier generation and his name appears in shipping directories some two decades prior to Furness.

Whereas the Furness family took their name and origin from the Furness district, Houlder roots lay further south, in Lancastria. By the time E S Houlder was born on 19 December 1828 the family were living at Heathfield, Sussex. His father lost heavily at gambling and as a last resort fled abroad, abandoning his wife and seven children. In such straitened circumstances Edwin was raised and, in 1844, commenced working for Ionides Sgouta and Company, a firm of Greek merchants in London.

With the encouragement of his employers he branched out, commencing business for his own account on reaching the age of twenty one. This was an opportune time. The repeal of the Navigation Acts and the introduction of free trade heralded a massive and continuous growth in Britain's overseas trade which would continue until World War I. During the same period the sailing ship reached its zenith and steam came of age. Single expansion engines led to compounding, triple expansion and, later, the turbine. On this wave of growth British shipowners rode until half the world's steamers flew the Red Ensign and were seen in every port of the world.

Edwin Houlder retained his old job and used the address of Sgouta and Company until about 1853. By then the scale of his trade warranted independent premises and an office was taken in Gracechurch Street as E S Houlder and Company, ship and insurance brokers.

Early in his career Houlder saw the potential of the remote colony of Australia. Settled originally as a convenient convict prison, slow growth had been given a massive impetus in 1851 with the discovery of gold by Edgar Hargreaves. Sydney became a ghost town within a week and when news reached England by the Aberdeen White Star liner *Phoenician* early in February 1852, thousands clamoured for a passage to fortune, over 100,000 arriving in Victoria that year alone. Few were to find it, but most were to settle in a new homeland. The populations of Victoria and New South Wales jumped overnight, and within eighteen months the populations of Melbourne and Geelong had trebled. When gold fever abated the colonies, who were at the time in the process of establishing local self government, settled back from the disruption of the Gold Rush into a pattern of steady growth and development.

Mineral wealth abounded. As well as gold the country had riches of silver, copper, lead, zinc and tin. In 1883 mining of the rich silver-lead-zinc deposits at Broken Hill commenced. Elsewhere coal seams had long been worked and were to provide a regular cargo for ships calling at Newcastle, NSW. Another important source of wealth lay in sheep. Early in the century the Merino sheep had laid the foundation for a trade still important in the Australian economy today. In 1821 less than 100 tons of wool was shipped; by 1850 this had grown to about 20,000 tons and continued to increase. In the main the wool was shipped to the London sale rooms. Grain also constituted a growing export whilst the sailing of *Strathleven* from Sydney and Melbourne to London at the end of 1879 proved the value of refrigeration in Antipodean trade and opened new markets for Australian meat and perishable commodities.

Improved communications and raw materials, ranging from consumer goods to railway lines and rolling stock, were required to fuel the growth of the Australian economy. Edwin Houlder recognised this need and, like others, responded by chartering and loading ships from London to Melbourne and Sydney. By 1860 he was advertising monthly sailings to Melbourne and twice monthly to Sydney, employing chartered British and American clippers. The outbreak of the American Civil War was to change the pattern of chartering and also introduce his firm to shipowning. Prior to the outbreak of the Civil War in 1861, the American merchant marine had been challenging the British for supremacy in world trade. However, the depredations of the civil war with Confederate commerce raiders like *Alabama* at sea were to change all that. Many ships became casualties of the conflict and others were sold abroad to avoid war risks. When peace returned to the continent not only had the merchant fleet been decimated but the eyes of Americans had turned from the sea to the vast prairies with the cry 'Go West, Young Man'.

The first ship owned and managed in Houlder's office was to be the wooden sailing ship *Golden Horn* built in Maine in 1854 and purchased in 1861. Two years later, in 1863, the fleet of sailing ships reached its zenith with five bought: *Golden City*, *Glendower*, *Lucibelle*, *Empress* and *Eagle Speed*. Apart from *Golden Sea*, bought in 1866, the fleet were all softwood ships built in New York or Maine and ranging from 779 to 1418 tons.

As shipowners and not merely charterers another problem had to be met. Australia had, at the time, little return cargo to offer and after discharge many ships had to seek it elsewhere. Some sailed for China and others turned north-west to India or loaded coal for America. As charterers, Houlders could engage ships for the outward passage and be left with no responsibility for homeward freight. Now, as owners this responsibility could not be avoided. The answer was provided by an employee, J T Cayford. Following a serious illness he was sent on a voyage from England to New Zealand to recuperate. Whilst there he became interested in the guano, coconut and copra trade of the Pacific and after returning home formed J T Arundel and Company with E S Houlder as one of the partners. Houlder ships could now load such cargo home. A reminder of this lies in loss records, for in July 1866 *Golden City* was driven ashore and wrecked on Lady Elliott's Island whilst loading guano and *Lucibelle* drifted ashore in a calm during May 1871 at Starbuck Island after arrival from Melbourne via the Kermody Group and Carolina Islands seeking guano. Not all Houlder's ships followed this route however, for in July 1865 *Eagle Speed* had been wrecked in the Mutlah River carrying coolies and rice for Calcutta.

In 1896 the interests of J T Arundel and Company were amalgamated with those of James Morrison and Company in a new undertaking, The Pacific Island Company Ltd. Their interests in guano, copra, mother of pearl and island trading were to lead to phosphate discoveries at Ocean and Nauru Islands. The early association of Houlders with companies, such as Arundel, responsible for the development of Pacific island trade, including the Pacific Phosphate Company Ltd and, later, British Phosphate Commissioners was to be responsible for the formation in 1914 of the British Empire Steam Navigation Company with the carriage of phosphates as a prime business.

By 1877 all the wooden sailing ships had been sold or lost and only *Queen of the North* remained to fly the Houlder flag until 1890. In the meantime Edwin Houlder and his partners, E S Houlder and Company had become Houlder Brothers and Company with the admission of his brothers Alfred and Augustus in 1856 and 1867, followed by Ebenezer Cayford in 1880, were exhibiting the customary Victorian entrepreneurial habits, developing all opportunities. Contracts were undertaken, for example, to ship coal to railways in India and South Africa prior to the development of indigenous supplies. For South Africa alone this rose to nearly 200,000 tons a year before the Natal coalfields were developed and replaced British supplies.

In 1878 Alfred Houlder had literally to run for his life when a volcano erupted in Hawaii. Sadly, having a weak heart he died shortly afterwards. Three years later Edwin Houlder visited Argentina with his sons Frank and Maurice to study possibilities and laid the foundations of the trade for which Houlders were to become best known, the carriage of frozen meat. Frank Houlder's introduction to business had started with a sea trip on *Golden Sea* when aged 14; later he was to go on and obtain his mate's ticket.

During their visit to Argentina the Houlders, father and sons, had recent refrigeration trials and experiments in mind. Like Australia and New Zealand, the Argentine had a surfeit of animals and no market for them. The Houlders came home with a contract from the River Plate Fresh Meat Company Ltd to ship frozen meat to Belgium and England. This company had been formed with the sole purpose of freezing and shipping meat to England, initially mutton, but after a few years beef was added to the output.

The Sunderland owned steamers *Meath* and *Wexford* were chartered and after being fitted with insulation were dispatched south. *Meath,* commanded by J J Ormiston, loaded her first cargo off Colonia (Uruguay), the frozen mutton being shipped down from Campana (Argentina) on the steamer *Nevera.* On 6 December 1883 loading was delayed as a fire broke out on *Nevera* and damaged some 1,600 carcasses. However, *Meath* sailed from Buenos Aires on 17 December and arrived at Antwerp on 21 January 1884. After part discharge she then moved on 1 February across to London where she landed the first Argentinian frozen meat to be handled at Smithfield: 7571 sheep carcasses and various parcels of by-products, tongues, skins, kidneys, tallow and dried blood. *Wexford,* Captain W Richardson, arrived at Rosario on 28 January 1884 before moving down to load at Campana. She arrived back at Antwerp on 6 April and London on 10 April, landing 9,432 frozen sheep carcasses and other produce at the latter port.

Both *Meath* and *Wexford* remained on charter until 1886. Also chartered, until 1893, were *Zenobia* and *Zephyrus* owned by Turner, Brightman and Company who, in due course, were to take the River Plate Fresh Meat contract from Houlders. Another contract was obtained, carrying material for the construction of harbour facilities at Buenos Aires for T Walker, the contractor. This provided welcome outward cargo to balance the refrigerated homeward trade.

An intriguing mystery of the period is the appearance of the names of two steamers in advertisements of 1881-2. After listing the sailing ships and steamers on berth for Australia they ended with "To follow" *Urmston Grange* and *Ovingdean Grange.* It is not now known if these ships were actually built and possibly sold prior to launch or completion.

With the growth of the frozen meat trade the decision was taken by Houlders in 1888 to build and operate their own refrigerated ships. First into the water at Middlesbrough was *Ovingdean Grange* on 29 November 1889, followed on 7 December by her sister *Hornby Grange.* Each was fitted with insulated chambers of 70,000 cubic feet capacity for the carriage of meat and other frozen cargo. Other ships followed including *Urmston Grange* in 1894 from Workman, Clark and Company, Belfast. Her building commenced a relationship which was to see eight refrigerated ships delivered from Belfast by 1902.

In 1898 the partnership of Houlder Brothers and Company was replaced by a new limited liability company, Houlder Brothers and Company Ltd, and the following year Houlder Line Ltd was formed to take over the fleet, which had been owned up to that time either in 64th shares or by single ship companies.

Houlder interests by now extended beyond shipping. In both Australia and Argentina they included land and processing plants, some being personal holdings of family members and others being held by the company. A meat works was established at Merinda (near Bowen, Queensland) in 1895 by Bergl (Australia) Ltd in which company Houlders held a large interest. In South America the Rio Seco works was opened in 1905, ten miles east of Punta Arenas. These works were owned by the South American Export Syndicate in which Houlders held a large interest.

The Frozen Meat Trade

The association with Houlder Brothers and the 1910 meat contracts marked a major Furness Withy development into the frozen meat trade, for although refrigerated ships had long been owned, these had in the main been chartered to other managers.

In 1890 the new *Pakeha* had featured briefly in the fleet list prior to her sale to Shaw, Savill and Albion Company and her sister *Rangatira* was laid down originally for Furness Withy. In due course Manchester Liners converted *Manchester City* into a refrigerated carrier and the *Guardiana* of 1906 was also fitted. After the Furness Withy foray into the River Plate meat trade had ended these ships were chartered to Anglo-Argentine Shipping Company. Anglo-Argentine, however, defaulted on mortgage payments on their two owned ships, *La Blanca* and *El Argentino,* in 1908 and the mortgagees took possession and formed Argentine Cargo Line Ltd to own them. In 1911, control of Argentine Cargo Lines passed to British and Argentine Steam Navigation Company.

The first meat freezing plant in the world had been built at Sydney, NSW, in 1861, followed closely by another at Melbourne. Initially serving the local market the owners, Thomas Mort and James Harrison respectively, both recognised the potential markets abroad and early experimented with the carriage of frozen cargo at sea. Harrison chartered *Norfolk* in 1873 and Mort used *Northam* during 1876. Both trials failed. Elsewhere limited success attended French experiments. Charles Tellier first attempted refrigerated carriage on *City of Rio de Janeiro* in 1868 but was defeated by a machinery breakdown. A trial using *Frigorifique* fitted with ammonia compressors in 1876 for a return voyage from France to Argentina met with partial success. The shipment of 5500 carcasses of mutton by *Paraguay* in 1877/8, also using ammonia machines, was the first entirely successful carriage of frozen meat at sea. After this French efforts were abandoned. The year *Paraguay* sailed from France to Argentina had seen the Bell-Coleman cold air refrigeration machine patented, to be first fitted on the Anchor Line *Circassia* in 1879 for the North Atlantic trade.

Andrew McIlwraith and other Queensland interests decided to hold further trials, having inspected *Paraguay* in France. They chartered *Strathleven*, fitted Bell-Coleman machines and loaded forty tons of meat at Sydney and Melbourne in November and December 1879. Arriving in London on 2 February 1880 the cargo outturned in perfect order. *Protos* and *Europa* followed from Melbourne and in 1881 the Orient Line commenced fitting their ships, the first being *Cuzco*, for the carriage of frozen cargo whilst New Zealand saw the Albion Line sailing ship *Dunedin* load her first cargo in February 1882, followed by her sister *Marlborough*.

In September 1910 Furness, Withy and Company signed contracts with Swift Beef Company Ltd and La Sociedad Anonyme La Blanca de Carnes Congeladas, to which a year later they added The Smithfield and Argentine Meat Company Ltd. Jointly with Houlder Brothers, with whom an agreement was signed in December 1910, a fleet of dedicated refrigerated meat carriers would now be built. In addition to those registered in the name of Houlder Line Ltd they would be owned by British and Argentine Steam Navigation Company Ltd and its subsidiary Argentine Cargo Line Ltd, and the new Furness-Houlder Argentine Lines Ltd.

On the outbreak of war in 1914 the Furness Withy and Houlder Group could boast one of the largest fleets of such ships, some of which were already fitted with defensive weapons in case of the outbreak of war. When writing "A History of the Frozen Meat Trade" in 1912 J T Critchell and J Raymond listed the 41 companies, all British apart from seven, operating refrigerated ships in trades from South America and Australasia to Europe and the East. The companies owned 251 ships with a total capacity of 43,951,822 cubic feet. The combined Furness and Houlder fleets controlled twenty ships with a capacity of 4,363,890 cubic feet. Only Nelson Line (20 ships, 5,754,959 cubic feet), New Zealand Shipping Company (18 ships, 4,826,000 cubic feet) and Shaw, Savill and Albion Company (17 ships, 4,729,000 cubic feet) provided greater refrigerated space. The Furness and Houlder fleet was listed as —

Argentine Cargo Line Ltd	3 ships	1,107,000 cubic feet
Furness, Withy & Co Ltd	3 ships	222,201 cubic feet
Gulf Line Ltd	1 ship	88,000 cubic feet
Houlder Brothers & Co Ltd	11 ships	2,541,694 cubic feet
Manchester Liners Ltd	2 ships	404,995 cubic feet

The Pre-War Shipbuilding Programme

With the upturn in the freight market after 1910 the Group undertook a massive newbuilding programme with over seventy ships delivered or ordered, quite apart from the Empire Transport Company programme of 1910. With Sir Christopher Furness having an interest in Empire Transport it was not surprising that the ships of this 1910 programme were, in the main, placed with Furness Withy shipyards, Irvine's and Northumberland.

A brief examination of the deliveries from 1911 onwards gives an interesting insight into the make up of the Group. Of the 75 ships involved, a total of 50 were to come from Irvine's and Northumberland, with the balance spread over a dozen other builders, Sir Raylton Dixon and Company having seven orders, Alexander Stephen and Sons three and the rest one or two each. About 350,000 tons gross of new ships were commissioned, most of them in time to be of service when war was declared.

The most varied group were the ships delivered to Furness Withy itself. In the main these were smaller colliers, including the pioneer motorship *Eavestone*, the "monitor" *Wingate* and "arch deckers" *Bedale* and *Pensacola*. Four were coastal ships, three were larger general cargo ships, and two were the refrigerated meat transports *El Uruguayo* and *La Rosarina*. *El Uruguayo* was transferred soon after completion, and *La Rosarina* prior to completion, to British and Argentine Steam Navigation Company. Then there was *Digby* for the Canadian service. The company was now returning to the North Atlantic passenger trade, abandoned a decade earlier with the sale of the beautiful *Loyalist* and *Evangeline*. A more modern, but nice looking, steamer of 3966gt, *Digby* was launched in December 1912 and the following year entered service to St John's and Halifax. Fitted to carry 58 1st and 32 2nd class passengers she was to remain on this run, apart from war service, until replaced by new tonnage in 1925/6.

Gulf Line and Neptune received ten cargo ships averaging 4,000gt each, and another, laid down as *Pentland Range* for Neptune, was sold to Russia and completed in 1915 as *Krasnoiarsk*. Norfolk and North American not only commissioned three cargo ships in 1911/2, they were later to receive a series of liners which adopted

The shipbuilding programme undertaken after 1910 included *Digby* for the service from Liverpool to Newfoundland and Canada.

Completed in 1914 *Clutha River,* pictured as *Rhodesian Transport,* was intended for general trading.

With a new North Pacific service planned through the Panama Canal, *Northwestern Miller* was completed in 1915.

a new naming system, the suffix *Miller. Dominion Miller* was transferred prior to completion to the new Furness-Houlder Argentine Lines as their *Abadesa,* but *Northwestern Miller* and *Southwestern Miller* entered service, followed by *Start Point* in 1916. With the needs of the newly acquired Warren Line in mind, the short lived *Bay State* entered service in 1915.

Houlder Brothers received the two refrigerated carriers and five cargo ships for Houlder Line, Empire Transport received a further dozen deliveries from Irvine's and Northumberland and formed a new subsidiary, British Empire Steam Navigation Company Ltd who received ten ships between 1914 and 1916. Furness Withy's refrigerated interests were incorporated as British and Argentine Steam Navigation Company (originally established in 1909) which received three big meat carriers, *El Uruguayo* being the largest insulated ship afloat when launched with her capacity of 400,000 cubic feet. Furness-Houlder Argentine Lines Ltd was also incorporated in 1914 and orders were placed for five refrigerated ships, although the war delayed the delivery of four until 1918.

Eavestone

Sir Christopher Furness' interest in new technology was again confirmed following the much publicised introduction of the first ocean going motorships in Denmark and Holland.

Two 1,700gt sisters were ordered from the Middlesbrough yard of Sir Raylton Dixon and Company Ltd to test the new motive power. First, in January 1912, came *Saltburn* as a steamer. Her sister, the diesel powered *Eavestone,* was launched by Lady Furness and entered service in August.

Eavestone, the first British owned deep-sea motorship.

Designed in Belgium by Carel Freres of Ghent, *Eavestone's* internal combustion engine was erected by Richardsons, Westgarth and Company Ltd, Middlesbrough. Carel Freres supplied the cylinders, valves and camshafts whilst the frames and other parts were manufactured on Teesside. A four cylinder two-stroke, single-acting unit with 20 inch bore and 36 inch stroke it produced 800bhp at 95rpm and resembled a steam engine, with open crank pit, box columns supporting the cylinders and outside crossheads.

The compact nature of the diesel when compared with steam resulted in an engine room eight feet shorter in length and the ability to carry an extra 400 tons of cargo on a 30 day voyage.

Captain T Weber made two short proving trips, to Antwerp and the Baltic, before sailing from Hartlepool on 10 October 1912 for a transatlantic voyage. Calling at Barcelona, Pomarao and Savannah, *Eavestone* was back in Rotterdam on 2 March 1913. The protracted voyage, nearly five months, was due to engine trouble, and in January she had been lying at Fayal with two piston heads and covers cracked and other damage.

It was May 1914 before she was trusted on another transatlantic voyage; in the meantime she ran to the Baltic. Following the second visit to America she was again kept in the coastal and short sea trades, within easy reach of engineers as the engine was still causing problems.

Finally the decision was made to end the diesel experiment. Arriving in the Tees on 10 March 1915 she went into shipyard hands and emerged three months later transformed into a steamer. As such she continued in service until being captured and sunk by *U45* on 3 February 1917.

Canada Steamship Lines Ltd

Although the name Canada Steamship Lines was born late in 1913 its genesis lay two years earlier when Grant Morden, a young Canadian financier resident in London and with little in the way of a track record in the financial field, proposed to Sir Christopher Furness that Canadian Great Lakes and St Lawrence shipping, which was largely fragmented into numerous uncoordinated lines, was ready for amalgamation and merger. This audacious scheme appealed to Furness; probably he saw a parallel between himself in his early years and this young Canadian.

The premier Canadian inland shipping company was Richelieu and Ontario Navigation Company. Before endeavouring to acquire such an important prize Morden had to start elsewhere. Gathering a group of associates, including J R Binning, manager of Furness Withy's Montreal office, he commenced with the knowledge that another of the associates, James Playfair, would bring Inland Navigation Company, which he controlled, into the combine. With Furness finance Playfair began, as a front man, buying the shares of Northern Navigation Company and rapidly acquired over 90%.

Now, with two companies in hand, Morden could look towards the biggest prize, Richelieu and Ontario Navigation Company. In March 1911 Morden and his associates, who had been buying all the shares they could get, met the board of directors and laid proposals for amalgamation before them. The three companies would become one, with Morden and his associates elected directors. If the proposal was not accepted the accumulation of shares would continue until a controlling interest had been built up and then they would have little choice but to submit. At the same time there was the attraction of association and links with Furness Withy and Manchester Liners' ocean services. By the end of April the merger was complete as the board bowed to the inevitable.

Two years of outward calm followed. Grant Morden, however, was working to achieve full control of the board on which ten directors, headed by Sir Rodolphe Forget, could veto proposals from Morden and his group of five directors. The question of control was settled at the annual meeting on 19 February 1913 when Morden proposed five new directors to replace the five who were retiring and who had submitted their names for re-election. If elected the newly nominated directors would give Morden and the Furness interest a two-thirds majority. Balloting took all day and at the end gave complete victory to Morden.

Three important acquisitions were made in 1912, of Niagara Navigation Company, Thousand Islands Steamboat Company and St Lawrence River Steamboat Company.

Finance to form the new combine had been raised in Britain, mainly from Furness Withy and Vickers Ltd, who were extending their engineering interests in Canada. Influence with a customer such as Canada Steamship Lines would benefit the shipyards owned by Vickers by directing business their way. As financial control now lay with the British interests, a London Advisory Committee was established during 1913 in addition to the board in Montreal. Headed by Sir Trevor Dawson, managing director of Vickers, this committee was anything but advisory. It made all the major decisions, the Montreal board being limited to local day-to-day control, often having to send representatives to London to appear personally before the Advisory Committee and explain matters.

As was common with many such mergers the financial arrangements concealed a time bomb, which in the case of Canada Steamship Lines was nearly to explode a decade later. Many of the assets were entered in the accounts at cost rather than depreciated or market value, much of the capital was raised in the form of cumulative preference shares and mortgage debenture stock and an intangible asset, "good will", was entered at $8 million.

In 1913, following the general meeting, James Carruthers (dubbed "the Wheat King of Canada") was appointed president. However, real power and control lay with Morden who was to pursue an expansionist policy which nearly ruined the company. That year a further four acquisitions were made, Ontario and Quebec Navigation Company, Lake Ontario and Bay of Quinte Steamship Company, Canadian Interlakes Lines and Quebec Steamship Company.

With the outbreak of war in 1914 many of the fleet were sent down river to cross the Atlantic and take part in the war effort. On arrival in England, they were naturally placed under the management of Furness, Withy and Company, but the condition of many caused concern. Furness Withy therefore arranged extensive overhauls to fit them for the task ahead and to satisfy the requirements of Lloyd's Register of Shipping. With shipyards busy on Admiralty work these overhauls were expensive and the costs incurred led to differences between Furness Withy, the Advisory Committee in London and the board in Montreal, resulting in Furness Withy distancing themselves from Canada Steamship Lines and starting to dispose of their shareholding. As Sir Christopher Furness had been the one link holding his loose knit empire together, his death in 1912 resulted in a slow loosening of the ties with Canada Steamship Lines until they parted completely in 1919.

In Montreal, Canada Steamship Lines fell increasingly under the influence of Joseph Norcross, Vice-President and Managing Director. Whereas Carruthers was cautious and conservative, Norcross was expansionist and optimistic. The end result was Carruthers' resignation in 1919, Norcross becoming his successor. Like many others in both shipping and industry, Norcross viewed the post-war world through rose coloured spectacles. This optimism, and his consequent actions, were to be highly dangerous to the good health of the company and lit the fuse that nearly set off the time bomb.

In 1919 Canada Steamship Lines moved into ocean shipping, and the following year bought Montreal Transportation Company, also investing $2.5 million in Davie Shipbuilding and Repairing Company. Ill-considered, these acquisitions merely added to Canada Steamship Lines' mounting financial problems and did nothing to remedy them. One small remedial step in 1919, however, was to sell the Quebec Steamship Company ships and services to the West Indies, South America and Bermuda to Furness Withy for $2 million. This cash, however, did little to resolve the problems being faced.

Attempts to raise finance for the ailing undertaking met with no response. Morden was busy with another merger, the British Empire Steel Company which was being formed from the steel companies of Nova Scotia and he proposed including Canada Steamship Lines as one arm of the new company. However, the collapse of the freight market in 1920 and the general relapse of the economy after the war saw British Empire Steel facing their own difficulties, so this hope for salvation faded.

The solution lay in New York. In desperation Norcross turned to the investment firm of Kissel, Kennicott and Company. The New York management firm of Coverdale and Colpitts were instructed to review the finances, trade and operations of the invalid concern and William H Coverdale was in due course appointed President to implement their recommendations. He had correctly identified the root cause of the problem as being the original financial structure, aggravated by the optimistic attitude and expenditure during the intervening years. He was to nurse the invalid back to health and remained President until his death in 1949.

One important outcome of Coverdale's intervention in 1922, and the infusion of aid from New York, was to limit the power of the London Advisory Committee which survived in only limited form until being wound up in 1932. Control had returned to Montreal with supervision from New York until Coverdale led Canada Steamship Lines into full independence.

Manchester Liners Ltd

After the first few years of meteoric growth Manchester Liners found themselves faced with maintaining their services despite the recession gripping the shipping industry. With a fleet of fourteen ships in 1904

Manchester Liners major role in serving Manchester was early recognised in this cartoon. *(Syren and Shipping)*

the company looked to diversification, such as the River Plate service already mentioned, which operated from 1906 to 1908. Three of the ships were employed outside the United Kingdom to Canada trade and showed the best return on investment of any of the fleet.

The problems facing shipowners come through clearly when Manchester Liners' annual accounts are examined. No dividend was paid to ordinary shareholders between 1903 and 1912, and even preference shareholders were five and a half years in arrears by 1911. An upturn in the freight market at that stage was welcome, although it was to take the effect of World War I fully to remedy the deficit and allow reserves to be built up for the future.

The developments in Canada which led to the formation of Canada Steamship Lines also brought benefit to Manchester Liners, resulting in working arrangements which enabled them to offer through services, with transhipment at Montreal, to destinations on the Great Lakes.

The size of the fleet reflected the market. Following the delivery of sisters *Manchester Port, Manchester Merchant* and *Manchester Mariner* in early 1904, it was to be February 1912 before another order was placed. As a result of this order, in August 1912 Northumberland Shipbuilding delivered *Manchester Citizen,* and she was followed three weeks later by the Irvine's built *Manchester Civilian.*

Change of Chairman

Ever since Furness, Withy and Company Ltd was incorporated in 1891 Lord Furness had been chairman. But in September 1912 his health caused concern and, on doctor's advice, he resigned the chairmanship of Palmer's Shipbuilding and Iron Co Ltd and returned home to Grantley Hall, near Ripon, to rest. His health continued to deteriorate until early on Sunday, 10 November 1912, he died at the age of 60.

For the first time the Furness Withy offices were to be without his restless presence. His energy had been channelled in many directions as his industrial empire had developed. Always interested in new inventions and processes he was eager to adopt any that enhanced his interests. His activities when a Liberal Party Member of Parliament for Hartlepool, in addition to his business interests, were recognised by a knighthood in 1895 and elevation to the peerage in 1910 as Baron Furness of Grantley.

The chairman's cloak fell naturally on his nephew, Stephen Furness, who had succeeded him as Liberal Member of Parliament for Hartlepool in 1910. Furness, Withy and Company continued to develop under the leadership of the new chairman, who was made a baronet in 1913. However, tragedy was to strike when least expected. Sir Stephen and Lady Furness were staying at a hotel in Broadstairs on 6 September 1914 when, being a light sleeper, he rose at 1am to open a window, lost his balance and fell to his death from the 5th floor.

At this juncture Frederick Lewis was the logical choice to assume the chair, from his long association with the business and standing in the office; he had also been a director since 1899. However, he chose to defer to the young Marmaduke Furness, born in 1883 and now Lord Furness, both in deference to the memory of Christopher Furness and in recognition of the size of the family shareholding. But, in view of Marmaduke's lack of experience, it was agreed he would take no decisions without prior consultation with Lewis.

Warren Line

In 1912 the Liverpool shipowner George Warren approached Furness, Withy and Company, initially looking for new Boston agents. Having succeeded his father, who had died in 1880, and been in sole control of the line since his brother's death in 1901, Warren now had retirement in mind. At the same time he faced the problem of raising capital for renewal of an ageing fleet: the youngest ship, *Iowa*, dated from 1902. Negotiations rapidly developed into Furness Withy acquiring, for £81,000, a controlling interest in the small, but complementary, White Diamond Steamship Company Ltd with their Liverpool to Boston service and four ships —

Name	Built	GRT	Name	Built	GRT
MICHIGAN	1887	4935	SACHEM	1893	5354
SAGAMORE	1892	5197	IOWA	1902	8370

The name White Diamond recalled the origin of the Warren Line as an American packet line running from Boston to Liverpool, established by Enoch Train in 1839 and identified by a red houseflag with a white diamond. Many of the line's early packets were built by Donald McKay who was to become one of the best known Yankee shipbuilders.

Sachem joined Furness Withy as part of the Warren Line fleet, remaining in service until broken up in 1926.

During 1848 an office was opened in Liverpool to replace the existing agency arrangement, and in 1853 George Warren moved from Boston to manage it. Ultimately he was to take over full control of the enterprise which became closely identified with his name. The outbreak of the American Civil War in 1861 led to the ships being transferred to the British flag and thereafter it increasingly became a British organisation.

Steam was introduced with chartered tonnage in 1863, followed by owned steamers in and after 1875. The first to be purchased was the Guion liner *Manhattan* built in 1866, and renamed *Massachusetts* on hoisting the Warren flag. With owned and chartered tonnage the service was maintained, with a ship sailing about every three days in 1895/6. Cattle were a major cargo, an annual average of 40,000 cattle being landed by the company at Liverpool. During 1904 a service from Galveston was commenced with the new *Iowa*, which landed some of the largest cotton cargoes brought into the Mersey.

The attraction to Furness Withy was the opportunity to integrate the service with their own Newfoundland and Canadian run, whilst the future management needs and capital injection posed no problem. *Iowa* was sold to the Hamburg America Line soon after the purchase, whilst *Michigan* passed to the Admiralty after the outbreak of war and was expended as a blockship at Mudros. When needed, extra ships were obtained from other Furness Withy companies to run alongside the Warren ships.

During 1913 *Sagamore* and *Sachem* had accommodation fitted for 60 2nd class passengers; *Michigan* continued with berths for only twelve passengers. In December 1915 a new ship joined the fleet when Laing completed the 5064gt *Bay State*, but just over two years later she was sunk by *U66*.

Marine Losses—1903 to 1914

The losses sustained by the fleet in this period reflect the concentration of company interests on the North Atlantic and in the coal trades.

One loss, although not from marine causes, occurred in the Far East. For many years rivalry between Japan and Russia had been growing as both tried to extend their spheres of influence in the Far East. On 8 February 1904 Japanese forces made a pre-emptive strike against the Russian fleet at Port Arthur, commencing the war that ended with Japanese victory and the Treaty of Portsmouth in September 1905. The Trans-Siberian Railway was still under construction, so maritime supply lines were vital to both belligerents. The financial returns to neutral shipowners were such that many risked belligerent warships to run supplies. Both Russia and Japan seized and condemned, as prizes of war, ships bound for enemy ports. The largest group of prizes were eleven ships stopped and taken in by Japanese warships whilst trying to run the blockade of Vladivostock, including Furness Withy's *Sylviana* with a cargo of coal loaded at Cardiff. Captured in February 1905, she was condemned and sold to become the Japanese *Goto Maru*. As such she went missing in the Pacific late in 1907.

Early in 1903 Manchester Liners were to suffer two losses. *Manchester Merchant* was nearing the end of a passage from New Orleans with a cargo mainly of cotton, but including lumber, turpentine, resin and maize for Manchester when fire was discovered on 12 January. It gained rapidly and she ran for the nearest port of refuge, which was Dingle Bay. Captain Couch brought her in at midnight two days later with the fire raging forward of the bridge and scuttled her in an attempt to extinguish the conflagration. Although the salvage vessel *Ranger* attended from Liverpool she lay in a position exposed to the Atlantic and ten days later bad weather saw her breaking up. Three months later, on 26 April, *Manchester Market* was outward bound from Manchester with general cargo for Philadelphia when, in fog, she ran onto Gipsy Rock, Tuskar. *Ranger* also attended here but heavy seas saw *Manchester Market* start to break up three days later and by 1 May she had broken in two.

Fleet losses—1903 to 1914

MANCHESTER MERCHANT—15 January 1903 on fire, scuttled in Dingle Bay. New Orleans for Manchester, cotton, lumber & maize.
MANCHESTER MARKET—26 April 1903 wrecked on Gipsy Rock, off Tuskar. Manchester for Philadelphia, general.
LOYALIST—27 September 1904 wrecked at Freshwater Cove, Trepassey Bay NF. St John NB and Halifax for London, apples & general.
DAMARA—7 February 1905 struck floating ice or submerged object in snowstorm. Sank off Jedore Head, Musquodoboit NS (SE of Halifax). Liverpool for Halifax, general.
SYLVIANA—February 1905 captured by Japanese warships, condemned. Cardiff for Vladivostock, coal.
TAMPICO—19 October 1907 abandoned in 38N 33W. Baltimore for Rotterdam, grain & general.
CRAMLINGTON—21 October 1908 collision, sunk on Haile Sand, mouth of the Humber. Dunston (Tyne) for Seville & Oran, coal, coke & caustic.
DAGENHAM—8 April 1909 wrecked on North West Grunes, Cobo Bay, Guernsey. Howden Dock (Tyne) for St Malo, coal.
AMANA—21 February 1912 posted missing. Sailed Leith 1 December 1911 for Philadelphia, general.
FLORENCE—20 December 1912 wrecked at Marine Cove, St Mary's Bay NF. Halifax for Liverpool, general.

The other seven casualties of the period can be grouped into two, five lost on the remaining liner services to North America and the other two colliers outward bound for European destinations.

Tampico foundered in the North Atlantic. Heavy weather had caused extensive damage, with bridge, boats and bulwarks carried away and decks burst so the holds and engine room were partially flooded. For two days the crew tried to bale out the engine room with buckets before the derelict was sighted by the steamer *Indiana* and her crew taken off. *Amana* was posted missing in 1912, likely a victim of the winter weather on the same ocean.

Loyalist, *Damara* and *Florence* were all casualties of the dangerous North American coastline. *Loyalist* went ashore on the Newfoundland coast and within a few days had broken up in a gale. *Damara* was feeling her way blind through a snowstorm when she hit Musquodoboit Harbour Ledges and foundered whilst *Florence* was another victim of the Newfoundland coast, wrecked near Cape Race with the loss of her captain and 21 men drowned. Only five survived, spending two days in a lifeboat before being rescued.

The two collier losses were *Cramlington* and *Dagenham*. *Cramlington* was run down by the steamer *Cadeby* at midnight off the mouth of the Humber. Struck abaft the engine room, the flooding soon reached the boilers and she drifted ashore where she broke up in heavy weather shortly after. *Dagenham* was wrecked off Guernsey, breaking in two soon after striking.

Johnston Line

In 1914 Furness Withy acquired a 50% interest in the fleet managed by William Johnston and Company Ltd, Liverpool, the other 50% being purchased two years later in 1916.

Chance played a role in this transaction, Frederick Lewis was playing golf on Formby Golf Course when he noticed a ship ashore in the Mersey. This would have been *Ulstermore*, wrecked on 22 January 1913 on Taylor's Bank Revetment in the Crosby Channel, inward bound with general cargo from Baltimore. Casually asking his companion who she belonged to the conversation then turned to the likelihood of William and Edmund Johnston being interested in selling the enterprise. An enquiry elicited a favourable response, so without delay the deal was struck, adding to Furness Withy's North Atlantic interests and opening up a new area—the Black Sea. On the Atlantic, Johnston's routes ran from Liverpool to Baltimore and also Galveston and other Gulf ports.

The fleet in 1914 consisted of eighteen ships and one tug; four of the eighteen were large Atlantic traders and the other fourteen smaller Mediterranean and Black Sea ships. Previously owned by numerous small single ship companies, the fleet was amalgamated by Furness Withy during 1914 into Johnston Line Ltd.

The war was virtually to wipe this fleet out, and the Black Sea trade was suspended when Turkey entered the war as an ally to Germany and closed the Dardanelles. Only *Cranmore* was still in service at the end of 1918, along with the Mersey based tug *Amore*.

Name	Built	GRT	Name	Built	GRT
FENMORE	1894	2300	CRANMORE	1905	3157
VEDAMORE	1895	6330	EDENMORE	1909	3667
AMORE (tug)	1896	155	FOYLEMORE	1911	3831
HEATHMORE	1898	3147	BARROWMORE	1911	3832
INCEMORE	1898	3060	JESSMORE	1911	3911
QUERNMORE	1898	7302	KENMORE	1912	3919
GORSEMORE	1899	3079	LARCHMORE	1912	4355
ROWANMORE	1900	10320	DROMORE	1913	4398
ARRANMORE	1904	3045	SWANMORE	1913	6373
BARNESMORE	1905	3158			

Kenmore, one of the latest Johnston Line ships.   **(WSS)**

The Johnston Story

William and Edmund Johnston had commenced business at Liverpool in 1872 with the small steamer *Plynlymmon*. With several ships bought soon after, they opened a service to the Mediterranean and Black Sea the following year. In 1874 the *Ardmore* introduced the Johnston Line nomenclature, the suffix *-more*.

On 21 September 1877 Johnston's *Olga* sailed from Alexandria with Cleopatra's Needle in tow for England. On 14 October 1877 Captain Booth lost the tow in heavy weather off Cape Finisterre. The derelict was picked up the following day and taken into Ferrol by the steamer *Fitzmaurice* of Burrell and Son, Glasgow. The Needle was finally brought to London by the tug *Anglia* early the following year and a salvage award of £2,000 was made in favour of *Fitzmaurice*. Burrell offered to forego the salvage award if the needle was erected at Greenock; however the offer was declined and a site on the Embankment in London chosen instead. The needle is one of a pair, the other being taken to Central Park in New York.

In 1880 a transatlantic service between Baltimore and Liverpool was inaugurated in conjunction with the Baltimore and Ohio Railroad, followed ten years later by another between London and Boston. During 1894 a pooling arrangement on the Boston service was agreed with Furness Withy, and the same year a Liverpool to Montreal service was founded. Neither of these—the Boston and Montreal routes—survived long into the 20th century.

The Johnston brothers were impressed in 1891 when the American whaleback steamer *Charles W Wetmore* arrived in Liverpool. They turned to William Doxford and Sons for a ship of this design, and *Sagamore* was launched in 1893. Due to problems with classification and load line under the British flag, she was registered in Belgium and owned by Belgian-American Maritime Company Ltd (this company was a 50:50 partnership between Johnston and Doxford). She was employed mainly on Black Sea routes, being a handy vessel for grain cargoes. In addition she is known to have carried sugar from Cuba, manganese ore from Poti, copper concentrates and iron ore from Spain and phosphates from Sfax. Johnston also purchased several of Doxford's turret ships, *Ashmore*, *Noranmore* and *Beechmore*, which were also placed under the Belgian flag.

In November 1898 *Vedamore*, commanded by Captain Robert Bartlett, saved the majority of the crew from the sinking *Londonian* (see Wilson's and Furness-Leyland Line), for which Captain Bartlett was presented with a silver cup. Sixty years later Miss Olive Bartlett donated this cup to the cadet ship *Conway* as a trophy for life-saving competitions.

When the Furness Withy interest in the company emerged the brothers, after more than forty years in business, were happy to consider the offer. With retirement in mind here was an opportunity to see their company placed in secure hands for the future whilst they were enabled to enjoy the fruits of their long years' labour.

Three generations of Johnston and Furness towing at Liverpool. Top: *Amore* of 1896 *(B Feilden).* Centre: *Beemore* of 1929, also seen proceeding down the Mersey in choppy conditions *(B Feilden).* Bottom: The third generation *Kilmore* of 1958 assisting *Nova Scotia* of 1965 *(Elsam, Mann & Cooper Ltd).*

4. The War to End all Wars— 1914 to 1918

Two shots rang out in the streets of Sarajevo on 28 June 1914 and reverberate to this day. Like the pebble that starts an avalanche, nobody could guess the holocaust those shots would provoke.

A product of the confused Balkan politics of the period, a young Serbian nationalist, Gavrilo Princip, fired the shots that not only killed the heir to the Austrian crown, Archduke Franz Ferdinand, and his wife Sophie, Duchess of Hohenberg, but kindled the flames of world war. The Archduke had been warned of the risk attaching to his visit to one of the restless minority nations of the fragile Austro-Hungarian Empire, which for years had sought independence.

In West Hartlepool the directors of Furness Withy could have had little inkling of the changes that were about to be wrought both in their fleet and the British mercantile marine. Although civilian manned, merchant shipping would be very much in the front line and take heavy casualties, Furness Withy companies were to record the loss of 88 ships, and 340 lives from their crews, before peace returned. As Viscount Grey of Fallodon wrote, "the lamps are going out all over Europe; we shall not see them lit again in our lifetime."

Events gained momentum. On 28 July Austria declared war on Serbia. Like a giant ripple Germany, France and Russia were drawn into the whirlpool. At 11 pm on 4 August it was Britain's turn to declare war on Germany, Germany having struck at France through Belgian territory, an enveloping movement to get behind the fortresses along the French border. Britain honoured its treaty pledge to maintain Belgian neutrality.

That Ungentlemanly Weapon

Without delay, an indication was given of what was to come at sea. The following afternoon Leutnant Hensing, commander of the German submarine *U21*, watched the British light cruiser *Pathfinder* come into range. His one torpedo exploded in the forward magazine, and the fore part of the ship disintegrated. Rescue craft saved 54—another 259 men died with their ship.

Two weeks later Leutnant Weddigen with *U9* sighted the old British cruisers *Aboukir*, *Cressy* and *Hogue* off the Dutch coast. Soon after dawn on 20 September *Aboukir*, hit by one torpedo from *U9*, rolled over and sank. *Hogue* stopped to pick up survivors and presented a sitting target, as did *Cressy* in her turn. Within an hour all three had sunk with the loss of nearly 1,400 lives.

For merchant seamen the first indication of what was to come occurred on 20 October. Salvesen's *Glitra* on passage from Grangemouth for Stavanger was sighted by *U17* some 14 miles off the Norwegian coast. Stopped and boarded, her seacocks were opened to make her the first merchant ship sunk by a U-boat. Oberleutnant Feldkirchner towed the lifeboat towards the Norwegian coast, a humane action. As will be seen, neither side had a monopoly on angels.

Furness Withy Goes to War

For Furness Withy companies the war was to start quietly. Only two ships became victims of enemy action in 1914 —

7.10.14	LA CORRENTINA—captured by KRONPRINZ WILHELM
26.10.14	MANCHESTER COMMERCE—mined

La Correntina was one of the first liners to be fitted with two 4.7 inch guns prior to the outbreak of war, a move instigated by Winston Churchill during March 1913 in view of heightening international tension. By the end of December 1913 five of the fleet controlled by Houlder Brothers had been equipped, *La Correntina*, *La Rosarina*, *La Negra*, *El Uruguayo* and *El Paraguayo*. In May 1914 the press was able to report that 42 merchant ships were armed—White Star and Royal Mail 11 each, Wilson Line 6, Houlder Brothers 5, Aberdeen Line 3, Federal and New Zealand Shipping two each and single vessels owned by Scottish Shire and Shaw, Savill and Albion.

Homeward bound from La Plata with frozen meat consigned to Liverpool, *La Correntina's* defensive armament was of no value when *Kronprinz Wilhelm* was sighted in the South Atlantic on 7 October. Although fitted with guns the ships, including *La Correntina,* carried no ammunition, in case objections should be raised by the authorities at ports of call! Norddeutscher Lloyd's *Kronprinz Wilhelm,* a North Atlantic liner, was anything but ideal as a commerce raider as her appetite for coal severely limited her scope. However, equipped with two 88mm guns from the cruiser *Karlsruhe,* she had two advantages, speed and ammunition. Had *La Correntina* carried shells for her heavier weapons the outcome might have been different. Instead, her weapons were transhipped to *Kronprinz Wilhelm* before she was scuttled on 14 October.

Another Norddeutscher Lloyd ship was responsible for the loss of *Manchester Commerce* later the same month. *Berlin* had been fitted as a minelayer and laid a minefield off Tory Island and NW Ireland. On 26 October the battleship *Audacious* was sunk, as also was *Manchester Commerce,* outward bound from Manchester for Montreal. Sinking within seven minutes of the explosion, only one lifeboat could be launched. Captain Payne and 13 others were drowned. The trawler *City of London* picked up the 30 survivors and landed them at Carnlough Bay in County Antrim.

One Furness Withy Group ship, Warren Line's *Michigan,* was chosen as one of fourteen ships to form the "10th Battle Squadron", a unit totally unable to live up to its title. The ships were sent to Belfast where Harland and Wolff carried out alterations to make them look, at a distance, like various battleships and battle cruisers. As such they were intended to mislead the enemy as to the current whereabouts of the real ships. Later the Squadron was renamed the S C Squadron, or Special Coastal Squadron. The crews involved thought Scare Crow Squadron might be a more apt name.

Michigan, with her silhouette altered by the careful use of steel scaffolding and canvas, assumed the role of HMS *Collingwood* in December 1914 and later was sent to the Mediterranean where she was scuttled as a blockship at Mudros in January 1916.

First Losses to Submarines

The year 1915 witnessed the sinking of five more ships, all at the hands of submarines. They were —

27. 3.15	SOUTH POINT—torpedoed by U28	
28. 4.15	MOBILE—sunk by gunfire from U30	
8. 5.15	QUEEN WILHELMINA—torpedoed by U9	
23. 6.15	TUNISIANA—torpedoed by UB16	
4. 9.15	NATAL TRANSPORT—sunk by gunfire from U34	

With the exception of *Tunisiana,* all were captured before being sunk. The war had not developed to the stage where a surfaced U-boat was at risk from defensive weapons or Q-ships. *Tunisiana* had sailed from Montreal on 5 June with grain for Hull, and in the early afternoon of 23 June was off Lowestoft when a torpedo from *UB16* hit her aft. Captain Buckley steered for the beach and put her aground on Newcombe Sand, but to no avail as within ten days she had sunk into the sand.

Lord Fisher had, prior to the war, correctly forecast the development of submarine warfare, although his views were met with disbelief. Time was soon to see him vindicated. As the danger to the U-boats increased— the first Q-ship was commissioned in late 1914—warfare began to degenerate into a sink at sight policy. In 1915, however, this had not yet developed as Germany was still too concerned about affronting American feelings and risking the United States becoming actively involvement in the war. The sinking of *Lusitania* in May 1915, with 1,198 deaths, provoked public outrage, and the sinking of *Arabic* in August caused Germany to impose restrictions on their U-boats as three American lives were lost. The effect of the sinking of *Arabic* on American public opinion was somewhat nullified later the same day when the Q-ship *Baralong* came upon *U27* attacking the steamer *Nicosian.* Having sunk the submarine, a boarding party from *Baralong* pursued the unarmed German survivors who had clambered aboard the abandoned *Nicosian.*

The first Furness Withy loss of 1915 was *South Point,* captured by *U28* on 27 March. A torpedo was used to dispatch her 60 miles west of Lundy Island. Her crew spent ten hours in their boats before being picked up by the steamer *Hollington* which landed them in Portugal. A month later *Mobile,* employed as an Admiralty collier under 'sealed orders', was stopped by *U30* 25 miles off the Butt of Lewis, soon after noon on 28 April. One of her lifeboats was used by the German boarding party who placed bombs on board to sink her. Six hours later the crew landed at Carloway, later being picked up by the patrol boat *Golanthe* and taken to Stornoway. The third loss within six weeks was *Queen Wilhelmina,* captured by *U9* on 8 May. Having sailed from Leith on 7 May, in ballast for Fowey, *Queen Wilhelmina* was sighted by the submarine at 3.45pm. Captain Dickinson turned and ran towards the land but the submarine overtook her and opened fire with her gun. After the crew had abandoned ship a torpedo was fired into the engine room and, as she settled, another hit No 2 hold. The crew were picked up by the patrol boat *Recolada* and landed in the Tyne. Meanwhile *Queen Wilhelmina* had remained afloat and was taken in tow by destroyers and trawlers which beached her a mile offshore in Druridge Bay where she subsequently broke up. The final loss of the year was *Natal Transport,* chased and captured by *U34* during the early evening of 4 September and sunk by gunfire 40 miles west of Gavdo Island, Crete. Abandoning ship under fire, the crew sailed and rowed for Crete where they landed the following afternoon.

The real defence against submarine attack was to convoy the ships. At the Admiralty the early theory expounded was that this provided sitting targets for U-boats, whereas designated and patrolled routes protected vulnerable merchant ships. It took most of the war to prove how wrong this theory was. In the meantime a stream of single ships followed Admiralty orders and provided targets for the growing fleet of German submarines.

A new offensive commenced in March 1916 aimed at bringing the Allies to the negotiating table and an early victim was *Sussex,* sunk by *UB29* on 24 March with the loss of 25 American lives. Yet again the German Navy had political, artificial restrictions placed on the U-boat offensive, but with lessening Government weight behind it.

Lull Before the Storm

The Furness Withy losses, two sunk in 1914 and five in 1915 proceeded to grow to nine in 1916 and, after the commencement of unrestricted submarine warfare, 53 in 1917 and 19 in the last year of the war. The list of losses for 1916 was —

27. 3.16	MANCHESTER ENGINEER—torpedoed by U44	8.10.16	WEST POINT—captured, sunk by U53
28. 3.16	EAGLE POINT—torpedoed by U70	26.10.16	RAPPAHANNOCK—torpedoed by U69
14. 4.16	SHENANDOAH—mined (laid by UC6)	26.10.16	ROWANMORE—torpedoed by U57
23. 4.16	PARISIANA—torpedoed by U19	9.12.16	CAMBRIAN RANGE—sunk by raider MÖWE
26. 5.16	EL ARGENTINO—mined (laid by UC1)		

Two were lost to enemy mines, *Shenandoah* on 14 April in the Channel and *El Argentino* off the East Coast on 26 May. In December *Cambrian Range* became a victim of one of the most successful of the German commerce raiders when stopped by *Möwe,* 600 miles off Cape Race; *Shenandoah* had two killed in the mine explosion, the crew of *Cambrian Range* became prisoners-of-war. In February 1917 they would be joined by the crew of *French Prince* when she became a victim of the same raider.

Six of the nine losses were due to submarine action. In two days, 27 and 28 March, *Manchester Engineer* and *Eagle Point* were both sunk. *Manchester Engineer* had been purchased to replace the previous ship of the name sunk in 1914 and now fell victim to *U44* while nearing the end of her passage from Philadelphia. The day after, *U70* shelled *Eagle Point* at dawn 100 miles WSW of Bishop Rock and, after she had been abandoned, dispatched her with a torpedo in the engine room.

Parisiana had sailed from London on 20 April for Newport News. On Sunday 23 April a U-boat was sighted alongside a barquentine. Captain Dickinson turned away and a chase developed with *U19* firing at *Parisiana.* An hour later with her superior speed the submarine was close alongside. Captain Dickinson abandoned his unarmed ship at 9.15am and half an hour later *U19* fired a torpedo into her. The boats made their way towards the Norwegian steamer *Braske* whilst *U19* left to chase and sink the British *Ribston,* whose crew were also picked up by *Braske* and landed the following day at Falmouth.

Later in the year, on 8 October, *U53* was responsible for the sinking of another company ship. Earlier in the year the German merchant submarine *Deutschland* had visited neutral America. Now, as a veiled warning to the United States, *U53* was dispatched across the Atlantic to call at Newport, Rhode Island, and return without taking fuel or supplies. The message was clear, German submarines could interdict American coastal shipping. Kapitänleutnant Hans Rose brought his boat into harbour on 7 October. Sailing later the same day *U53* commenced stopping and searching shipping in International waters off the Nantucket Lightship. *Strathdene* and *Chr Knudsen* were sunk before *West Point* was sighted. She had sailed from London on 23 September on the same service as *Parisiana,* and despite all Captain Harden's efforts, and those of the engine and boiler room crew, *U53* had overtaken her within half an hour. Bombs were placed on board to sink her and save a torpedo for another target and the boats containing the crew were towed towards the Lightvessel. Picked up by the US destroyer *Drayton,* the crew proceeded to New York and embarked on *Adriatic* for passage

Jupiter was damaged by a submarine on 7 October 1916 but was towed in and repaired.

to Liverpool four days after the loss of their ship. *U53* then stopped and sank *Blommersdijk* and *Stephano* before commencing her return home across the Atlantic. On the one day five ships of over 20,000 tons fell victim to *U53*.

The tragedy of the year was the loss of *Rappahannock*. Sailing from Halifax on 17 October for London she never arrived at her destination. Mounting concern for her culminated in three events on 8 November. Germany issued claims to have sunk her, a body identified as that of a greaser, Joseph Theuwkens, was washed ashore near Perranporth, Cornwall, and the Allan Line's *Corinthian* reported passing wreckage 60 miles west of the Scillies which was reminiscent of the deck cargo loaded on *Rappahannock*, deals, barrels, wood pulp and apples. She had in fact been sunk by *U69* on 26 October with the loss of all 37 crew.

Finally, the same day as *Rappahannock* was sunk, *Rowanmore*, also bound East on passage from Baltimore for Liverpool, was chased and shelled by *U57*. Abandoned, she was sunk with a torpedo and her master taken prisoner. The rest of the crew were picked up by a patrol ship and landed at Bantry on 27 October.

Prince Line Ltd Purchased

In August 1916 it was announced that Furness Withy had purchased Prince Line for £3 million, probably the purchase which had the profoundest effect on the future of the Group. Furness Withy had previously been largely confined to Atlantic and Mediterranean trades; even after the association with Houlder Brothers, the Antipodean routes had been sold and Houlders limited to South American lines. Prince Line was to add world wide operations to those already in being.

Prince Line only came on the market because of the war. James Knott was an entrepreneur in the same mould as Furness. With three sons entering the business he could look forward to handing on his thriving empire to the next generation. But as with so many other families, the war negated such plans, Captain Henry Basil Knott was killed at Ypres on 7 September 1915, aged 24, and less than a year later Major James Leadbetter Knott, DSO, was killed in action at the Somme, on 1 July 1916. The two brothers lie side by side in Ypres cemetery. Both Henry and James had worked their way up in the company before answering the call to the colours, James becoming deputy managing director and Henry heading the coal trade interests. Their older brother, Thomas Garbutt Knott, had preferred the company of his drinking partners, rather than spend his time in the office. He also was missing, believed dead. In fact he had been captured at Gallipoli and was a prisoner-of-war, but this was not known until some time later.

James Knott had placed much hope on his sons in the future of the business he had built. These hopes were dashed in 1916 and, shattered, he withdrew from business, sold his interests and moved to Jersey where he died in 1934. He was created a baronet in 1917.

Furness Withy found themselves the owners of another 38 ships of 145,871 tons, although by the time of the Armistice in 1918, 12 of these were to have been sunk by enemy action and another three lost by wreck and collision. Established lines were operated by Prince Line between the U S A and South Africa, the Far East and South America, and from the U K and Continent to the Mediterranean and River Plate. Knott had also been an early operator in the oil trade. *Gluckauf* of 1885 is generally recognised as the first successful tanker, and only three years later the first *Russian Prince* was commissioned. In 1916 Furness Withy found four tankers in the taken over fleet — *Georgian Prince, Mexican Prince, Russian Prince* and *Roumanian Prince* — built for the the oil trade from the Black Sea and America to Europe. In 1918 this interest was abandoned and the tankers sold.

Name	Built	GRT	Name	Built	GRT
KAFFIR PRINCE	1891	2228	ASIATIC PRINCE	1910	2887
CARIB PRINCE	1893	1975	EASTERN PRINCE	1910	2885
CREOLE PRINCE	1893	1988	SCOTTISH PRINCE	1910	2897
GEORGIAN PRINCE	1893	3245	BURMESE PRINCE	1911	4825
ITALIAN PRINCE	1893	3083	CHINESE PRINCE	1911	4834
MEXICAN PRINCE	1893	3028	JAPANESE PRINCE	1911	4876
TROJAN PRINCE	1896	3196	SIAMESE PRINCE	1911	4847
NORMAN PRINCE	1900	3464	SERVIAN PRINCE	1901	4831
SOLDIER PRINCE	1901	3118	FRENCH PRINCE	1900	4766
EGYPTIAN PRINCE	1902	3117	HIGHLAND PRINCE	1901	3390
MERCHANT PRINCE	1902	3092	BELGIAN PRINCE	1901	4765
AFGHAN PRINCE	1903	4923	PORTUGUESE PRINCE	1912	4981
AFRICAN PRINCE	1903	4916	RUSSIAN PRINCE	1912	4158
TUDOR PRINCE	1903	4292	STUART PRINCE	1899	3597
WELSH PRINCE	1903	4934	ROUMANIAN PRINCE	1913	4147
BLACK PRINCE	1903	3925	TUSCAN PRINCE	1913	5275
CORSICAN PRINCE	1900	2776	MOORISH PRINCE	1914	5943
OCEAN PRINCE	1907	5101	ROMAN PRINCE	1914	5284
ROYAL PRINCE	1907	5547	POLAR PRINCE	1895	3611

Sir James Knott

Born on the last day of January 1855, James Knott was the son of a customs official turned publican. He spent his childhood in close proximity to the Tyne at Newcastle where he started work aged thirteen in a shipbrokers office on Newcastle Quay. Six years later he ventured into business on his own account. From shipbroking to ownership and management was a short step and at the age of 23 he made this step with a quarter interest in the collier brig *Pearl*, borrowing £185 to finance the deal. Lord Runciman, in his book "Collier Brigs and their Sailors" states that Knott —

> " . . . bought a large fleet from Blyth, Whitby, Sunderland and Shields, for an old song. Sir James bought thirty two of these old vessels and made astonishing profits, but he had the instinct to gauge aright the time to sell and get rid of them, and go into steamers as new expenses hit the sailers.
> They were mostly sold to Scandinavians, who in turn were reputed to make a fortune with them."

After nine years, in 1887, all the sailing ships were sold and Knott concentrated on steam, his first steamer having been *Saxon Prince* built in 1881. His other interests were far ranging: he purchased Togston Colliery in 1899, formed the Acklington Coal Company and held an interest in the Welsh Primrose Coal Company. Holder of a master's certificate, he also studied law and was called to the Bar in 1899, practising as a member of Gray's Inn for four years. Politically a Conservative, he stood for Tyneside in 1906 and lost, but in January 1910 was elected Member of Parliament for Sunderland. That parliament only lasted a matter of months and for health reasons he did not stand at the election in December 1910.

Building Prince Line

Saxon Prince was followed by a further eight ships within two years, *Sailor Prince* and *Norman Prince* in 1882 and *Crown Prince, Soldier Prince, Merchant Prince, Black Prince* and *Highland Prince* in 1883. Limited liability was first employed with The Steamship Welsh Prince Company Ltd at the end of 1884 and in 1895 the Prince Line (1895) Ltd came into existence to consolidate a large, expanding and financially healthy undertaking.

The fleet was employed in six trades: Knott went on record as stating that the tankers were a good "bread and butter trade", giving steady returns on the run from the Gulf of Mexico and Philadelphia to Europe. Another early line ran from Italian ports to the United States, employing ships like *Trojan Prince* and *Tartar Prince* with large steerage accommodation for emigrants. This trade came to a premature end in 1907 with Italian legislation reserving the emigrant trade to Italian flag vessels. At the time two big 12,000 ton liners were under construction designed specially for the route, but these were sold on the stocks to Italian owners. For some twelve years Knott ran a service from Genoa and Marseilles to the West Indies and Central America but despite all efforts it was not economically viable, so with the emigrant trade closed the decision was taken in 1910 to abandon this service also.

Austrian Prince of 1901 was renamed *Servian Prince* in 1915 and sold in 1923.

69

Far greater success came with the services to Brazil and the River Plate, commenced soon after steamers entered the fleet and operated both from North America and from Europe. One of the earliest Prince Line services had been to the Mediterranean; in due course this was to become the last survivor of the Line's services. The opening of the Manchester Ship Canal in 1894 gave a boost to Prince Line as the Liverpool based James Moss & Company declined to trade up to Manchester so Knott instituted a direct line, loading cotton from Egypt for discharge at the head of the Canal and greatly strengthening the Mediterranean operation.

Around 1902 Knott commenced to run ships from New York to South Africa, India and the Far East, and also to East Africa. The opportunity offered by the opening of the Panama Canal in 1914 was readily grasped and the line extended to become a Round the World service.

Such was the shipping empire that became associated with Furness Withy in the summer of 1916, although the war had already badly disrupted the smooth running of operations and had seen *Indian Prince, Sailor Prince, Orange Prince* and *Swedish Prince* fall victim to enemy action. Knott's first steamer, *Saxon Prince*, sold as long ago as 1895 and latterly the Leith owned *Glitra*, had the doubtful distinction, as mentioned earlier, of being the first ship sunk by a U-boat in the war.

The Portuguese Charters

The outbreak of war in 1914 had repercussions on the economies and shipping fleets of not only the belligerents, it also affected the neutral nations. One such was Portugal, whose merchant fleet was limited to a total of 33 ships. She had previously relied on the services of British, Norwegian and other owners to fill many of her shipping requirements such as the import of coal and grain.

After war had commenced numerous German merchant ships seeking sanctuary from capture by British and French warships arrived at Portuguese ports. Soon, seventy two German and two Austrian ships were to be found at anchor, thirty five off Lagos in the sheltered waters of the River Tagus and the rest in other Portuguese home or colonial harbours. Included were a number of liners, a large number of cargo ships, three sailing ships, a tug and a tender.

To Portugal this idle tonnage offered a means to fill the need for ships to carry her cargoes once British vessels were no longer readily available. Attempts were made to purchase or charter from the German owners, but to no avail. At the same time British diplomatic efforts were being directed to persuading Portugal to seize the ships and make them available to Britain for the war effort.

On 24 February 1916 the decision was made. That day by decree all German ships in Portuguese waters were requisitioned "for the service of the State". As might be expected, Germany reacted and declared that a state of war existed with Portugal. To reactivate the ships, make repairs to both sabotage and routine damage, and then manage the new fleet, Transportes Maritimos do Estado was organised. An obvious mark of the requisitioning was the renaming of the ships with place names from the territories where the ships were taken over.

In July 1916 the Portuguese Prime Minister and Finance Minister visited London and agreement was reached to lease "those requisitioned steamers that were not necessary for Portugal's own requirements". Fifty one ships were to be time chartered, with Portuguese crews, at a cost of £1.5 million per annum and Furness Withy were appointed managers by the British Government.

Whilst the full list of ships seized by Portugal is easy to prepare, no list of the ships chartered has survived and it has not proved possible to compile such a list with accuracy. The first six were handed over to Furness Withy's Lisbon agents, Casa Torlades, in September 1916, *Alentejo* (ex *Uckermark*), *Madeira* (ex *Petropolis*), *Cascais* (ex *Electra*), *Mira* (ex *Rolandseck*), *Nazare* (ex *Minna Schuldt*) and *Sines* (ex *Milos*). A number of ships were early losses and it is impossible to say whether they were ever taken over by Furness Withy, for example *Sao Nicolau* (ex *Dora Horn*) which was sunk by *UC26* on 17 November 1916 while on passage from Lisbon for Le Havre where it is believed she was to be handed over, and *Desertas* (ex *Wittenburg*) which went ashore south of Aveiro soon after sailing from Lisbon. It was to be 1918 before she was refloated.

It is believed that in all twenty six of the ships intended for Furness Withy management were lost, seventeen by enemy action and the rest from marine risks, collision, fire, grounding and foundering. The charter had provided for the return of the ships to Portugal "six months after the end of the war". Several were returned to Portuguese control before the war ended, many others returned during 1920 and the last is believed to have been *Inhambane* (ex *Essen*) which appears to have returned about April 1921.

Following the return of the ships Transportes Maritimos do Estado found itself with a fleet which faced the post war recession in shipping, with trade at pre-war levels and a world fleet far larger than that of 1914. After the needs of the Portuguese colonial empire had been met there was still an excess of tonnage. Between 1923 and 1926 the fleet was auctioned and then Transportes Maritimos do Estado was placed in liquidation. The ships passed to the ownership of private Portuguese companies and many were destined to give long service to their new flag.

The Japanese Orders

Prior to World War I, Japan was little known as a shipbuilding nation, yet within a short time they extended their facilities to supply the ships needed in the fight against Germany. From six yards capable of building ships of over 1,000 tons prior to the war, the industry had grown to 57 such yards by the end of 1918. By 1915 destroyers were being built and during that year series construction commenced of standardised merchant ships, a total of 236 being delivered to six main designs.

Twenty standard ships of four types were purchased by the British Government and given *War* names. These were purchased through the agency of various shipping companies, notably Federal Steam Navigation Company and Furness Withy, and registered in the names of the companies even though they were Government owned.

The Furness Withy order was the largest, for twelve ships from Kawasaki Dockyard Company Ltd, Kobe. Nine were 385ft 9160dwt vessels of a class totalling some fifty seven examples, two were larger 445ft 10,400dwt vessels of the Japanese "T" type and the largest, *War King*, was of the 475ft long Japanese "A" type. When *U63* sank *War Council* in October 1918, it was the last in the long list of company war losses.

Name	Built	GRT	Name	Built	GRT
WAR KING	1917	9394	WAR ADMIRAL	1917	5875
WAR SOLDIER	1917	7446	WAR WOLF	1917	5875
WAR SAILOR	1917	7522	WAR LION	1917	5875
WAR QUEEN	1917	5844	WAR TIGER	1917	5875
WAR PRINCE	1917	5870	WAR HERO	1917	5875
WAR COUNCIL	1917	5875	WAR PILOT	1917	5875

Japanese built, *War King* seen in camouflage paint.

Glendhu was renamed *Stuart Prince* in 1922.

The Rio Cape Line Ltd

In 1917 a further purchase was made by Furness Withy, and was placed in the Prince Line fold. J Gardiner and Company, Glasgow, had been operating a service from Rio de Janeiro to Cape Town, principally carrying coffee, after which the ships went on tramp charter to the Far East and home to Europe. This line was bought by Furness Withy with a fleet of eleven steamers, plus another nearing completion. To operate this service and the ships purchased, Rio Cape Line Ltd was formed and the ships placed in its ownership. The close association with Prince Line was to be made more obvious five years later when Prince Line names were given to the Rio Cape Line fleet. The purchased fleet consisted of —

Name	Built	GRT	Name	Built	GRT
GLENELG	1904	4160	GLENETIVE	1911	5212
GLENAFFRIC	1905	4144	GLENSPEAN	1912	5221
GLENDHU	1905	4129	GLENNEVIS	1917	5119
GLENDEVON	1907	4169	GLENCARRON	1917	5117
GLENORCHY	1909	4737	GLENLYON	1917	4933
GLENSHIEL	1909	4798	GLENLEE	1918	4915

The Storm—Unrestricted Submarine Warfare

Losses sustained in 1917 were to make the earlier years seem quiet in comparison. In an effort to break the stalemate which had developed on the Western Front, with trench warfare bogged down across France and Belgium, Germany turned to an all out submarine campaign to force Britain into submission. From 1 February 1917 a policy of unrestricted submarine warfare commenced, and any ship in the war zone was liable to be sunk without warning. With larger numbers of patrolling warships and more merchant ships fitted with defensive guns and thus able to put up a fight against their attackers, U-boat commanders became increasingly careful in risking their boats. The increase in the number of Q-ships, innocent looking steamers and sailing vessels trailing their skirts across the sea lanes and inviting attack, also came high in the thoughts of U-boat commanders. None wished to find himself close alongside what suddenly revealed itself to be a heavily armed warship able to deal a death blow to the frail structure of the submarine.

Examination of the merchant ship loss figures prepared by Lloyd's of London make sombre reading. The total loss figures, for Allied and neutral shipping, from enemy action by all means, submarine, surface craft and mines, were —

1914	165 ships	323,626 tons
1915	772	1,323,114
1916	1,410	2,367,368
1917	3,267	6,350,414
1918	1,313	2,724,008
Total	6,927 ships	13,088,530 tons

Looking at the monthly figures, the effect of the decision to commence unrestricted warfare from February 1917 become apparent. Whereas in 1915 average monthly losses were slightly under 100,000 tons they climbed steadily during 1916 to double that figure with the period from October 1916 to January 1917 higher still at between 330,000 and 380,000 tons a month. February, however, returned 545,000 tons and the peak came in April when 458 ships of 882,227 tons were listed as lost. At the end of 1917 the average monthly toll for the year was to be over 500,000 tons and, whilst in 1918 figures fell, they remained at a dangerously high level.

Submarines were the principal enemy means of waging maritime warfare, accounting for a total of 5,798 ships of 11,311,971 tons during the war. In the catastrophic month of April 1917 they alone sank 425 ships totalling 844,725 tons.

Furness Withy losses for the year make desolate reading. The mother company lost ten ships, another nine came from the fleet of Johnston Line whilst Manchester Liners with seven and Prince Line with nine, each sustained heavy casualties.

18. 1.17	MANCHESTER INVENTOR—torpedoed by U57	
26. 1.17	TABASCO—torpedoed by U45	
3. 2.17	EAVESTONE—sunk by U45	
4. 2.17	TURINO—torpedoed by U43	
6. 2.17	CROWN POINT—torpedoed by U83	
7. 2.17	VEDAMORE—torpedoed by U85	
7. 2.17	CORSICAN PRINCE—torpedoed by UB34	
10. 2.17	JAPANESE PRINCE—torpedoed by UC47	
16. 2.17	FRENCH PRINCE—sunk by raider MÖWE	
19. 2.17	LADY OLIVE—sunk in action with UC18	
23. 2.17	TROJAN PRINCE—torpedoed by U39	
3. 3.17	SAGAMORE—torpedoed by U49	
9. 3.17	EAST POINT—torpedoed by U48	
22. 3.17	STUART PRINCE—torpedoed by U66	
28. 3.17	SNOWDON RANGE—torpedoed by UC65	
11. 4.17	IMPERIAL TRANSPORT—torpedoed by UC34	
17. 4.17	BRISBANE RIVER—sunk by U35	
19. 4.17	ANNAPOLIS—torpedoed by U61, damaged. Sunk following day by torpedo from U69	
25. 4.17	SWANMORE—torpedoed by U43, U93 & U50	
26. 4.17	MANCHESTER CITIZEN—torpedoed by U70	
27. 4.17	DROMORE—torpedoed by U58	
12. 5.17	EGYPTIAN PRINCE—sunk by U38	
13. 5.17	JESSMORE—torpedoed by U48	
4. 6.17	MANCHESTER TRADER—sunk by U65	
5. 6.17	MANCHESTER MILLER—torpedoed by U66	
9. 6.17	EGYPTIANA—torpedoed by U70	
10. 6.17	BAY STATE—torpedoed by U66	

11. 6.17	SOUTH POINT—torpedoed by UB32	
14. 6.17	NEW ZEALAND TRANSPORT—torpedoed by UC23	
21. 6.17	ORTONA—torpedoed by U50	
7. 7.17	CONDESA—torpedoed by U84	
21. 7.17	AFRICAN PRINCE—torpedoed by U66	
22. 7.17	ROTA—torpedoed by UB40	
29. 7.17	MANCHESTER COMMERCE—torpedoed by U39	
30. 7.17	MANCHESTER INVENTOR—sunk by U94	
31. 7.17	QUERNMORE—torpedoed by U82	
31. 7.17	BELGIAN PRINCE—torpedoed by U55	
12. 8.17	ROANOKE—sunk by UB48	
16. 8.17	MANCHESTER ENGINEER—torpedoed by UC16	
20. 8.17	INCEMORE—torpedoed by U38	
25. 8.17	SYCAMORE—torpedoed by UB61	
26. 8.17	KENMORE—torpedoed by U53	
26. 8.17	DURANGO—sunk by U53	
30. 8.17	EASTERN PRINCE—torpedoed by U62	
3. 9.17	LA NEGRA—torpedoed by UC50	
27. 9.17	SWAN RIVER—torpedoed by U39	
2.10.17	LUGANO—mined (laid by U79)	
6.10.17	BEDALE—torpedoed by U96	
23.11.17	LA BLANCA—torpedoed by U96	
11.12.17	OLDFIELD GRANGE—torpedoed by U62	
12.12.17	CHARLESTON—sunk by UB65	
16.12.17	FOYLEMORE—torpedoed by UB55	
28.12.17	MAXTON—torpedoed by U19	

At least three incidents with the Furness Withy fleet remind us that the U-boats did not always get things their own way. On 19 February 1917 the loss returns noted *Lady Olive*, sunk in action with *UC18*. Listed as a "Special Service Ship", this was a euphemism for a Q-ship. One of the small coasters built for London

Brisbane River, photographed from *U35* as she sank on 17 April 1917.

Welsh S S Company as *Tees Trader*, she had been chartered to British and Irish Steam Packet Company from 1914 to 1916 as *Lady Olive*. After return to her owners she was taken up by the Admiralty as *Q18*, fitted with one 4 inch and four 12 pounder guns and commissioned on 18 December 1916 under the command of Lieutenant F A Frank, RNR. On the morning of 19 February she was steaming in the Channel (49.15N 02.34W) when sighted by *UC18*, a small 400 ton minelaying submarine. *UC18* opened fire, and the "panic party" abandoned *Lady Olive* leaving the rest of the crew hidden and waiting. When *UC18* closed the true identity of the ship was revealed, fire was opened and *UC18* fatally damaged. But during the earlier shelling *Lady Olive* had been badly hit in the engine room and was settling in the water. Frank and his crew had to abandon ship and were in their boats until picked up late the following day by the French destroyer *Dunois*.

The ordinary merchant ship, too, was fighting back. On 9 March Kapitänleutnant Busz of *U48* sighted *East Point* which, when attacked, turned towards the submarine and tried to ram her. In this she was only partially successful, but Busz and one of his crew, Adolf Bergmann, lost their lives as *U48* crash dived. This did not save *East Point* as *U48* continued the attack and sank her with a torpedo. Later in the year *U49*, sister of *U48*, was not so fortunate. At noon on 11 September she sighted *British Transport* under the command of Captain Pope. By this time *British Transport* mounted a 4 inch defensive gun and a duel developed which continued for five hours. After dark *U49* continued to stalk its prey and at 9pm missed with two torpedoes. Half an hour later Captain Pope and his officers sighted the U-boat on the port bow and successfully steered to ram. This was one of the few occasions during the war when merchant ships managed to sink their attackers. Captain Pope was honoured by appointment to the Distinguished Service Order and, later, received Lloyd's Silver Medal for Meritorious Conduct. The Chief and 2nd Officers and Chief Engineer received the DSC,

Harold Mugford, V C

Between 1911 and 1914 Harold Mugford worked in the Chartering Department of Furness, Withy and Company. A member of the Territorial Army, he was called to the colours and active service soon after the outbreak of war in August 1914.

Present at many of the major battles of the war, including Ypres, Loos and the Somme, he was, by 1917, a Lance Corporal with the Machine Gun Corps.

On the morning of Easter Monday, 9 April 1917, he went into action at the village of Monchy-le-Preuz, near Arras. Getting his machine gun into a forward and exposed position he was soon alone, his Number Two killed and himself severely wounded. Refusing to go back to the casualty post he continued to operate his gun and was responsible for breaking up an enemy counter attack. Wounded again, with both legs broken, he continued in action until removed to the dressing station.

His valour and initiative was recognised with the award of the Victoria Cross, Britain's highest award for valour.

His terrible injuries confined Harold Mugford to a wheelchair for the rest of his life, and prevented his return to work. Furness Withy granted him a pension for life, and this was continued to his widow after his death in 1958. Following his wife's decease the Victoria Cross was bequeathed to the company, ''in gratitude''.

another seven of the crew the DSM and three were mentioned in dispatches. The Admiralty made an award of £1,000, matched by an anonymous donor through Lloyd's Register. The Committee of Lloyd's and the owners added £250 each and the Ministry of Shipping £100 to Captain Pope and a month's wages to all the crew.

Early in the year *U45* sank *Tabasco* on 26 January and then, only a few days later on 3 February, stopped the pioneer motorship *Eavestone* (albeit now converted to a steamer) on passage from Barry for Gibraltar with a cargo of Admiralty coal and sank her with gunfire. The crew of *Tabasco* had been fortunate, no lives were lost and they were only in their boats for a few hours before being picked up by *Bristol City* and landed at Liverpool. On *Eavestone* however the master and four of the crew were killed by shellfire, the survivors being picked up from their boats by a Norwegian barque.

Two sad cases with heavy loss of life during the year were *Sagamore* and *Belgian Prince*. *Sagamore* had sailed from Boston on 27 February, bound for Liverpool with 59 crew and a general cargo. When 150 miles west of Fastnet a torpedo from *U49* hit her amidships on the port side. Before she sank half an hour later three boats had got away, only to be dispersed in a gale that blew up during the first night. Two boats were never seen again, and the third had only seven survivors left when it was sighted by the outward bound *Deucalion* on 12 March. Ten had died in this boat but the rest were cared for on board *Deucalion* until she arrived in Cape Town on 6 April when they were hospitalised, five unfortunately losing their feet due to frost-bite and the onset of gangrene.

Another loss was that of Johnston Line's *Quernmore*, torpedoed by *U82* on 31 July some 160 miles west of Tory Island. She was one of a small number of merchant ships taken up by the Royal Navy as Commissioned Escort Ships. Fitted with a heavy armament (she had three 6 inch guns) they flew the white ensign and acted as convoy escorts whilst at the same time carrying a full commercial cargo.

The year 1917 was noteworthy for the number of Furness Withy ships damaged but brought safely to port. Having been hit by a torpedo in the Atlantic, *Cranmore* made it to Galway whilst in the Mediterranean her sister *Incemore* was towed into Marsa Scirocco. Another two were damaged in September, *Scottish Prince* being beached at Cawsand Bay and later refloated and repaired whilst *Glenelg* was in the North Sea on passage from the Tyne for Archangel when she was hit, being later beached at Lerwick to save her from sinking. Finally in December both *Sedbergh* and *Sachem* were hit and damaged in the English Channel, being towed into Plymouth within a week of each other.

7. 6.17	CRANMORE—torpedoed by U66		12. 9.17	GLENELG—torpedoed by UC40	
15. 7.17	INCEMORE—torpedoed by unknown submarine		9.12.17	SEDBERGH—torpedoed by UB40	
7. 9.17	SCOTTISH PRINCE—torpedoed by UC77		15.12.17	SACHEM—torpedoed by UB31	

The *Belgian Prince* Atrocity

Belgian Prince is remembered as the victim of one of the atrocities of the war. Having sailed from Liverpool on 28 July 1917 for Newport News she was intercepted by *U55* at 8pm on 31 July when 175 miles north west of Tory Island. Following her capture the ship was dispatched by torpedo and the lifeboats were ordered alongside the submarine. Captain Hassam was taken below as a prisoner of war, the rest of the crew were lined up on deck, their lifejackets taken, and the oars and plugs removed from the lifeboats which were then set adrift. Getting under way, *U55* suddenly started to submerge 20 minutes later, at 9 pm, leaving the crew of *Belgian Prince* floundering in the water. For 39 of them this was the end. With the coming of dawn a patrol boat sighted the only three survivors, Willie Snell, the American cook, George Sileski, a Russian seaman and Thomas Bowman, the British Chief Engineer.

Belgian Prince was not the only such atrocity. Earlier in the year the Cardiff owned *Torrington* had been sunk by *U55* on 8 April and her crew had received similar treatment.

The Neutral Requisitions and Charters

Various means were adopted by the British Government to maintain the supply of shipping required to meet the war needs of the country. The most obvious was the emergency programme with ships built not only in the United Kingdom but also in the United States, Canada, Japan, Hong Kong and China, but this programme only really commenced to produce results in 1917 and many ships were not completed until after the Armistice.

Other sources were the large fleets of neutral countries such as Norway, Denmark and Holland. High freight rates were one obvious attraction, against which owners had to weigh the risk of sinking by German submarines. The Allies also applied political and diplomatic pressure to ensure that the ships kept calling at British ports. One ploy was to refuse sailing permission until another equivalent vessel under that flag arrived. Finally, with the massive increase of sinkings during the unrestricted submarine campaign, thought was given to requisitioning ships. Before this dire action was taken discussions led to a compromise in some instances, the neutral countries undertaking to charter agreed numbers of ships to the British Government; these ships would be transferred to British ownership and flag, and given British crews and armament.

Furness Withy were appointed managers of many of these ships, which were registered in the names of Group companies. Some were part-completed ships in British yards, others were transferred from abroad.

One group consisted of the fleet of the associated Dutch company. As with other groups of ships, losses were heavy and the remainder were, in the main, returned to their owners in 1919 and 1920.

The Norwegian ships were taken over from various companies. Four of them were ships ordered from British yards by Wilh Wilhelmsen, Christiania (now Oslo), and consisted of the following which were registered in the name of Norfolk and North American Steamship Company, apart from *Ortona* which went to Gulf Line —

Name	Built	GRT	Name	Built	GRT
ABERCORN	1917	5385	GLASTONBURY	1917	6041
APPLEBY	1917	6041	ORTONA	1917	5425

Another Wilhelmsen ship, *Rinda* (built 1916, 5509gt) had been chartered to Furness Withy but was still under the Norwegian flag when she was wrecked on 9 January 1917.

Fearnley and Eger, also of Christiania, had four ships registered under the name of Furness Withy.

Name	Built	GRT	Name	Built	GRT
ALLENDALE	1917	2153	HASLEMERE	1917	2126
BEAUMARIS	1917	2372	KEIGHLEY	1917	2149

Other Norwegian owners with ships taken over by the British Government and registered in the name of Furness Withy Group companies included A/S Gro, Bergen, who had their newbuilding steamer *Gro* taken over and renamed *Tenterden*; Ivar An Ivarans Rederi, Christiania, whose *Modesta* was requisitioned; Bruusgaard and Kiosterud, Drammen, with *Hermelin*; Wilhelm Torkildsen, Bergen with *Pacific* and Jacob R Olsen, Bergen, with *Sedbergh*. Several ships were under construction in Canadian yards when requisitioned—*Alaska* to the order of D/S A/S Alaska (Christian Haaland), Haugesund, *Porsanger* and *Samnanger* for Westfal-Larsen and Company, Bergen, *Tento* for J W Prebensen, Risor, and *Asp* for Thv Heistein and Sonner, Kristiansand.

Name	Built	GRT	Name	Built	GRT
TENTERDEN	1917	4127	PORSANGER	1918	4363
ALASKA	1918	5825	SAMNANGER	1918	4305
ASP	1918	2350	SEDBERGH	1917	4275
HERMELIN	1918	2232	TENTO	1917	2350
PACIFIC	1915	6034	MODESTA	1917	3832

The Dutch flag fleet managed by NV Furness' Scheepvaart- & Agentuur Maatschappij, Rotterdam, consisted of five ships, viz

Name	Built	GRT	Name	Built	GRT
EIBERGEN	1914	4767	RIJSBERGEN	1897	3658
KELBERGEN	1914	4751	UBBERGEN	1911	1877
VEENBERGEN	1905	4281			

In March 1918 the decision was taken by the Allies to requisition all Dutch ships within their ports, under the Right of Angary of International Law. Whilst protesting the move and denying the right of the requisitioned ships to continue flying the Dutch flag, and also stating that Dutch seamen could refuse to serve, many in Holland looked upon the move with relief. The seizure enabled the Dutch to avoid the risk of war with Germany, which might have erupted had they been a party to chartering ships to the Allied belligerents. Although the number of ships seized in British ports is not known, America took over 38. Two Dutch ships were placed under Furness Withy control, apart from the five mentioned above and the following miscellaneous Greek, Chinese and Danish vessels

Name	Built	GRT	Name	Built	GRT
NOORDDIJK	1914	3241	ARISTIDES	1884	2179
YILDUM	1913	3234	HWAH HSIN	1905	1643
ANTONIOS M. MAVROGORDATOS	1901	3771	ROTA	1915	2171
			CRESSWELL	1917	2829
ARGO	1892	2444			

The *Cresswell*, requisitioned whilst under construction by William Gray and Company for Rederi A/S Dannebrog, Copenhagen, was registered in the name of Furness Withy, the others were chartered or requisitioned by the British Government and placed under Furness Withy management by the Shipping Controller.

Managed Ships

In addition to the Japanese built ships registered in the name of Furness Withy, the company managed four Standard ships on behalf of The Shipping Controller. They were constructed in Canada (three) and the United States (*War Knight*) —

Name	Built	GRT	Name	Built	GRT
WAR HORUS	1918	2266	WAR KNIGHT	1917	7951
WAR KARMA	1918	2271	WAR WITCH	1918	1961

Manchester Civilian fitted with minesweeping gear during World War I.

and after the surrender of the German merchant fleet to the Allied Shipping Commission several ships were placed under Furness Withy management following their allocation to Britain.

Name	Built	GRT	Name	Built	GRT
SANTA FE	1902	5342	SAUERLAND	1918	10800
ERIKA	1906	2666	WENDLAND	1919	11446
PARIA	1916	6086			

whilst Houlder Brothers and Company were appointed managers of two ex German ships seized by Uruguay and chartered to Britain.

Name	Built	GRT	Name	Built	GRT
TREINTA-Y-TRES	1906	4775	RIO NEGRO	1901	4819

Newbuilding Programme During the War

On the outbreak of war the intervention of the Admiralty with urgent orders for warships disrupted the orderly pattern in the shipyards. William Doxford and Sons recorded in their Minute Book the instruction to give preference to such orders. This, plus the extra problems of getting supplies of plates, steelwork capacity having been diverted to supply the Admiralty orders, caused delayed delivery of merchant ships to become a problem. Some ships were completed to clear the yard, other hulls were laid up pending completion. Some yards became extremely busy with war work, especially those with a record of warship construction. Others, like Russell and Company on the Clyde, became chronically short of work as, being solely merchant ship builders, they received no Admiralty contracts.

Some Furness Withy orders suffered extensive delays, the worst probably being the refrigerated meat carriers ordered before the war for Furness-Houlder Argentine Lines. Apart from *Condesa*, delivered in 1916, the others did not come into service until 1918. The list of ships delivered between 1914 and 1918 can be misleading as it includes the various requisitioned ships built in British yards for Norwegian and other owners, and the Japanese orders, which were built for the Government and registered in the name of Furness Withy or associated companies. Furness Withy themselves registered no new ships until 1917, when six requisitioned

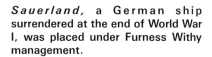

Sauerland, a German ship surrendered at the end of World War I, was placed under Furness Withy management.

ships were entered and one other, *Sidlaw Range* which carried a Neptune Steam Navigation name. After completion of the pre-war orders in 1915-6, Neptune themselves did not receive another ship until *Grampian Range* and *Norfolk Range* were completed in 1918.

Norfolk and North American completed delivery of their pre-war orders with *Start Point* in 1916, then took over four of the requisitioned ships in 1917. Gulf Line registered four ships in 1916-7, *Ortona* and *Modesta* are known to have been Norwegian charter/requisitions and it is suspected the other two, *Lugano* and *Rapallo* may have been as well. Likewise Houlder Line, British Empire and Empire Transport completed their pre-war orders and then adding no new construction until after the war. Prince Line did not commission a new ship until 1918, Warren's White Diamond Line purchased a hull under construction for Glasgow owners and completed her as *Rhode Island* in 1918. Johnston Line were the only company in the Group to take delivery of tonnage which may have been ordered after the outbreak of war, four ships in the 1916 to 1918 period —

Name	Built	GRT	Name	Built	GRT
MAPLEMORE	1916	4330	REXMORE	1918	6512
THISTLEMORE	1917	6506	VALEMORE	1918	6629

Sycamore and *Oakmore* were also commissioned in 1918 but they were both purchased whilst under construction for other owners.

The Last Year of the War

The entry of America into the war during April 1917 gave the Allies renewed strength, although as 1918 opened the outcome of the war was still anything but certain. Russia had fought to a standstill and then collapsed into Revolution whilst the attrition of both men and materials in the other theatres of fighting was still at horrifying levels, the like of which had never before been visualised. At sea heavy losses of shipping continued despite the introduction of the convoy system, but every effort was now being made to replace at least some of the losses with ships of the emergency shipbuilding programme which had been initiated by the Shipping Controller. Furness Withy took part in this, ordering a fleet of ships to be built in Japan to help fill the need—one of these, *War Council*, was to be the last Furness Withy loss of the war.

Although the worst year, 1917, was past, heavy loss of life was sustained in two of the sinkings in January 1918. *Barrowmore* was torpedoed by *U94* in 49.58N 07.54W whilst on passage from Huelva with copper ore for Barry. 25 lives were lost, and two days later another 27 went with *Cheviot Range*, torpedoed by *U102* South of the Lizard when nearing home on passage from India. Six other of the losses involved loss of life, a further 12 casualties. The crew of *Beaumaris* were able to beach their ship in Whitesand Bay after she was torpedoed, but to no avail as she became a total wreck.

However, at last the final sinking was reported: employed as an Admiralty collier, *War Council* was sighted and torpedoed by *U63* on 16 October in 35.44N 21.00E whilst on passage from Barry with coal for Port Said.

Delivery of *Baronesa*, one of a large class of refrigerated meat carriers ordered before the war, was delayed until 1918.

12. 1.18	WHORLTON — torpedoed by UB30	11. 4.18 HIGHLAND PRINCE—torpedoed by UB50
13. 1.18	RAPALLO—torpedoed by U28	20. 4.18 LOWTHER RANGE—torpedoed, probably by U91
22. 1.18	MANCHESTER SPINNER—torpedoed by U27	30. 4.18 CONWAY—torpedoed by UB105
	(Austro-Hungarian)	30. 5.18 ASIATIC PRINCE—torpedoed by U63
5. 2.18	CRESSWELL—torpedoed by U46	25. 6.18 AFRICAN TRANSPORT—torpedoed by UB88
7. 2.18	BEAUMARIS—torpedoed by U53	9. 8.18 GLENLEE—torpedoed by UB57
19. 2.18	BARROWMORE—torpedoed by U94	23. 8.18 AUSTRALIAN TRANSPORT—torpedoed by UC27
19. 2.18	GLENCARRON—torpedoed by U82	22. 9.18 GORSEMORE—torpedoed by UC53
21. 2.18	CHEVIOT RANGE—sunk by U102	3.10.18 WESTWOOD—torpedoed by UB112
3. 3.18	CASTLE EDEN—torpedoed by U110	16.10.18 WAR COUNCIL—torpedoed by U63
25. 3.18	ALLENDALE—torpedoed by U101	

Two others ships had been hit by torpedo during the year and damaged, but lived to be repaired and continue in service. Both were in the English Channel, *Canonesa* being off Worthing and *Tuscan Prince* not far away off Dungeness. *Canonesa* was brought into Southampton, where she was abandoned to the Government who undertook repairs and then sold her to Blue Star; *Tuscan Prince* was towed into Dover and returned to Prince Line service after repair.

    1. 5.18   CANONESA—torpedoed by UB57
    5. 8.18   TUSCAN PRINCE—torpedoed by UC49

At 11am on 11 November 1918 the sound of gunfire died away. With the Armistice the "war to end wars" came to an end and the survivors could look forward hopefully to a return to sanity. For Furness Withy and the crews of their ships the task was now to repair the damage done to the fleet and trades and to rebuild. What an unbounded relief the coming of peace was to all merchant seamen, whose civilian profession had suffered proportionately higher casualties than any of the fighting services.

Marine Losses

The horrendous submarine losses largely overshadowed those arising from marine risks, which however saw five ships end their service with the company. Even of these five though, two can be said to have been partially war losses for both *War Knight* and *Denby Grange* were in collision with other ships in their convoys.

War Knight was in collision with the American tanker *O B Jennings* which was carrying a cargo of naphtha. This exploded, killing almost all on board the two ships. Towed towards the Isle of Wight by destroyers, *O B Jennings* burned for ten days in Sandown Bay. To make matters worse *War Knight* struck a mine while under tow and, still on fire, was sunk by gunfire close to Freshwater Bay. When she started to break up bacon and lard floated ashore, to the joy of the local population.

London Trader foundered off Penzance in a gale, four survivors being picked up by the steamer *Forward*, whilst *Heathmore* went ashore when entering Garston. Breaking in two she was considered a total loss, but later her cargo was salved and she was recovered and repaired, although not retained in the fleet.

Fleet Losses — 1914 to 1918

LONDON TRADER (London Welsh Steamship Company Ltd)—5 February 1915 foundered off Penzance. Dublin for London, general.

HEATHMORE (Johnston Line Ltd)—17 February 1916 wrecked at entrance to Garston. Huelva for Garston, iron pyrites. Recovered, re-registered 1919 (transferred W.R. Davies & Co, 1919).

WAR KNIGHT (Shipping Controller)—24 March 1918 collision with O B JENNINGS in convoy, caught fire 15 miles off St Catherine's Point. Taken in tow, broke adrift, struck mine. Again taken in tow, beached Freshwater Bay, where she broke up. New York for London, oil & lard.

AFGHAN PRINCE (Prince Line Ltd)—30 July 1918 wrecked off Gabarus, CB, Baltimore, for La Pallice, general.

PENTLAND RANGE (Neptune Steam Navigation Company Ltd)—4 September 1918 foundered off the River Plate. Rosario for Liverpool, maize & general.

DENBY GRANGE (Houlder Line Ltd)—24 October 1918 collision with WAR ISLAND in convoy, sank in 39.52N 05.32E. Newport for Spezia, coal.

Amongst the other casualties that did not result in total loss of the ship was that experienced by *Mendip Range*. One of a convoy of sixteen ships escorted by the armoured cruiser *Drake* in October 1917, orders were given to disperse as they neared Rathlin Island. Passing outside the island, *Drake* was torpedoed by *U79*. Meanwhile *Mendip Range* had passed inside the island and as she cleared the island sighted the damaged *Drake* bearing down on her. Despite using both rudder and engines *Mendip Range* could not avoid *Drake*, which rammed her amidships. *Drake* became a total loss whereas *Mendip Range*, which had been beached, was recovered and returned to service.

Steel and Bennie Ltd

In 1917 Houlder Brothers acquired a controlling interest in the Clyde based towage company Steel and Bennie Ltd. The company dated from 1856 when James Steel, previously a manager with Clyde Shipping Company, established his own lighterage business between Greenock and Glasgow. The first tug, *Admiral*, was commissioned in 1866. Changing transport methods saw the last of the lighters sold in 1925, leaving Steel and Bennie as one of the two principal tug fleets serving the Clyde.

The outbreak of war in 1939 led to the Clyde becoming a major port facility as traffic was diverted from ports in the south of England threatened by enemy action. The two Clyde tug fleets (Steel and Bennie Ltd and the Clyde Shipping Company Ltd) joined forces under common control and were strengthened by tugs from the south. These moved north with barges and dockers to handle the much increased traffic. Steel and Bennie's *Warrior* of 1935 was also taken as the model for a class of tugs ordered by the Ministry of War Transport.

Houlder Brothers retained their interest until 1969 when the holding was sold to R and J H Rea Ltd, who were themselves controlled by William Cory and Son Ltd. Renamed Cory Ship Towage (Clyde) Ltd the following year they continue to operate on the Clyde with a reduced fleet of three tugs (compared with eight to ten in the later years of Houlder ownership), reflecting the current level of shipping movements on the river.

Shipbuilding

The years leading up to the outbreak of war in 1914 had been prosperous with full order books for the Group shipyards. The start of the war was followed by a further increase in the workload, although with a change of emphasis as Admiralty requirements came ahead of merchant shipping. Many shipyard workers joined the Army and Navy, leading to shortages of skilled workers which, in fact, became so serious that, in some instances, skilled men had to be released from the armed forces to keep the yards working. Demands for raw materials also increased and this caused delays in merchant shipbuilding. The following statistics for the number and tonnage of merchant vessels produced by British shipyards illustrates how the necessities of war submerged normal business —

1913	1,424 ships	1,977,600gt
1914	1,294	1,722,150
1915	517	649,340
1916	413	582,300

The increasing German submarine campaign led to a change in policy, and emergency steps were taken to build replacement tonnage for Government account. This caused the tonnage for 1917 to recover to 1,163,474gt.

Many changes were to take place in the Group's shipyards. In 1909 the Furness Withy yard in West Hartlepool had been transferred to the ownership and management of Irvine's Shipbuilding and Dry Docks Company Ltd. Now, with interest, effort and investment being expended on new shipbuilding yards at Chepstow and Haverton Hill-on-Tees, the decision was taken to sell the old yards.

A remote Irish outpost joined the Group in 1917 when the Queenstown Dry Docks, Shipbuilding and Engineering Company Ltd at Passage West was purchased for £50,000, to be retained until sold to William Beardmore and Company for a similar figure in 1929.

The shares in Irvine's Shipbuilding and Dry Docks Company were accordingly sold in 1917 for £347,500, to a syndicate acting through the Commercial Bank of London. The following year the Northumberland Shipbuilding Company also passed, for £835,000, to new owners led by R A Workman of Workman, Clark and Company, Belfast.

The subsequent history of the Irvine's and Northumberland shipyards was brief. At West Hartlepool the syndicate behind the purchase included, in addition to R A Workman, the names of John Esplen, Clarence Hatry, P Haig Thomas and S W Lund. Initially business was good, a new company was formed and the capital structure increased. With the heavy slump in post-war shipbuilding the last year to show a profit was 1921. Dividends on ordinary shares were not paid after 1920 and preference shares went into arrears after 1922. A debenture issue that year never received a dividend. The last ships to be built in both the Middleton shipyard and the Harbour dockyard went into the water in 1924. Liquidation was decided upon in 1930 and the assets were placed on the market. Finally in 1938 National Shipbuilders Security Ltd purchased and dismantled the yards, although the fitting out berth was kept busy with war work and the dry-dock continued to find some use for many years to come.

On the Tyne sale of the Northumberland Shipbuilding Company was concluded in November 1918. The new owners were associated with merchant bankers Sperling and Company, and used the company as a vehicle to create a shipbuilding combine, the largest of its kind in Britain. The combine included Workman, Clark and Company, Lancashire Iron and Steel Company, William Doxford and Sons, Blythswood Shipbuilding Company, Fairfield Shipbuilding and Engineering Company and Monmouth Shipbuilding Company. When purchased in 1918 the Northumberland share capital was £500,000: within a year this was raised to £7 million. £5.5 million of this was in preference shares (£500,000 10% cumulative and £5 million 6% non-cumulative).

The optimism of the new owners shows clearly in the contract signed in March 1920 with Dorman, Long and Company, for the supply of 300,000 tons of steel plates and sections in the period to the end of 1923. Following the collapse of the shipping market in 1920 orders for new ships became hard to find, many of the contracts held were cancelled and other shipowners involved were in no position to proceed with their commitments, thus effectively cancelling the agreements. Such a large tonnage of steel could no longer be absorbed and the contract with Dorman, Long and Company had to be re-negotiated. The new agreement involved the yards taking 50% of their needs from the steelmakers and paying compensation payment of £300,000.

During the recession of the early 1920's the Northumberland Group came under increasing pressure, their large capital, debenture and loan structure becoming a growing burden until, in 1926, the combine crashed. The Northumberland yard at Howden-on-Tyne was taken over by a new concern, the Northumberland Shipbuilding Company (1927) Ltd, but the onset of the Great Depression saw its last ship, *Briarwood*, launched on 27 May 1930. In 1931 the yard was sold to National Shipbuilders Security Ltd, to be dismantled and sold.

At the instigation of Sir James Caird, various shipowners and shipbuilders, including P&O, British India, Federal, Orient and Andrew Weir, joined forces in 1916 to form the Standard Shipbuilding and Engineering Company Ltd. In the names of the British Maritime Trust and Frederick Lewis, Furness Withy took 10% of the capital of £300,000.

The small shipyard of Edward Finch and Company and land at Chepstow were acquired and a start was made in laying down a new yard for the construction of merchant ships to fill the immediate and urgent needs of British owners. Initial plans were for ten berths up to 600ft long, together with a nearby "Garden City" to house the large number of workers needed. The following year the venture was nationalised, purchased by the Government and completed for their emergency shipbuilding programme of vessels to be owned by The Shipping Controller.

Although the identity of the initiator of the Haverton Hill-on-Tees shipyard project is not known, it is likely that it was Marmaduke, Lord Furness. To build and operate the projected yard the Furness Shipbuilding Company Ltd was formed in 1917 with a nominal capital of £650,000.

A site extending to some 85 acres was purchased with a 2,500ft frontage on the Tees. The major problem was that over 50 acres of the 85 lay under water at high tide. When permission to proceed was given by the authorities in late 1917 the first task was to raise the ground level and over a million tons of slag, sand and ash were used to do this. With the war raging, manpower was in short supply, with the result that much of this reclamation, which raised the land level by some 15ft, was undertaken by women.

In the centre of the site a six acre fitting out basin, 1,000ft by 250ft, divided the yard into two sections. The West Yard had eight building berths ranging from 450ft to 700ft in length, and served by twelve rail mounted cranes. The East yard had four 365ft berths served by twenty revolving derricks. The first keel was laid in the West Yard during May 1918, and the first launch took place on 29 April 1919 when Mrs Walter Furness sent *War Energy* into the water.

Such was the pace of development at Haverton Hill that office staff initially ate, slept and worked in disused railway carriages. By the summer of 1920 over 3,000 people were employed, and to accommodate them the Belasis Model Village was erected. A hostel for 500 men and over 500 houses were soon occupied.

The shipyard project was initially budgeted at £1.5 million, but by the time it was completed some £4 million had been spent. Sir Frederick Lewis was greatly relieved when its voracious appetite for capital was removed from the Group with its transfer to the Furness family along with the other engineering and industrial interests.

Littlewoods Challenge Cup

The elaborately engraved solid silver Littlewoods Challenge Cup is believed to be enjoying at least its third incarnation.

Made by Turner Bradbury and hallmarked 1895 the cup stands 2ft 9ins tall and weighs 3.789kg. It is believed to have originally been a racing trophy, with Ripon Racecourse suggested as the venue.

With the founding of the Haverton-Hill on Tees shipyard by Furness Shipbuilding Company Ltd in 1917 the cup became the Viscountess Furness Football Cup, presented to the winners of the interdepartmental football competition. This annual competition continued until 1968, the yard closing the following year.

Thereafter the whereabouts of the cup are obscure until found in 1985 by the Littlewoods Organisation plc and refurbished to grace their sponsorship of the Football League, commencing with the 1986/1987 season. The Football League, the world's oldest league, celebrated its centenary in 1988 during Littlewoods' sponsorship.

The Football League Cup started with the 1960/1961 season, became the Milk Cup in 1981/1982 and then Littlewoods' Challenge Cup in 1986/1987. The prize of £75,000 made it the largest team prize in British sport.

Winners of the Cup have been Arsenal in the 1986/1987 season, Luton Town in 1987/1988, and Nottingham Forest in both the 1988/1989 and 1989/1990 seasons.

5. Recession and Depression—1919 to 1939

When the Armistice came into effect at 11am on 11 November 1918, the Furness Withy fleet stood with horrendous gaps in the ranks. The combined fleet had lost 89 ships to enemy action and another eight to marine risks and faced the future with the survivors in need of attention to remedy the wear and tear of war service. At the same time, fighting continued in Russia, between the forces of the White Russians and the Communist Red Russians, the end result of which would influence world events, and the pattern of Furness Withy trade, down to the present day.

As the war had progressed, Frederick Lewis found himself spending an increasing amount of time on Government duties. After the formation of the Ministry of Shipping, he was spending only about one and a half hours at Furness Withy each day, leaving decisions in the hands of the chairman, Marmaduke, Lord Furness. Now, with the return of peace, Lewis was able to reverse this and increasingly concentrate on the future of the company, and with it the need to restore services and rebuild the fleet.

Rapidly it became apparent that all was not well. In 1914 Lord Furness had agreed, when accepting the chairmanship, to consult with Lewis on all matters. For the first few years this had worked well, but concurrent with the period that Lewis spent at the Ministry of Shipping a coolness developed and now, in 1919, it became clear that Lord Furness considered the agreement to be no longer applicable.

The attitudes of the two men were diametrically opposed: Furness was an optimism and Lewis a pessimist. Whilst the war still raged, Furness had been the principal promoter of the new shipyard being built on the Tees. He also established a full order book for the shipowning side of the company, placing orders for post-war delivery with various yards at enhanced wartime prices.

Many, at the end of 1918, looked forward to a bright future, believing that the buoyant economy with its greatly enlarged manufacturing capacity would continue with full order books and growth expectations. Some entrepreneurs during the war organised companies which were soundly conceived at birth; their mistake, however, was to retain cost values in the balance sheets, or write the values up to boom levels, in order to capitalise or distribute profits rather than conserve them as reserves. A few were able to reorganise their capital structure but many found this impossible with heavy mortgages on assets which, after the freight market collapsed in 1920, retained insufficient break-up value to cover liabilities.

Lewis had early had his doubts about such a view of the post-war world. At the Annual General Meeting of 29 July 1916 he had spoken, saying —

"Whilst I am not by any means of a pessimistic turn of mind, I think it is essential that shipowners should keep before them the fact that they are passing through a period of prosperity which is unhealthy, inasmuch as it is due to un-natural and abnormal causes. Sooner or later, the high rates of freight which are now prevailing may be expected to abate very rapidly, and we must be prepared to meet adversity and competition which will inevitably arise. When that time comes, it will be found that a reserve fund is better than a bank overdraft." (Fairplay)

He was not alone in his views, for shipowners such as William Burrell, Walter Runciman and Arthur Sutherland all considered the boom bubble must burst. They sold their fleets whilst the market was high and declined to re-enter active shipping operations until saner counsel prevailed. Burrell effectively retired, Runciman and Sutherland returned to shipowning in the early 1920's.

The optimists included owners like Edgar Edwards who, between 1915 and 1920, built Western Counties Shipping Company Ltd from nothing into an undertaking with a capital of £2.5 million. Two years later the company, forecast in 1920 to make a profit in excess of £1 million a year, was in the hands of receivers, the fleet being sold for thousands of pounds rather than millions. Another collapse, mentioned in the last chapter, was that of the Northumberland Shipbuilding Company group organised by Sperling and Company, and formed round the Furness Withy Tyne shipyard, the Northumberland yard having been sold by the Group in 1918. Other notorious collapses from the same malaise included the empires rapidly constructed by Gould and Slater, which collapsed like packs of cards. The greatest and most lasting casualty of this post war optimism, however, was undoubtedly that of Lord Kylsant's Royal Mail Steam Packet Group in 1930.

Management Buyout

In the summer of 1919 the shipping press reported the resignation of Lord Furness from the Board of the Furness Withy companies; no detail was given of the reason and a decade or more later writers were still wondering how it had been arranged.

Lewis had rapidly reached the conclusion that he could not continue working in harness with Furness. Two people pulling in different directions at the head of an organisation is a recipe for disaster and the more Lewis discovered in those early months of 1919, the greater became his concern for the future. It became clear that if he was allowed to continue, Lord Furness was going to saddle the company with a financial burden beyond what it was capable of carrying. Funds were being poured into the shipyard far beyond budget and no ships had yet been built. Originally the cost had been estimated at £1.5 million; by the summer of 1919 well over £2 million had been spent and the final cost was now being forecast at £3 million. Furness was treating Furness Withy as if it were his own private property and not a public company, employing company funds and assets for his personal use and convenience.

In Lewis' eyes there were two choices open when it became clear that proper co-operation was not working. Either he or Furness must leave the company. Considering the lifetime of effort that he had devoted to the undertaking since entering the office in 1883, helping it grow from small beginnings to the present size, he immediately dismissed the possibility of his own departure. How, though, could Marmaduke, Lord Furness, be persuaded to withdraw? Lewis' private memorandum records how the subject developed between the two men; in essence, Lewis expressed the opinion that if the Furness family funds, which were mainly in the form of over 600,000 shares held by the Furness Trust, were sold at £10 each and the funds were reinvested they would, at 5% interest, yield twice the income that could be expected from the shipping concern. Furness agreed with this proposition and opened negotiations with Lord Pirrie to sell to the Royal Mail Group. Furness Withy assets stood at £17 10s 0d per share, Furness was looking for £10 a share and after Pirrie refused to offer more than £9, negotiations ceased.

Following the collapse of these negotiations it was agreed that Lewis should prepare and submit his own offer. In consultation with Mr Goodenough, chairman of Barclays Bank, he drew up his proposals, which were that the Furness Trust and other family shares in Furness, Withy and Company Ltd should be purchased at a price ultimately agreed at £12 each. Payment was to be made up of the new shipyard at Haverton Hill-on-Tees, to be retained by the Furness family and be valued at the sum already invested in it, the steel, coal and iron shares held by Furness Withy valued at the highest price in the current year and the balance in cash. Another vital clause was a reduction in the number of ships on order for Furness Withy with the Furness yard, from 44 to 26.

This 1921 photograph at Dartmouth evidences the post-war recession, with ten Prince Line ships laid up. Top left are *Siberian Prince, Servian Prince* and *Spartan Prince.* Centre are *Arabian Prince, Siamese Prince,* and *Burmese Prince,* with in the foreground, *Manchurian Prince, Trojan Prince, Korean Prince* and *Grecian Prince.*

The total cost of the 849,066 Furness Trust and family ordinary shares so purchased was £10,188,792 and payment was —

Shipyard, coal, iron & steel interests	£	3,800,000
Government stock		3,167,724
Cash		3,221,068

The timing was fortunate for Lewis. With the high level of wartime trade, many shipping companies, along with other major industrial undertakings, had very large cash reserves. In many cases these profits and reserves were capitalised: in July 1919 a board meeting of the directors of Furness, Withy and Company decided to realise the accretion of capital assets by increasing the ordinary capital from £2 million to £4 million, distributing one fully paid up ordinary share for each one already held.

Those shipowners who resisted the temptation to spend money and buy ships at inflated prices, were in many cases able to survive the recession of the 1920's and depression of the 1930's with the aid of these reserves built up during the war. In the case of Furness Withy Group these reserves provided the funds to finance the purchase of the Furness Trust and family shareholdings.

The procedure arranged started with Barclays Bank purchasing the industrial (coal, iron and steel interests) shares from Furness Withy, who then used the cash to buy Prince Line shares, which could not be valued as they were not quoted on the Stock Exchange, from the subsidiary companies who had acquired them in 1916. These subsidiaries then, with their own reserves and the cash received for their Prince Line holdings, purchased the Furness Trust and family shares in Furness Withy. In the coming years the shares so purchased were slowly placed on the market and the cash realised was returned to the companies concerned. With the help of the Bank, the division of the business empire built by Christopher Furness was soon completed.

This change in control was discreetly explained at the Annual General Meeting held on 2 October 1919 by Lewis saying that Viscount Furness (Marmaduke had been elevated to be Viscount Furness in 1918) wished to "devote himself more particularly to the shipbuilding, steel and coal interests of the company, with the result that now the stress of war was over he felt he would prefer to concentrate the whole of his energies in the development of those concerns."

Rebuilding

During the later years of the war, ships continued to be delivered to Furness Withy, ships which had been ordered before or during the early years of the conflict. After the Armistice, a number of these ships continued to enter service, such as the 420ft shelter deckers ordered from various builders such as Irvine's (who delivered *Thistlemore*, *Manchester Brigade* and *Manchester Division* in 1917/8), Laing (*Rexmore* of 1918) and Dixon (*Valemore* of 1918). The post war deliveries were —

Name	Built	GRT	Owning Company
BARRYMORE	1920	6656	Johnston Line
PARISIANA	1921	6640	Furness Withy
CYNTHIANA	1922	6629	Furness Withy

Most of these ships were powered by triple expansion machinery, the exception being the steam turbine powered *Parisiana*.

The other additions of Company-designed ships were the long delayed meat carriers, five of which had been ordered pre-war for Furness-Houlder Argentine Lines. *Condesa* had been commissioned late in 1916, only to be sunk the following year. Her four sisters were finally commissioned in 1918 as *Baronesa*, *Duquesa*, *Marquesa* and *Princesa*. Finally, in 1921, William Hamilton and Company delivered a further sister as *Hardwicke Grange* to Houlder Line.

Within a matter of months the first steps were been taken to replace some of the ships lost during the war and, more important, introduce new designs to meet developing needs. Like many other owners, Furness Withy took the opportunity to buy a number of the standard ships being built in many yards for Government account. However, unlike the Royal Mail and P & O Groups, Furness Withy limited their acquisition to eleven

Name	Built	GRT	Class	Owners	New name
WAR HIND	1918	5263	B	Prince Line	GRECIAN PRINCE
War Isthmus	1919	3089	C	Prince Line	ALGERIAN PRINCE
WAR JACKDAW	1918	5214	B	Prince Line	TARTAR PRINCE
War Minerva	1920	8286	G	Furness-Houlder Argentine Lines	CANONESA
WAR PERCH	1918	5226	B	Prince Line	TROJAN PRINCE
War Planet	1919	3071	C	Prince Line	CYPRIAN PRINCE
WAR PYTHON	1918	5155	B	Gulf Line	ARIANO
War Rock	1919	3072	C	Prince Line	SYRIAN PRINCE
War Sable	1919	4565	J	Johnston Line	GALTYMORE
WAR SHARK	1919	5247	B	Prince Line	SPARTAN PRINCE
WAR SPANIEL	1918	5227	B	Gulf Line	CASTELLANO

Typical of the latest ships in 1918 were *Gothic Prince* and *Valemore* pictured after being renamed *London Citizen*. *(WSPL and A Duncan)*.

ships, six of the B-class, three C-class and one each of the G and J classes. The first to join the fleet became the Gulf Line's *Ariano* and *Castellano* in January 1919, others followed during the year and the last, purchased on the stocks, entered service in 1920 as *Canonesa* for Furness-Houlder Argentine Lines.

These purchases were followed by five modern second- hand ships which came from Lang and Fulton, Greenock in May and June 1919. Three ships had been purchased from these owners earlier, two in 1917 which became Johnston Line's *Sycamore* and *Hartland Point* for Norfolk and North American and one the following year renamed *Manchurian Prince* for Prince Line. The latest 1919 purchases were shared four to Johnston Line and one to Gulf Line. The price paid for four (excluding *Ardgay*) was £628,000.

Name	Built	GRT	Owners	New name
ARDGARRY	1914	4526	Johnston Line	STANMORE
ARDGRANGE	1916	4543	Johnston Line	WIGMORE
ARDGAY	1918	4593	Johnston Line	ERNEMORE
ARDGORM	1918	4618	Gulf Line	COMINO
ARDGROOM	1918	4882	Johnston Line	TULLAMORE

Few other second-hand ships were purchased after the war. In 1920 the small coaster *Waterland* (built 1903, 494gt) was bought to become *Egyptian Prince*, followed in 1922 by *Gowerian* (built 1921, 449gt). They were sold in 1922 and 1923 respectively. Apart from the ships on the Bermuda and West Indies run from North America acquired in 1919/20, to which reference will be made later, the other second-hand purchase was one ex-German ship, *Altenfels*, in 1920 to become Prince Line's *Eastern Prince*. Virtually unique, Lewis ensured that Furness Withy took little part in the purchase of ex-enemy tonnage, unlike Lord Inchcape and Lord Kylsant, whose groups—P & O and Royal Mail—took large numbers of surrendered German ships.

Whilst concerned with the number of orders placed by the Group, and taking steps to come to terms with the yards and cancel some of them, Lewis was not averse to occasional purchase, as witness those mentioned above and the early Doxford diesel powered ships to be mentioned shortly.

In 1920, the first of the wartime orders started to enter service. There were two main classes, or groups, and it is not easy to allocate them to specific Group companies as time was to see many moved between trades and owning companies, names and trades at times changing without transfer of ownership. Some of the changes of service, though, are obvious from a study of the names chosen.

One of a large class of ships built at the Furness shipyard for Group trades was *Egyptian Prince* of 1922.

The larger of the two classes were six turbine powered cargo ships of 7900gt (see "Whisky Galore" below), products of the new Furness yard on the Tees. The other was a group of fourteen smaller single deck steamers and motorships of between 3478 and 4099gt from both Irvine's and Furness. Basic dimensions were similar, a length of 360-364ft, beam 52ft and depth 24ft. Although built to the same basic design, there were differences such as the filling in of the well deck on the two completed as motorships. These diesel powered vessels, *Sycamore* and *Tramore,* were powered by Italian designed Tosi diesels, licence built by Richardsons, Westgarth and Company Ltd. As problems were experienced with the machinery, further ships were not fitted with this marque of diesel and when an opportunity came to sell the two ships to Russia in 1933, they passed from the fleet.

Name	Built	GRT	Owning Company
AVIEMORE	1920	4060	Johnston Line
DROMORE	1920	4096	Johnston Line
INCEMORE	1921	4098	Johnston Line
PERUVIANA	1921	4099	Furness Withy
1924 JESSMORE			1923 to Johnston Line
PERSIANA	1921	3493	Furness Withy
1922 CHICKAHOMINY,			1924 to Rio Cape Line
1924 CORSICAN PRINCE			
TUNISIANA	1922	3482	Furness Withy
1922 LANCASTRIAN PRINCE			1922 to Prince Line
ITALIAN PRINCE	1921	3478	Prince Line
EGYPTIAN PRINCE	1922	3490	Prince Line
ALLEGHANY	1922	3489	Furness Withy
1924 CASTILLIAN PRINCE			1924 to Rio Cape Line
1926 SICILIAN PRINCE			
APPOMATTOX	1922	3491	Furness Withy
1924 SARDINIAN PRINCE			1924 to Rio Cape Line
KENMORE	1923	3783	Johnston Line
QUERNMORE	1923	3787	Johnston Line
SYCAMORE	1923	3493	Johnston Line
1926 CASTILLIAN PRINCE			1926 to Prince Line
TRAMORE	1924	3493	Johnston Line
1925 BRAZILIAN PRINCE			1926 to Prince Line

A further two steamships of the class were sold prior to completion to Wilh Wilhelmsen of Oslo, entering their service as *Louisiana* (intended name *Egyptian Prince*) and *Delaware*.

In the years that followed, these Furness Withy ships were to be transferred between many of the Group companies, given new and more appropriate names following those transfers and, apart from the two motorships, generally gave long service.

Whisky Galore

Although *Politician,* inspiration for Sir Compton Mackenzie's comedy "Whisky Galore", was at the time of her loss a Harrison Line vessel, she had been built originally for Furness Withy as one of the six turbine shelter deckers of 7,900gt on a length of 450ft delivered by Furness Shipbuilding Company in 1922 and 1923. Initially they were employed on North Atlantic service but the developing recession, American subsidised competition and high fuel consumption led to withdrawal of all except *Manchester Regiment*.

Manchester Liners had initially agreed to take three ships but later reduced this to one in view of the high price. *Manchester Regiment* lasted until she was sunk in collision with *Oropesa,* owned by the Pacific Steam Navigation Company, on 4 December 1939.

Royal Prince, one of a class of six ships that included *London Merchant,* later famous as *Politician.*　　(A Duncan)

After withdrawal from the North Atlantic, several of the ships were transferred in 1928 to Prince Line for service to South Africa, being given Prince Line names but without change of registered ownership.

Name	Built	GRT	Owning Company
FELICIANA	1922	7896	Furness Withy
1922 LONDON MARINER			1923 to Gulf Line
1929 IMPERIAL PRINCE			1929 to Furness Withy
MANCHESTER REGIMENT	1922	7930	Manchester Liners
LONDON IMPORTER	1922	7895	Furness Withy
LONDON MERCHANT	1923	7899	Neptune
LONDON SHIPPER	1923	7939	Norfolk & North American
1929 BRITISH PRINCE			
LONDON COMMERCE	1923	7886	Furness Withy
1928 ROYAL PRINCE			

London Importer was sold to the Admiralty for £46,000 in 1933, becoming the Fleet Supply Ship *Reliant.* Later named *Anthony G* then *Firdausa,* she was scrapped in 1963. The other four went to Harrisons in 1935 for a total of £123,000. The Prince Line ships became *Collegian, Craftsman* and *Statesman,* whilst *London Merchant* was renamed *Politician. Collegian* was broken up in 1948, *Craftsman* was sunk by the raider *Kormoran* in the South Atlantic on 9 April 1941, and *Statesman* fell victim to bombing by a Kondor of KG40 on 17 May 1941 some 200 miles west of *Politician's* wreck.

Politician was lost when she stranded as she sailed north from Liverpool to join an outward bound convoy. Her cargo included many luxury items such as whisky being exported to help finance the war effort. In bad weather, she went ashore on 5 February 1941 in Eriskay Sound and although most of the ship was later salved and scrapped, her stern section still lies there as a reminder of the myth, speculation, gossip and entertainment with which her name has become associated.

In addition to the two abovementioned classes, totalling eighteen ships, built in the Furness shipyard at Haverton Hill, a further two 2866gt colliers, the last to be built for Furness Withy, were delivered in 1923 as *Eldon* and *Throckley.* They were followed in 1925 by two ships for Manchester Liners, *Manchester Commerce* and *Manchester Citizen.* The contracts placed with the Furness Shipbuilding Company had been reduced from 44 to 26 as part of the agreement for the purchase of the Furness shareholding in 1919, but it has not been possible to establish if the balance of the agreed total number of orders were cancelled or, like the two Norwegian ships, sold to other owners prior to launch or completion.

River Syndicate Ltd and Danube Navigation Company Ltd

After four years of war, Europe was in dire straits. The economic blockade, collapse of the Austro-Hungarian Empire and diversion of so much of the economy to the war effort had resulted in extensive disorganisation and economic distress. In this situation, the British Government requested Sir Frederick Lewis to chair a consortium of London Merchant Banks and others to consider the proposals of a British representative who had returned from Central Europe with details of Danube shipping and with options to buy control of the three major Austrian, German and Hungarian shipping companies operating there. Many of the craft on the river had been sunk or damaged, and many of the warehouses and other shore installations were damaged.

The River Syndicate was floated to negotiate. Lewis and a delegation visited Vienna and Budapest, returning with signed agreements to purchase Erste Donau Dampschiffahrt G/S (Austrian)—49%; Magyar Kiralyi Folyam es Tengehajosas Resvenytarsas A.G. (Hungarian)—49% and Sud Deutsche Donau Dampschiffahrt G/S (German)—100%

To own these holdings, Danube Navigation Company Ltd was formed in 1920 with a capital of £1,200,000. The three companies retained their identities but were subject to supervision from London.

Early optimism for this new venture was soon clouded by problems, such as the cabotage laws on the Roumanian section of the Danube which reserved trade between Roumanian ports for Roumanian flag vessels. Experience soon revealed the difficulties of controlling a venture on the Danube, with differences of opinion on the interpretation of agreements, obstructive actions by local Governments, companies and individuals and the questions of ownership, seizure and compensation under the Treaties of Versailles, Trianon and St Germain to be resolved. The major problem, though, was the massive depreciation of currencies during the post war years, as a result of which the balance sheet retained large amounts in local currencies since to convert into sterling would have brought massive exchange losses. Consequently within a few years, the holdings in the three companies were sold back to national interests.

Following this sale, Furness Withy purchased the interest of their partners in both Danube Navigation and River Syndicate for 8s 9d per £1 share and henceforth both continued as investment companies owned by British Maritime Trust.

Watson and Youell Shipping Agency Ltd and Russo-British Grain Export Company Ltd

In 1921, an interest was taken in the firm of Watson and Youell, merchants long established in the Roumanian and Black Sea Trade. Shipping activities, based in Roumanian ports on the Danube and hence complementing the Danube Navigation Company's interests, were reorganised as Watson and Youell Shipping Agency Ltd.

Following the Russian Revolution, the Communists had consolidated control of Russia under the leadership of Lenin. Being a realist he soon perceived the impossibility of an immediate application of the doctrine of state capitalism. In order to feed the population, restore the damage caused by years of fighting and encourage industrial growth, Lenin turned to the quasi-capitalist New Economic Policy, which allowed controlled capitalistic investment.

One result of this Policy was the Russo-British Grain Export Company Ltd, half owned by the Russian Government. Prior to the outbreak of war in 1914, Southern Russia had been the bread basket of the world, the Black Sea grain trade being a large employer of tramp tonnage long before the trades in North American, Australian and River Plate grain developed. With Turkish participation in the war as a German ally, the trade had ceased and now the Russian Government sought to re-establish this important trade. During 1924 Furness Withy took an interest in Russo-British Grain Export Company and for some years satisfactory results were achieved.

After several years of ill health, Lenin died in January 1924, being succeeded by Stalin. In 1926 the Russian Trade Agreement was suspended and the Grain Company became a casualty. Stalin took a far more severe line than Lenin who, fearing the consequences for the Russian people, had tried unsuccessfully to keep him away from power. Stalin soon abandoned the New Economic Policy and in 1928 introduced a massive programme of industrialisation, collectivisation of agriculture and social reorganisation. In the years that followed, this was achieved at the price of destroying not only the grain production and export trade of Southern Russia, but also the lives of all who differed during the many purges of the era.

Quebec Steamship Company

The purchase of the Quebec Steamship Company interests and assets from Canada Steamship Lines in 1919 introduced Furness Withy to the trade with which it was to become closely identified, the Bermuda holiday industry. In actual fact Furness Withy were already familiar with the trade as for years the New York office had acted as port agents for Quebec Steamship Company. The ships involved in the transaction were

Name	Built	GRT	Name	Built	GRT
BERMUDIAN	1904	5530	KORONA	1886	2874
PARIMA	1889	2990	GUIANA	1907	3657

Quebec Steamship Company had been founded in 1867 as the Quebec and Gulf Ports Steamship Company with Canadian Government subsidy, to connect the Maritime and inland provinces of the new Canadian Confederation.

An additional service commenced in 1874 when a contract, with a £4,000 annual subsidy, was signed with the Bermudan Government for a three-weekly service from New York to the island. This was mainly a cargo service with Canima (692gt) arriving at Bermuda on 21 January 1874 on the first sailing with cargo and twelve passengers.

The opening of the Intercolonial Railway in 1876 blighted the Canadian routes, the subsidy was cancelled and competition from the railway rapidly saw services and routes wither away. The following year another contract was obtained, from the Venezuelan Government for a service from New York to Puerto Cabello and La Guaira. Only two years later this was repudiated following a revolution, after which the company

Guiana, purchased with the Quebec Steamship Company interests in 1919.

concentrated on developing an un-subsidised service from New York to the Windward and Leeward Islands, Venezuela, Demerera and Trinidad. Another new service was from New York north to New Brunswick and Nova Scotia.

The change of emphasis, with services from New York to Newfoundland, Bermuda and the West Indies, was recognised when, in 1880, the company was renamed Quebec Steamship Company.

Steadily the tourist potential of Bermuda grew and the company responded with *Orinoco* of 1880, accommodating 100 passengers, *Trinidad* of 1884 carrying 180 and finally in 1905 *Bermudian* entered service with 340 berths. In February 1895, the company instituted winter cruises from New York to the West Indies with *Madiana.*

When Canada Steamship Lines gained control of Quebec Steamship Company in 1913, *Bermudian* and *Trinidad* operated the Bermuda service (*Trinidad* also maintained the Canadian service) whilst *Korona, Parima* and *Guiana* ran to the West Indies. In 1914 an agreement was signed with the Bermuda Government for an improved service, to be undertaken by two new 10,000 ton ships to be specially built for the trade.

World War I disrupted the regular service pattern and effectively negated the two proposed new ships. *Bermudian* was taken up in 1914 to carry the Strathcona Horse, part of the first contingent of Canadian troops to fight in Europe; she then returned to the Bermuda run until being requisitioned in June 1917 for Mediterranean trooping. To serve the needs of the island, the elderly cruiser *Charybdis,* dating from 1894, was converted into a cargo ship and served as a most unsuitable substitute from the Spring of 1918 until the end of 1919. Meanwhile *Bermudian* had sunk in harbour at Alexandria, been refloated and repaired before being released to her owners. *Trinidad* had been sunk by *U101* in March 1918 but the three cargo ships survived and with *Bermudian* were sold to Furness Withy.

Trinidad Shipping and Trading Company Ltd

When, in 1920 Furness Withy purchased the Trinidad Shipping and Trading Company, they became the owners of a line which for many years had competed with the ships of Quebec Steamship Company on the route from New York. Although only three ships were involved, there were extensive trading interests in Trinidad. The fleet consisted of

Name	Built	GRT
MAYARO	1900	3896
MATURA	1901	4556
MARAVAL	1903	5144

The business had been founded by Gregor Turnbull who had arrived in the island in 1831. Over the years he built up his business based on sugar estates and encompassing the shipping required to carry the produce to Glasgow, and also the supplies and equipment needed in Trinidad.

In 1889, the Trinidad Government had contracted with Turnbull, Stewart and Company for the provision of coastal steamer services and a route to New York. The company themselves also contracted with the developers of the Pitch Lake in Trinidad to ship their asphalt to New York. In 1895 Trinidad Shipping and Trading Company Ltd was established to take over this New York service.

Initially Furness Withy endeavoured to purchase the shipping interests only, but to no avail. They therefore completed negotiations by taking over all Trinidad Shipping and Trading's business including Queens Park Hotel, the principal hotel in the island, Trinidad Estates Company Ltd, cold storage and ice making facilities, ship repair shops and a slipway, plus timber and sawmilling and limestone quarries.

The shipping and marine interests were absorbed by Furness Withy, whilst in 1921 Trinidad Trading Company Ltd was formed to operate the various other interests. Sugar estate interests were passed to Caroni Sugar Estates (Trinidad) Ltd in 1924 and subsequently to Tate & Lyle.

Bermuda and West Indies Steamship Company Ltd

In 1921 the shipping interests purchased from Quebec Steamship Company, also those of Trinidad Shipping and Trading Company Ltd, were amalgamated into the newly formed Bermuda and West Indies Steamship Company, apart from *Korona* which had been sold earlier that year.

To these assets Furness Withy also contributed the two ships bought from Adelaide Steamship Company in 1919, *Willochra* and *Wandilla* (renamed *Fort Victoria* and *Fort St George*) to provide effectively the enhanced service envisaged in 1914. With *Fort Hamilton* the two ships carried the growing tourist trade from New York which the company proceeded to develop. An important factor was undoubtedly the introduction of Prohibition into America in 1919. This law banned the sale of alcohol in the USA, although once outside territorial waters a ship was free of the limitation and could open the bar for the sale of liquor. The statute not only proved unpopular but also impossible fully to enforce so was repealed in 1933.

Fort Victoria and *Fort St George* were soon refitted and altered from three class to two class ships with berths for 380 1st and 50 2nd class passengers. They were also fitted with refrigerated space and deep tanks to carry fresh water. Bermuda had a water shortage problem, hence the ships carried supplies which were pumped ashore for the use of the hotels.

Fort St George was out of service for a while following a collision with *Olympic* in March 1924. *Fort Hamilton* was sold during 1926 and the decision was taken to build a new ship for the service. The keel of this ship was laid in Belfast on 13 October 1926 and was provisionally named *Mid Ocean*, although this was changed to *Bermuda* prior to launch. She was to be a ship that would greatly outclass those already employed on the service, and was a departure in all ways from the previous three Forts. At 19,086gt she dwarfed them, being constructed to the largest dimensions that could enter Hamilton Harbour. Launched on 28 July 1927, she accommodated 616 1st and 75 2nd class passengers and was powered by four Doxford diesels.

Entering service in January 1928, *Bermuda* had *Fort St George* and *Fort Victoria* as running mates until *Fort Victoria* sank following a collision with *Algonquin* on 18 December 1929. At the time of the sinking she was dropping the pilot after leaving New York. As the wreck obstructed the Ambrose Channel, it was shortly afterwards blown up. In March 1930, therefore, a contract worth £1,160,000 was signed with Vickers-Armstrong, Newcastle, for the speedy construction of a suitable companion for *Bermuda*, which was launched on 17 March 1931 as *Monarch of Bermuda*. Even larger than *Bermuda*, the new ship was given turbo-electric machinery rather than diesels.

Whilst she was fitting out, news was received from Bermuda that *Bermuda* herself had had a disastrous fire on 16 June 1931, whilst berthed alongside at Hamilton. To maintain the service until *Monarch of Bermuda* was ready in December, resort had to be made to chartering, including ships such as Cunard's *Franconia*, Holland-America's *Veendam* and Canadian Pacific's *Duchess of Bedford*. The damaged *Bermuda* was returned to her builders in Belfast for repair but as these were on the point of completion, another fire erupted and this time the damage saw her condemned as a constructive total loss. Vickers, who had designed and built *Monarch of Bermuda*, immediately put in hand a sister to her, which entered service in 1933 as *Queen of Bermuda*. Unlike the *Bermuda*, these two new liners were registered as owned by Furness Withy, not Bermuda and West Indies Steamship Company, the New York to Bermuda service having been transferred to Furness Withy in April 1932 for £150,000. Henceforth Bermuda and West Indies Steamship Company would be confined to the West Indian and Newfoundland services.

Meanwhile changes had taken place with the ships on the West Indies service. *Parima* was broken up in 1924, followed by *Guiana* in 1925, *Mayaro* in 1929 and *Maraval* in 1933 with *Matura* converted into a coal hulk at Trinidad during 1934. Only one ship had joined the service in this period, when in 1925, *Digby* was transferred to Bermuda and West Indies Steamship Company and renamed *Dominica*. Originally built for Furness-Warren Line to operate on the Liverpool to St John's NF, Halifax and Boston route, she had been displaced by the new *Newfoundland* and *Nova Scotia*. Refitted and with extended passenger accommodation to take 100 1st and 66 2nd class passengers, she was to spend the next decade on the run from New York to the islands.

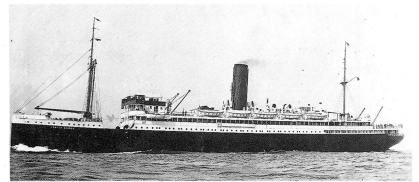

Built for Australian coastal service as *Wandilla*, *Fort St George* served on the Bermuda route from 1919 to 1935.

A contrast in size, the new 19,000gt *Bermuda* and *Bermudian,* the 200gt tender at Bermuda. (*L Dunn*)

A final link in the Canadian services was forged in 1929 with the purchase from C T Bowring and Company of their Red Cross Line from New York to Halifax and St John's. With it came three ships

Name	Built	GRT
NERISSA	1926	5583
ROSALIND	1911	2390
SILVIA	1909	3589

The Red Cross Line service had competed with the old Quebec Steamship Company route north, now operated by Bermuda and West Indies Steamship. Henceforth the Furness flag would fly over the ships operating from New York to Newfoundland as Furness Red Cross Line.

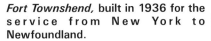

Fort Townshend, built in 1936 for the service from New York to Newfoundland.

Silvia, purchased in 1929 with the Red Cross Line.

In 1935/6, the two oldest Red Cross ships, *Silvia* and *Rosalind*, were sold, to be replaced by two new ships named after the forts at the entrance to St John's harbour, *Fort Amherst* and *Fort Townshend*. Both were registered as owned by Furness, Withy and Company, like the two Bermuda liners *Monarch*, and *Queen, of Bermuda*. As war clouds loomed on the horizon, the fleet based on New York serving Canada, Bermuda and the West Indies was

Name	Built	GRT	Name	Built	GRT
Bermuda & West Indies Steamship Company Ltd			Furness, Withy and Company Ltd		
BERMUDIAN	1915	237	MONARCH OF BERMUDA	1931	22424
CASTLE HARBOUR	1929	730	QUEEN OF BERMUDA	1933	22575
NERISSA	1926	5583	FORT AMHERST	1936	3489
			FORT TOWNSHEND	1936	3489

Bermuda Tourism and Bermuda Development Company Ltd

In the first year of Furness Withy ownership of the service from New York to Bermuda, 22,000 passengers were carried to the island. The importance of the tourist trade was highlighted by the revenue of $2,000,000 which compared with the $500,000 received by Furness Withy for the carriage of freight.

To complement the ships, the St George Hotel, with 100 rooms, was purchased in 1920, reconditioned and extended. A swimming pool and golf course were added and in 1923 the tender *Bermudian* entered service to carry passengers from ship to hotel. Built in 1915 as *Arctic Whale*, she had been a patrol vessel built on whaler lines for the Admiralty, being sold by them in 1920.

At the same time, 645 acres of land was acquired at Tuckers Town and the Bermuda Development Company Ltd was formed to develop it. Here the Mid Ocean Club and golf course was completed in 1923, the year a majority holding was taken in the Hotel Bermudiana, a 247 room hotel with golf course being built at Hamilton. Finally, the even larger Castle Harbour Hotel with 287 rooms was opened at Tuckers Town in 1931 to complement the order placed in 1930 with Vickers-Armstrong, Newcastle for the ship which was launched as *Monarch of Bermuda*. As were most of the newbuildings for the Bermuda service she, too, had initially been named *Mid Ocean*.

In view of the unacceptably high tenders received for the building of Castle Harbour Hotel, the construction had been undertaken by Furness Withy. Some 600 Portuguese labourers were brought in from South America whilst all the materials were shipped in from the United Kingdom. Johnston Line's *Incemore* carried much of the material and the small cargo vessel *Newton Bay*, completed in 1919 as the Kil class gunboat HMS *Kilmuckridge*, was purchased to tranship the material, being renamed *Longbird*. An order was placed with Blythswood Shipbuilding Company for a tender, the 730gt *Mid Ocean* completed in 1929 and renamed *Castle Harbour* the following year.

The Doxford Diesel

After the first experimental Doxford oil engine had run in 1912, the war delayed practical application apart from an experimental submarine engine and shipboard generators.

In February 1917 Doxford booked two of their standard 420ft 9300dwt shelter deck steamers (yard numbers 519 and 521) for Royalist Steamship Company Ltd (shortly afterwards renamed Grindon Steamship Company Ltd). Also, through Clarksons, they contracted with various Norwegian owners for post-war delivery of thirty three similar ships at prices ranging from £240,000 to £247,500.

After the Armistice in November 1918, the Norwegian orders were commenced as numbers 544-576. The 1920 collapse of the freight market led to cancellation of nineteen of the orders and renegotiation of the prices for others, down to about £85,000. Permission was also received from the Admiralty to commence work on yard numbers 519 and 521, or, as the Doxford Minute Book records, they were "released to roll".

Grindon Steamship Company was managed by B J Sutherland and Company, of Newcastle. With Sutherland's long association as Doxford sales agents and the Doxford shareholding in Grindon, it was no surprise when yard number 521, launched on 20 March 1920, was chosen to take the first of the new diesels.

Dominion Miller, later *Pacific Commerce,* the first British ship powered by a Doxford diesel. *(WSPL)*

Rederi A/B Transatlantic, Gothenburg, who purchased three of the Norwegian contracts, took delivery of two (numbers 549 and 556) and deferred the third (number 561), finally cancelling it in 1928. They also amended the contracts from steam to diesel. To speed delivery, the engine for number 521 was diverted to number 549, launched as *Yngaren* on 28 September 1920. The second engine was used to power number 521.

In August 1921 Grindon Steamship Company sold number 521 to Norfolk and North American Steam Navigation Company Ltd for whom she was completed as *Dominion Miller,* with a proviso that if the new owners were not satisfied with the engine, Doxford would take her back. Sir John Esplen, Bt, a director of both Furness Withy and Doxford was to be the adjudicating expert in the event of the clause being invoked.

The Swedish *Eknaren* (number 556) followed, being launched on 25 July 1922. These three were the first large single screw motorships, all previous motor vessels having had twin screws as an insurance against the risk of breakdown.

Similar engines were chosen for *Pacific Shipper* and *Pacific Trader* which entered service two years later. Furness Withy also ordered three smaller shelter deckers from Doxford with three, rather than four, cylinder engines. They were subsequently sold to Silver Line, entering service as *Silverelm, Silverfir* and *Silvercedar* although *Silverfir* had been launched on 3 May 1924 as *Oristano* for Furness Withy.

New Funnel Colours and Nomenclature

For many years the simple blue rectangular flag with a white F had identified the Furness Withy fleet whilst the plain black funnel had been relieved about 1913 by the addition of a blue band with a white F. Now, following the buyout of the Furness interest, new funnel markings were adopted.

As far as can be ascertained, the new colours were chosen late in 1919. In October, shortly after the Furness buyout, Frederick Lewis arrived in New York en route for Bermuda, and whilst there admired the smart appearance of *Moorish Prince.* With the New York manager, various schemes were considered until finally the Prince Line funnel, which had caught his eye, was adopted as a basis. The Prince of Wales feathers would be deleted for all except Prince Line ships and a new eighteen inch red band added above the broad red band already carried. The first ship to carry the new colours was *Merchant Prince* in 1920.

The houseflag continued unchanged and it was to be another thirty years and after another World War before a new design was adopted.

Never, since Christopher Furness had watched *Chicago* sail on her ill fated voyage in 1878, had a recognisable system of naming been applied to the whole fleet. In the early days the suffix *City* was common. When new fleets were founded, or purchased, suitable naming systems were chosen or the old ones retained. Now in the early post-war years a reversion was made, not for the subsidiary companies but for Furness Withy itself, to the system employed by British Maritime Trust. This was the suffix *-iana.* The scheme was virtually stillborn for as ships were allocated to particular services, more appropriate names were adopted and only six ships carried *-iana* names when they entered service. Details of another eight intended names have survived.

Also during the 1920's, two other new systems of nomenclature were introduced for specific services. On the North Atlantic the prefix *London* was adopted and for the North Pacific the prefix *Pacific,* both in 1923.

North Atlantic Services

During the post war years, the services to Canada and the United States, based both on what remained of the old Furness Withy routes plus those previously operated by Group companies such as Neptune, Johnston, Warren and Chesapeake & Ohio, saw ships calling at St John NB, Halifax and St John's NF in Canada, also Baltimore, Newport News, Boston and Philadelphia in the U S A. Regular British ports of call included London, Liverpool, Hull, Belfast, Glasgow, Leith and Dundee. In 1922, New York returned to the list of ports served, despite opposition from the established lines. The fast cargo service to Philadelphia and New York was opened by *London Mariner.*

Undoubtedly the finest ships on the routes were the big 450ft turbine sisters mentioned under "Whisky Galore", but the state of the trade saw them transferred to Prince Line routes, and after the Depression started in 1929 such big and expensive ships were laid up. Even the smaller vessels, burning less fuel, that took

Nova Scotia and **Newfoundland,** of 1925/6, replaced **Digby** on the service from Liverpool to Canada. **Digby** was refitted and renamed **Dominica** for the New York service to the West Indies.

their place on the North Atlantic were unable to weather the severe trading conditions that followed and with the arrival of *Corsican Prince* in London on 21 January 1932, the New York service was suspended.

The ships on the Warren Line Boston service had, by the end of the war, been reduced to only *Sachem*, although a ship building for Raeburn and Verel, Glasgow, was bought and completed as *Rhode Island* in 1918. So the Furness Withy and Warren services were combined into a new Liverpool, St John's, Halifax and Boston route served by *Sachem* and *Digby* until, in 1925/6, two new ships replaced them. Appropriately named *Newfoundland* and *Nova Scotia*, the new ships carried rather more passengers than either *Digby* or *Sachem*, 105 cabin and 80 3rd class. On completion, *Sachem* was scrapped and *Digby* refitted and renamed *Dominica* for the New York to West Indies service where she was to serve a further decade. Interestingly *Digby*, as *Baltrover*, was to return to the Furness Withy North Atlantic service during World War II.

During 1926 negotiations commenced between a British consortium led by Furness Withy and International Mercantile Marine, for the purchase of the White Star Line. This would have taken Furness Withy into the top ranks of British shipowners. The shipping press reported that P A S Franklin of the I M M wanted between £7 and £7.5 million for White Star, whereas the Furness Withy Minute Book mentions an asking figure of £10 million. This was considered too high, so by July negotiations had ended. They were revived soon after by Lord Kylsant and by December a sale had been agreed under which White Star was bought by Lord Kylsant's Royal Mail group for £7 million. This was one of the liabilities which helped to bring the Royal Mail Group to its knees within a few years.

The changes wrought in Furness Withy by 1926 were such that the Editor of "Fairplay" was led to write (29 April 1926) —

"the present chairman, Sir Frederick Lewis, has raised its status to a level that probably never entered into the mind of the founder of the firm, who was far more concerned with 'tramp' vessels than with liners."

The increased route network of Group companies led to rumours of further developments, such as in 1924 when one shipping journal stated rumours were heard in Liverpool that Johnston Line were to open a service to South America and would be ordering two 7,000 ton motorships for it.

By 1934, however, the North Atlantic routes had been decimated and all that remained was the Furness-Warren Line from Liverpool to Boston, Halifax and St John's. This led to the decision in 1934 to merge the three Liverpool based companies, Neptune, Warren and Johnston into a combined Johnston Warren Lines. It was to be 1939 before the needs of war led to the reopening of the New York service.

The North Pacific Route

In September 1921 *Mongolian Prince* headed through the Panama Canal and turned north to the Pacific Coast ports of America, opening a service which was to be developed in the years to come. This service was not a new project, the potential of the Panama Canal, which opened in 1914 shortly after the outbreak of war, had been realised from the beginning and the ordering of ships, completed in 1915/1916, to be named *Northwestern Miller*, *Southwestern Miller* and *Dominion Miller* under the ownership of Norfolk and North American Steamship Company hints at the intention to develop this trade. The onset of the war delayed implementation until more normal times returned.

Various other Prince Line ships were employed on the service and were joined in 1923 by the new *Dominion Miller* with her pioneer Doxford diesel. The earlier *Northwestern Miller* and *Southwestern Miller* followed together with ships such as *London Shipper*, *London Merchant* and *London Importer*. With the decision to introduce a new nomenclature having the *Pacific* prefix, *Dominion Miller* was renamed *Pacific Commerce* and continued to serve with new ships specially designed for the service.

The Shipbuilding Programme of the 1920's

With the new tonnage ordered during the war entering service, Lewis and his managers reviewed the long term needs of the Group services. Furness Withy was now a different company from a decade ago. The connection with coal and steel interests had been broken and with it the traffic which they had generated for Furness Withy Group shipping. Hence the short service to be given by the colliers *Eldon* and *Throckley* before they were sold in 1929. Furness Withy was now reliant on the liner trades of constituent companies such as Johnston and Prince Lines, plus the new Bermuda and Pacific trades opened in its own name.

In placing orders for ships to be delivered during the decade commencing 1924, the company was to exhibit an awareness of changing technology, adopting the diesel engine for all except two Manchester Liners and the turbo-electric system of *Monarch of Bermuda* and *Queen of Bermuda*. Of the twenty ships with *Pacific* or *Prince* names, all but four would be powered by Burmeister and Wain designed engines, the other four taking Doxfords. Houlder's five ships in the same period were to have three Sulzer, one Werkspoor and one Burmeister & Wain.

Inter-company competition. The *Manchester Corporation* cricket team ready for the match against Johnston Line's *Wheatmore* at Montreal in 1924.
(D Attenborough)

Pacific Trader transiting the Panama Canal, and *Sutherland Grange* passing through the Kirk Narrows, Straits of Magellan, in 1925.

As mentioned earlier, two Doxford built ships were commissioned in 1924 as *Pacific Shipper* and *Pacific Trader*. A further seven *Pacific* ships were to be commissioned between 1927 and 1930. British Maritime Trust also became shipowners again for a brief spell in 1923 with two tankers, the Northumberland built *Modum* just completed for Norwegian owners, bought and renamed *Peruviana*, and the *Cynthiana*. They were sold in 1925 and 1926 respectively to Argentine and German interests.

Name	Built	GRT	Name	Built	GRT
PACIFIC SHIPPER	1924	6304	PACIFIC PRESIDENT	1928	7114
PACIFIC TRADER	1924	6327	PACIFIC GROVE	1928	7114
PACIFIC RELIANCE	1927	6717	PACIFIC RANGER	1929	6866
PACIFIC ENTERPRISE	1927	6722	PERUVIANA	1923	4302
PACIFIC PIONEER	1928	6723	CYNTHIANA	1923	3374
PACIFIC EXPORTER	1928	6723			

A major order, announced in March 1925 on behalf of Prince Line, caused a furore in the press, dismay and consternation in British shipbuilding circles. Tenders had been invited for five ships to upgrade Prince Line's Round-the-World service and the contract had been awarded to Deutsche Werft A G, Hamburg, whose tender of £153,000 per ship was £60,000 less than the lowest British yard. This was the first major order placed by a British owner with a foreign yard and came during a period when excess capacity was the nightmare facing British yards. Lewis expressed a preference to build in Britain and even offered to place the order with any yard who would accept a price £10,000 above the German tender. Even with this offer, it proved impossible to retain the order in Great Britain. Subsequently it was reported that Deutsche Werft actually built the ships at a loss.

Name	Built	GRT	Name	Built	GRT
ASIATIC PRINCE	1926	6734	JAVANESE PRINCE	1926	6734
CHINESE PRINCE	1926	6734	MALAYAN PRINCE	1926	6734
JAPANESE PRINCE	1926	6734			

The enormous discrepancy in prices created considerable uneasiness and led to a Joint Committee of Inquiry being formed by the Shipbuilders Employers' Federation and the Trade Unions. With a brief to devise some means of reducing costs to meet foreign competition, the shock of the Prince Line order secured a measure of unanimity in a trade that had anything but a creditable record of disputes and demarcation troubles. The

Monarch of Bermuda, completed in 1931.

first of the Inquiry reports highlighted working hours, in Britain 47 per week as opposed to the German and Dutch 54, and the need to ease demarcation rules to allow interchangeability and agree that it would be possible to secure greater elasticity without infringing the broad principle of craftsmanship. The second report also protested against the ending of the Trade Facilities Act and urged that it be continued and enlarged, saying "We … cannot think that the Chancellor of the Exchequer can have had the conditions of employment in shipbuilding in mind when he declared that this Act had exhausted its usefulness."

Dating from the early years of the post war recession, the Trade Facilities Act provided Treasury guarantees to secure loans to obtain and finance contracts. Not originally intended for use in the shipbuilding industry, it was subsequently extended to include ships built for both British and foreign owners. Many British shipowners used the facilities thus afforded, with Lord Kylsant and the Royal Mail Group leaders in the field. The Furness Withy Group employed it when financing a number of orders —

Company	Sum	In respect of
Manchester Liners Ltd	£140,000	2 ships (MANCHESTER COMMERCE and CITIZEN)
Warren Line Ltd	£155,400	1 ship (probably NOVA SCOTIA)
Houlder Line Ltd (withdrawn)	£250,000	1 ship (probably UPWEY GRANGE)
Norfolk & North American S S Co Ltd	£400,000	2 ships (PACIFIC RELIANCE and ENTERPRISE)
Gulf Line Ltd	£400,000	2 ships (PACIFIC PIONEER and EXPORTER)
Prince Line Ltd	£840,000	4 ships (The Compass boats)

In addition to orders placed in connection with Trade Facilities guarantees, Prince Line went to Blythswood Shipbuilding Company for two more ships to join their Round-the-World service. The four "Compass Boats", for the prestige route from New York to Brazil and the Plate, were ordered two each from Lithgows and Napier and Miller.

Pacific President, of 1928 transiting the Manchester Ship Canal.

Built in Germany for Rio Cape Line, *Javanese Prince* was employed on the Round-the-World service.

Name	Built	GRT		Name	Built	GRT
SIAMESE PRINCE	1929	6607		NORTHERN PRINCE	1929	10917
CINGALESE PRINCE	1929	6625		SOUTHERN PRINCE	1929	10917
EASTERN PRINCE	1929	10926		WESTERN PRINCE	1929	10926

Meanwhile Houlder Brothers had instituted and carried through a smaller investment programme consisting of three refrigerated ships for the South American service and two tankers for British Empire Steam Navigation Company and Empire Transport Company.

Name	Built	GRT		Name	Built	GRT
UPWEY GRANGE	1925	9130		CARONI RIVER	1928	7807
DUNSTER GRANGE	1928	9494		IMPERIAL TRANSPORT	1931	8022
EL ARGENTINO	1928	9501				

Cairn Line of Steamships Ltd

In 1928 the first company to join the Group since the war was Cairns, Noble and Company Ltd, Newcastle. Initially the intention had been to purchase the shipowning company Cairn Line of Steamships Ltd, but a rise in the market price of that company's shares had led to second thoughts. The alternative path was then taken, purchasing the management company and effectively gaining control of the fleet. The price paid

Both built for service to South America, Prince Line's *Eastern Prince* ran from New York, whereas Houlder Line's *Dunster Grange* was on the route from Britain.

for the £50,000 capital of Cairns, Noble and Company Ltd was £267,500, the bulk of which (£220,000) was in Furness Withy shares. This was considered a good purchase, able to return profits of some £40-50,000 a year. At the same time, 50,000 Cairn Line shares were purchased from Sir William Noble in exchange for 25,000 Furness Withy shares.

Cairn Line had for many years been under the control of Sir William Noble, who had lost his son and heir killed in action in Flanders on 26 April 1915, and Major Russell Cairns, son of the founder. Effectively retiring with the sale, Sir William Noble became a director of Furness, Withy and Company, Ltd, was raised to the peerage as Lord Kirkley in 1930 and died in 1935. Russell Cairns remained active in Cairn Line management until retiring in 1949.

Continuity of management and the need for financial strength in the adverse business climate of the period were the reasons for this small company becoming associated with Furness Withy.

The firm dated from 1876 and the formation of the shipbroking partnership of Starks and Cairns and shipowning had commenced in 1883, the year in which a second partnership, Cairns and Young, was formed. At the end of 1888 both partnerships were terminated in favour of a new one, Cairns, Young and Noble which commenced on 1 January 1889. At the end of December 1903 Lindsay Young retired and the firm was renamed as Cairns, Noble and Company, until becoming a limited liability company in 1915. Meanwhile some of the ships managed by the firm had, in 1892, been placed in the newly formed Cairn Line of Steamships Ltd. Initially engaged in the Baltic, Mediterranean and West African trades, Canadian routes were added with the take-over of Thomson Line early in 1908.

The Thomson roots were even older, dating back to Captain William Thomson of Pittenweem, Fife, who owned and commanded his own ships prior to his death at sea in 1829. Starks and Cairns had first acted as Newcastle agents for Thomson's ships in March 1877 when the steamer *Strathtay* loaded for Leghorn and Drontheim. They first handled a Thomson ship for Montreal in June 1880, when *Avlona* was placed on the loading berth.

Although the London to Montreal service taken over from Thomson was sold to the Cunard Line in 1911, together with the three passenger and cargo ships involved, the Cairn-Thomson Line continued to run refrigerated and general cargo services on a weekly basis from Newcastle and Leith to Montreal (summer), St John NB and Halifax NS (winter). This service complemented and fitted in well with the services already operated by Furness Withy on the North Atlantic.

Cairnmona gave over 20 years service before being sunk in October 1939.
(Stewart Bale Ltd)

The fleet of Cairn Line in 1928 consisted of nine ships, several of which had been built for the trade. Two, however, were B-class war standard ships laid down as *War Camel* and *War Oriole*, sold and completed as *Cairndhu* and *Cairngowan*. The other vessel not built for Cairn Line was *Scatwell*, purchased second-hand in 1920 for onward sale to an Italian owner, whose death frustrated the transaction.

Name	Built	Acquired	GRT	Name	Built	Acquired	GRT
CAIRNMONA	1918	--	4666	CAIRNROSS	1921	--	5494
CAIRNVALONA	1918	--	4929	CAIRNTORR	1922	--	5387
CAIRNDHU	1919	--	5250	CAIRNESK	1926	--	5007
CAIRNGOWAN	1919	--	5295	CAIRNGLEN	1926	--	5019
SCATWELL	1911	1920	4410				

Cairnross, Cairnesk and *Cairnglen* were steam turbine powered. Cairn Line had, in 1912, ordered the previous turbine steamer *Cairnross* in order to compare her performance with that of the triple-expansion engined *Cairngowan* of 1911. The company had earlier taken great interest in Charles Parson's experiments of 1910 with geared turbines for cargo ships, which were tested in *Vespasian* (ex *Eastern Prince)* of 1887. Cairns, Noble and Company in fact purchased *Vespasian* in 1913, but sold her for scrap and ordered a new hull from Doxford in which to fit her turbines. War intervened, the order was cancelled and the hull completed in 1917 as *Lord Byron* for London Greek owners. The pre-war *Cairnross* was torpedoed in 1918, being replaced by the new

Cairnross in 1921, whilst the sisterships *Cairnesk* and *Cairnglen* followed in 1926.

Soon after the purchase, *Scatwell* was sold whilst *Cairntorr* was wrecked on the Labrador coast in October 1928. The Depression followed and the first half of 1931 saw only two ships (*Cairnesk* and *Cairnglen)* operating, the other five being laid up. In 1935 the two war standard ships, *Cairndhu* and *Cairngowan*, were sold, *Cairngowan* having, apart from one spell of four months, been laid up continually since May 1930. This left a reduced fleet of five ships to handle the needs of the service.

Although prior to the outbreak of war in 1939 new tonnage had been planned, when launched the new ship was commissioned as *Welsh Prince* for Prince Line.. It was to be 1946 before any addition was made to the Cairn Line fleet.

Gulf Line Ltd

It was many years since Gulf Line had operated its own services, as related earlier the conference rights in the route to the West Coast of South America had been sold and Gulf Line had withdrawn from the Australian trade. Since then the fleet had been employed on other Group services. Now, in April 1929, there was no reason to retain the company in existence so the decision was made to liquidate and transfer the ships owned, *Ariano* and *London Mariner* going to Furness Withy, *Pacific Pioneer* and *Pacific Exporter* to Norfolk and North American.

Thomas on Stowage

Born at Pwllheli in 1873, R E Thomas went to sea at 18 as an apprentice on the barques *Colony* and *Inversnaid*. Obtaining his Second Mate's certificate he went into steam, serving on Black Sea tramps. Having passed for Master in 1902, Thomas left tramping and served for a short time with the Cunard Line before joining Prince Line in 1903, after meeting Sir James Knott during an Atlantic crossing.

Commencing as second officer on *Afghan Prince* in August 1903, his first command was *Eastern Prince* at the end of 1905. Thomas continued in command of various ships until October 1916 when the Marine Superintendent's post becoming vacant and he was invited to come ashore and fill it, which he did until retiring in 1938.

During the years superintending Prince Line ships, he sat on many maritime committees including the Runciman Steering Committee and the Merchant Ship Defence Advisory Committee. Thomas was also Shipping Adviser to Imperial Airways.

An active member of the Honourable Company of Master Mariners, he originated the scheme to have a floating headquarters. The ship originally chosen to lie alongside the Embankment in London was the four-masted barque *Archibald Russell*, a plan defeated by the outbreak of war in 1939. After the end of hostilities the plan was revived and led to *Wellington* being commissioned as the Headquarters ship.

His inventions included roller hatch beams, hatch locking bars and thief proof hose connections. However, his name will always be linked to the volume "Stowage Properties and Stowage of Cargo" - colloquially known to many as "Thomas's Stowage". First published in 1928 under the title "Stowage" the work went through numerous editions and in 1983 was again revised as "Thomas's Stowage" which is currently in its 2nd edition.

After retirement Captain Thomas returned to his home town of Pwllheli where his activities included setting up the Ministry of Food Organisation for the district and acting as Advisor to the Admiralty on experiments to protect lifeboats.

After a long and active life he died in 1960 aged 87.

Immingham Agency and Hadley Shipping

From the early days under the guidance of Christopher Furness, it had been common for senior managers to have an interest in, and manage, ships outside the Furness Withy fleet, provided the time expended thereon was not considered excessive. Only one manager was considered to have overstepped the mark and left as a result.

Hadley Shipping is a company that was cast in this mould, and because of its post 1950's position in Houlder Brothers' offices in London many people believed it to be a Houlder Group company. Although a small Houlder and Furness Withy interest has in fact existed, it has always been a small minority shareholding.

The story commences in 1912 when Maurice Houlder and Walter Warwick established Immingham Agency Company Ltd in partnership with S H Kaye to offer services to ships calling at Humber ports. Consequent on the war, the Immingham Agency office was closed and post-war the company business consisted of a coal sales agency and a share with Houlder Brothers and Kaye, Son and Company in servicing coal supply contracts to Patagonian meat packing plants. *Beacon Grange*, when lost in 1921, was laden with such a cargo.

In 1924 a one-third interest was taken by Immingham Agency in the French flag *Glacière* which was "operated as a Houlder Line boat", the only one under the French flag. This lasted for eighteen months until the share was sold to another of the partners in the *Glacière* venture, Arthur Rappaport.

Walter Warwick and his fellow Furness Withy director, Sir John Esplen, were at the time looking for employment for their sons, and hearing of the Anglo-Saxon Petroleum Company sale of ten year old tankers with a ten year charter-back, they negotiated the purchase of *Cepolis* and the formation in 1926 of a new company to own the ship, Hadley Shipping Company Ltd. During 1929 a second Shell "sale and charter back" tanker was purchased, *Cliona* with the remainder of her charter.

Sir John Esplen's other business interests included coastal tankers and these later came under the management of Immingham Agency. For the next fifty years, Hadley would continue to operate from a corner of the Houlder offices with a small fleet of tankers, dry cargo ships and bulk carriers until after the Tung take-over when finally the company moved into new premises, although still under the active management of the Warwick family.

The Great Depression

The Wall Street Crash of 1929 ushered in a period of unemployment and lack of work just when most shipowners were anticipating a few years of prosperity. Their hopes, based on experience of trade cycles over many years, were completely dashed and many owners who had placed orders with the shipyards during the years prior to 1929 in confident expectation suddenly found themselves facing bankruptcy: their cash reserves built up during the War had been whittled away in surviving the recession of the 1920's and there was now little or no prospect of raising finances to meet their obligations. In a number of instances the financial institutions acted to recover what they could and new ships were available on the market at prices far below their actual cost.

The Depression saw Furness Withy shed the last vestiges of its role, two decades earlier, as a tramp and collier owner. British Empire and Empire Transport, the two tramp ship fleets managed by Houlder Brothers, sold all their tramps built in the period prior to World War I, a total of seventeen going for scrap or further trading between 1929 and 1934. At the end of the sale they were left with just two ships, the tankers *Caroni River* and *Imperial Transport*. Lack of cargoes was evident when *Imperial Transport* was delivered in 1931; she went straight into lay up and remained there for two years.

Furness Withy were to survive because, as The Economist expressed it, "... under the chairmanship of Sir Frederick Lewis (now Lord Essendon), the Furness Withy Group had maintained a reputation for ultra-conservative finance and shrewd reluctance to take anything but the right step at the right time, which went far to explain its acknowledged position as one of the strongest shipping organisations in the world".

Despite the strength of the Group, cut backs and rationalisation were required. The Atlantic services which had been reopened a decade earlier were closed, leaving only the combined Johnston, Warren and Furness Withy service to Newfoundland and Nova Scotia, employing the two ships named after those colonies. Prince Line and Rio Cape Line were together losing £250,000 a year on the New York routes to South America and Far East, so in 1932 agreement was reached with the competing Silver Line to join forces in a service which enabled them to withdraw one and Prince Line two ships from the service. Prince Line also reduced the number of ships on the South American route from four to three.

The Kylsant Crash

Although the financial collapse of the Royal Mail Steam Packet Group was in no way related to Furness Withy, it was to result in several companies joining the Furness Withy Group in the decades that followed, first Shaw, Savill and Albion Company Ltd and then Royal Mail Lines Ltd and Pacific Steam Navigation Company Ltd.

In 1903 Owen Philipps (created Lord Kylsant in 1923) became chairman of the ailing Royal Mail Steam Packet Company. Having restored the company to financial health he commenced to build an interlinking group of companies in concert with Lord Pirrie of Harland and Wolff, the Belfast shipbuilders. Using cross shareholdings to bind the companies to Royal Mail and Harland and Wolff, their first major acquisition in 1910 was Elder, Dempster and Company, purchased from the executors of Alfred Jones.

Kylsant, a noted optimist, continued to develop his interests during the post war recession. One useful tool in this was the ability, under the accounting and company law of the period, to retain hidden reserves which could be brought forward into the annual accounts and permit a false impression of financial health to be maintained. This practice could only work whilst the reserves existed; the shipping recession finally exhausted these reserves and by 1929 it was no longer possible to maintain the facade.

The first crack to appear was at Lamport and Holt, who were suffering from the loss of trade on their route from New York to South America following the foundering of *Vestris* on 12 November 1928 with the loss of 112 lives. In 1929 the need for more capital at Lamport and Holt was initially to have been met by a cash call on unpaid shares, but this intention had to be abandoned when it was realised the amount realised would be far less than expected due to the network of cross shareholdings between the companies. These cross holdings hid the fact that although the total group capital was some £52 million, the actual cash involved was only £20 million.

Royal Mail Steam Packet Group Companies

1907	Shire Line (50%, balance in 1911)		1917	McGregor, Gow and Holland Ltd
1908	Forwood Line		1917	Argentine Navigation Co (N Mihanovich) Ltd
1910	Elder, Dempster and Company Ltd and associated companies		1917	John Hall, Junior and Company
1910	Pacific Steam Navigation Co		1919	J and P Hutchison
1911	Glen Line Ltd		1919	Bullard, King and Company
1911	Lamport and Holt Ltd		1919	David MacIver and Company Ltd
1912	Union-Castle Mail Steamship Company Ltd		1919	Scottish Steamship Company Ltd
1913	Nelson Line (Liverpool) Ltd, Nelson Steam Navigation Company Ltd and H and W Nelson Ltd		1925	British Motorship Company Ltd
1914	RMSP (Meat Transports) Ltd formed		1926	Dundalk & Newry Steam Packet Company Ltd
1916	Moss Steamship Company Ltd and James Moss and Company		1926	Michael Murphy Ltd
			1927	Oceanic Steam Navigation Company Ltd (White Star)
1916	R MacAndrew and Company Ltd		1927	Shaw, Savill and Albion Company Ltd
1917	Coast Lines Ltd and associated companies		1927	Aberdeen Line (G Thompson and Company Ltd)
			1928	David MacBrayne Ltd
			1928	Australian Commonwealth Line

As the edifice started to crumble major creditors (banks and insurance companies), the City Institutions and the Bank of England came together, realising the harm that would result in all quarters from the looming bankruptcy. A salvage sale of the assets, with the world in the throes of the Great Depression, would be an unmitigated disaster. The alternative, to save jobs and investment, was to enforce a moratorium on debts, appoint trustees to keep the business working and then reorganise the assets and sell them in suitable packages as the market allowed. Although much of the reorganisation was completed by the time war again broke out in 1939, the repercussions of the affair continued to be felt long after, the Company Act, 1948, being one result. In fact some forty years were to pass before the last file was to be closed on the debacle.

Shaw, Savill and Albion Company Ltd

In 1935 control of Shaw, Savill and Albion passed to Furness Withy, and with it a fleet of nearly thirty ships and the services from the United Kingdom to Australasia. Shaw, Savill and Albion had been largely owned by John Ellerman (50%) and Oceanic Steam Navigation Company (White Star) (40%) when, in 1927, Royal Mail had purchased White Star from the International Mercantile Marine. Ellerman had little faith in Kylsant and was loath to be in partnership with him so, soon after the transaction, he sold his holding to Kylsant, giving control to Royal Mail.

Along with Union-Castle, Shaw, Savill and Albion was one of the Group companies that remained profitable through the Kylsant collapse. However, its services were run as a joint undertaking with White Star whose financial status was the opposite. Joint ownership of the ships, including four built with the aid of Trade Facilities Act guarantees (*Zealandic*, *Coptic*, *Taranaki* and *Karamea*) posed problems that took several years to disentangle.

With White Star defaulting on their mortgage payments for these four ships, and Shaw, Savill and Albion meeting their payments on due dates, the Treasury guarantees were invoked, but the Registrar of Ships could not register the Treasury mortgage interest on half a ship!

The first step, in May 1933, towards resolving the difficulties was the issue of 20,925 £5 shares to raise capital to purchase, jointly with P & O, the Aberdeen and Commonwealth Line from the Royal Mail Trustees. These new shares were taken up by Furness Withy. At the end of the year the Shaw, Savill and Albion capital was doubled to £600,000 and the new shares distributed as a rights issue. The next step was taken in September 1934 with the purchase by Shaw, Savill and Albion of Oceanic's West Australian rights and *Ceramic* for £75,000. Finally, in 1935, Furness Withy paid £1.1 million to the Trustees for the Shaw, Savill and Albion shares held by Oceanic (34,636) and White Star Line (43,184), together with Oceanic's interest in twelve Shaw, Savill and

Largs Bay **joined the Group in 1935 with the Shaw, Savill and Albion and Aberdeen and Commonwealth Line.**
(Skyfotos)

Albion ships. With a holding now of over 98,000 of the 120,000 shares, this gave full control to Furness Withy. The only outstanding matter was cleared up in 1937 when the Treasury interest in the four ships built with Trade Facilities Act guarantees was purchased for £370,000.

The fleet of Shaw, Savill and Albion in 1935 consisted of —

Name	Built	GRT	Name	Built	GRT
KIA ORA	1907	6567	RARANGA*	1916	7956
AKAROA	1914	15128	MAHANA*	1917	8740
KUMARA	1919	7926	MAHIA*	1917	7914
MATAROA	1922	12333	OTIRA*	1919	7995
TAMAROA	1922	12354	MAIMOA*	1920	8011
THEMISTOCLES	1911	11231	TAIROA*	1920	7983
FORDSDALE	1924	9949	MATAKANA*	1921	8048
IONIC*	1902	12352	COPTIC*	1928	8281
TAINUI*	1908	9965	KARAMEA*	1928	8281
PAKEHA*	1910	7909	TARANAKI*	1928	8286
MAMARI*	1911	7924	ZEALANDIC*	1928	8281
WAIMANA*	1911	7852			

Aberdeen & Commonwealth Line Ltd

ESPERANCE BAY	1922	14176	LARGS BAY	1921	14184
HOBSONS BAY	1922	14198	MORETON BAY	1921	14145
JERVIS BAY	1922	14164			

*jointly owned with Oceanic S N Co Ltd.

Under Furness Withy ownership, this fleet was shortly to be upgraded by the addition of several modern refrigerated cargo ships, and within a few years would commission the largest motorship in the world, *Dominion Monarch*.

Origins of Shaw, Savill and Albion Company Ltd

Formed in 1882 to combat competition from the New Zealand Shipping Company, which had been founded ten years earlier, the company brought together in an amalgamation two firms long established in the Australasian trade. These were Shaw, Savill and Company of London and the Albion Line managed by P Henderson and Company, of Glasgow.

Patrick Henderson, merchant, had founded his business in Glasgow during 1834, whilst shipowning can be traced back to his brother, George Henderson, a shipmaster and owner from 1829 of *Tom and Jessie*. Initially employed on trade from the Clyde to Italy, the growing fleet of sailing ships later extended their field to South America and India. In 1853 the company embarked on a venture to run steamers to Panama, connecting to a Pacific service which served the Californian goldfields. The outbreak of the Crimean War that year saw the two steamers taken up as troopships by the French Government, and after the war they were employed to fulfil a British government mail contract, overland at Suez and thence to Australia. Sadly this venture failed.

The Henderson name was already associated with New Zealand. The southern province of Otago was settled by the Free Church of Scotland, through the Otago Association, with the first settlers landing near Dunedin in 1848; shortly afterwards ships chartered by Hendersons were trading to the new province. The first owned ship to sail for New Zealand was *Lady Douglas* in 1857. Within a few years Henderson ships were being advertised as "The Albion Line" and in 1864 the Albion Shipping Company was registered, in 1877 becoming the Albion Shipping Company Ltd.

Until 1882, the Albion Line was noted as the owners of a fine fleet of sailing ships named after the partners, their wives and in due course cities and provinces of New Zealand. The most famous of these was the iron ship *Dunedin*, launched from Robert Duncan and Company's yard into the Clyde on 3 March 1874 at a cost of £23,750. She was chosen to load the first cargo of frozen meat exported from New Zealand to Europe. Sailing from Port Chalmers on 15 February 1882 she was in London on 26 May where her cargo was received with enthusiasm by the traders at Smithfield Market. Shortly afterwards she was followed by *Marlborough*.

At the other end of Britain, Shaw, Savill and Company dated from 1858 when Robert Shaw and Walter Savill left Willis, Gann and Company to form their own firm. Willis, Gann and Company were London loading brokers for the New Zealand trade and the new venture initially placed chartered tonnage on the berth, mainly to the English settlements in North Island. It was to be 1865 before Shaw, Savill and Company purchased their first ship, the wooden *Cossipore*. Like Hendersons, they built up a fleet of high class sailing ships and the two companies continued to trade without serious competition between them.

The appearance, in 1872, of the New Zealand Shipping Company, based in that country, had the effect of causing the long-standing informal friendly relationship between Hendersons and Shaw, Savill and Company to grow, until in 1882 the inevitable merger took place. The opening of the frozen meat trade and the proposal by New Zealand Shipping to introduce steamers called for a serious look at future plans.

In November 1882 the agreement to amalgamate was signed and Shaw, Savill and Albion Company Ltd came into being. Twelve Albion Line ships were purchased by the new company for £200,157 and nineteen came from Shaw, Savill and Company. Valued at £285,110, the Shaw, Savill ships were paid for with £100,000 shares, £100,000 debentures and the balance in cash.

A joint service agreement was made in 1884 with Oceanic Steam Navigation Company (better known as White Star). White Star provided three ships, *Coptic, Doric* and *Ionic* whilst Shaw, Savill and Albion built *Arawa* and *Tainui* on the Clyde.

Houlder Brothers

Having, during the war, lost over a dozen ships from the fleets under their control, Houlder Brothers were, like the other Group companies, slow to replace tonnage. As the economic climate developed this conservative policy proved to be correct.

Led by Walter Warwick, Frank Houlder and Maurice Houlder the interests in both Australia and South America were consolidated and a perceived opportunity to establish a meat extract plant at Mwanza, processing Tanganyikan cattle, was promoted in 1928 through a company named Meat Rations Ltd. This failed to develop satisfactorily, so in 1935 it was wound up.

Some of the refrigerated tonnage lost during the War was replaced by the delayed orders placed pre-war, especially the Furness-Houlder Argentine Lines ships. The *War Minerva*, building in Belfast, was purchased and became *Canonesa* in 1920, followed by *Hardwicke Grange* the following year. The next newbuilding was the first motorship in the Houlder fleet, fitted with Fairfield built Sulzer engines. She was named *Upwey Grange* in 1925, followed three years later by a pair of sisters, *Dunster Grange* and *El Argentino* with similar machinery.

W C Warwick.

The loss of *Beacon Grange* and *Ocean Transport*, both wrecked, and the disposal of all the British Empire and Empire Transport tramps during the Depression was offset by the building of two motor tankers, *Caroni River* in 1928 for British Empire and *Imperial Transport* of 1931 for Empire Transport. This marked the entry of Houlders into the tanker trades.

Another opportunity was seized in 1935 when three ships and their charters were taken over from the Buenos Aires and Great Southern Railway Company, shortly after Frank Houlder died. Plans were also in hand to introduce new tonnage for meat carriage and these came to fruition with the motorship *Beacon Grange,* powered by Hawthorn built Werkspoor engines.

As peace drained away and the country started to prepare for War, Houlders were a much slimmer organisation than two decades before, the Plate meat trade had been consolidated despite adverse conditions and the lost tramp trades had been replaced by a small presence in the tanker field. All the ships carrying the Houlder Line suffix *Grange* at this time were to be lost in the War years that followed, apart from *Dunster Grange* which was still in company service in 1945.

The Furness Withy Shipbuilding Programme of the 1930's

The Great Depression settled on the world following the Wall Street Crash of "Black Tuesday" 29 October 1929. Along with industry, shipping suffered; millions of tons of ships were laid up without employment and cases of ships crewed entirely by certificated officers received widespread publicity. The optimism and anticipation which had seen increased orders and deliveries from shipyards in the late 1920s evaporated and

Lancastrian Prince **opens the new Haifa harbour, 31 October 1933.**

by early 1931 most shipbuilding yards had delivered the last ships on their order books, laid off their workforce and effectively closed down. Some were able to retain a skeleton of key workers and kept drawing office staff preparing new and more economic designs in readiness for an upturn in the economy; others shut entirely. So great was the over capacity in the industry that National Shipbuilders Security Ltd was established, financed by a levy on future production, to purchase obsolete and redundant yards, dispose of their equipment and sterilise them from returning to shipbuilding for many years to come.

The only Furness Withy orders to be placed in this period were for the two liners employed on the Furness Bermuda run from New York. *Monarch of Bermuda* and *Queen of Bermuda* were welcome orders to the industry, albeit too little to make much of an impression in the prevailing conditions. The delivery of orders placed prior to the Depression finished with the tanker *Imperial Transport* in 1931.

The Depression period saw, according to some shipowners, the worst five years they had ever experienced. Various proposals were mooted to alleviate the situation, and finally in 1935 the British Shipping (Assistance) Act was passed to make funds available to owners placing orders with British yards, also to make payments to tramp owners who agreed to apply and enforce minimum freight rates. Prince Line was the only Group company to apply for a Treasury loan under the act, proposing to build four Mediterranean service ships. The Act required the scrapping of twice the tonnage built, hence the term "Scrap and Build". *Sailor Prince, Stuart Prince, London Citizen* and *London Exchange* were submitted for scrapping. Ultimately it was agreed to scrap the elderly *Sailor Prince* and *Stuart Prince* (built in 1907 and 1905 respectively) against a loan to build *Arabian Prince* and *Syrian Prince,* costing £65,000 each. The other two sisters, *Palestinian Prince* and *Cyprian Prince* were financed from other sources, *London Citizen* was sold to James Chambers of Liverpool and broken up against their "Scrap and Build" loan whilst *London Exchange* was sold to Ben Line for further trading.

Prince Line were later to be the only Group company to make use of the British Shipping (Assistance) Bill, 1939, which failed to reach the statute book due to the outbreak of War. However, the Government honoured its undertaking to provide finance for shipbuilding, and Prince Line commissioned four Mediterranean and one larger vessel paid for with Treasury loans, *Norman Prince, Lancastrian Prince, Tudor Prince* and *Stuart Prince* were sisters to the earlier class of four Mediterranean traders, whilst the larger ship, *Welsh Prince,* had been laid down for Cairn Line and transferred to Prince Line prior to launch.

From 1934 until the outbreak of War in September 1939, member companies of the Furness Withy Group were to commission a total of twenty ships and had ten then under construction which were delivered during the first eighteen months of the war. They also purchased two ships second-hand, *Manaqui* in 1937 for the service south from New York to the West Indies, and *Sutherland* (renamed *British Prince*) built in 1935 for B J Sutherland and Company, the first of Doxford's new economy design of cargo motorship from a yard which had lain idle since 1931.

The first of the twenty deliveries were orders placed by Shaw, Savill and Albion prior to their coming into the Group, the first of the "W" class Empire Food Ships. *Waipawa* and *Waiwera* entered service in 1934 and were followed by three others prior to the outbreak of war. Furness Withy commissioned two new ships

Newbuildings ranged in size from *Palestinian Prince* (1960gt) of 1936 to *Dominion Monarch* (27,155gt) of 1939.

for the New York to Newfoundland service of the Furness Red Cross Line, named for the two forts at the entrance to St John's harbour, *Fort Amherst* and *Fort Townshend*. Houlder Line and Empire Transport Company took delivery of two general cargo ships and one meat carrier, Manchester Liners commenced a series of deliveries with *Manchester Port* in 1935, whilst Prince Line and the associated Rio Cape Line ordered two series of ships, small Mediterranean traders and larger deep sea tonnage.

The most important order after the delivery of *Queen of Bermuda*, was undoubtedly *Dominion Monarch* which entered Shaw, Savill and Albion service to New Zealand in 1939.

Name	Built	GRT	Name	Built	GRT
Furness, Withy and Company Ltd			Prince Line Ltd		
FORT AMHERST	1936	3489	ARABIAN PRINCE	1936	1960
FORT TOWNSHEND	1936	3489	PALESTINIAN PRINCE	1936	1960
			SYRIAN PRINCE	1936	1988
Renfrew Navigation Company Ltd			CYPRIAN PRINCE	1937	1988
ARGENTINE TRANSPORT	1935	4684	AFRICAN PRINCE	1939	4653
			LANCASTRIAN PRINCE	1940	1914
Houlder Line Ltd			NORMAN PRINCE	1940	1913
LYNTON GRANGE	1937	5029	TUDOR PRINCE	1940	1913
BEACON GRANGE	1938	10119	WELSH PRINCE	1940	5148
			STUART PRINCE	1940	1911
Manchester Liners Ltd					
MANCHESTER PORT	1935	5469	Shaw, Savill and Albion Company Ltd		
MANCHESTER CITY	1937	5600	WAIPAWA	1934	10801
MANCHESTER PROGRESS	1938	5620	WAIWERA	1934	10800
MANCHESTER MERCHANT	1940	7264	WAIRANGI	1935	10796
MANCHESTER TRADER	1941	5671	WAIMARAMA	1938	11092
			DOMINION MONARCH	1939	27155
Rio Cape Line Ltd			WAIOTIRA	1939	12823
SCOTTISH PRINCE	1938	4917			

In addition Shaw, Savill and Albion had another W-class ship under construction at Harland and Wolff, Belfast. Yard number 1091, she was taken over by the Admiralty and converted, being launched as the aircraft carrier *Campania*. Unlike other merchant hulls converted to that role, she was not returned to her intended state after the war and remained an aircraft carrier until broken up in 1955. However, *Campania* was to be associated with the company as, with Great Britain returning to civilian life in the post-war era, she embarked a touring version of the Festival of Britain which was open to the public in various ports. In this guise she was manned and managed by the company.

Johnston Warren Lines Ltd

In late 1934 the decision was taken to amalgamate the Liverpool based companies. The Depression had seen the suspension of so many routes that only the old Warren Line from Liverpool to St John's NF, Halifax NS and Boston, together with Johnston Line's Black Sea and Mediterranean services survived. No justification remained for having three companies so an amalgamation took place between Neptune Steam Navigation Company Ltd, Warren Line (Liverpool) Ltd and Johnston Line Ltd.

Quernmore sailing from Ramsden Dock, Barrow.

Warren Line (Liverpool) Ltd had been established in 1898 as White Diamond Steamship Company Ltd, under the management of George Warren and Company, Liverpool. Renamed in 1922, a further renaming now occurred on 13 December 1934, to become Johnston Warren Lines Ltd. The ships and assets of Neptune Steam Navigation Company and Johnston Line were transferred and the two companies wound up.

Following the amalgamation, Johnston Warren Lines found themselves the managers of a fleet consisting of ten ships and three tugs employed on the Mersey —

Name	Built	GRT	Name	Built	GRT
Neptune Steam Navigation Company Ltd			CEEMORE (tug)	1929	186
LONDON EXCHANGE	1921	6640	DEEMORE (tug)	1930	187
LONDON MERCHANT	1923	7899	AVIEMORE	1920	4060
Warren Line (Liverpool) Ltd			DROMORE	1920	4096
NEWFOUNDLAND	1925	6791	INCEMORE	1921	4098
NOVA SCOTIA	1926	6796	JESSMORE	1921	4099
Johnston Line Ltd			KENMORE	1923	3783
BEEMORE (tug)	1929	186	QUERNMORE	1923	3787

London Merchant was sold to T & J Harrison in 1935, followed by *London Exchange* which passed to Ben Line during 1938 whilst *Kenmore* and *Quernmore* were sold to French-buyers in 1937. The two Warren Line ships continued on the service for which they had been built, to St John's, Halifax and Boston and the four Johnston Line vessels were sufficient to maintain the line to Greece, Turkey and Roumania until war broke out in 1939 when they were diverted to other duties.

Frederick Lewis, Lord Essendon

Following the buyout of 1919, Frederick Lewis was elected to be the fourth chairman, a position held until his death in 1944. He not only occupied that seat for longer than anyone before or since but must rank alongside Christopher Furness as having had most influence on the direction, and survival, of Furness Withy.

Frederick Lewis was born at West Hartlepool in 1870, his father Edmund Lewis, from South Wales, working for Christopher Furness. Prior to Edmund's death, Furness had promised to give his son a job, so Frederick commenced work as an office boy in 1883. Later posted to the London office opened by R B Stoker, he became manager there on the transfer of Stoker to Manchester in 1898 as Managing Director of the newly formed Manchester Liners. The following year Lewis was appointed a director of Furness, Withy and Company, Ltd.

On the unexpected death of Sir Stephen Furness in 1914, Lewis was his logical successor, but chose to defer to the memory of his mentor Christopher Furness, and the Furness family financial interest in the company. He therefore suggested Marmaduke Furness, the second Lord Furness, be chairman, with himself as deputy-chairman. In view of the lack of experience of the new chairman it was agreed Marmaduke would only make decisions after full consultation with his deputy.

During World War I, Walter Runciman, President of the Board of Trade, invited Lewis to be one of the original members of the Ships Licensing Committee, of which Lewis was appointed deputy-chairman. This was followed in 1916 by membership of the Shipping Control Committee. Later he chaired several sub-committees of the Ministry of Shipping, one of the most important being the Neutral Tonnage Committee. For these services he was created a baronet in 1918.

Having become chairman of Furness Withy in 1919 Sir Frederick Lewis continued to devote much time to wider issues. Vice-President of the Chamber of Shipping in 1921, he was President the following year and elected chairman of the Shipowners' Parliamentary Committee in 1924. Numerous other public duties, some allied to shipping, were recognised in the 1932 Birthday Honours with the granting of a Barony as Lord Essendon of Essendon.

His wisdom and imagination, coupled with a conservative policy, was at the heart of both the changing role of the company, from a largely tramp ship operation to one primarily concerned with liner trades, and the maintenance of the company in a healthy financial state which enabled it to survive the difficult inter-war years when some companies of similar repute and standing crashed.

At the same time he led the company in developing imaginative interests such as the Bermuda holiday trade and the North Pacific route, whilst taking the opportunity to acquire assets, sometimes a controlling interest and at others a minority holding. Amongst these can be listed Cairn Line, Shaw, Savill and Albion, Royal Mail Lines and Pacific Steam Navigation. His standing was acknowledged by the number of directorships held outside the Group.

When war came again in 1939 his experience was enlisted by the Ministry of Supply and his first duty was as chairman of the Wool Disposal Committee, followed by membership of the Advisory Council of the Ministry of Shipping.

As a person he is remembered as a competent organiser who obtained decisions by consultation rather than dictate, always accessible and acting in a kind, courteous manner to all. One biographer wrote "Probably few peers of the realm are known to such a large circle by their christian names."

At the time of his death, on 24 June 1944, he had completed 61 years of service to the company.

Bermuda on fire at Hamilton, Bermuda, 16 June 1931.

Marine Losses

The pattern of losses sustained in the period between the wars, thirteen ships from various causes, well illustrates the changed character of the Furness Withy Group. Whereas previously all had been lost on the North Atlantic or in the Baltic, the casualties between 1919 and 1939 were scattered world wide, from Ocean Island to Cyprus, Vancouver to the Plate. Until 1923 each year was to see losses reported, thereafter nothing until four ships went in 1928. After that only one in 1931 and another in 1938, both from fire, to complete the list.

Fleet losses 1919 to 1939

APPENINE (Gulf Line Ltd)—4 March 1919 wrecked on Witless Point Icepack NF. Liverpool for St John's NF, general.

MESSINA (Gulf Line Ltd)—14 December 1919 abandoned in 47.29N 38.11W. St John NB for Antwerp, grain & foodstuffs.

GLENORCHY (Rio Cape Line Ltd)—1 March 1920 wrecked off Victoria Bar, Brazil. New York for Victoria, general.

ITALIAN PRINCE (Prince Line Ltd)—10 November 1920 on fire at Evdimou, taken to Limassol and beached 11.11.20. Cyprus for Liverpool, beans & general.

BEACON GRANGE (Houlder Line Ltd)—6 September 1921 wrecked on Banco Oliver, entrance to Rio Gallegos. Newport News for Rio Gallegos, coal.

WELSH PRINCE (Rio Cape Line Ltd)—29 May 1922 collision with IOWAN, sunk in Columbia River. Baltimore & Portland (Oregon) for Kobe, steel & timber.

TUSCAN PRINCE (Prince Line Ltd)—15 February 1923 wrecked on Village Island, Barclay Sound. Tyne & Antwerp for Vancouver, general.

OCEAN TRANSPORT (Empire Transport Co Ltd)—30 January 1928 lost propeller, wrecked at Ocean Island.

ASIATIC PRINCE (Rio Cape Line Ltd)—23 May 1928 posted missing. Sailed New York 28.2.28 and Los Angeles 16.3.28 for Yokohama, general.

CYNTHIANA (Furness, Withy & Co Ltd)—23 June 1928 wrecked at Cape Mala, Panama Bay. Bellingham for Grangemouth, lumber.

CAIRNTORR (Cairn Line of Steamships Ltd)—23 October 1928 wrecked on Island Rock, Cocoacho Bay (50.7N 60.17W). Montreal for Tyne & Leith, grain & general.

BERMUDA (Bermuda & West Indies S.S. Co Ltd)—19 November 1931 badly damaged by fire, CTL, at Belfast undergoing repairs and reconstruction after serious fire 16.6.31 at Hamilton, Bermuda. Sold 1932 and dismantled. 30 April 1932 hulk wrecked whilst in tow for breaking up.

ITALIAN PRINCE (Prince Line Ltd)—6 September 1938 on fire, abandoned 30m S 21°W of Finisterre. London for Alexandretta, passengers & general.

Three of the losses could be said to be in traditional Furness Withy territory. Gulf Line's *Appenine* went ashore on the Newfoundland coast in early March 1919, running at eight knots and with only 400 tons of cargo, she grounded on high tide. Salvage attempts were hindered by the ice which, with storms, caused increasing damage until she was abandoned on 21 April with most of her bottom torn out. Later the same year *Messina* was abandoned in 47.29N 38.11W. Bound for Europe, heavy seas tore tarpaulins and hatch covers from holds 2 and 3, carried away the steering gear and caused other damage. Flooding, and with pumps choked, she was abandoned and the crew were rescued by the steamer *Regina* which landed them at Philadelphia. The final North Atlantic loss was Cairn Line's *Cairntorr,* a new addition to the fleets controlled by the Group. Bound down the St Lawrence, she failed to clear the estuary before being wrecked on 23 October 1928. The crew got away in two boats and were picked up by Donaldson's *Salacia. Cairntorr* had broken up and disappeared by the end of the month.

Ocean Transport, seen on 16 June 1929, eighteen months after being wrecked at Ocean Island.

Three ships were wrecked on the Atlantic coasts of Central and South America. *Cynthiana* went ashore in Panama Bay on 23 June 1928 and despite the efforts of salvage contractors Merritt, Chapman and Scott, broke up and had to be abandoned in mid August. Rio Cape Line's *Glenorchy* hit the rocks approaching Victoria Bar on 1 March 1920 and was abandoned two days later whilst Houlder Line lost *Beacon Grange* on 6 September 1921. With coal for the meat packing plants, she was approaching her destination, Rio Gallegos, with the pilot on board when she grounded. A week later her back was broken and she was adjudged a total loss.

The Pacific was to see the loss of four ships, three of them Prince Line. Empire Transport's *Ocean Transport* was on charter to Andrew Weir and Company, to load phosphates at Ocean Island. Moored and waiting to load she was ordered to sea to ride out approaching bad weather. Slipping the moorings at noon on 30 January 1928, her propeller struck the mooring buoy and a blade was lost. With this damage *Ocean Transport* was unable to clear the land and a squall drove her broadside onto a reef where she broke up.

Tuscan Prince was on the new North Pacific service bound for Vancouver when she grounded in a blinding snowstorm in Barclay Sound. Wrecked on 15 February 1923 in an exposed position, the crew were rescued by the American coastguard cutter *Snohomish* and much cargo was recovered by Pacific Salvage Company before she slipped into deep water. Further south, *Welsh Prince* was lost on 29 May 1922, sunk in collision in the Columbia River. Ten miles from Astoria she was in a bow to bow collision with the American steamer *Iowan* which cut 50 feet into *Welsh Prince's* starboard bow, killed seven firemen and drove timbers in the cargo (she was loaded with 3,600 tons of steel and two million feet of timber for Japan) through the bulkheads allowing the engine room and forward holds to fill with water so that she sank in thirty minutes. Settling on the river bed, fire started and by the end of the month her back was broken. At the subsequent inquiry, the pilot on board *Iowan* was found responsible.

The disappearance of *Asiatic Prince* in 1928 remains one of the mysteries of the sea. On the Round-the-World service, she had sailed from New York on 28 February and Los Angeles on 16 March bound for Yokohama. As in most such cases many rumours abounded, pirates after the bullion on board being typical. What is most likely is she succumbed to heavy weather north of Hawaii as garbled distress calls were received and, at the time, not immediately linked to her. She was posted missing at Lloyd's on 23 May.

Two ships named *Italian Prince* were lost on the Prince Line Mediterranean service. On 10 November 1920, the first of that name was loading a cargo of locust beans in Cyprus for carriage to Liverpool when a bunker fire was discovered. This spread rapidly and the following day she had to be beached at Limassol where she was abandoned as a total loss. Eighteen years later another ship of the same name was bound from London for Alexandretta when fire was discovered and she also had to be abandoned, off Finisterre.

Not all casualties were total losses. *Thistlemore* ashore at Cape Cod in 1922 was refloated and returned to service.

Last, but in fact the largest ship ever to be lost in peacetime under the Furness flag, was the 19,086gt *Bermuda*. Only four years old and built for the New York to Bermuda tourist trade, she was alongside at Hamilton when fire was discovered in the early hours of 16 June 1931. Although extinguished, extensive damage had been sustained and she was returned to her builders for repairs. These were nearly completed when, on 19 November, fire broke out again at Belfast. This time the fire ravaged the whole ship which was declared a total loss. Her builders, Workman, Clark and Company, purchased the wreck, removed the engines for further use and sold the hull to shipbreakers. Finally, under tow of the tug *Seaman*, she left for Rosyth only to go ashore on the Scottish coast and become a total loss.

Furness Withy ships were also able to help others in distress. On 8 September 1934, the Ward Line's *Morro Castle* was nearing the end of her passage from Havana to New York when fire broke out. Of the 547 passengers and crew on board, 137 lost their lives. When distress signals were sent out, *Monarch of Bermuda* was one of those to respond and she was able to save 79 lives.

Bowater's Paper Boats

In 1938 Bowaters took over the pulp and paper mill at Corner Brook, Newfoundland. The facility operated as International Power and Paper Company of Newfoundland Ltd, being renamed Bowater's Newfoundland Pulp and Paper Mills Ltd following the change of ownership.

The company owned two ships built to carry newsprint to the American market, *Humber Arm* and *Corner Brook*. In 1939 a contract was negotiated for Furness Withy to manage these ships, and others to follow.

Name	Built	Acquired	GRT	Name	Built	Acquired	GRT
HUMBER ARM	1925	--	5758	WATERTON	1928	1941	2140
CORNER BROOK	1925	--	5767	LIVINGSTON	1928	1941	2115
NORTH BROOK	1919	1940	2373	KITTYS BROOK	1907	1941	4031
BETTY	1919	1940	2323	SANDLANDS	1925	1943	2170
PORTIA	1904	1941	978				

During the war, seven ships were purchased to ensure tonnage was available for the company trade, in addition to a number of tugs and barges used on the American coast. Five ships fell victim to enemy submarine action.

The cost of charters during the Korean War led to Bowaters deciding to build a new fleet of tonnage designed for their trade. To own these ships, Bowater Steamship Company Ltd was formed and during 1955 the first two ships, *Margaret Bowater* and *Sarah Bowater*, came into service, to be followed by another seven. However, the Furness Withy contract ended in 1957 and thereafter Bowaters managed their own affairs.

Name	Built	GRT
MARGARET BOWATER	1955	6841
SARAH BOWATER	1955	6471

6. The King's Enemies—World War II 1939 to 1945

After the horrors of trench warfare in World War I, few looked forward to another global conflict with equanimity. But for some years the storm clouds could be seen gathering on the horizon. The after effects of the previous conflict in Germany, the rampaging inflation of the Weimar Republic and the general world economic climate were good breeding grounds for extremists offering better things, illusory or otherwise. In Germany this brought Hitler into power, whilst Mussolini came to the fore in Italy. Initially their regimes were beneficial in establishing prosperous economies, but behind this lay the latent time bomb of their extreme totalitarian doctrine.

Both European powers flexed their muscles. Italy turned to conquest in Abyssinia (October 1935) and Albania (April 1939). Germany sought to recover territory lost under the 1919 Versailles Peace Treaty and extend her borders to achieve Lebensraum (living space) for the German speaking race. The Saar was reunited with Germany in January 1935 and the German army reoccupied the demilitarised Rheinland in March 1936. The Anschluss of March 1938 brought union of Austria and Germany, soon followed by claims for the Sudeten area of Czechoslovakia. The pattern was clear for all who had the courage to look. It would only be a matter of time. The outbreak of the Spanish Civil War in 1936 gave both Hitler and Mussolini the opportunity they sought, to develop and perfect the new weapons and tactics available to them. Meanwhile, in the Far East, the ambitions of Imperial Japan sent her forces into China in 1937. The Berlin-Rome alliance, or "Axis", came into existence in May 1939 and extended to Tokyo in September 1940.

In 1938 the German demands for the return from Czechoslovakia of the Sudetenland, with its largely German speaking population, led to the British and French Premiers, Neville Chamberlain and Edouard Daladier, meeting Hitler at Munich in September 1938. The resulting agreement ceding the Sudetenland to Germany, signed without consulting Czechoslovakia, led to Chamberlain announcing, on his return, "Peace in our time". There was little conviction in his heart however: knowing the state of the British Empire, he was buying time to permit rearmament to proceed in a race against time.

The conviction that it was a matter of when, not if, war would come was evident on board Furness Withy ships. By early 1939 they all carried sealed Admiralty orders, to be opened on the outbreak of war. The ships on the North Pacific service carried an even more obvious sign, aircraft stowed on deck for the passage to England. Some of the ships even had their lifeboats swung out to enable extra aircraft to be secured on their boat decks. Devised by the Los Angeles office of Furness Withy a method of deck stowage was perfected and about seven aircraft could be carried on deck making the best possible use of the space available. Between 1939 and 1942, 326 Lockheed, 941 North American and 52 Douglas aircraft were shipped to the United Kingdom. A further 477 were shipped to India and 724 to Australia.

Sadly, on Sunday morning, 3 September 1939, Chamberlain announced to the country that the sands of time had finally run out. Germany had failed to respond to the ultimatum to withdraw her forces from Poland and a state of war existed between the two countries. As the British Expeditionary Force embarked for France, the country was still far from fully prepared, although a number of important decisions had already been taken. These included the design, several years before, and ordering of aircraft such as the Spitfire and Hurricane, without which the air war would have been lost, and the ordering of the first escort ships of the "Flower" class corvette, developed from the whale catcher *Southern Pride* recently built by Smith's Dock Company, Middlesbrough. The development of the corvette started soon after the Munich Crisis; the Naval Staff assumed war would have been declared by 1940 and the design proceeded with urgency, enabling the first orders to be placed in July 1939. First into the water was HMS *Gladiolus*, launched on 24 January 1940. She was also the first of the class to sink a submarine, being credited jointly with a Sunderland aircraft of 10 Squadron RAF, with the destruction of *U26* on 1 July 1940, south-west of Ireland.

The lessons for British merchant shipping of the previous war had been learned well. The very real possibility of enemy submarine sinkings bringing the country to its knees was appreciated and the remedy was known and applied immediately. All British shipping was brought under Government control and convoys were introduced without delay. Even so, the submarine had been refined as a weapon and was to prove a formidable opponent which would take several years of effort to control, if not defeat. In addition to the growing fleet of escort ships one of the major factors in the battle would be air cover.

Although not one of the fighting forces, the merchant marine was in fact in the front line to a greater degree than most of the armed forces. The estimate of over 31,000 deaths from a profession which never numbered more than 185,000 is horrendous and a larger percentage of merchant seamen lost their lives from enemy action than in any of the fighting forces. Moreover the estimate does not include the gunners or passengers who faced the same dangers and died alongside the seamen.

 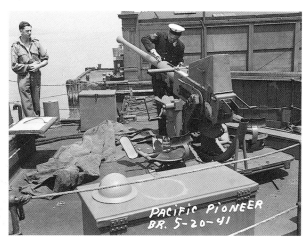

Defensive armament of *Pacific Pioneer*, May 1941.

From the Furness Withy fleet, over sixty ships were to fall victim to enemy action, ships either owned by Group companies or managed on behalf of the Ministry of War Transport and others. Ships totalling nearly 450,000 tons went down and with them over 2,700 lives, crew and passengers. Company ships would be seen in all theatres of war, serving as armed merchant cruisers, troopships, hospital ships and in a variety of other guises; as well as carrying the vital cargoes of war.

Soon after the outbreak of war, three of the Shaw Savill fleet were taken over and, as in the previous war, converted into dummy warships. *Pakeha* and *Waimana*, dating from 1910/1, posed as the battleships *Revenge* and *Resolution*, whilst *Mamari* was converted to resemble the aircraft carrier *Hermes*. Having been purchased in 1939 by the Admiralty, they were transferred to the Ministry of War Transport when this role ended in 1941; *Pakeha* and *Waimana* reverted to their cargo ship role under management by Shaw Savill & Albion and were given *Empire* prefixes to their names. Repurchased by the company in 1946, they went to the breakers during 1950. *Mamari* was not so fortunate, because on her way to the shipyard for reconversion she hit the submerged wreck of the mined tanker *Ahamo* in the Wold Channel, off Cromer, on 3 June 1941, was beached and then torpedoed by an E-boat to became a total loss.

Many Furness Withy ships were destined to play a more active role, *Jervis Bay* and *Queen of Bermuda* became armed merchant cruisers, *Southern Prince* and *Manchester City* were commissioned as minelayers. *Monarch of Bermuda* was employed as an LSI(L)—Landing Ship Infantry (Large)— fitted with landing craft to enable her troops to be landed as part of the assault on enemy coastline, whilst *Stuart Prince* became an LSF— Landing Ship Fighter Direction—equipped with radio equipment, plotting rooms and personnel to control fighter aircraft, vectoring them to enemy formations intent on attacking Allied forces during the invasion of Europe.

Quiet Before the Storm—1939

Within two weeks of the outbreak of war the first Furness Withy loss was reported. In the first attack, 16 September 1939, by a submarine on a convoy (OB4 to North America) U31 hit Johnston Warren Lines' *Aviemore* with two torpedoes and she went down in thirty seconds with the loss of 23 lives. Another three lives were lost when Cairn Lines' *Cairnmona* was sunk by U13 on 30 September, off Rattray Head as she was nearing the end of a voyage from Canada to the Tyne in company with *Cairnglen* and *Cairnvalona*. Houlder Line's *Royston Grange* was also nearing the end of her voyage from Buenos Aires, and was heading towards Liverpool when U28 sighted her in 49.1N 9.16W and dispatched her with a single torpedo, fortunately without loss of life.

| 16. 9.1939 | AVIEMORE | torpedoed by U31 | 25.11.1939 | ROYSTON GRANGE | torpedoed by U28 |
| 30.10.1939 | CAIRNMONA | torpedoed by U13 | 2.12.1939 | TAIROA | sunk by ADMIRAL GRAF SPEE |

On passage from Australia, Shaw Savill's *Tairoa* had sailed from Durban on 27 November bound for Britain. Hearing the distress calls from *Doric Star,* under attack by *Admiral Graf Spee,* her course was altered, but to no avail and the German pocket battleship sighted her the following morning, 2 December 1939. *Tairoa* was hit by 59 shells before she surrendered and was so damaged that she had to be sunk by scuttling charges and gunfire after the crew had been taken off. Captain Starr and most of the crew were later transferred to the tanker *Altmark,* being rescued by HMS *Cossack* in Jossing Fjord on 16 February 1940. The five wounded remained on board *Admiral Graf Spee,* were present at the Battle of the River Plate and were landed at Montevideo before the battleship was scuttled.

British Prince at Cape Town in wartime grey paint.

The Furness Withy Offices at War

The outbreak of war and requisition of all ships led to a complete change in the operation of the various offices who now managed the ships on behalf of the Ministry of Shipping (later Ministry of War Transport). A gaggle of new organisations were soon active and amongst these the Sea Transport Department of the Royal Navy, the Ministry of Supply and the Ministry of Economic Warfare were to be closely involved with shipping.

At Furness Withy the departure of members of staff for active duty with the forces or to take up posts with various Ministries was a clear reminder of the change. Heading those seconded for other duties was the Deputy Chairman, Ernest Murrant, who became Special Representative of the Minister of War Transport in the Middle East, responsible for the supervision of all Allied shipping from Turkey to Aden. He remained at this post until the death of the Chairman, Lord Essendon, required his return to the office in London.

A large number of ships were placed under Furness Withy management, in addition to those owned by Group companies, by the Minister of War Transport. On the invasion of Norway in 1940 the company was instructed to charter all available Norwegian ships and temporarily managed them until the Ministry designated managers. At one time as many as 56 such ships were operated, and a Norwegian Department was established in Glasgow which continued to manage 25 to 30 Norwegian ships for the Minister, apart from technical superintendence and crew matters which remained with the Norwegian Shipping & Trade Mission. This fleet of Norwegian ships included the liners *Bergensfjord* and *Oslofjord* of the Norwegian America Line.

Other ships under the Dutch, Danish and Finish flags were also included in the managed fleet. Interestingly two of the Dutch ships had previously been managed in 1917, *Eibergen* and *Kelbergen* owned by NV Zuid Hollandsche Scheepvaart Maatschappij under the management of NV Furness Scheepvaart en Agentuur Maatschappij, a company which had, of course, once been part of the Furness Withy Group.

The tide of German victories brought them to the Channel coast in June 1940. With the air blitz of London, extensive damage to the docks and shipping and the proximity of the enemy coast stretching from North Cape to the Spanish border it became increasingly dangerous to bring shipping into the Thames. Consequently the Furness Withy service from North America was transferred to Cardiff and, later in the war, the ships were directed to various ports according to the availability of berths to handle them. Tugs, barges, equipment and dockers from London were also transferred, many being sent to the Clyde which experienced a massive increase in shipping handled.

Christopher, Lord Furness

Brantford City, of 1880, the third steamer owned   *(A Henderson)*

Furness Line sailing card issued in 1899

Jervis Bay in action with *Admiral Scheer,* 5 November 1940 *(Painting by Montague Dawson)*

Sir Frederick Lewis, Lord Essendon, chairman from 1919 to 1944

Sir Ernest Murrant, KCMG, chairman from 1944 to 1959

The meat carrier *Duquesa* of 1949   *(Paisajes Españoles)*

Arriving from Bermuda early in 1933, *Monarch of Bermuda* meets the new *Queen of Bermuda*, arriving from Liverpool to commence service
(Painting by Stephen J Card — courtesy of H. H. Outerbridge Collection)

H.M. Queen Elizabeth II launched *Southern Cross* in 1954

H.M. Queen Elizabeth, the Queen Mother, launched *Northern Star* in 1961

Welcome for Her Majesty, arriving at Wellington on the Royal yacht *Gothic*

Andes was completed in 1939 to mark the centenary of the formation of the Royal Mail Steam Packet Company

Ocean Monarch, launched in 1950 to replace the lost *Monarch of Bermuda*

Westbury of 1960 proceeding down Channel   *(Skyfotos)*

Northern Star passing The Needles outward bound   *(Skyfotos)*

Uncle John at sea in heavy weather

The offshore oil support vessel *Orelia*

Modern image. The SD14 Liberty ship replacement *Derwent* and the gas tanker *Humboldt*

Walton Container Terminal (above)
at Felixstowe and (below)
Manchester Challenge at Montreal

Empire Stevedoring's Vancouver container terminal

The container ship *Andes* operating as the Pacific Steam Navigation Company
contribution to Eurosal, the consortium serving the West Coast of South America,
and *Orenda Bridge,* a bulker chartered to Seabridge Shipping Ltd

Hornby Grange at sea in heavy weather   *(F Fletcher)*

Presentation to John Houlder on completing 50 years with Houlder Brothers, 1985.
(left to right) John Houlder, Captain R. Hedger OBE and Cyril Warwick

The Mahe Hotel in the Seychelles (above) and Caravel Motor Hotel, Rotorua, New Zealand (below)

Saxon Inns at:

Northampton

Blackburn

Peterborough

Memorial window (above) for *Royston Grange,* and (left) the Furness Withy Group war memorial and designer, Mrs Lesley Alexander

Operation Fish

In 1940 the rampage of German armies through Europe left Britain alone, standing with her back to the sea. Invasion threatened and vital supplies were coming across the Atlantic from North America. In the United States the law did not allow the sale of the much needed supplies on credit, especially as many considered Britain a lost cause.

To avoid the possibility of British gold reserves falling into Nazi hands, and similarly those which had been shipped to Britain before the owning countries fell to the invaders, arrangements were made to ship these reserves across the Atlantic to Canada for safety. Negotiable documents, shares in North American companies and other assets which could be realised on that Continent were also collected and moved out of Great Britain.

The value of gold shipped was £827.75 million; the value of the stocks and shares was never calculated. Furness Withy played a major role in this evacuation during 1940 and company ships carried a total of £96.75 million in gold, or 11.6% of the total amount shipped.

Monarch of Bermuda, with gold valued at £40 million on board, was one of the ships engaged in the largest single movement. Aboard her and the liners *Batory* and *Sobieski*, the cruisers *Emerald* and *Bonaventure*, and the battleship *Revenge*, gold valued at £222 million was shipped in July 1940 from Greenock to Halifax.

During the period of operations, five Prince Line ships moved a total £19.75 million: two consignments by *Western Prince* amounted to £2 million, four by *Eastern Prince* added up to £10.75 million, *Northern Prince* stowed one consignment of £1 million whilst *British Prince* and *Welsh Prince* each carried single consignments of £3 million.

Manchester Liners were responsible for shipping £25 million in eight ships: *Manchester Merchant, Manchester Brigade* and *Manchester Progress* each carried two consignments, *Manchester Merchant* and *Manchester Brigade* totalling £4.5 million each and *Manchester Progress* £5 million. The others carried single shipments, *Manchester Commerce* valued at £3 million and for *Manchester Exporter, Manchester Division, Manchester Port* and *Manchester Citizen* £2 million each.

Four Furness Withy ships carried single shipments of £3 million to total £12 million. They were *Newfoundland, Pacific Pioneer, Pacific President* and *Pacific Shipper*.

The *Jervis Bay* Convoy

One of five sisters built by Vickers and Beardmore for the Australian Commonwealth Line, *Jervis Bay* was launched at Barrow on 17 January 1922. Of 13,839gt she had geared turbines giving a speed of 15 knots. Originally accommodation was provided for 12 first and 712 third class passengers, but a 1931 refit saw this reduced to 542 tourist class.

The Australian Commonwealth Line was sold to White Star Line in 1928. The collapse of the Royal Mail Group, owners of White Star, led to a reorganisation of assets during which these five sisters were transferred to Aberdeen and Commonwealth Line, jointly owned by Shaw, Savill and Albion and P & O, with Shaw Savill management.

With the outbreak of war, four of the sisters were taken up as armed merchant cruisers. In London *Jervis Bay* was fitted with eight 6 inch and two 3 inch guns and was commissioned on 23 September 1939. On 1 April 1940, Captain E S F Fegen RN was appointed to command.

Edward Stephen Fogarty Fegen was born in 1891, the son and grandson of serving naval officers. Entering the Navy, he survived the sinking of the cruiser *Amphion* on 5 August 1914 and between the World Wars was awarded a Dutch lifesaving medal and received an Admiralty commendation for the rescue of the crew of the steamer *Hedwig*, ashore in the South China Sea.

Originally intended for service on the Northern Patrol, damage to the windlass delayed *Jervis Bay* and her place there was taken by *Rawalpindi*, herself destined for a short career, ending when she became a victim

Monarch of Bermuda as a troop transport.

to the overwhelming gunfire of the German battlecruiser *Scharnhorst* in late November 1939. *Jervis Bay* instead steamed south to join the Freetown Escort Force, later being transferring to Bermuda and Atlantic convoys.

On 28 October 1940 *Jervis Bay* sailed from Halifax as the sole ocean escort for convoy HX84, 38 ships bound for Britain. On 5 November in 52.45N 32.13W the convoy was steaming at nine knots in good visibility when, at 3.40pm, *Rangitiki* reported smoke, and this was followed at 5pm by *Empire Penguin* sighting a ship— fortunately dusk would soon fall to protect many of the convoy from the attention of the stranger. Thoughts that the she was British were soon dispelled when the approaching ship opened fire and was identified as *Admiral Scheer* (Kapitän Theodor Krancke), a German pocket battleship armed with six 11 inch and eight 5.9 inch guns, intent on annihilating the convoy.

Fegen immediately turned *Jervis Bay* towards the enemy and ordered the convoy to scatter. *Jervis Bay* was hopelessly outgunned and outranged, for while *Admiral Scheer* opened fire at 17,000 yards *Jervis Bay's* guns had a maximum range of 14,000 yards and she immediately started to take lethal punishment. Hit by the third German salvo the bridge and fire control gear were wrecked and the action turned into a massacre. But *Jervis Bay* had delayed *Admiral Scheer* long enough for many of the convoy to escape into the gathering dusk. Fegen was killed in the action and 190 of the crew were lost with him, 65 survivors being picked up by the Swedish *Stureholm* which courageously turned back to the scene after having scattered with the other members of the convoy.

After leaving *Jervis Bay*, the raider managed to find and sink five ships of the convoy, *Beaverford*, *Fresno City*, *Kenbane Head*, *Maidan* and *Trewellard*. The tanker *San Demetrio* was also hit and abandoned, but some of her crew later reboarded the burning wreck and brought her safely to port. Although *Admiral Scheer* failed to destroy the convoy, her presence roaming the high seas seriously disrupted the flow of shipping for a while.

A fitting recognition of the bravery of Captain Fegen and his crew was the posthumous award of the Victoria Cross, presented to Captain Fegen's sister by King George VI at Buckingham Palace on 12 June 1941.

Backs to the Wall—1940 and 1941

Undoubtedly the action of *Jervis Bay* was the event that comes first to mind when 1940 is recalled, resulting in a posthumous Victoria Cross being awarded to Captain Fogarty Fegen. Nearly two weeks after sinking the armed merchant cruiser, *Admiral Scheer* stopped the Furness-Houlder Argentine Lines' *Duquesa* on 18 December, just north of the Equator. Loaded with foodstuffs, she was kept afloat to supply both surface raiders and submarines with provisions until the supplies were exhausted, by which time the crew of *Admiral Scheer* were sick of the sight of eggs. Her crew were then transferred to the captured tanker *Sandefjord* and eventually landed at Bordeaux, faced with the prospect of a prison camp.

Earlier in the year *Duquesa* had been one of the last ships to get away from Le Havre before it was occupied by advancing German forces and on 7 September 1940 had been one of five steamers in London's Victoria Dock when the big daylight raids started on the City. Two days later she was the only one still afloat.

Nineteen ships were lost by Furness Withy during the year, four of them ships managed for the Government. Apart from 1942, these were to be the highest number of losses sustained in any year of the War. The actual losses between 1939 and 1945 were as follows —

Year	No	GT	Raider	Sub	Mine	Aircraft	E-boat
1939	4	23,910	1	3			
1940	19	161,118	4	11	4		
1941	16	101,175	2	9	1	4	
1942	20	142,248		18		1	1
1943	10	68,674		7		3	
1944	1	2,115		1			
1945	1	7,219			1		

Two other ships fell victim to surface craft in 1940. Shaw Savill's *Maimoa* was three days out from Fremantle on 20 November when she was captured after a long chase by the raider *Pinguin*. Her crew were transferred to the captured Norwegian tanker *Storstad* and were landed at Bordeaux on 5 February 1941. The 4th and 5th engineers escaped from the train taking them on to Germany and travelled through France and Spain to reach freedom. Earlier, on 20 September, the raider *Atlantis* had sunk the French steamer *Commissaire Ramel* which had been placed under Shaw Savill management following the fall of France. Three of her crew were killed, and the others were landed at Mogadishu and faced life in an Italian prisoner-of-war camp until the town was captured by British forces in February 1941.

17. 1.40	CAIRNROSS—sunk by mine (U30)	12.10.40	PACIFIC RANGER—torpedoed by U59
20. 1.40	CARONI RIVER—sunk by mine (U34)	18.10.40	EMPIRE BRIGADE—torpedoed by U99
4. 3.40	PACIFIC RELIANCE—torpedoed by U29	5.11.40	JERVIS BAY—sunk by ADMIRAL SCHEER
9. 6.40	EMPIRE COMMERCE—sunk by mine	20.11.40	MAIMOA—sunk by PINGUIN
8. 7.40	HUMBER ARM—torpedoed by U99	1.12.40	OSLOFJORD—sunk by mine
8. 8.40	UPWEY GRANGE—torpedoed by U37	2.12.40	PACIFIC PRESIDENT—torpedoed by U43
14. 8.40	BETTY—torpedoed by U59	14.12.40	WESTERN PRINCE—torpedoed by U96
20. 9.40	COMMISSAIRE RAMEL—sunk by ATLANTIS	18.12.40	DUQUESA—captured by ADMIRAL SCHEER
21. 9.40	CANONESA—torpedoed by U100	25.12.40	WAIOTIRA—torpedoed by U95
26. 9.40	MANCHESTER BRIGADE—torpedoed by U137		

Empire Faith on trials, 26 June 1941, fitted with aircraft catapult for convoy protection.

Mines were responsible for the loss of four ships, two in January and one each in June and December. *Cairnross* was outward bound from the Mersey on 17 January when she hit a mine which had been laid by *U30*, commanded by Fritz-Julius Lemp who had sunk *Athenia* at the beginning of the war. The tanker *Caroni River* was carrying out armament trials in Falmouth Bay three days later when she detonated a mine laid by *U34*. Less than two hours later she slipped beneath the water. Both these sinkings were reminders of how close the enemy could approach British ports. The third ship to find a mine was *Empire Commerce*, on 9 June off Margate, the first ship managed by the company for the Government to be lost. Finally one of the largest Group losses took place when the managed Norwegian liner *Oslofjord*, a modern vessel completed in 1938, triggered a mine as she approached the Tyne. Fortunately only one life was lost, but after being beached at South Shields she broke her back and became a total loss during the bad weather that followed.

Eleven ships were victims of submarine attack. *Pacific President*, sunk by *U43*, was to suffer the heaviest loss of life in the fleet in 1940, apart from *Jervis Bay*, as there were no survivors from her crew of 52 when she was torpedoed by *U43* while in convoy OB251, bound in ballast for New York. Two other of the ''Pacific'' boats, *Pacific Reliance* and *Pacific Ranger* were also lost, *Pacific Reliance* was off the Longships on coastal passage from London for Liverpool, following arrival from the North Pacific, when she was sighted and sunk on 4 March by *U29*, while *Pacific Ranger* was in convoy HX77 when she was attacked by *U59* whilst homeward bound from Seattle. The crews of both ships escaped without loss of life.

Houlder losses in 1940 were *Upwey Grange* and *Canonesa*. *Upwey Grange* was sunk on 8 August with the loss of half her crew, the survivors being picked up by the trawler *Naniwa* two days later. *Canonesa* was part of the homebound convoy HX72 when torpedoed by *U100* on 21 September. Thoroughly outclassed, the escort could do little against attacks which sank twelve of the 41 ships in the convoy. *U100* took station in the middle of the convoy and picked off seven ships one at a time. During this happy hunting time for the U-boats, Manchester Liners lost *Manchester Brigade* on 26 September, the first sinking in convoy OB218. The prize *Elios*, which had been renamed *Empire Brigade* when Italy entered the war in June 1940, was the next loss. Managed by Cairns, Noble and Company, she was sunk by *U99* when convoy SC7 was torn apart and scattered with the loss of half the merchant ships.

Bowater's Newfoundland Pulp and Paper Mills fleet, enlarged by purchases after the outbreak of war, lost two ships to submarine action. One of the original sisters, *Humber Arm*, was torpedoed by *U99* when she was nearing the end of her passage from Corner Brook to the Mersey on 8 July, fortunately without loss of life. The crew of *Betty* were not so fortunate, when on 14 August she went down in two minutes after being hit by *U59*. Also bound for the Mersey, with rice from Saigon, she took thirty of her crew down with her when she sank some 35 miles off Tory Island. There were only four survivors.

December brought 1940 to its conclusion with the loss of two valuable ships. Prince Lines' *Western Prince*, one of the four Compass Boats built for the New York to South American service, was on the North Atlantic run when she was sighted by *U96* and sunk on 14 December. Amongst her survivors were members of the

Pacific Grove, with a deck cargo of aircraft, locomotives and trucks.

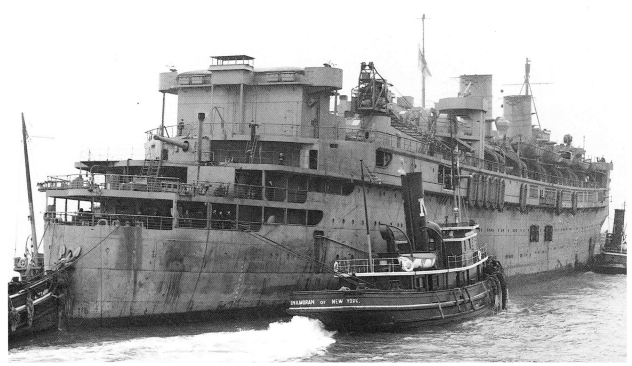

HMS *Queen of Bermuda* as an armed merchant cruiser.

British Merchant Shipbuilding Commission returning from a visit to North America where orders had been placed with United States and Canadian yards for an emergency shipbuilding programme. Christmas Day saw Shaw Savill's food carrier *Waiotira* torpedoed on passage from New Zealand, although she remained afloat until sinking the following day.

As the New Year dawned, England and the Empire stood alone against Hitler. France had fallen, but a large number of British and Allied troops had been rescued through Dunkirk and other ports in early June, although much of their arms and equipment had been lost. Holland, Denmark and Norway had fallen to the swastika. Italy had taken up arms alongside Germany.

Although probably not recognised clearly at the time, Hitler was to take decisions and actions in 1941 which were to make certain his ultimate defeat. On June 22, without warning, he turned on Russia and sent his panzers towards Moscow. Six months later, on December 7, Japan struck at the American fleet in Pearl Harbor and Hitler declared war on the United States. The war of attrition would take over three years, but the power of the opposition was now decisively against Germany and her Axis partners.

At sea, 1941 was to be a repeat of the previous year with heavy losses sustained by merchant shipping. Slowly the escort forces gained experience and developed methods to combat the enemy submarines. The flow of emergency tonnage started, ships which would fill the gaps caused by the losses sustained and play a material role in the coming victory.

Nine of the sixteen losses suffered by the Group during the year were to be sustained by Prince Line and their associated Rio Cape Line. Two ships were lost to surface raiders whilst an increasing number became victim to air attack.

German heavy surface units sallied into the Atlantic early in the year as "Operation Berlin", a concerted effort to disrupt and destroy the vital convoys to Britain. The battlecruisers *Scharnhorst* and *Gneisenau* sailed from Kiel on 22 January, followed by the heavy cruiser *Admiral Hipper* from Brest on 1 February.

Admiral Hipper found convoy SLS64, homeward bound from Freetown. At the time, 12 February 1941, the convoy was unescorted so she sailed down the centre between the columns of ships and when she had finished, eight of the ten had been sunk and the two survivors were damaged. *Oswestry Grange* received twelve 8 inch shells in her side, rolled over and sank. Fortunately only five of her crew were lost, the other 37 crewmen being picked up by the damaged *Lornaston* and landed at Funchal two days later.

A month later, on 16 March, *Sardinian Prince* was to become a victim of *Scharnhorst*, her crew being taken prisoner. Despite the dispatch of forces which included the battleships *Rodney*, *King George V* and *Nelson*, the battlecruiser *Renown* and the aircraft carrier *Ark Royal*, the tally for "Operation Berlin" was 22 ships of some 115,000 tons sunk, a figure which fails to convey the full extent of the additional damage caused to the war effort by delayed or cancelled convoys. With the arrival of *Admiral Hipper* at Kiel on 28 March "Operation Berlin" ended, the two battlecruisers having reached Brest four days earlier.

Greece had been invaded by Italy in October 1940. The Italians were being kept at bay by Allied forces, so German troop reinforcements were dispatched early in April 1941 and by the end of the month had fully occupied the country. *Northern Prince* was caught in this theatre by German aircraft and sunk between Greece and Crete on 3 April, when bound for Piraeus with military stores. Two days later, on the night of 6 April, eleven He111 aircraft of 2/KG4 attacked Piraeus harbour. They hit *Clan Fraser* which caught fire and four hours later blew up, spreading devastation around the harbour. *Cyprian Prince* was hit by a parachute mine in the raid and had to be abandoned as a total loss, whilst *Cingalese Prince* was damaged but managed to get away. The raid and the explosion of *Clan Fraser* sank thirteen ships, 60 lighters and 25 sailing ships.

The wreck of *Elstree Grange* at Liverpool, May 1941.

Another air raid led to the loss of *Elstree Grange*. On the night of 3 May 1941, a large German force targeted Liverpool. Several days earlier *Elstree Grange* had completed discharge and was undergoing repairs when she was hit amidships by a land mine. She caught fire and sank at her berth. A tangled mass of wreckage, she was refloated and on 14 May towed out of the docks to be beached and broken up during the summer. Also hit in the raid was Brocklebank's *Malakand*, loading ammunition. On fire, she blew up at 7am, causing extensive damage to installations and other craft.

16.	1.41	ZEALANDIC—torpedoed by U106	27.	4.41	BEACON GRANGE—torpedoed by U552
12.	2.41	OSWESTRY GRANGE—sunk by ADMIRAL HIPPER	30.	4.41	NERISSA—torpedoed by U552
			3.	5.41	ELSTREE GRANGE—CTL, by aircraft
17.	2.41	SIAMESE PRINCE—torpedoed by U69	20.	5.41	JAVANESE PRINCE—torpedoed by U138
17.	2.41	BLACK OSPREY—torpedoed by U96	3.	6.41	EIBERGEN—torpedoed by U75
16.	3.41	SARDINIAN PRINCE—sunk by SCHARNHORST	12.	6.41	CHINESE PRINCE—torpedoed by U552
			20.	9.41	CINGALESE PRINCE—torpedoed by U111
3.	4.41	NORTHERN PRINCE—sunk by aircraft	26.	9.41	BRITISH PRINCE—sunk by aircraft
6.	4.41	CYPRIAN PRINCE—sunk by aircraft		7.12.41	WELSH PRINCE—sunk by mine

Two ships were to be lost with every soul on board. Three days after sailing from Liverpool for Australia, *Zealandic* was sunk by *U106* on 16 January, north-west of Ireland and took all 73 on board with her. A month later, on 17 February, *U69* found *Siamese Prince* and sank her with all 67 on board. No distress calls were heard but she was assumed to have sunk as wreckage was sighted the following day. Amongst those lost with *Siamese Prince* was Wilbert Widdicombe, one of only two survivors from *Anglo-Saxon* (Nitrate Producers' Steamship Company Ltd) sunk by the raider *Widder* on 21 August 1940. The two men had drifted 2,500 miles in 71 days before landing on Eleuthera Island.

Heavy loss of life was also suffered in four other sinkings. The first of these was *Black Osprey*, one of the many American owned ships built at the end of World War I and recently purchased by the British Government. Now owned by the Ministry of War Transport and managed by Cairn Line, she was carrying a cargo of steel and trucks when torpedoed by *U96* on 17 February with the loss of 25 out of her crew of 36. Even greater loss of life occurred when *Nerissa* was sighted by *U552* off St Kilda on 30 April as she was nearing the end of her voyage from Canada to Liverpool. A gale was blowing when she was hit and as a result 83 of her crew and 124 passengers lost their lives, only 29 crew and 51 passengers surviving. On 12 June, *Chinese Prince* was in the Western Approaches, nearing the end of a long haul from Port Said via South Africa when *U552* sank her with the loss of 45 men. *U552* was responsible for the sinking of three company ships during the year, *Nerissa*, *Chinese Prince* and *Beacon Grange*. Another Rio Cape Line ship, *Cingalese Prince*, had the doubtful privilege of being the first merchant ship to be sunk by a U-boat south of the Equator when *U111* caught her south of St Paul's Rocks on 20 September with a heavy cargo of ore and general cargo from Bombay. 56 of the crew were lost, the survivors spending twelve days on a raft before being sighted by the Spanish steamer *Castillo Montjuich*.

As mentioned above, *U552* was also responsible for the loss of *Beacon Grange* south of Iceland on 27 April. Outward bound for the Plate and routed independently, it was a marvel that only two lives were lost. 39 of the survivors in one lifeboat were picked up on 2 May by the trawler *Edward Anseele*, the other 41 in a second boat having already been rescued by HMS *Gladiolus. Javanese Prince* was also a victim of submarine action, this time by *U138*, when bound from South Wales for New York in ballast. Two members of her crew were killed, the 58 surviving passengers and crew being picked up from their boats by the tug *Assurance* and HMS *Heather*. Transferred to the rescue ship *Toward*, they were subsequently landed at Greenock.

The second half of 1941 was relatively quiet, the only two losses after *Cingalese Prince* being *British Prince*, caught by aircraft on 26 September, bombed and sunk off the Humber homeward bound from New York, and *Welsh Prince* which exploded an acoustic mine off Spurn Head and had to be put ashore where she broke in two. Happily no lives were lost in either of these incidents.

The Trials of *Imperial Transport*

One of the few ships built by British yards during 1931, in the depths of the Great Depression, the motor tanker *Imperial Transport* was a product of the Clyde yard of Blythswood Shipbuilding Company, launched on 17 February to the order of Empire Transport Company Ltd.

During the war she was to lead a charmed, if somewhat dangerous, life, being twice torpedoed, salved and repaired. After the war she was sold to Norwegian owners in 1947 and under the names *Mesna* and *Rona* survived until going to the breakers in 1958.

Her first encounter with the dangers of submarines came on 11 February 1940, when she was outward bound in ballast from Scapa Flow for Trinidad. The day after she sailed, *U53* hit her aft of the bridge with a torpedo. In less than five minutes she had broken in two and the forepart sank. Two of the crew were lost as they took to the boats, but the rest of the crew reboarded the derelict stern section the following day and commenced steaming it towards Scotland at 2.5 knots. On 14 February destroyers were sighted and the crew were taken on board HMS *Kingston* the day after, as a gale was approaching, and the ability of *Imperial Transport* to survive was causing concern. At day-break on 16 February the tug *Buccaneer* arrived and took the derelict in tow. Captain Smail and his crew were unable to reboard so they were landed at Scapa Flow whilst the remains of their ship was towed into the Clyde and beached at Kilchattan Bay. A new bow section was launched in December and the repaired *Imperial Transport* subsequently returned to service.

Again outward bound in ballast, this time from the Tyne for Curacao, in convoy ON77, she was hit by two torpedoes from *U94* in the early hours of 25 March 1942. Initially abandoned, an inspection was carried out at dawn and endeavours were made to get the damaged ship under way again. Most of the crew, on board a French corvette of the escort, then proceeded to St John's, Newfoundland, leaving a skeleton crew on board another corvette. On 26 March further attempts were made, ballast was moved to compensate for the damage and that afternoon she was got under way, and, although very tender, reached St John's on 30 March. After temporary repairs she was able to leave on 24 August, bound for New York and permanent repairs.

New fore-end for *Imperial Transport*, December 1940. *(J Hall)*

Operation Pedestal—The Malta Convoy

When Italy declared war on Britain on 10 June 1940, the conflict widened into Africa, with the island of Malta destined to play a key role.

Long before the war, Malta had been discounted by the Admiralty as a secure base for the British fleet, its normal role in peacetime. Situated in the centre of the Mediterranean, it lay athwart both the Allied lines of communication from west to east and the Axis supply routes from north to south. Whilst the Allies were never able to make much use of the Mediterranean route after June 1940, until the Italian surrender and the landings in Italy, they had available the alternative of routing south round Africa, even though this added six weeks to transit times. The German and Italian forces had no alternative supply line to their forces in Africa and Malta was to prove a major thorn in their side. The strategic Axis error, failing to invade and capture Malta when this was feasible, was one of the greatest magnitude and had a material bearing on the length of the war. The situation in Malta was also closely linked to the progress of the land campaign in North Africa. When, in the Spring of 1942, constant bombing had reduced the island to comparative helplessness, the Axis forces were able to take the initiative and push the British army back into Egypt. Conversely, when sufficient supplies reached the Malta garrison to enable them to take the offensive, the sinking of Axis supply ships soon slowed the progress of the Afrika Korps and their Italian allies.

From June 1940 until the Italian surrender in September 1943, Malta was supplied by a number of key convoys as well as by single ships. In times of desperation submarines and the fast minelayer *Welshman* ran urgent supplies. To seamen used to the North Atlantic, where often a large convoy would be covered by a handful of small escort ships, the sight of a Malta convoy with its fighting escort of battleships and aircraft carriers, as well as numerous cruisers and destroyers, was something beyond belief. Typical was the force assembled to take the supply ship *Breconshire* from Alexandria to Malta in December 1941, six cruisers and sixteen destroyers to protect a single ship.

The convoys continued until Malta was finally relieved in December 1942 and Furness Withy, through the medium of Shaw, Savill and Albion, were to be involved in the most famous of them all. This was the August 1942 "Operation Pedestal", better known to many as the "Ohio Convoy", carrying much needed supplies for the island where sufficient remained for only three weeks. Consisting of one tanker, *Ohio*, and thirteen dry cargo ships it included two Shaw, Savill owned and one managed vessel, all three of which were to be lost before reaching their destination. A list of the merchant ships in the convoy emphasises the importance of the island to the Allied cause and the difficulty of running supplies there, as they included some of the fastest and most modern ships in the British merchant marine, as well as several fast American vessels.

Ships in Convoy WS521S—Operation Pedestal			
Name	Built	GRT	Owners
ALMERIA LYKES	1940	7773	Lykes Brothers S S Co Inc, New Orleans.
BRISBANE STAR	1936	12791	Union Cold Storage Co Ltd (Blue Star Line Ltd), London.
CLAN FERGUSON	1938	7347	Clan Line Steamers Ltd, London.
DEUCALION	1930	7516	Ocean S S Co Ltd (A. Holt & Co), Liverpool.
DORSET	1934	10624	Federal S N Co Ltd, London.
EMPIRE HOPE	1941	12688	Ministry of War Transport (Shaw, Savill & Albion Co Ltd), London.
GLENORCHY	1939	8982	Glen Line Ltd, London.
MELBOURNE STAR	1936	12806	Union Cold Storage Co Ltd (Blue Star Line Ltd), London.
OHIO (tanker)	1940	9265	Ministry of War Transport (EagleOil & Shipping Co Ltd), London.
PORT CHALMERS	1933	8535	Port Line Ltd, London.
ROCHESTER CASTLE	1937	7795	Union-Castle Mail S S Co Ltd, London.
SANTA ELISA	1941	8379	Grace Line Inc (W R Grace & Co), New York.
WAIMARAMA	1938	12843	Shaw, Savill & Albion Co Ltd, London.
WAIRANGI	1935	12436	Shaw, Savill & Albion Co Ltd, London.

The escort was led by the battleships *Nelson* and *Rodney*, and included four aircraft carriers, *Argus*, *Eagle*, *Furious* and *Indomitable*, seven cruisers, 33 destroyers, two oilers, four corvettes and a salvage vessel. When the cost was added up after the operation it was seen that the four dry cargo merchant ships and one tanker that arrived landed 47,000 tons of cargo, whilst the ten that were lost took with them 100,000 tons of supplies and 350 men. The aircraft carrier *Eagle* was sunk, as were the cruisers *Cairo* and *Manchester* and the destroyer *Foresight*. The aircraft carrier *Indomitable*, two cruisers, *Nigeria* and *Kenya*, and the destroyer *Ithuriel* were damaged.

The convoy sailed from the Clyde on 2 August 1942, and Gibraltar was passed on 10 August. Arrayed to meet them was a formidable force including some nineteen Axis submarines, surface forces of six cruisers and eleven destroyers and massive air power. Action started the day after passing Gibraltar with *U73* sinking *Eagle*, but air attacks were driven off without loss. On the 12th, *Deucalion* was damaged and fell behind, *Indomitable* was put out of action by Ju87s of StG3 and *Foresight* was torpedoed. The day ended with torpedo hits on the cruisers *Cairo*, *Nigeria* and *Kenya*, also *Brisbane Star*, *Clan Ferguson* and the tanker *Ohio*. The first Shaw Savill victim was *Empire Hope*, hit, with *Glenorchy*, by bombs from a wave of Ju88 bombers. The Italian submarine *Bronzo* then found *Empire Hope* and sank her with a torpedo.

The following day, 13 August, the action continued, and in four hours there were fifteen attacks by German and Italian torpedo boats. The cruiser *Manchester* was hit and had to be sunk, *Glenorchy*, already damaged, was sunk as were also *Santa Elisa*, *Almeria Lykes* and *Wairangi*. *Rochester Castle* was damaged. Air attacks hit *Waimarama*, *Dorset*, *Port Chalmers* and *Ohio* again. Later in the day the first ships of the badly mauled convoy reached Malta, *Melbourne Star*, *Port Chalmers* and *Rochester Castle*, followed later by *Ohio* so badly damaged that she came in with the destroyers *Ledbury* and *Penn* secured alongside her. The following day the last surviving merchantman, *Brisbane Star*, arrived. Of the five ships to survive, three were damaged.

Waimarama suffered the greatest loss of life in the convoy. Laden with petrol and ammunition, she was hit by bombs from Ju87 Stuka dive bombers and blew up, destroying one of the attacking aircraft in the blast. Of the 104 passengers and crew, 83 died despite the endeavours of the destroyer *Ledbury*. Fortunately no lives were lost with either *Wairangi* or *Empire Hope*. The crew of *Empire Hope* were taken off by the destroyer *Penn* and were on board her when she entered Valletta Harbour lashed alongside *Ohio*. The crew of *Wairangi* were saved by the destroyer *Eskimo* and came home from Malta in the Blue Funnel *Troilus*.

Furness, Withy and Company, North America

The network of offices in North America, with the New York office controlling eight others in the United States and four in Canada, also Furness (Pacific) Ltd at San Francisco, Los Angeles and Vancouver were all to play a major role in the war effort.

The network of services radiating from New York largely ceased on the outbreak of war. Only three sailings were made on the Bermuda service which ended two weeks after the declaration of war. The island was thereafter reliant on the American War Shipping Administration for a service to meet the needs of the civilian population, which was coupled with serving the American base there. The South American service ended abruptly and the four "Compass" boats reopened the New York to London service. The South African and Round-the-World services ceased in the early autumn of 1939 as the ships were diverted to more important duties, followed by the West Indies service at the end of 1940. Only the route north to Newfoundland continued despite enemy action, to serve St John's which soon became an important base both for ocean escorts and air service to Britain. *Fort Amherst* and *Fort Townshend* made 217 round trips, many as Commodore ship of the coastwise convoys, and chartered tonnage brought the number of voyages during the war up to 323.

The Chief Engineer Superintendent at New York became Technical Adviser to the Ministry of War Transport in New York and, with his technical staff in the various offices, was responsible for the commissioning of a large number of ships. First, late in 1940, thirty ships of World War I vintage, laid up for many years, were purchased by the British Government and Furness Withy were made responsible for the reconditioning and

Fort Amherst at war. Note slight bow damage, probably incurred in berthing.

The hospital ship *El Nil*, fitted out and managed by Furness Withy.

preparation of these vessels for sea, a task completed by December 1941. Another task was the conversion of various ships for their new duties, including the Egyptian pilgrim ship *El Nil* refitted as a hospital ship at New York. The offices accepted, as Ministry of War Transport agents, 104 Liberty ships and various others, including tugs, coasters and Landing Ships (Infantry). Similarly on completion the 60 "Ocean" class ships, ordered from American yards by the British Shipbuilding Commission, were taken over and readied for sea. The first of these was *Ocean Vanguard* , taken over on 27 October 1941 and placed under the management of W H Seager and Company, Cardiff.

In addition to the above duties all the offices handled greatly expanded duties in loading and dispatching a wide variety of ships and cargo. The war activity report from the St John's office is typical of the increase in workload. Regular liner calls on the Johnston Warren Line from Liverpool would, in peacetime, have been 40 to 45, plus some 20 tramps. The average number of ships handled throughout the war was 267, with the peak being 321. Further south, at St John NB, the office was responsible, commencing January 1943, for the dispatch of 95 Swedish ships with relief cargo for Greece.

The Montreal office was also appointed by the Park Steamship Company, the Canadian Government owned company formed to act as owners of the Canadian war emergency fleet, to manage ten of their ships. *Jasper Park* became a war loss, the other nine survived the conflict and were *Riverdale Park, Westmount Park, High Park, Rideau Park, Yamaska Park, Belwoods Park, Lakeview Park, Strathcona Park* and *Champlain Park*.

Stemming and Turning the Tide—1942 to 1945

The greatest losses sustained by the Group were during 1942 when twenty ships of over 140,000 tons were lost, including three, *Waimarama, Wairangi* and *Empire Hope,* which were sunk in two days in the same Malta convoy. The increased Allied power at sea meant that most of the losses sustained by Furness Withy during this period were caused by submarine action rather than by surface craft, although aircraft were involved in two sinkings.

After a couple of quiet months, the first loss of the year was *Manaqui,* which was torpedoed and sunk by *U504* off Barbados on 15 March. Bound for Jamaica there were no survivors and she was posted as "Untraced" on 29 April. It was only much later that the true cause of her loss at the hands of *U504* was ascertained. Two days after *Manaqui* had been sunk, Rio Cape Line lost *Scottish Prince* off Freetown with the loss of one life. Prince Line, after the heavy losses of 1941, was only to lose one ship in 1942: *Norman Prince* torpedoed by *U156* in the Caribbean. Sixteen of her crew were lost, the survivors being picked up by the Vichy French steamer *Angoulême.* Landed at Fort de France, Martinique, they were held for over four months in "concentration camp" conditions before being repatriated. Later in the year, on 12 September, *U156* was to sink the liner *Laconia.* Finding that she was a transport full of prisoners of war, *U156* appealed for help in plain language by radio and was joined by *U506, U507* and the Italian submarine *Cappellini.* British and French ships were ordered to the rescue but, before they arrived, a Liberator of the USAAF 343rd Bombardment Squadron sighted the submarines, flying Red Cross flags, laden with survivors above and below deck and towing strings of lifeboats. The Liberator attacked the submarines but only succeeded in hitting lifeboats; as a consequence of this event all German U-boats were ordered not to rescue survivors (The "Laconia Order").

The increasing range of the German submarines was by now taking them south to the Cape of Good Hope, which they rounded to foray into the Indian Ocean, and along the American coast into the Caribbean. Off the coast of Trinidad *Castle Harbour,* built for service at Bermuda, was torpedoed by *U160* whilst on a ballast passage to Pernambuco. The two losses sustained by the ships of Bowater's Newfoundland Pulp and Paper Mills Ltd also illustrate how dangerous the American coast had become for merchant ships. On 11 October, *Waterton* was sunk by *U106* in the St Lawrence while she was on passage from Newfoundland for Cleveland, whilst earlier, on 10 May, *U588* had sunk *Kittys Brook* off Cape Sable, while she was bound from New York with US Army stores for Argentia in Newfoundland.

16. 3.42	MANAQUI—torpedoed by U504	11.10.42	WATERTON—torpedoed by U106
17. 3.42	SCOTTISH PRINCE—sunk by U68	16.10.42	CASTLE HARBOUR—torpedoed by U160
10. 5.42	KITTYS BROOK—torpedoed by U588	27.10.42	ANGLO MAERSK—torpedoed by U509 and U604
28. 5.42	NORMAN PRINCE—torpedoed by U156		
31. 5.42	FRED W GREEN—sunk by U506	21.11.42	EMPIRE STARLING—torpedoed by U163
12. 6.42	HARDWICKE GRANGE—sunk by U129	21.11.42	EMPIRE SAILOR—torpedoed by U518
29. 6.42	WAIWERA—torpedoed by U754	28.11.42	NOVA SCOTIA—torpedoed by U177
29. 7.42	PACIFIC PIONEER—torpedoed by U132	6.12.42	CERAMIC—torpedoed by U515
12. 8.42	EMPIRE HOPE—sunk by aircraft and Italian submarine BRONZO	28.12.42	LYNTON GRANGE—torpedoed by U406 and U628
13. 8.42	WAIMARAMA—bombed by aircraft	28.12.42	EMPIRE SHACKLETON—sunk by U225, U123 and U435
13. 8.42	WAIRANGI—torpedoed by E-boat		

The tragedy of the year, and in fact for the complete war so far as Furness Withy was concerned, came with the loss of Johnston Warren Lines *Nova Scotia,* torpedoed by *U177* off Lourenco Marques on 28 November. She is amongst the "top ten" Allied merchant ships lost in terms of loss of life. Bound from Aden with prisoners destined for Durban and a prisoner-of-war camp in the sun of South Africa, she had 1,055 on board, 139 crew, 6 passengers, 780 Italian prisoners-of-war and 130 guards. The survivors were picked up by the Portuguese sloop *Alfonso de Albuquerque*. At the final count 863 had lost their lives: 120 crew, 5 passengers, 650 prisoners and 88 guards. Shortly afterwards, on 6 December, Shaw Savill lost *Ceramic*, sunk by *U515* west of the Azores. Bound for Australia with 278 crew and 378 passengers, heavy winter gales were responsible for all except one being lost after the sinking. The one survivor, a Royal Engineers sapper, was picked up the following day by *U515*. The same gales resulted in two other ships sunk in the same area on 7 December suffering heavy loss of life. *Peter Maersk* was a victim of *U185*, and all 67 on board perished whilst from *Henry Stanley*, sunk by *U103*, only Captain Jones survived as a prisoner on the submarine, the 64 other lives being lost.

Houlder Line saw their fleet depleted due to two further sinkings, fortunately with only three crew lost in the engine room of *Hardwicke Grange* when she was sunk on 12 June by *U129* in 25.45N 65.45W, on passage from the United States to the Plate. For nearly two weeks the survivors, in four lifeboats, made for safety, landing on the coasts of the Dominican Republic, Haiti and Turks Island whilst the other one was picked up by the tanker *Athelprince*. *Lynton Grange* was outward bound for the Middle East in convoy ONS154 when nineteen U-boats attacked and sank thirteen of the 45 ships, including *Lynton Grange* on 28 December. She was damaged by *U406* and finished off by *U628*. There was no loss of life amongst the crew, who were picked up by HMS *Milne*. Also lost in this convoy was *Empire Shackleton*, managed by Houlder Line on behalf of the Ministry of War Transport. Completed in 1942 she was a CAM-Ship (Catapult Aircraft Merchant Ship), a merchant ship fitted with a catapult forward carrying a Hurricane fighter for use in convoy protection against attacks by long range German Focke-Wulf Kondor reconnaissance bombers. Of the 34 ships so fitted, eleven were lost in service but during their 170 voyages they launched their aircraft on eight occasions, destroying seven enemy aircraft and damaging a further three. Furness Withy companies managed three CAM-ships, none of which were to launch their aircraft in defence of the convoy. But in submarine actions a Hurricane was of little use. Torpedoed by *U225*, and again by *U123*, *Empire Shackleton* was finally sunk by gunfire from *U435*. The fifty on board included the Convoy Commodore and his staff. Survivors were picked up by HMCS *Shediac* (seven) and the steamer *Calgary* (eleven), but most by the Q-ship *Fidelity* which was later sunk by *U435* with the loss of all 374 on board, including the survivors from *Empire Shackleton*.

On the North Atlantic, *Pacific Pioneer* fell victim to *U132* on 29 July whilst in convoy ON113, and the homeward bound *Waiwera* sank on 29 June after two torpedo hits by *U754*. Eight lives were lost and the 97 survivors spent four days in the boats until rescued by the Norwegian *Oregon Express*. The growing fleet of the Ministry of War Transport was to suffer the remaining losses under Furness Withy Group management. *Fred W Green*, an elderly 1918 built ship, was sunk by gunfire from *U506* during passage from America to West Africa. The

Empire Allenby in 1945. Fully armed and in grey paint but with Furness Withy funnel markings.

The troopship *Empire Anvil*.

Danish tanker *Anglo Maersk,* under Houlder management, had straggled from convoy SL125 due to engine trouble and was catching up when she was sighted and hit by *U509,* to be later sunk by *U604.* Both *Empire Starling* and *Empire Sailor* were sunk on 21 November, *Empire Starling* by *U163* off the West Indies, fortunately with no loss of life, and *Empire Sailor* by *U518* whilst on passage in convoy ON145 from Liverpool for St John NB.

Empire Sailor, managed by Cairn Line, had in her cargo some 270 tons of phosgene and mustard gas. The torpedo hit the hold containing this lethal cargo and the sinking *Empire Sailor* found herself enveloped by a cloud of gas as she was abandoned. Of her crew 22 died, most of them from the effects of gas and only two of the survivors did not have to be treated for exposure to gas. Although the threat to use gas existed throughout World War II it was never used in action, the case of *Empire Sailor* and the Bari tragedy being the only two instances where gas was released, albeit by accident. The Bari tragedy occurred on 2 December 1943 when a force of German Ju88 bombers attacked the congested harbour, sinking 17 ships and damaging 8 others. The American ammunition ship *Joseph Wheeler* took a direct hit and blew up, and the nearby *Fort Athabasca* took fire and blew up when two captured German rocket bombs were engulfed. Another American ship, *John Harvey,* also blew up. She had on board 100 tons of mustard gas which spread over the harbour. Over 1,000 died and 800 were admitted to hospital, the majority suffering from the effects of the gas.

The turning of the tide against the U-boats became apparent in 1943. Increased numbers of escorts, air cover and the formation of hunter/killer groups saw the sinkings of submarines increase inexorably and convoys started to get through without loss. The hunter/killer groups were co-ordinated with the convoy escorts, remaining behind to stalk the enemy to the kill.

The year 1943 brought some relief to Furness Withy and, although losses were still recorded, the worst was past and only ten sinkings were to take place during the year. Three were managed ships, *Empire Trader* and *Empire Stanley,* plus *Jasper Park* managed by the Montreal office. Built in 1908 as *Tainui, Empire Trader* had been sold by Shaw, Savill and Albion to shipbreakers just prior to the outbreak of war. Retrieved by the Government, she was renamed *Empire Trader* and returned to Shaw Savill management until torpedoed by *U92* on 21 February 1943. Convoy ON166 had a five day battle with U-boats and lost fourteen ships. *Empire Trader* was damaged and diverted for the Azores but was later sunk by her escort on Admiralty orders. The convoy rescue ship *Stockport* was dropping behind the convoy to pick up the crew of *Empire Trader* when she was herself sunk by *U604* with the loss of all hands including 91 survivors. Both *Empire Stanley* and *Jasper Park* were sunk in the Indian Ocean, off the coast of South Africa.

Most of the Group's losses took place in the Atlantic. One, however, occurred in the Mediterranean and serves as a reminder of the course of the War. Johnston Warren Lines' *Newfoundland* had been converted into a hospital ship and was lying off Salerno on 13 September waiting for casualties, the landings having taken place on 9 September, when hit by German aircraft. Fortunately there were only two patients on board with the crew of 106 and 188 medical staff, but 4 crew and 15 medical staff died as *Newfoundland* burnt, and she had finally to be sunk by gunfire from a warship.

Manchester Liners were to lose two ships during the year. *Manchester Merchant* was sunk by *U628* in convoy ON166 on 25 February, the same convoy but the day after *Empire Trader.* There was heavy loss of life, 29 only surviving from her crew of 65. On 9 July, *U508* found *Manchester Citizen* on a ballast passage from Freetown to Lagos and sank her with the loss of 15 lives. Prince Line also lost two of their ships. *Lancastrian Prince* was part of convoy ON176 when she was attacked and sunk by *U613* east of Newfoundland, going down with all her crew of 45. *Indian Prince* was in the Mediterranean, part of convoy KMS31 bound from Liverpool to India when nearly fifty enemy aircraft launched an attack off Oran on 11 November. Four ships were sunk for the loss of seven German aircraft, and they included *Indian Prince* which was taken in tow but sank five hours later.

21. 2.43	EMPIRE TRADER—torpedoed by U92	
25. 2.43	MANCHESTER MERCHANT—torpedoed by U628	
11. 4.43	LANCASTRIAN PRINCE—torpedoed by U613	
12. 4.43	PACIFIC GROVE—torpedoed by U563	
6. 7.43	JASPER PARK—torpedoed by U177	

9. 7.43	MANCHESTER CITIZEN—torpedoed by U508	
26. 7.43	EL ARGENTINO—bombed by aircraft	
17. 8.43	EMPIRE STANLEY—torpedoed by U197	
13. 9.43	NEWFOUNDLAND—bombed by aircraft	
11.11.43	INDIAN PRINCE—torpedoed by aircraft	

The other two ships sunk during the year were *Pacific Grove* and *El Argentino. Pacific Grove* was part of convoy HX232 when she was sunk on 12 April by *U563* early on her passage from New York to Glasgow, whilst *El Argentino* was north-west of Lisbon when attacked in convoy OS52 by an FW200 Kondor and sunk on 26 July. Of the 54 crew and 16 passengers on *Pacific Grove,* twelve crew were lost whilst 4 crew died out of the 98 crew and 6 passengers on board *El Argentino.*

With the sinking of *Indian Prince* on 11 November 1943, the list of Furness Withy Group losses ends. During the final eighteen months of the war, two further losses were sustained, but both were amongst the managed ships. On 3 September 1944, Bowater's *Livingston,* on passage from Boston and Halifax for St John's NF was caught by *U541* and sunk with the loss of half her crew. Finally, the managed Liberty ship *Sampa* was mined early in 1945, with the loss of fifteen lives, ten miles North of Ostend. She was one of several victims of mines laid on the convoy route from the Thames to the Scheldt by E-boat flotillas.

3. 9.44	LIVINGSTON—torpedoed by U541	27. 2.45	SAMPA—sunk by mine

123

Samcalia was managed until purchased in 1947 and renamed *Pacific Liberty*.

The War Shipbuilding Programme

Following the outbreak of war, the Admiralty assumed a controlling role in shipbuilding and rapidly a pattern emerged. Whilst orders already placed were allowed to continue to completion, priority would go to naval orders in future. Soon a Shipbuilding Commission was dispatched to North America where orders were placed both in the United States and Canada for two series of standard ships subsequently identified by the prefix *Ocean* and *Fort*. The *Ocean* series would develop in due course into the Liberty ship. Capacity over and above naval requirements in the United Kingdom was employed in building cargo ships and tankers for Government account, and these ships were given the prefix *Empire* to their names. The Government tonnage, registered in the name of the Ministry of War Transport, was allocated to various shipowners to manage.

By the time *Manchester Trader*, last of the pre-war orders, was delivered in May 1941, Government planners were already starting to look ahead to the post war years and it was decided to permit limited private building under licence during the war years to replace some of the tonnage which owners had lost to enemy action. These vessels would either be of the standard designs already under construction or approved owners' designs where such vessels were of value to the war effort, albeit with many austerity features rather than those normally required by the owners. Additionally there was the Tonnage Replacement Scheme under which various "Empire" ships were allocated to owners who had suffered heavy losses, to be managed by them during the war and sold to them on the return of peace.

The Furness Withy Group were to take delivery of ten ships built under licence prior to the end of the war in 1945. These consisted of three reefers to Houlder Brothers and Shaw, Savill and Albion designs and seven general cargo ships for Prince Line, Rio Cape Line and Manchester Liners.

Name	Built	GRT		Name	Built	GRT	
CONDESA	1944	10367	Furness-Houlder Line Agentine Lines	ENGLISH PRINCE	1943	7275	Prince Line
				SCOTTISH PRINCE	1944	7138	Prince Line
RIPPINGHAM GRANGE	1943	10365	Houlder Line	JAVANESE PRINCE	1944	8875	Rio Cape Line
MANCHESTER SHIPPER	1943	7881	Manchester Lines	WELSH PRINCE	1944	7354	Rio Cape Line
HIGHLAND PRINCE	1942	7043	Prince Line	WAIWERA	1944	12028	Shaw, Savill and Albion
CHINESE PRINCE	1943	9485	Prince Line				

In addition, the Ministry of War Transport ordered four austerity versions of Shaw, Savill's W-class from Harland and Wolff. The first two, *Empire Hope* and *Empire Grace* were placed under Shaw, Savill and Albion management. As already noted *Empire Hope* was lost on the Malta Convoy of August 1942 and *Empire Grace* was purchased by the company in 1946 and renamed *Wairangi*. The second pair, *Empire Mercia* and *Empire Wessex* followed in 1946 and were sold prior to completion, becoming *Empire Star* and *Port Hobart* with Blue Star and Port Line respectively. Commencing with *Waipawa* and *Waiwera* in 1934, a total of eleven orders had been placed for this highly successful design.

The Tragedy of *Zyunyo Maru*

Lying off the west coast of Sumatra, the submarine HMS *Tradewind* sighted a 5,000 ton steamer moving north along the coast and at dusk on 18 September 1944 sank her with two torpedoes, little realising the tragedy this would be.

That steamer was *Zyunyo Maru*, known in British ports between 1917 and 1921 as either *Hartland Point* of Norfolk and North American Steamship Company or Johnston Line's *Hartmore*. Passing from the British register to Japanese owners in 1927, she was now employed as a transport in the Japanese war effort.

At Tandjong Priok (Batavia) she had received orders to embark prisoners-of-war and Javanese forced labour (romushas) being sent north to work on constructing the Pakanbaroe railway to connect the east and west coasts across central Sumatra. Conditions there were akin to those on the equally notorious Burma railway.

No exact record of numbers embarked survive, the most likely estimate being 2,170 prisoners, mainly Dutch but including 200 British, Australian and American, and 4,860 romushas when she sailed on 16 September, heading through the Sunda Straits past Krakatoa towards Padang. The meeting with *Tradewind* two days later meant she was never to arrive.

Only 680 prisoners and 200 romushas survived, some 6,150 lives being lost from their ranks when *Zyunyo Maru* sank. Of the fifteen Japanese ships sunk with prisoners on board, she sustained by far the greatest loss of life and ranks with losses like *Lancastria, Wilhelm Gustloff, Goya* and *General von Steuben* in the tragic annals of the Second World War at sea.

Marine Losses

The risks facing shipping during wartime were not limited to enemy action. Radar was still in infancy, highly classified on the secret list and the few sets available went to warships and not merchant vessels. Convoys of ships, with few or no lights and in close proximity brought enhanced risks of collision whilst the suppression of many navigation beacons made the navigators' task all the more difficult. An examination of the losses sustained during the war amply illustrates these risks.

Three ships were lost in collision, *Manchester Regiment* at the end of 1939 was proceeding without lights when she was run down and sunk by Pacific Steam's *Oropesa* detached from an eastbound convoy. The Dutch flag *Driebergen* was nearing the Tyne, with her first cargo of grain since being taken under management, when sunk in collision with *Port Darwin*. Later, *Jessmore* was outward bound in convoy during February 1941 when she was hit twice in the engine room by *Baron Pentland*. Although taken in tow, she sank two days later an hour after the tug *Assurance* had arrived to assist.

The other three losses were all by grounding. *Matakana* was wrecked in the West Indies, *Cairnglen* on the British East coast when nearing the end of her voyage from Canada and *Incemore* on Anticosti Island.

Fleet Losses—1939 to 1945

MANCHESTER REGIMENT (Manchester Liners Ltd)—4 December 1939 collision with OROPESA, abandoned in 44.50N 55.30W. Manchester for St John NB, general.

MATAKANA (Shaw, Savill & Albion Co Ltd)—1 May 1940 ashore in heavy weather on Mayaguana Island, about 150 miles North of Haiti. Napier for UK, refrigerated & general.

DRIEBERGEN (Minister of War Transport)—28 August 1940 collision with PORT DARWIN north of the Tyne (55.25N 1.22W). Bahia Blanca for Tyne, wheat.

INCEMORE (Johnston Warren Lines Ltd)—16 September 1940 ashore East Cape, Anticosti. Manchester for Montreal, wool, glass & machinery, &c. Wreck sold.

CAIRNGLEN (Cairn Line of Steamships Ltd)—22 October 1940 ashore near Souter Point, South of the Tyne. Montreal for Tyne & Leith, bacon & wheat.

JESSMORE (Johnston Warren Lines Ltd)—19 February 1941 collision with BARON PENTLAND South-west of Rockall (54N 16.56W). Hull for Table Bay, Piraeus & Turkey. Taken in tow but abandoned 20.2.1941 in 53.11N 16.7W. Sank 21.2.1941.

---

7. Rebuilding fleets and services—1946 to 1960

As the sound of gunfire died for the second time this century, the battle scarred British merchant fleet could lick its wounds and turn its eyes to the future. Six years of war had decimated not only the fleets of Furness Withy but also the services, staff and offices round the world. It would take years to complete the restoration work.

Some shipowners looked over their shoulders and remembered the years following the Armistice of 1918. Eighteen months of prosperity had been enjoyed before the freight market collapsed in the summer of 1920. Would the same thing happen again?

With the coming of peace, the Government started to remove the wartime controls and to return ships to their owners, enabling them to recommence services which had been out of their control since the beginning of the war. Although shipowners had continued to operate during that period, Government control of imports had meant that they were effectively acting on behalf of various Government Departments and using what ships were available for allocation to the routes when required by national needs and the flow of freight.

Shipyards all over the world experienced a period of full order books. Ships being returned to owners were in need of reconditioning, whilst many had accumulated long lists of minor damage which had remained unrepaired in the face of more important matters. Repairs were now taken in hand at the end of the Government charters. At the same time, owners were clamouring for new tonnage both to replace ships lost in the war and to upgrade and modernise their fleets.

The flow of traffic generated by the Marshall Plan, the American sponsored and financed assistance programme to rebuild and restore the war ravaged countries of the world—followed by the outbreak of war in Korea during 1950—boosted demand for shipping and kept the shipping market buoyant, as also did the closure of the Suez Canal for a brief period in 1956 to 1957. Thus, from 1945 a period approaching fifteen years of prosperity lay ahead of shipping before changing times and recession were to be felt.

However, a more insidious and fundamental change was to take place in the two decades following the war. Entirely outside the control of British shipowners, it was ultimately to place their future survival in jeopardy. The British Empire had developed into the British Commonwealth of Nations. The status of this Commonwealth had first been defined in the "Balfour Declaration" at the Inter-Imperial Relations Committee in 1926 and given legal substance by the Statute of Westminster in 1931. In the two decades following 1945, a steady flow of colonies achieved statehood and with that status commenced to encourage their own shipowners and industrialists, rather than remain reliant on the United Kingdom.

At the same time, from limited proposals on coal and steel in 1950, the concept of the European Community started to develop, leading to the Treaty of Rome in 1957. Commencing with six member nations, the Community has been enlarged over the years with Britain signing the Treaty of Accession in 1972. This turning of British eyes towards Europe was ultimately at the expense of the Commonwealth, the members of which increasingly looked for other trading partners. Then, the move by some countries to restrict shipping to the fleets of the two nations concerned at either end of a trade route affected shipowners in other countries who were totally or partially cross traders (operating between countries none of which is their home state).

Rebuilding the Fleet

Furness Withy did not quickly turn to the shipyards with massive orders for replacement tonnage. They chose rather to take suitable ships from the large number of Government owned vessels and prizes being offered for sale. Purchases, for Group companies and others associated with the Group, such as Hadley Shipping Company and companies managed by Kaye, Son and Company, totalled 42 ships. Included were 21 "Empire" ships, split into fifteen of the various general cargo types, one each of the Norwegian class tanker (*Empire Coral*), fast cargo (*Empire Regent*), refrigerated (*Empire Grace*) and Ocean class (*Ocean Valley*) ships; two old Shaw, Savill and Albion ships repurchased and one German vessel taken as a prize in 1945 (*Empire Kent*). From the United States came ten Liberty ships, four Victory and one C1-M class (*Hickory Mount*), whilst five Canadian built *Fort* and *Park* ships completed the roll-call.

Name	Built	Acquired	GRT	Renamed	
		Alexander Shipping Co Ltd			
EMPIRE GLEN	1941	1945	6327	AYLESBURY	
EMPIRE CLIVE	1941	1946	7115	CHARLBURY	
EMPIRE STALWART	1943	1946	7066	EASTBURY	
EMPIRE BALLAD	1942	1946	6582	BIBURY	
EMPIRE CANYON	1943	1946	7081	HOLMBURY	
SAMTAMPA	1943	--	7219	23.4.1947 wrecked	Liberty
SAMLAMU	1944	1947	7246	KINGSBURY	Liberty
SAMDAK	1943	1948	7265	LEDBURY	Liberty
		British Empire S N Co Ltd			
EMPIRE CORAL	1941	1946	8602	DERWENT RIVER	tanker
SAMSOARING	1944	1947	7210	FRASER RIVER	Liberty
		Cairn Line of Steamships Ltd			
EMPIRE SNOW	1941	1946	6327	CAIRNAVON	
		Claremont Shipping Co Ltd			
SAMEARN	1943	1947	7219	CLAREPARK	Liberty
		Empire Transport Co Ltd			
SAMTYNE	1944	1947	7283	ARGENTINE TRANSPORT	Liberty
		Furness, Withy & Co Ltd			
SAMCALIA	1943	1947	7219	PACIFIC LIBERTY	Liberty
SAMAVON	1943	1947	7219	PACIFIC NOMAD	Liberty
SAMDARING	1944	1947	7282	PACIFIC RANGER	Liberty
SAMTREDY	1943	1947	7259	PACIFIC IMPORTER	Liberty
TUSCULUM VICTORY	1945	1947	7640	PACIFIC STRONGHOLD	Victory
		Furness (Canada) Ltd			
OUTREMONT PARK	1944	1946	7158	BRAZILIAN PRINCE	
ELGIN PARK	1945	1946	7160	ROYAL PRINCE	
ALBERT PARK	1945	1947	7157	BEACON GRANGE	
SAPPERTON PARK	1943	1947	7166	ROYSTON GRANGE	
	Hadley Shipping Co Ltd (Immingham Agency Co Ltd)				
SAMKANSA	1943	1947	7265	CERINTHUS	Liberty
		Houlder Line Ltd			
EMPIRE BUCKLER	1942	1946	7046	OVINGDEAN GRANGE	
EMPIRE PIBROCH	1942	1946	7051	URMSTON GRANGE	
EMPIRE PENNANT	1942	1947	7071	LANGTON GRANGE	
SAMETTRICK	1943	1947	7272	ELSTREE GRANGE	Liberty
EMPIRE BALFOUR	1944	1949	7201	BARTON GRANGE	
FORT ASH	1943	1950	7131	ROYSTON GRANGE	
		Johnston Warren Lines Ltd			
EMPIRE FAITH	1941	1946	7061	JESSMORE	
EMPIRE KENT	1939	1947	4769	OAKMORE	
HICKORY MOUNT	1945	1947	3825	HEATHMORE	
		Kaye, Son & Co Ltd			
EMPIRE ALMOND	1941	1946	6860	MARQUITA	
EMPIRE GANTOCK	1946	1946	7369	MARTITA	
EMPIRE KEDAH	1946	1946	7311	MARSHALL	
EMPIRE PROME	1945	1947	7086	MARTAGAN	
		Renfrew Navigation Co Ltd			
ATCHISON VICTORY	1944	1946	7677	KHEDIVE ISMAIL	Victory
UNITED VICTORY	1944	1946	7677	MOHAMED ALI EL KEBIR	Victory
		Rio Cape Line Ltd			
EMPIRE REGENT	1943	1946	9904	BLACK PRINCE	
STAMFORD VICTORY	1945	1947	7681	BRITISH PRINCE	Victory
		Shaw, Savill & Albion Co Ltd			
EMPIRE GRACE	1942	1946	13478	WAIRANGI	
EMPIRE PAKEHA	1910	1946	8115	PAKEHA	
EMPIRE WAIMANA	1911	1946	8129	WAIMANA	
SAMRICH	1943	1947	7219	CUFIC	Liberty
SAMSYLVAN	1943	1947	7219	TROPIC	Liberty

Typical of the ships purchased after 1945 were the British built *Empire Stalwart*, renamed *Eastbury* photographed at Durban *(Natal Photo)*,

the Liberty ship *Samtredy*, renamed *Pacific Importer,*

the Victory ship *Atchison Victory* which became *Mohamed Ali El Kebir,*

and the surrendered German *Empire Kent* which was renamed *Oakmore (A Duncan).*

In 1946 an offer was made to buy ships from the Canadian Government-controlled Park Steamship Company. Initially, the purchase of two ships, plus a further two on charter, was agreed together with the acquisition of Park Steamship's interest in the Canada to South American trade. For political reasons, the Canadian Government required the ships to be retained under the Canadian flag so Furness (Canada) Ltd was formed to own the four ships ultimately purchased. For the same reason other buyers such as Bristol City Line and Elder Dempster had to form Canadian subsidiaries to own Canadian ships purchased at this time. The names chosen indicate that the Furness Withy ships were employed on Prince Line and Houlder Line services.

During the summer of 1947, the Company's offer to buy four Liberty ships for the North Pacific service was accepted at a price of $544,506 each, the ships being renamed *Pacific Nomad, Pacific Ranger, Pacific Liberty* and *Pacific Importer*. At the same time, a contract for the purchase of two Victories, renamed *Pacific Stronghold* and *British Prince* was concluded. Interestingly, later in the year a much smaller C1-M was obtained for Johnston Warren Lines which cost $693,862, considerably more than the Liberties.

The tragedy amongst the purchases was the loss of *Samtampa* with all her crew, and that of the Mumbles lifeboat. Her purchase for Alexander Shipping had been agreed and at the time of her loss (see page) she was on a ballast passage from Middlesbrough for Newport, Mon, where she was to be handed over.

Building the New Fleet

The Group was in no hurry to place orders, preferring to consider the post-war needs of the services in the light of current trade levels. In fact, several companies had to wait until the early 1950s before new tonnage was commissioned, the Empire and Liberty ships proving capable of servicing the routes in the meantime.

Even before the war in Europe had ended the first order had been placed. This was with Vickers for post-war delivery of two ships to replace *Nova Scotia* and *Newfoundland* on the Johnston Warren route from Liverpool to Canada. Six months later Burntisland and Laing received contracts for new North Pacific ships. However, the most important order placed was for a ship to replace the burnt out *Monarch of Bermuda*. A smaller vessel was perceived to be better suited for the post-war route, so Vickers were instructed to commence work on *Ocean Monarch* for March 1951 delivery.

Early postwar fleet renewals included the Mediterranean trader *Maltese Prince* and *Nova Scotia* for Johnston Warren Lines.

Shaw, Savill and Albion were the main orderers of new tonnage, to serve the demands of the trade from New Zealand. In 1945, orders were placed with Harland and Wolff, Swan, Hunter and Wigham Richardson and Cammell Laird for four 15,000 ton cargo-passenger vessels (the first two were laid down as cargo ships and altered during construction), to be named *Athenic*, *Corinthic*, *Ceramic* and *Gothic*. These were followed by a series of cargo ships, the first being the motorships *Delphic* and *Doric*, followed by a trio of sisters to the *Athenic* group, but without passenger accommodation - *Persic*, *Runic* and *Suevic*.

The other company to place the most numerous orders was Prince Line. Two ship types can be identified, the large 8,000 ton sisters *Cingalese Prince* and *Eastern Prince*, completed by Vickers in 1950, for world wide service, and the smaller Mediterranean traders, which came from Burntisland. Prince Line's first post-war delivery was *Maltese Prince* in 1946, followed by seven others over the decade that followed. *Cyprian Prince* was a sister, *Sycamore*, *Egyptian Prince* and *Afric* were a slightly larger version and *Beechmore*, *Pinemore* and

Black Prince were slightly larger again. These ships were to serve not only Prince Line, but Johnston Warren Lines and Shaw, Savill and Albion.

Bermuda and West Indies also received a new ship in 1949, *Fort Avalon* delivered by Scotts. The same year Furness-Houlder Argentine Lines received the first replacement for the Plate frozen meat fleet in the shape of *Duquesa*.

A New Houseflag

In 1946 Furness, Withy and Company hoisted a new houseflag, even though there are still those who maintain the only "true" flag for the company was the plain blue flag carrying a white "F" in the centre, which had remained in use for 60 years and under which the fleet had fought two world wars.

The new flag of 1946 was a burgee with, in the centre, a black ball carrying two red stripes of unequal width as on the funnel. In the upper hoist was a white "F". Subsequently variations on this flag appeared, in 1980 Furness Withy (Shipping) Ltd adopted a variation with the letter "F" deleted, and about the same time Furness Withy (Chartering) Ltd introduced another variation on the funnel colours, a black flag with the two unequal red bands.

Bermuda Tourism

In 1945 the possibility of leasing out the Furness Withy tourist property in Bermuda was developed. The first proposal was to lease the Hotel Bermudiana, Castle Harbour Hotel, St George's Hotel and Mid Ocean Golf Course and Clubhouse to an operating company which would also lease three hotels owned by Sir Howard Trott's Princess Hotels. The failure of the Princess Hotels shareholders to ratify the agreement placed the proposal in abeyance.

The wish to divest the company of the Bermuda operation arose largely from difficulties in controlling the undertaking from London. Staffing problems and strikes were proving troublesome and the desirability of passing control to a local body was recognised.

In 1947 a new strategy was evolved. Instead of leasing the hotels, the shares in the owning Bermuda Development Company would be marketed, with up to 80% to be sold and management of the hotels would pass to the Hilton group. By the end of October, two-thirds of the shares had been sold and effectively the land-based tourist trade passed from company control, although the shipping service with *Queen of Bermuda* and *Ocean Monarch* was to be retained for many years to come. A minority 25% holding in Bermuda Development Company was retained until it was sold to Robert Benson, Lonsdale and Company in 1958.

Alexander Shipping Company Ltd

In 1946 the announcement was made that Houlder Brothers had acquired control of Alexander Shipping Company Ltd, with management to be transferred the following year. Thus was cemented a long standing association between the two firms.

The purchase was a reminder of the very early days of the Furness Withy history, Edward Alexander having been a partner in Edward Withy and Company until he withdrew in 1874 and moved to Cardiff to join his cousin, Captain Capper, in business as a shipowner and manager.

Born in London in 1839 Edward Hall Capper went to sea as an apprentice on board the London ship *Irene* in 1857. Rising to command of the *Phoenix* in 1864, he came ashore about 1872 to establish his shipbroking business in the rising coal metropolis of Cardiff where he was joined by Edward Alexander. Capper then moved to London and about 1880 opened an office there. Suffering from a heart condition, he was sent on a sea voyage by his doctor. Landing at Sydney from the *Iberia* in March 1883 he went, with his wife, to stay with friends at Newcastle NSW where he was well known from his years in command. Sadly, three weeks later he died and is buried there.

Now head of the firm, Edward Alexander moved to London, closing the Cardiff office about 1886 and, until his death in 1925, building a small but active fleet of steam tramps. The Alexander Shipping Company was formed in 1914 to consolidate the ownership of the fleet. For many years the traditional trade of the Alexander fleet was the carriage of coal to the River Plate where, after discharge, the ships were placed in the hands of Houlder Brothers for loading. Some were placed on the Houlder homeward liner berth, others loaded bulk cargo. This

Sir Frank S Alexander, Bt *(R Alexander).*

close working association was strengthened in 1937 when Houlder Brothers took a minority financial holding in Alexander Shipping. This led logically to the sale in 1946, which brought with it the strength of the Furness Withy/Houlder Group.

The Burntisland built *Tenbury* on trials.   *(J Campbell Harper Ltd)*

Controlled now by Edward Alexander's three sons, Charles, Frank and Waldemar, the future security of the firm was at the forefront of their minds as the war came to its close in 1945, the events of the years after 1918 causing them concern. They were all getting older, in fact Charles, who took a leading share in the management of the business, died early in 1945. Frank also devoted much time to wider interests, being a member of the board of the Port of London Authority, chairman of the Baltic Exchange throughout the war and Lord Mayor of London in 1944/5. His services to both shipping and London were recognised by the granting of a knighthood when Sheriff in 1942, being elevated to a baronetcy in 1945. The surviving brothers wished to see the business in a secure position to face an expected recession.

The company started the war in 1939 with twelve ships, plus another building, but all had been lost when the war ended. They were replaced by the purchase of a series of war built standard ships, five Empires and two Liberty ships. Sadly a third Liberty ship, *Samtampa*, was lost on her delivery passage with heavy loss of life.

Name	Built	Acquired	GRT	Name	Built	Acquired	GRT
AYLESBURY	1941	1945	6327	LEDBURY	1943	1948	7265
CHARLBURY	1941	1946	7115	NEWBURY	1951	--	11199
EASTBURY	1943	1946	7066	QUEENSBURY	1953	--	6175
BIBURY	1942	1946	6700	SHAFTESBURY	1958	--	8532
HOLMBURY	1943	1946	7081	TEWKESBURY	1959	--	8532
KINGSBURY	1944	1947	7246	WESTBURY	1960	--	8533

Employed in the tramping side of Houlder Brothers' interests, the Alexander fleet was to have only five additions in the next fifteen years. The first of these introduced Alexander Shipping to a new trade with the commissioning of the Lithgow-built tanker *Newbury* in 1951. She was followed two years later by the cargo ship *Queensbury*, a product of Burntisland Shipbuilding, which was employed on the Houlder Line general cargo service to South America. Later Burntisland built three sisters, developments of *Queensbury*, which were delivered in 1958/60 and were employed as general traders.

Only two further ships with traditional Alexander names were to be commissioned, *Tenbury* in 1965 and *Banbury* (named *Iron Banbury* while under charter to Broken Hill Proprietary of Australia) in 1971, although with the various reorganisations of the Group companies, Alexander Shipping became, from 1975, the registered owners of the various Houlder owned bulk carriers and tankers until they were transferred to Furness Withy (Shipping) Ltd in 1981. Finally the Alexander Shipping Company was included in the list of dormant companies being wound up in 1990.

The Royal Tour

In 1950 Shaw, Savill and Albion were approached in connection with the planned 1952 visit of King George VI and Queen Elizabeth to New Zealand and Australia. The Royal Yacht *Victoria and Albert* was too old and the new *Britannia* was still on the drawing board. The search for a British ship with both the speed and suitable accommodation had led to Shaw Savill and the four ships of the *Athenic* class. *Gothic* was the final choice, with her sister *Ceramic* listed as standby should any accident prevent *Gothic* taking the role. *Gothic* was taken in hand and converted in readiness for the honour.

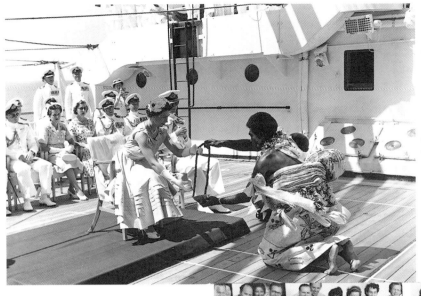

Her Majesty Queen Elizabeth II being greeted on board *Gothic* at Fiji (left). Crossing the line ceremony. *(The Times)*

Tragedy was to upset all the plans. The illness of King George led to Princess Elizabeth stepping in to undertake the tour with Prince Philip. As the Princess was already scheduled to visit Kenya, *Gothic* was routed to Mombasa to commence her duties, rather than London as previously planned. Departure from Mombasa was scheduled for 7 February 1952; but the death of the King was announced the previous day and the Royal Party immediately returned to London, the tour cancelled.

Following the Coronation, the Royal visit to Australia and New Zealand was again rescheduled with *Gothic*, which had meantime traded with her royal suites locked, taking the Queen on board at Jamaica and sailing on 27 November 1953. The tour visited Tonga, Fiji, New Zealand, Australia and Ceylon, ending at Aden on 28 April 1954. The Royal Party then travelled south to complete the East African visit interrupted two years earlier, before joining the new Royal Yacht *Britannia* at Tobruk. *Gothic*, her duties completed, sailed direct from Aden to Malta and England.

Into the Great Lakes

Stretching into the centre of the North American continent, the five Great Lakes offered the possibility of cheap water routes from the Atlantic to important industrial centres such as Detroit and Chicago. The St Lawrence River from the sea and the river connections between the lakes, however, nullified the attraction as shallows and rapids voided any hope of sending ships to the head of the lakes.

From the early days of European settlement, canals to join the lakes and to avoid obstacles such as the Niagara Falls had been planned and built. For many years seagoing ships had been able to traverse the Lachine,

Gothic meets the Royal Yacht ***Britannia*** at Malta.

Welland and Soo Canals but the locks limited the size of these ships to about 260ft long, 44ft beam and 14ft draft. Various agreements between the United States and Canada led to the appointment of a joint Deep Waterways Commission in 1895 to investigate how best to improve the river and canal links between the lakes. Following World War II, after fifty years of studies, discussions and prolonged negotiations, the St Lawrence Seaway concept, a joint power and transport development, got under way with the first sod turned on 10 August 1954. The Seaway formally opened on 26 June 1959, dedicated by Queen Elizabeth II and President Dwight D Eisenhower. Taking the Welland Canal locks as the standard, ships up to 766ft long, 80ft beam and taking 27ft of water could now navigate to the heart of the continent.

For many years a small number of shipowners had operated a through service using ships specially built to fit the Lachine Locks. Easily recognised with their vertical stem and tucked in sterns these ships were colloquially known as "Lakers". Amongst these companies were the Dutch Maatschappij Zeetransport NV managed by Anthony Veder and Company, Rotterdam (the Oranje Line), the Norwegian Olsen and Ugelstad, Oslo (Fjell Line) and the German firm of Sartori and Berger, Hamburg.

With the prospect of the Waterway becoming a reality, other owners active in the trade to North American East Coast ports decided to commence through services in anticipation of the opportunities the Waterway would open up. Amongst these were Manchester Liners who, in the Spring of 1952, opened the first all-British service into the Lakes. They had Cammell Laird build two ships specially for the service, and the following year purchased a third from Norwegian owners. As the service developed, a further pair of sisters entered service in 1956, built by A G Weser. With the Lakes closed to shipping in the winter, the ships were employed elsewhere in wintertime, including charter to Yeoward Line for the fruit trade from the Canary Islands.

Name	Built	Acquired	GRT	Name	Built	Acquired	GRT
MANCHESTER PIONEER	1952	--	1805	MANCHESTER VANGUARD	1956	--	1662
MANCHESTER EXPLORER	1952	--	1805	MANCHESTER VENTURE	1956	--	1662
MANCHESTER PROSPECTOR	1948	1953	1400				

Manchester Pioneer, first of the ''Laker'' fleet.

Although *Manchester Pioneer* was lengthened in 1960, the opening of the St Lawrence Seaway in 1959 and the economies this introduced with the use of larger vessels, soon saw the five "Lakers" withdrawn and, as opportunity offered, they were sold for further service. The Weser built sisters went to the General Steam Navigation Company whilst *Manchester Explorer* was bought by Canadian interests.

Into the Air

Like many other shipping companies, Furness Withy took the opportunity to amend its Memorandum of Association to permit diversification into the new field of aviation, which had developed so rapidly under the impetus of war.

The increased powers enabled a substantial interest to be acquired in Airwork Ltd early in 1954, in association with Blue Star Line Ltd. Airwork had been founded in 1928 and, prior to the outbreak of war in 1939, had been interested in training and maintenance. It assisted in the formation of Egyptair in 1932 and Indian National Airways the following year. Wartime work had been centred on the training of Royal Air Force personnel.

Post-war, a fleet of Vikings started to come into service in 1947, mainly operating charter and trooping services because under the Air Corporations Act, 1949, all internal and international scheduled services were reserved for the Public Corporations and their associate companies. In 1948-9, a number of flights were undertaken on the Berlin Airlift.

The best known Airwork operation commenced in 1952, with the inauguration of the Safari Service between the United Kingdom and Nairobi, Lagos and Salisbury. Units of the fleet were to be seen in many parts of the world, with a 1954 Far East trooping contract and transatlantic freight service. During 1958 the replacement of the ageing Vikings commenced, with their more modern Viscount sisters entering service.

Johnston Warren Lines

Having lost five out of their fleet of six ocean going ships during the war, *Dromore* being the only survivor, Johnston Warren Lines were in dire need of tonnage in 1945 to resume their services. Included in the losses were both the North Atlantic passenger ships, *Newfoundland* and *Nova Scotia*.

The replacement *Newfoundland* and *Nova Scotia* were amongst the first ships to be delivered by shipbuilders to any Furness Withy company after the war. In the meantime three ships were purchased, *Empire Faith* (which had been one of the CAM-Ships—fitted with a catapult, they had carried a Hurricane for convoy protection) for the North Atlantic route, the ex German *Empire Kent* and an American C1-M class for the Mediterranean services.

Name	Built	Acquired	GRT
JESSMORE	1941	1946	7061
OAKMORE	1939	1947	4700
HEATHMORE	1945	1947	3825

The two passenger ships recommenced the service from Liverpool to St John's, Halifax and Boston whilst the smaller ships reopened the Mediterranean and Black Sea routes which had been closed for the duration of the war. With the political changes in Roumania, now a Communist state, the Black Sea service was never to regain its old status and closed, although those to Greece and Turkey were able to continue.

The steady contraction of the Lines can be seen in the renaming of ships on charter to other group lines, or to other owners. In fact *Mystic* was built in 1959 for charter to Shaw Savill and Albion and three of the fleet were to assume Prince Line names in 1965. As well as deep sea ships, Johnston Warren also ordered three new tugs for their Mersey operation to replace those built in 1929/30.

Name	Built	GRT	Name	Built	GRT
NOVA SCOTIA	1947	7438	ROWANMORE	1956	8495
NEWFOUNDLAND	1948	7437	FOYLEMORE	1958	208
SYCAMORE	1950	3343	KILMORE	1958	208
BEECHMORE	1954	3291	ROSSMORE	1958	206
PINEMORE	1955	3597	MYSTIC	1959	6656

As the North Atlantic passenger trade withered, *Nova Scotia* and *Newfoundland* were withdrawn in 1962 and sold to Dominion Navigation Company (managed by H C Sleigh Ltd) for operation between Australia and Japan. They were replaced on the North Atlantic by two cargo only ships with the same names, ships which served the route for another decade until closure in the face of containerisation.

The start of the merging of Furness Withy interests can possibly be detected in this mid-1950's period with the appearance of ships carrying readily identifiable names but owned by other Group companies. In the case of Johnston Warren the bulk carriers *Sagamore* and *Edenmore* of 1957, followed by *Newfoundland* and *Nova Scotia* of 1965, carried Johnston Line names but were in fact always owned by the parent company, Furness, Withy and Company.

Prince Line Ltd

After the war Prince Line, with the largest liner network of any Furness Withy company, was faced with the task of rebuilding the four areas of operation. The Mediterranean service had, pre-war, employed six ships; the other services, all based on New York, were the South African and South American routes (three and four ships respectively) and the round-the-world service with five. To the 1939 fleet of twenty ships, eleven had been added during the war, offsetting in part the toll of fourteen sunk by enemy action.

The pride of the fleet had undoubtedly been the four "Compass" boats on the New York to River Plate service. Two of them had been sunk and neither of the others was to return to service with Prince Line. *Southern Prince* had been employed as a minelayer and, before being sold to Italian owners, was employed as accommodation for men rebuilding the ports at Hong Kong and Singapore, whilst *Eastern Prince* was bought by the Ministry of Transport and, in due course, renamed *Empire Medway*. The passenger service from New York to South America was not revived after the war.

The fourth *Black Prince* served Prince Line from 1955 to 1971. *(Skyfotos)*

Name	Built	GRT	Name	Built	GRT
MALTESE PRINCE	1946	2361	NORMAN PRINCE	1956	2709
CYPRIAN PRINCE	1949	2358	AFRIC	1950	3364
CINGALESE PRINCE	1950	8827	NORTHUMBRIAN PRINCE	1956	2709
EASTERN PRINCE	1950	8827	SOUTHERN PRINCE	1956	7917
EGYPTIAN PRINCE	1951	3364	LANCASTRIAN PRINCE	1960	4800
BLACK PRINCE	1955	3271	STUART PRINCE	1960	12959
WESTERN PRINCE	1955	7917			

Although the post-war rebuilding programme enabled the services to continue, changing circumstances saw it becoming increasingly difficult to operate them profitably. In 1954 the Rio Cape Line subsidiary was wound up, the last ship owned, *Welsh Prince,* being transferred to Furness Withy ownership.

The result of the problems was an increase in the number of ships chartered to other companies such as Shaw Savill and Albion; *Afric* was in fact launched with a Shaw Savill name in 1950 for service between Africa and Australia. An examination of the above building list will indicate how many Prince Line ships were chartered out in this manner.

At the end of 1959, with worsening results from the round-the-world service, the decision was taken to withdraw the three ships left on the route. This only left the Mediterranean operation and even here it was found necessary to cancel an order for a sister to *Lancastrian Prince.*

Manchester Liners Ltd

In 1947 delivery was taken of *Manchester Regiment,* a near sister of the war built *Manchester Shipper.* The following year a rebuilding programme commenced in order both to replace war losses and to renew the fleet.

Two specific groups of ships were to be commissioned in the decade that followed: the larger ships for the traditional service to Montreal and other Canadian ocean ports and, after the decision was taken to enter the Great Lakes trade, the smaller canal sized Lakers. We will return to the Lakers and the St Lawrence Seaway later. Another route pioneered, during the summer months, was to Churchill in Hudson Bay using, the first year, *Cairnavon,* whilst an older service was resumed to the southern United States ports of Charleston, Savannah and Jacksonville.

Blythswood delivered their last Manchester Liner in 1951 as *Manchester Merchant.* Thereafter the company placed orders with a variety of builders; Cammell Laird in Birkenhead receiving orders for two Lakers and also the larger *Manchester Spinner* (1952) and *Manchester Mariner* (1955)—*Manchester Spinner* and the first Laker, *Manchester Pioneer,* being launched on the same day. Austin and Pickersgill Ltd received orders for two sisters of 4,460gt—half the tonnage of the trans-Atlantic ships—designed for the St Lawrence Seaway trade or for service as fruit carriers from the Mediterranean. These ships were delivered in 1959 as *Manchester Faith* and *Manchester Fame.* The same year, Harland and Wolff Ltd completed *Manchester Miller* in their Belfast yard, the largest ship yet owned. After a decade of service as a break bulk general cargo ship, she was destined to be sent back to the shipyard in 1970 for conversion into the cellular container ship *Manchester Quest* as the trade changed.

The 1950's also witnessed Manchester Liners taking part in deep sea lifesaving. The first time was in 1954 when *Manchester Shipper* and *Manchester Pioneer* answered distress calls from a United States Air Force Convair RB36 bomber which had force-landed in the sea, and they were able to rescue the four survivors. Three years later *Manchester Trader* picked up and relayed the last radio messages from the sinking sail training ship *Pamir*. On the outbreak of World War II *Pamir* had been seized by the New Zealand Government and employed on trans-Pacific routes. Returned to her Finnish owners after the war Shaw, Savill and Albion loaded her with a full cargo for the voyage to Europe.

Name	Built	GRT		Name	Built	GRT
MANCHESTER REGIMENT	1947	5888		MANCHESTER FAITH	1959	4459
MANCHESTER MERCHANT	1951	7651		MANCHESTER FAME	1959	4462
MANCHESTER SPINNER	1952	7815		MANCHESTER MILLER	1959	9297
MANCHESTER MARINER	1955	7850				

Cairndhu on charter to Manchester Liners and renamed *Manchester Exporter*.

Cairn Line of Steamships Ltd

Although Cairn Line itself was not wholly owned by Furness Withy until 1967, it was under Group control as it was managed by the wholly owned Cairns, Noble and Company Ltd, Newcastle.

The three surviving ships, the elderly *Cairnvalona* and *Cairnesk* together with the war-built *Cairnavon*, were able to continue the service from the North East Coast of Britain to Canada until the delivery of new tonnage took place. Three ships were delivered, two in 1952 and the third in 1958. These enabled the older units of the fleet, *Cairnvalona* the oldest dating from 1918, to be retired and sold.

Name	Built	GRT
CAIRNGOWAN	1952	7503
CAIRNDHU	1952	7503
CAIRNFORTH	1958	8105

As the traffic on the route dropped, all three were chartered to Manchester Liners in 1965 and placed on the thriving West Coast service, being replaced on the service from the North East Coast by two smaller Manchester Liners ships, *Manchester Faith* and *Manchester Fame*, which were renamed *Cairnesk* and *Cairnglen*. In 1969 the company was placed under the control of Shaw Savill and Albion and, following containerisation on the North Atlantic, the service was withdrawn.

The company remained in existence and the Cairn Line nomenclature and colours were adopted for the fleet of mini-bulkers commissioned by the Group in the following decade.

The North Pacific Routes

Apart from the New York to Bermuda run, the service with which the Furness Withy name was most closely associated was the North Pacific route through the Panama Canal and north to Vancouver. Of the eight ships employed on this service, and registered as owned by Furness, Withy and Company or Norfolk and North American Steamship Company when war broke out, only three were to survive and one of these (*Pacific Enterprise*) was to be wrecked in 1949. The other two, with over twenty years of service each, did not survive much longer, *Pacific Shipper* being broken up in 1950 and *Pacific Exporter* was sold the following year to Italian owners.

The immediate post-war needs of the service were met by the purchase of four Liberty and one Victory ship in 1947, whilst the first newbuilding was commissioned the same year as *Pacific Fortune* under the ownership of Norfolk and North American Steamship Company. As there was now no reason to keep this company in existence, the decision was taken in 1950 to wind it up the following year, *Pacific Fortune* being transferred to Furness Withy at the same time with a valuation of £625,000. The other five *Pacific* boats built post-war were all registered from the beginning in the name of Furness Withy.

With a further four new ships commissioned in the period between 1948 and 1954, the Liberty ships were sold and the Victory *Pacific Stronghold* was renamed *Malayan Prince.* Rising costs thereafter saw the rationalisation of services on the route, especially with other operators. The full take-over of Royal Mail Lines in 1965 led to closer co-ordination, rationalisation and merger of interests, with *Pacific Envoy* being renamed *Loch Ryan* in 1967 to maintain the nomenclature and identity of Royal Mail Lines. All the post-war newbuildings were steam turbine powered, resulting in heavy fuel and operating costs which finally helped condemn the service to closure. Closure was part of the economy package for the Group adopted in November 1970, and as a result all four remaining *Pacific* boats were sold for breaking up or further service. Those which passed into other hands were not to survive for long, the last being scrapped in 1974. Doubtless, as cargo liners with a good speed, they were casualties of their own appetite for fuel and the consequent cost when compared with more economical motor vessels.

Name	Built	GRT	Name	Built	GRT
PACIFIC FORTUNE	1947	9400	PACIFIC NORTHWEST	1954	9442
PACIFIC UNITY	1948	9511	PACIFIC ENVOY	1958	9439
PACIFIC RELIANCE	1951	9442	PACIFIC STRONGHOLD	1958	9439

Pacific Unity, completed in 1948 for the North Pacific service. *(Turners (Photography) Ltd)*

Grant of Armorial Bearings (see frontispiece)

In 1957 Furness, Withy and Company, Ltd were granted corporate armorial bearings. In the language of chivalry the heralds described them as "Azure, three bars wavy Argent. In chief as many Capstans of the last, Cabled Or. And for the Crest Issuing out of a Coronet composed of four Trident heads set upon a Rim Or, a Sea Dog proper Guttée d'Eau Mantled Azure doubled Argent. On either side a Sea Hart proper attired hooves dorsal fin and tail Or".

In laymans terms the use of the wavy bars coloured alternately silver and blue alludes to water and is an ancient heraldic convention (also found in the arms of the City of Oxford and in those of London Livery Companies, such as the Merchant Adventurers, which were concerned with overseas trade) while the capstans in the chief, or upper part, of the shield show that the bearer's association with water is shipping.

The suitability of the coronet in the crest, formed from the heads of tridents, for a company concerned with ships is obvious, since the ancient sea god, Neptune to the Romans, Poseidon to the Greeks, was depicted holding a trident. The sea dog, however, requires some elucidation. The Medieval writers on natural history believed that all land creatures had their counterparts in the sea, and in armorial design, their principle is still followed when such composite monsters are required. The sea dog, in origin perhaps an otter (they have sometimes been observed far out in the sea) is depicted in heraldic art as a talbot dog, having webbed feet, a dorsal fin, and scales instead of fur. Two such animals, sprinkled with drops of water, were granted to Lord Furness in 1910 as the Supporters to his arms and it is to them that the demi sea dog in the crest refers.

The supporters on the sinister and dexter sides of the Arms are two Sea Harts which allude to West Hartlepool where the company was founded and which derive from the natural harts in unauthorised arms and crest used on their seal by the Borough Council. The Supporters and shield rest upon a Compartment Vert, with a Slipway thereon proper, alluding to the shipbuilding activities of the company.

The Armorial Bearings are completed by the motto "Quod Mare Non Novit", which translates "What Sea Has Not Known Us?" and refers to the world wide interests of the Group companies.

Furness Red Cross Line

During the war *Fort Amherst* and *Fort Townshend* had continued to run from New York to Newfoundland and following the return of peace their service was extended south to include Bermuda whilst the liners were being refitted.

The delivery of the new *Fort Avalon* to the Bermuda and West Indies Steamship Company in 1949 saw three ships now employed on the run. However, the route north from New York was soon to commence to decline and, in fact, the service was withdrawn completely in 1953. This was the result of Newfoundland becoming the tenth province of Canada in 1949. Previously Newfoundland had relied heavily on supplies from New York, but the new political situation saw a change of emphasis and an increasing volume of goods moving eastwards from Canada. The traffic flow north from the United States went into rapid decline and with it the economics of the service.

Fort Amherst was sold in 1951, becoming the Royal Fleet Auxiliary *Amherst*, whilst her sister *Fort Townshend* went the following year when she was sold to Haji Abdullah Alireza, Jeddah, for conversion into a yacht. She subsequenty spent some years as the cruise ship *Romantica* before being broken up.

One further ship was to join the service. This was Prince Line's *Stuart Prince* which dated from 1940 when she had been completed for the Mediterranean routes. She was renamed *Fort Hamilton* in 1951 and took up service from New York alongside *Fort Avalon*, replacing the two ships which had been sold.

Name	Built	Acquired	GRT
FORT AVALON	1949	--	3484
FORT HAMILTON	1940	1951	1911

Passenger Liners

As soon as they were released from Government control, the three Group passenger liners went to the shipyards for extensive renovation. Their service as armed merchant cruisers and troop transports had involved extensive alterations and these had to be made good.

Once again the Bermuda trade was to be beset by fire. The troopship *Monarch of Bermuda* went to the Tyne and was almost ready for her return to commercial service when, on 24 March 1947, fire virtually destroyed her. Abandoned as a constructive total loss, the demand for ships led the Ministry of Transport to buy the wreck for rebuilding as the emigrant carrier *New Australia* under Shaw Savill management. Later she became the Greek *Arkadia* and lasted until broken up in 1966.

This left her younger sister *Queen of Bermuda*, then under overhaul after war service as an armed merchant cruiser, alone when she returned to service in 1949, hence the order placed with Vickers in the summer of 1948 for *Ocean Monarch* to run alongside her. Completed in the Spring of 1951, *Ocean Monarch* was to remain with *Queen of Bermuda* on the service until the company withdrew from the route in 1966, the *Queen* then going for scrap whilst her younger consort was sold to Bulgaria and renamed *Varna*.

The third big passenger ship to survive the war was Shaw Savill's *Dominion Monarch* of 1939. Work on refitting her after trooping was completed in 1948 when she returned to the London to New Zealand service, supported by the new fleet of cargo-passenger ships.

The growing problems of operating mixed cargo and passenger ships, centred on dock labour disputes which increasingly disrupted the schedules of the ships, led to Shaw Savill deciding to isolate the two trades. Starting with a clean sheet of paper, the naval architects drew up an entirely new and, for the company, revolutionary concept which Harland and Wolff then turned into reality. On 17 August 1954, Queen Elizabeth II honoured the company by launching and naming *Southern Cross* which sailed on her maiden voyage from Southampton on 29 March 1955. Slightly smaller than *Dominion Monarch*, her outstanding feature, apart from not carrying cargo, was to move the machinery aft leaving the prime midship space for passenger accommodation.

Southern Cross and **Northern Star** meet as they transit the Panama Canal.

Having proved the concept, she was followed by a near sister, *Northern Star*, built by Vickers-Armstrong. When the new ship entered service in July 1962, *Dominion Monarch* was withdrawn and after a few months at Seattle serving as a floating hotel for World Fair visitors, she made the crossing of the Pacific to Japan where she was broken up.

Southern Cross and *Northern Star* operated, one eastabout and the other westabout, on their round the world service until the decision was taken to abandon the passenger trade to the Antipodes. Air travel had completely altered the pattern of sea travel and with it the economics of the service. *Southern Cross* was laid up in the River Fal in 1972 but early the following year put to sea again after sale to Greek owners for conversion into the cruise ship *Calypso*. Today she is still operating, as *Azure Sea*, in the Pacific. *Northern Star*, however, was not so fortunate; sold to Taiwanese shipbreakers, she arrived at Kaohsiung on 1 December 1974 for dismantling.

Shaw, Savill and Albion Ltd

An examination of the newbuilding programmes for the various Group companies in the post-war years is very revealing. When compared with their past record, it can give a good indication as to the prosperity not only of the company but also of the trades in which it was engaged.

On this basis, Shaw Savill and Albion were, for twenty or more years after the end of the war, to be one of the most prosperous and secure Group ventures. This is hardly surprising when it is recalled that two-thirds of New Zealand's foreign trade was with the United Kingdom, with the heavy flow of meat and dairy produce balanced by an equally steady movement of manufactured goods to New Zealand.

The company were fast off the mark with their tonnage replacement programme. Two ships which had been sold to the Ministry of War Transport were repurchased in 1946, together with one Empire ship built to a Shaw Savill design and two Liberty ships bought the following year.

Name	Built	Acquired	GRT	Name	Built	Acquired	GRT
WAIRANGI	1942	1946	13478	CUFIC	1943	1947	7219
PAKEHA	1910	1946	8115	TROPIC	1943	1947	7219
WAIMANA	1911	1946	8129				

In 1945, the company commenced their replacement newbuilding programme with the order for the four ships which would become *Gothic* and her sisters. Their ancestry in the pre-war refrigerated cargo ships was clear, and they were subsequently joined by a growing series of refrigerated cargo ships of similar size. By the end of 1950, five of these cargo only vessels were in service, both steam and diesel powered. Between 1952 and 1956 delivery of another five ships of the C class, led by *Cedric*, enabled the older units of the fleet to be sold for scrap or further trading. The latter included *Fordsdale* which went to a company controlled by C Y Tung who was destined one day to own Furness Withy, including Shaw Savill and Albion.

The period to 1960 was one of steady trading, without the problems which created headlines. The Royal Tour on board *Gothic* was one outstanding event, another was the design and building of *Southern Cross*. The reason for this revolutionary design has already been discussed, and the commissioning of *Southern Cross* in 1955 saw the Bay class, *Arawa* and *Esperance Bay* going to the breakers that year followed *Moreton Bay* and *Largs Bay* two years later.

Scarcely had *Southern Cross* entered service than the company was placing orders for a class of four 6,500gt general cargo ships, the first to be ordered since the war, which became *Arabic* and her sisters. They were followed by four I class developments of the refrigerated C class, the first of which was launched as *Ionic* in August 1958. With the I class under construction, consideration turned towards the ageing *Dominion Monarch*. *Southern Cross* had proved her worth as a passenger only vessel and the desirability of having a matching partner was clear. So in 1958 the decision was taken to commission an improved sister which would take the name *Northern Star* when launched in 1961.

October 1956 witnessed the first closure of the Suez Canal, consequent on the nationalisation of the canal by Egypt. The invasion by British and French forces followed; the canal was blocked with scuttled ships and it was to be April 1957 before it reopened for service. This resulted in the appearance of Shaw Savill ships in South African waters as they took the alternative eastward route to the Antipodes.

Lord Sanderson of Ayot, MC, Chairman of Shaw, Savill and Albion Company Ltd.
(Rex Coleman)

Name	Built	GRT		Name	Built	GRT
ATHENIC	1947	15187		CRETIC	1955	11151
CORINTHIC	1947	15682		SOUTHERN CROSS	1955	20204
CERAMIC	1948	15896		ARABIC	1956	6553
GOTHIC	1948	15902		CARNATIC	1956	11144
DELPHIC	1949	10691		AFRIC	1957	6553
DORIC	1949	10674		ARAMAIC	1957	6553
PERSIC	1949	13594		ALARIC	1958	6692
RUNIC	1950	13587		IONIC	1959	11219
SUEVIC	1950	13587		AMALRIC	1960	7791
CEDRIC	1952	11232		ICENIC	1960	11239
CYMRIC	1953	11182		ILLYRIC	1960	11256
CANOPIC	1954	11164				

The company did not limit themselves solely to the services from the United Kingdom to New Zealand and Australia however. As opportunities were identified services commenced between Australia and East and South Africa and also, with their Conference colleagues, the Crusader Shipping Company was founded to run north to Japan.

Crusader, first ship for Crusader Shipping. *(Green & Hahn)*

Crusader Shipping

In 1957, the development of the refrigerated trade from New Zealand to Japan led the New Zealand Conference members, Shaw, Savill and Albion with compatriots New Zealand Shipping Company, Port Line and Blue Star Line, to form a subsidiary under Shaw Savill and Albion management, to take part in the trade.

The Crusader Shipping Company, as it was named, turned to the Swedish Thorden Lines and purchased from them two small refrigerated ships which were under construction in Finland. Named *Crusader* and *Saracen,* they formed the backbone of the service, being joined in 1963 by a third ship, *Knight Templar.* Seasonal increases in trade were met by chartering ships from the fleets of Crusader's owning companies.

Name	Built	Acquired	GRT
CRUSADER	1957	--	3461
SARACEN	1958	--	3441
KNIGHT TEMPLAR	1948	1963	3791

Like the other routes which Shaw Savill and Albion transferred to Overseas Containers on the introduction of the ubiquitous container, Crusader Shipping was in due course containerised and today lives on in Crusader Swire Container Services Ltd.

Chairmen of Furness, Withy and Company, Ltd

Sir Ernest H Murrant KCMG   1944-1959
Frank Charlton   1959-1962

On the death of Lord Essendon in June 1944, his mantle was assumed by Ernest Murrant who had long been groomed for the role. In 1902 he had joined Furness Withy as a 13-year old with an annual salary of £20. Employed subsequently in the chartering department, he was responsible during World War I for the chartering of many foreign vessels for the British Government, for which services he was appointed an MBE.

Elected a director in 1924, he was appointed deputy chairman in 1935. On the outbreak of war with Germany for a second time in 1939, Murrant was appointed by the Minister of War Transport as his Special Representative in the Middle East, duties which he took up in the summer of 1941. His services, which covered an area from Turkey to Aden, led to his appointment as a KCMG.

Released from these duties in 1944 following the death of Lord Essendon, he returned to Furness Withy and was duly elected chairman. As chairman, he guided the Group through the years of reconstruction which followed the return of peace, until retiring from business in 1959. In 1947/8 he also served as president of the Chamber of Shipping.

Frank Charlton was a chartered accountant born in Jarrow who, for many years, was with the White Star Line in Liverpool. As a director of White Star he was closely involved in the merger with the Cunard Line following the Kylsant collapse, and became a director of both Cunard White Star and Cunard Steam Ship Company.

Elected a director of Furness Withy in 1944, deputy chairman in 1948 and chairman following the retirement of Sir Ernest Murrant in 1959, he found it necessary a couple of years later to reduce his business activities and so relinquished the chair in 1962, retiring from the board the following year.

Marine Losses—1945 to 1960

The years immediately following the war were to see four ships lost to marine causes, followed then by a decade with a clean slate. The Prince Line managed *Empire Patrol*, built as the Italian *Rodi* and captured at Malta when war was declared, was some 38 miles off Port Said with Greek refugees returning to Castelorizo when fire broke out on 29 September 1945. She sank two days later on 1 October with the loss of 33 lives. Heavier loss of life was experienced with the wreck of *Samtampa* on 23 April 1947. All 39 crew were lost when her anchor dragged in a heavy gale and she drove ashore at Skee Point, Porthcawl. In addition to those on board *Samtampa*, all the crew of the Mumbles lifeboat were lost when it capsized whilst trying to reach the casualty.

Fleet Losses—1945 to 1960

EMPIRE PATROL (Minister of War Transport)—29.9.1945 on fire about 38 miles off Port Said (31.56N 32.04E). Port Said for Castelorizo, refugees. 1.10.1945 sank.

MONARCH OF BERMUDA (Furness, Withy & Co Ltd)—24.3.1947 on fire at Palmer's drydock, Hebburn-on-Tyne. 25.3.1947 extinguished, CTL, sold.

SAMTAMPA (Minister of Transport)—23.4.1947 ashore at Sker Point, Porthcawl. Middlesbrough for Newport, Mon, ballast.

PACIFIC ENTERPRISE (Norfolk & North American S S Co Ltd)—9.9.1949 ashore on Wash Rock, 1 mile off Rock Beach, near Point Arena, California during fog. Vancouver for Manchester, passengers, grain, lumber and general.

The other two losses were owned ships. *Monarch of Bermuda* was nearing the completion of her refit at Newcastle when, on 24 March 1947, she took fire and was declared a total loss. After having survived the risks of war, the motorship *Pacific Enterprise* of 1927 had left Vancouver laden with grain, lumber and general cargo, and also passengers, bound south for the Panama Canal and Manchester when, on 9 September 1949, she went ashore in fog and became a total loss on Wash Rock, one mile off Rock Beach, near Point Arena, California.

The burnt out *Monarch of Bermuda,* afterwards rebuilt as the emigrant ship *New Australia.* *(The Scotsman)*

Houlder Brothers

To replace lost tonnage, the Houlder Brothers companies purchased a mixed selection of four Liberty, five Empire and three Fort class ships for Houlder Line, British Empire and Empire Transport. As mentioned earlier, two of the Fort class ships had to be registered under the Canadian flag for political reasons and hence they carried Houlder names under the ownership of Furness (Canada) Ltd. One of the two British Empire ships was the tanker *Empire Coral* which was renamed *Derwent River*.

The poor state of the South American trade can be gauged from the length of time some of the war built tonnage was retained, the last (*Elstree Grange*) not being sold until 1960. Changed economic and political consideration were making themselves felt. Since an Argentine Delegation to the United Kingdom in 1932 had placed demands on the table for participation in the carriage of meat exports from their country, matters had developed with the centralised buying of meat by a Government Ministry during World War II replacing

Royston Grange.

the operations of private trading firms. The nationalistic mood in Argentina and the Peronist government was to see shipping of frozen meat steadily diverted to Argentinian flag tonnage, whilst negotiations on prices at Governmental levels were to see shipments of meat cease for long periods.

Newbuildings for Houlder Brothers' companies were undertaken on only a limited scale, three of the nine ships built between 1946 and 1960 being tankers (*Clutha River, Imperial Transport* and *Denby Grange*), and only two were refrigerated ships (*Duquesa* and *Royston Grange*), the remaining four being general cargo vessels.

Name	Built	GRT	Name	Built	GRT
British Empire S N Co Ltd			Houlder Line Ltd		
CLUTHA RIVER	1952	12323	HORNBY GRANGE	1946	10785
			OSWESTRY GRANGE	1952	9406
Empire Transport Co Ltd			THORPE GRANGE	1954	8695
IMPERIAL TRANSPORT	1953	11365	DENBY GRANGE	1958	12576
			ROYSTON GRANGE	1959	10262
joint British Empire SN Co Ltd/Empire Transport Co Ltd					
SWAN RIVER	1959	9637			
Furness-Houlder Argentine Lines Ltd					
DUQUESA	1949	11007			

Ore Carriers Ltd

The formation of Ore Carriers Ltd stemmed from a chance meeting on the dockside at Port Talbot between John Houlder, Julian Spode (in charge of the British Iron and Steel Corporation shipping interests) and BISCO's ore buying director. *Star of Egypt,* an elderly multi-deck general cargo vessel, was unloading a bulk cargo of iron ore for the nearby steelworks. The three watched the grabs at work, at times tearing fittings out of the ship. The delays concomitant with the use of such unsuitable vessels led to a discussion about the possibility of building purpose designed bulk ore carriers.

In Houlder Brothers' London office, the design team soon produced the outline of what would become a large and successful class of bulk carriers with a deadweight of 9,000 tons. They had no 'tween decks, clear decks and wide hatches to enable shore discharging facilities to achieve fast rates of discharge and they also had the engine room and bridge placed aft—the first British ships of that size with this layout. The design at first brought adverse reaction, such as the Port Talbot pilots' dismay and demands for the bridge to be moved back to the normal forward pivotal point or at least to have a second docking bridge there for their use. This was resisted and in use the bridge-aft configuration was found to work well, although when *Orelia* went on trials there was a most embarrassing incident which could have rekindled the demands. Returning to the Tyne from trials she ploughed through a wooden jetty, virtually demolishing it. On investigation it was found that an unshielded mast-head light had blinded the officers on the bridge who had failed to see the jetty. The jetty was, in fact, waiting to be demolished so what could have proved to be an expensive claim finished as merely an embarrassment.

Orelia at Port Talbot.

Name	Built	GRT	Name	Built	GRT
ORELIA	1954	6858	OREPTON	1955	6859
OREOSA	1954	6856	OREMINA	1956	6858
OREDIAN	1955	6859	JOYA MCCANCE	1960	11871
OREGIS	1955	6858	MABEL WARWICK	1960	11632

Houlder Brothers and British Iron and Steel Corporation formed Ore Carriers Ltd as a joint venture and six of the new bulkers were ordered, to be placed on long term charter to British Steel. Escalation clauses were written into both the building and charter contracts, the first time this had ever been done. Despite initial objections on the basis that such clauses had never been seen before, they were retained and proved a great benefit over the years. Another six ships of similar design were ordered by Denholms, the traditional source of charter tonnage for British Steel.

Modern bulk cargo handling. *Sagamore* at Newcastle. *(Turners (Photography) Ltd)*

Houlders and Denholms were not the only partners of the British Iron and Steel Corporation in building their fleet of bulk carriers registered to jointly owned companies. J and J Denholm Ltd, Glasgow managed Scottish Ore Carriers Ltd and St Andrews Shipping Company Ltd whilst W A Souter and Company Ltd, Newcastle had the Bamburgh Shipping Company Ltd.

The trade for which the ore carriers were built was one way only, the import of iron ore. Rather than return to the loading ports in ballast, it was policy for the ships to take coal charters out. Coal exports at the time exceeded iron ore imports so it proved possible to finance the ships from outward earnings and treat the ore cargo homeward as a ballast run at cheaper freight rates. The design proved to be a handy and efficient one; the ships' quick discharge invariably earned bonus payments from charterers and they were always in demand.

Following the success of the 9,000 ton design, consultants suggested to British Iron and Steel Corporation that larger 18,000 ton deadweight ore carriers would prove even more economic. Many of these were built including two, *Joya McCance* and *Mabel Warwick* delivered in 1960, for the fleet of Ore Carriers Ltd, with charters to British Iron and Steel. In the event, the larger ships never proved such a success as their earlier, smaller sisters.

On completion of the charters, four of the ships were sold, leaving *Oregis* and *Oremina* of the original fleet. *Oregis* was transferred in 1973 to Comex-Houlder Ltd and was sent for conversion into an oil rig support and pipe laying vessel, later becoming a member of the fleet of Houlder Offshore Ltd. Initial plans for *Oremina* to be similarly converted were never implemented and she passed to the associated Vallum Shipping Company until sold in 1974.

As will be seen later, Ore Carriers bought the tanker *Beauval*, building in Norway, and later gave her the name *Joya McCance*. Then, in 1968, they commissioned *Orotava* to replace the smaller ships nearing the end of their careers. She was soon placed in the Seabridge Consortium as *Orotava Bridge*, being joined in 1972 by *Orenda Bridge*.

Finally Furness Withy sold their interest in Ore Carriers to British Steel Corporation and withdrew from the management in 1978.

Warwick Tanker Company Ltd

In 1960, two tankers were commissioned for the newly formed Warwick Tanker Company Ltd. British Petroleum were seeking finance for their newbuilding programme and one method employed was to float jointly owned companies such as Warwick Tanker. Two British Petroleum contracts for steam turbine tankers of about 36,000 tons deadweight, with Cammell, Laird and Company and R and W Hawthorn, Leslie and Company, were transferred to the new company and completed as *Bidford Priory* and *Brandon Priory* respectively.

Name	Built	GRT
BIDFORD PRIORY	1960	23065
BRANDON PRIORY	1960	23108

The funnel markings adopted gave a clear indication of the joint ownership, with the British Petroleum shield superimposed on Houlder's Maltese Cross.

Both ships were destined to spend all their lives in the ownership of Warwick Tanker, on charter to British Petroleum. Both were sold in 1975 for breaking up rather than further trading. Being steam powered, the market downturn following the Yom Kippur War between Israel and her Arab neighbours saw interest in such vessels much reduced.

Brandon Priory off Algeria, 28 September 1960.

8. Changing With the World — 1960 to 1980

As a new decade dawned, clouds of change filled the horizon, and although they were obvious to many observers, few could anticipate the changes the coming years would bring to Furness Withy and to British shipping in general.

The changing pattern of world trade was to see the next decade marked by the steady disposal of surplus units from the fleet as well as the sale of those at the end of their economic life.

The influences behind these changes were many and varied, but most were beyond the control of the directors who could only try and anticipate them and then respond in a manner calculated to protect company business and the futures of both shareholders and employees.

Despite world wars, and smaller conflicts and tensions, the 20th century had had relatively stable trade patterns with the world divided into areas of influence. British shipping lines served the Empire, and later the Commonwealth; French, Spanish, Portuguese and Italian lines their colonial possessions. Whilst there were cross traders, and countries such as Norway with extensive fleets, the spheres of influence were clear to those responsible for arranging the movement of export shipments. For instance British goods sold to traders in the Portuguese colonies would invariably be forwarded to Lisbon for transhipment, rather than being shipped direct. This pattern of influence and trade was now in the process of rapid dissolution. The independence movement, which brought the changes, could be gauged by the growing membership of the United Nations. Fifty nations signed the charter in 1945, membership passed the hundred mark in 1961 and continued to grow to 135 in 1974 and 157 nations a decade later.

Many of these new countries instituted steps to direct the flow of foreign trade into the holds of their own ships, enacted cabotage laws to limit coastal trade to their own nationals and eroded the business of British owners who had previously served those trades. At the same time, the post-war development of air travel hit passenger liner trades, especially following the introduction of large jet transports able to compete over long distances. In a different manner, the rapid growth of bulk carriers and container ship fleets was to have a major influence on the shape of companies in the years to come. The development of these ships was, in part, a reaction to the growing labour costs and discipline problems being met within major ports round the world, thus making it increasingly difficult, if not impossible, to operate a scheduled service with any certainty. As these specialist ships entered service many of the traditional breakbulk ships displaced were sold to "third world" and flag of convenience operators, and with considerable service life remaining were employed with cheap crews to compete with the remaining British tramp owners.

The 1960's were to witness Furness Withy undertaking a series of cost saving exercises, reluctantly cutting back where necessary in traditional trades but developing in several new directions with the future in mind, especially in the gas, container and offshore fields. The 1960's were to be followed by a decade of searching for the size and strength to face the future, and seeking a suitable partner for expansion. This seeking was to end in 1980 with the agreed take-over bid from C Y Tung, Hong Kong.

The confrontation between Israel and the Arab world was to continue to have a major effect on world shipping. In June 1967, the Suez Canal closed for the second time due to the fighting which erupted between Israel and Egypt. It was to remain out of use for the next eight years until reopening in 1975. During that period all traffic had to be routed via The Cape or transpacific through the Panama Canal. The extra time and distance involved was reflected in the number of ships employed and freight rates charged.

Another event, again in the Middle East, was to provide a short term financial windfall, although in the longer term it was as detrimental to the Group as it was to other shipowners. Following the Yom Kippur war between Israel and her Arab neighbours in October 1973, the Arab oil producing countries both increased the price of oil and used supply restrictions as an economic weapon against countries sympathetic to Israel. The fourfold increase in fuel oil prices hit shipowners hard and liner conferences had to add a fuel surcharge to their freight rates. Like all liner operators, the Group companies collected this surcharge, although they had signed new fixed price agreements with their bunker suppliers shortly before. Whilst the contract ran, the surcharge was a windfall lasting until subsequent fuel contracts reflected the greatly enhanced current prices.

Shipping Problems of the Decade

The companies faced a variety of problems, many of them small but between them causing considerable strain. The North Pacific service, for example, faced growing labour costs in North American ports. In a bid to overcome these, a team was set up by Furness Withy in the U K to organise planned stowage of cargo for these ports, thereby avoiding the expensive multiple movement of cargo to release that which was destined for the port at which the ship lay. Although the team was successful in achieving its aims, it only contained and controlled the problem of costs for a while, it did not defeat it. The costs continued to rise inexorably and ultimately the viability of the service as a whole had to be considered. In 1963 the decision was was also taken to rationalise the service with other owners and the resulting co-ordination enabled Furness Withy to withdraw two of its ships.

The Mediterranean posed its own problems. The Arab/Israeli conflict which started with the 1948 independence of Israel as a Jewish state, spawned the Arab Boycott of Israel. Any ship calling at an Israeli port was blacklisted and refused entry to Arab ports. Consequently, Prince Line and other owners serving the Levant had to operate two services, one to Arab destinations and the other to Israel and non-Arab countries: two sets of ships when one would have sufficed.

On the South American routes, there were fluctuations in the volume of frozen and chilled meat available for shipment from the River Plate and these made the scheduling of Royal Mail Lines and Houlder Brothers ships a nightmare. Following the severe drought of 1962, there was a dramatic contraction in shipments, the 1964 tonnage being only a third of the previous year. Fortunately the needs of the Antipodean trade of Shaw, Savill and Albion enabled *Drina* and *Durango* to be transferred there as the three passenger liners were able to handle most of the available cargo with their refrigerated cargo capacity. A few years later, in December 1967, the United Kingdom foot and mouth disease epidemic saw a complete ban on the importation of meat. This ban was not lifted until April 1968. Consequent on this, the three "Graces", *Amazon*, *Aragon* and *Arlanza* were transferred to Shaw Savill and Albion and renamed *Akaroa*, *Aranda* and *Arawa*.

Labour problems continued to rear their ugly head in many of the ports served. To these was added, in May 1966, a strike of British seamen which lasted for 47 days. By the end of the strike, nearly two-thirds of the Furness Withy fleet of 93 ships were immobilised and it was later estimated that the stoppage cost the Group £1.3 million.

The Group Structure

Until the 1960's, the size of the various fleets and their related services had allowed many of the companies to retain an autonomous status within the Group with dedicated offices caring for various duties. This had led to one definition of the Group being "a loose confederation of warring tribes", each with staff loyalties to the individual company rather than to the Group as a whole.

This structure, acceptable as it had been in the past, was obviously one that needed now in the 1960's to be rationalised in the light both of costs and the services required. The next two decades were to witness a continuing review of the Group structure which would undergo several administrative re-organisations. To the uninformed observer it presented a confusing picture as publicly the traditional route identities (Prince Line, Cairn Line, Royal Mail Lines, etc) were retained. But increasingly ships were registered in the names of companies which had no association with the service on which they were employed, or in the name of finance houses, and also, they were transferred between Group companies for financial, tax and other reasons. Typical were to be the Cairn Line mini bulk carriers registered as owned by Shaw Savill and Albion.

This fusion of identities can best be illustrated by *Derwent*, an SD14 type general cargo ship completed in 1979 for the joint Royal Mail/Houlder/Blue Star/Lamport and Holt service to South America (British Lines Joint Service to South America). One observer suggested that she was a mystery never intended to be solved. The order was placed by Houlder Brothers, who managed her although she was registered as owned by Shaw Savill and Albion Ltd and Welldeck Shipping Company Ltd (the name since 1966 of British Empire Steam Navigation Company Ltd). She carried a Royal Mail "River" name and buff funnel. Manned by Houlder Line sea staff, her Houlder black hull was, initially, matched to Shaw Savill upperworks (later changed to Houlder colours). In 1981 her ownership was transferred to Dee Navigation Ltd (the name since 1975 of Empire Transport Company Ltd) with joint Shaw Savill and Albion and Houlder Brothers management until she was sold in 1982 to become *Mountain Azalea*.

The decision was taken in 1963 to commence a simplification of the Group shareholding structure, by removing the cross holdings between various Furness Withy and Houlder Brothers subsidiaries, apart from the newly formed Furness-Houlder (Insurance) Ltd. A further programme was commenced to acquire the minority holdings in various of the companies, beginning in 1964 with British Maritime Trust Ltd, Prince Line Ltd and Fescol Ltd.

The major interest acquired at this time was undoubtedly the take-over, in the summer of 1965, of Royal Mail Lines Ltd which had, in recent years, been going through a period of poor trade. To finance this acquisition, the Furness Withy capital was increased from £11.5 million to £15 million. Although it was

Chairmen of Furness Withy: Frank Charlton, Sir Errington Keville and John A MacConochie.

anticipated that the Royal Mail refrigerated meat trade would continue to decline, the nature of the Royal Mail business and fleet presented real opportunities of rationalisation with Pacific Steam and Shaw Savill and Albion. These were realised with the transfer of routes and ships between the companies, as well as in the management restructuring.

Also in 1965 a further step in this rationalisation was seen in the appearance of Furness Ship Management Ltd to integrate under one management the ships and trades of Furness, Withy and Company, Ltd, Johnston Warren Ltd, the Pacific Steam Navigation Company, Prince Line Ltd and Royal Mail Lines Ltd. Better employment of the combined fleet was the immediate prize with, for instance, Houlder Brothers absorbing the Royal Mail offices in Buenos Aires and Montevideo; there was also a streamlining of the agency arrangements on the North Pacific services. Shaw, Savill and Albion, Houlder Brothers and Manchester Liners retained their autonomy.

With Sir Errington Keville, CBE, as chairman and Mr G N A Murrant as vice-chairman and managing director of Furness Ship Management, the Passenger, Freight, Superintendent's, Provedore, Personnel, Catering and other departments were merged, not only in London but also elsewhere in the United Kingdom and abroad.

Further purchases in 1965 included the minority holdings in Furness-Houlder Argentine Lines Ltd and Welldeck Shipping Company Ltd (previously British Empire Steam Navigation Company Ltd). Furness Withy did not hold a controlling shareholding in all the companies which were brought into subsidiary status, for example only 15% was held in the Cairn Line of Steamships Ltd when an offer was made in 1967 for the remaining 85% of the shares, with the aim of integrating all the Furness Withy Group North Atlantic services. The success of the bid effectively marked the end of Cairn Line North Atlantic liner service; henceforth its name and nomenclature would feature in the operation of a fleet of small short sea bulk carriers. The first of these, *Cairnventure* of 2,750 tons deadweight, entered service in 1969 by which time Cairn Line had become a subsidiary of Shaw, Savill and Albion.

Searching for the way forward led to notice being taken of the management seminars being held by Professor Roland Smith, the Joe Hyman Professor of Marketing at the Manchester Institute of Science and Technology. It was felt that these seminars would be of value and it was accordingly arranged for both directors and senior management to attend. Such was the success of the seminars that an invitation was extended to Professor Smith to join the board as a director, a position he held from 1969 until 1980. A change also took place in the structure of the directorate, it being felt that in addition to those directors with a lifetime of experience in company service, there would be value in recruiting non-executive directors from other business disciplines. In addition to Professor Smith, these included figures like Lord Beeching (a director from 1972 to 1975 and chairman between 1973 and 1975) and Sir Richard Clarke KCB OBE after he retired from a distinguished career in the Civil Service (a director 1971 to 1972). However, most of the new non-executive directors were drawn from the merchant banking field and were associated with major shareholdings in Furness Withy. From Kleinwort, Benson Ltd came Robert Henderson in 1968 until he resigned in 1971 on appointment as deputy chairman of the bank. From Rea Brothers in 1971 came S Wainwright who remained until he left to accept the post of managing director of the National Giro in 1977, and Sir James Steel CBE DL JP in 1972. Sir James remained a director, and was also chairman after 1975, until retiring in 1979. The third merchant bank represented on the board was Hambros who nominated a director, John M Clay, and an industrial adviser, Eric B Spencer MC, in 1972. They retained their seats until 1980 and 1976 respectively.

Furness Withy control of Houlder Brothers was achieved in 1968 when the shareholding reached 63%, and in the same year the Prince Line services from Manchester passed to the management of Manchester Liners Ltd. Manchester Liners themselves were not long to retain an associate status because in March 1970 the Furness Withy holding passed the critical 50% to achieve control shortly after the same thing had happened to the Economic Insurance Company Ltd.

With the commencement of the Overseas Containers service, together with pressures to reduce costs and the need to seek alternative sources of revenue, a radical reorganisation at Shaw Savill and Albion became necessary to match the structure to current requirements. In 1972 this was achieved with the creation of four Divisions. The Refrigerated Trades Division dealt with the remaining traditional Shaw Savill services, Crusader, the Royal Mail Brazil and River Plate service, and also refrigerated tramp work. The General Shipping Division was responsible for the Prince Line Mediterranean service, Gulf Container Line, Cairn Line and Furness Ship Management. The Passenger Division embraced not only passenger travel at sea but also the travel agencies such as Furness Travel whilst the Non-Shipping Division included areas such as hotels, insurance and stevedoring.

By the early years of the 1970's, Furness, Withy and Company, Ltd had attained the status of a holding company with the business controlled by specialist divisions. Each division had its own board of directors responsible, and reporting, to the main board. This was a blueprint for continued corporate good health, although such a restructuring was often hard to accept for individual staff members when job security was a paramount consideration and, in many instances, was at risk. "Black Friday", 13 November 1970, was the most obvious realisation of the insecurity many felt.

Progress does not stand still. Early in 1976 it was announced that Pacific Steam Navigation and Shaw Savill and Albion were to form a new General Shipping Division which would build a closer working relationship and seek the tangible benefits such co-operation had to offer. Some months later divisionalisation was announced within Houlder Brothers, with self-explanatory titles, the Bulk Shipping Division and the Offshore Division.

It had taken a decade to move from the loose-knit group of companies, often with duplicate service departments, to a single integrated structure.

Aviation Interests

The Civil Aviation (Licensing) Act, 1960, repealed the restrictions on scheduled services by independent operators which had been laid down in 1949. With this, Airwork Ltd merged in 1960 with Hunting-Clan Air Transport Ltd, and under the new name of British United Airways Ltd made applications for routes and ordered modern jet aircraft.

Although half of the applications were granted, delays built up into years as appeals by the National airline corporations were heard and the British Government negotiated with foreign governments on the planned services. By 1962 it had only been possible for British United Airways to commence services to Amsterdam, Barcelona, Genoa, Palma and Tarbes.

A further merger took place in January 1962; British United Airways joined with British Aviation Services Ltd, owners of Silver City Airways, under the control of a new holding company, Air Holdings Ltd, in which the Furness Withy holding was set at 18%.

In 1965, Blue Star Line was amongst the shareholders who wished to withdraw. Furness Withy decided to restrict its holding to 20% so, following the changes in holdings, British and Commonwealth Shipping Company Ltd emerged as the largest shareholder with 45.9%, Furness Withy and P&O each held 20% and the balance was in the hands of Lord Cowdray and Eagle Star Insurance Company Ltd.

Although a satisfactory profit was returned from the aviation field, the reduction in the percentage size of the Furness Withy holding following the various mergers resulted in a lessening of the control and influence the Furness Withy Board had on this associate company. There was also a continued need for more capital injection to finance the new generation of large jet aircraft—such as the order for fifty Lockheed TriStar 345 seat aircraft placed in 1968. The decision to withdraw from the aviation field was taken, and as a result, in 1971 Furness Withy sold their 20% stake from in Air Holdings Ltd for £1,649,700 to British Air Transport (Holdings) Ltd, a subsidiary of British and Commonwealth Shipping Company Ltd.

In 1970 a further merger had seen Air Holdings Ltd join with Caledonian Airways Ltd which, from 1972, became British Caledonian Airways Ltd and in due course was destined to merge with British Airways.

Travel and Hotels

In 1959, Houlder World Holidays was formed as an inclusive tour operator, Peter Warner being retained to develop the trade until, sadly, his death in Tangier during 1974. Houlder World Holidays was the first British operator to develop tours to the remoter areas of the world such as the Galapagos Islands and the Antarctic and built up a substantial business in the long-range package tour business.

However, in 1974, as there seemed to be no further growth potential in long-range tours, a view subsequently proved to be erroneous, Houlder World Holidays was sold to Kuoni Travel Ltd for a mere £210,000. The sale took place during Lord Beeching's chairmanship and undoubtedly his philosophy of concentrating on core interests and disposing of the peripherals had a bearing on the disposal. The sudden announcement caused consternation at British Overseas Airways who protested at not having been given an opportunity to bid for the company: being the air carriers employed, their interests could be materially affected by new ownership.

In 1973, Furness Travel Ltd had been organised, by a renaming of Aberdeen and Commonwealth Line Ltd, to bring under unified management the various travel agency outlets operated by Group companies. A total of forty three travel agency shops covered the United Kingdom from London to Aberdeen. This placed Furness Travel as one of the top three chains alongside Thomas Cook and Hogg Robinson. Here again a policy decision saw most of these agencies offered for sale in 1980, only three being retained, at Redhill (serving Furness Withy), Weybridge and Filton (both serving British Aerospace offices).

In the late 1960's, it was considered that hotels would constitute a growth area for the coming decade. Hence in 1968 Furness Withy moved into the hotel market, first by buying White Heron Lodge Ltd of Wellington, New Zealand. This New Zealand venture, owned through Shaw Savill, was extended by the purchase of other properties such as the Caravel Motor Hotel, Rotorua, and Waitomo Travel Lodge. Together with the New Zealand stevedoring and travel agency interests of Shaw, Savill and Albion, the hotels were sold in 1984, going to the local Owens Group.

This new development was a reminder of Sir Christopher Furness's ownership of hotels, such as the Grand Hotel, Harrogate, in the early years of the century. Arnold Bennett's novel "The Grand Babylon Hotel", published in 1902, is said to have been built on an incident in Furness's life, when the chief character in the novel purchases an hotel in order to sack the head waiter.

At the same time, in the United Kingdom control of Saxon Inn Motor Hotels Ltd was purchased, with properties at Whitley Bridge and Harlow. The Harlow hotel was extended and further developments undertaken at Huddersfield, Northampton, Blackburn, Peterborough and Gatwick before, in 1983, this venture was also sold.

Other hotel interests owned at this time and later sold were in Kenya and the Seychelles. From the base of Houlder World Holidays, Houlders Brothers launched into hotel ownership in Kenya with The Hotel Sindbad at Malindi in 1969, followed by the new Mahé Beach Hotel in the Seychelles, completed in time to open for business during 1975.

Newbuilding Programme of the 1960's

A review of the types of new ships delivered in the decade gives a good indication of those Furness Withy interests which were in recession and due to be cut out as deadwood, and those which were felt to have growth potential. The only two companies with series deliveries of new traditional tonnage were Manchester Liners and Shaw, Savill and Albion. Most of the orders went to British yards, although a few were placed abroad later in the decade when more specialised tonnage such as cellular container ships and bulk carriers were required for the fleet.

Manchester Liners took delivery of eight ships from Smith's Dock Company Ltd, plus a smaller vessel purchased whilst being built in Spain. The five ships built between 1963 and 1967 were traditional dry cargo ships, but with the introduction of containers, orders were placed for specialist tonnage and *Manchester Challenge* was the first container ship delivered, to be followed by her sisters *Manchester Courage* and *Manchester Concorde*. *Manchester Progress*, the most modern of the conventional fleet, was converted to cellular form in 1971 and renamed *Manchester Concept*. The older *Manchester Miller*, dating from 1959, also underwent this metamorphis, to emerge as the container ship *Manchester Quest*.

Name	Built	GRT	Name	Built	GRT
MANCHESTER COMMERCE	1963	8724	MANCHESTER CHALLENGE	1968	12039
MANCHESTER CITY	1964	8734	MANCHESTER COURAGE	1969	12039
MANCHESTER RENOWN	1964	8742	MANCHESTER CONCORDE	1969	12039
MANCHESTER PORT	1966	8938	MANCHESTER MERITO	1970	3414
MANCHESTER PROGRESS	1967	8176			

The other container ship orders were for *Jervis Bay* and *Botany Bay* for service with Overseas Containers Ltd. *Jervis Bay*, a product of Upper Clyde Shipbuilders, was the only British built member of the OCL fleet, *Botany Bay* coming from the yard of Howaldtswerke-Deutsche Werft in Germany.

Shaw Savill and Albion were the other company with a steady tonnage replacement programme throughout the decade, with the launch of *Northern Star* by H M Queen

The silver salt cellar presented by Queen Elizabeth the Queen Mother to *Northern Star* following her visit to the ship on 31 May 1974.

Elizabeth, the Queen Mother, on 27 June 1961 as the highlight. Built to replace the ageing *Dominion Monarch*, she was intended to operate in partnership with *Southern Cross* on the round-the-world service. The other orders were refrigerated cargo ships to operate on the route from New Zealand to Europe with meat and dairy produce. The favoured builders were Vickers-Armstrongs (Shipbuilders) Ltd for *Northern Star* and *Laurentic*, Swan Hunter and Wigham Richardson for *Megantic* and *Medic* and the Clyde yard of Alex Stephen and Sons for the other four.

Name	Built	GRT	Name	Built	GRT
IBERIC	1961	11248	LAURENTIC	1965	7964
MEGANTIC	1962	12226	ZEALANDIC	1965	7946
NORTHERN STAR	1962	24756	BRITANNIC	1967	12228
MEDIC	1963	12220	MAJESTIC	1967	12227

Two new ships, *Newfoundland* and *Nova Scotia* entered service with the Furness Warren Line. Taking the names of earlier ships, they differed in having no passenger accommodation. They came from Burntisland Shipbuilding Company, as did *Tenbury* for Alexander Shipping, whilst Houlder Brothers went to Hawthorn, Leslie (Shipbuilders) Ltd for *Hardwicke Grange* and *Ocean Transport*. Harland and Wolff Ltd launched *Orcoma* at Belfast for Pacific Steam Navigation service.

Name	Built	GRT	Name	Built	GRT
TENBURY	1965	8252	NEWFOUNDLAND	1964	6906
HARDWICKE GRANGE	1961	10338	NOVA SCOTIA	1965	6906
OCEAN TRANSPORT	1962	8608	ORCOMA	1966	10509

Ocean Transport.

The following list of oil and gas tankers and bulk carriers delivered during the 1960's gives a first indication of the future change in the composition of the fleet. Two of the oil tankers were British built, whilst *Beauval* was purchased whilst under construction in Norway. *Methane Progress* came from Vickers-Armstrongs (Shipbuilders) Ltd, whereas the other two gas tankers were French built. Both bulk carriers were British products.

Name	Built	GRT	Name	Built	GRT
tankers			JOULE	1964	2293
TUDOR PRINCE	1961	12958	CLERK-MAXWELL	1966	8298
ABADESA	1962	13571	HUMBOLDT	1968	5200
BEAUVAL	1964	26535	bulk carriers		
gas tankers			CLYDESDALE	1967	24024
METHANE PROGRESS	1964	21876	OROTAVA	1968	28880

The decade's final group of deliveries, in 1969/1970, were five ships for Cairn and Prince Lines, both now under Shaw, Savill and Albion control. A total of eighteen similar sized small ships of under 1,500gt were ordered during the next decade. Ten were single deckers built abroad, mini bulk carriers for operation with Cairn Line names, the others two-deck general cargo or container ships for Prince Line's Mediterranean services. The first Prince Line ships were British built, by Clelands Shipbuilding Company on the Tyne and by Grangemouth Dockyard Company (*Malvern Prince*), the first Cairn Line ship (*Cairnventure*) came from E J Smit en Zoon in Holland.

Name	Built	GRT	Name	Built	GRT
CAIRNVENTURE	1969	1436	MALVERN PRINCE	1970	1459
CHILTERN PRINCE	1970	1459	MENDIP PRINCE	1970	1459
COTSWOLD PRINCE	1970	1459			

Manchester Liners Ltd

A number of factors were to influence the fortunes of Manchester Liners in the 1960's. Port labour problems resulted in a continued drain on financial resources and the opening of the St Lawrence Seaway in 1959 not only instantly outdated the small Lakers but also opened the route to increased competition.

Fleet modernisation continued to cater for a good traffic flow. At the same under the leadership of R B Stoker, the third generation of the family to serve as chairman, Manchester Liners were laying innovative plans which were to result in the company commissioning the first British fully-cellular container ship on the North Atlantic in 1968—*Manchester Challenge,* capable of carrying 500 TEU, the first container ship to be ordered from British shipbuilders. *Manchester Challenge* was followed by her sisters *Manchester Courage, Manchester Concorde* and *Manchester Crusade.* By 1970 a container ship, owned or chartered, was sailing on the Manchester Liner berth from Manchester every 4.5 days. To handle cargo unsuited to containers, the associated Golden Cross Line operated with chartered conventional break-bulk tonnage.

At a single stroke the North Atlantic shipping scene changed out of all recognition. Whereas in the past several British companies' fleets had operated on the routes to North America, the capital intensive nature of containerisation saw the number of operators diminish rapidly. In Glasgow, Anchor Line withdrew from their joint service with Cunard, leaving Cunard to enter the Atlantic Container Line consortium for which Anchor Line acted as agents. Donaldsons considered the options and decided to liquidate their operation, selling their interests to the Belfast based Head Line, whilst in Bristol the Hill family and their Bristol City Line chose to enter the Dart Line consortium.

Manchester Liners absorbed the Cairn Line North Atlantic interests, and also Prince Line's Mediterranean service (purchasing the Prince Line loading brokers Gough and Crosthwaite) when Prince Line decided to withdraw from Manchester in 1968. Later, in 1975, the Furness Warren Line discontinued its North Atlantic service in the face of competition from container carrying companies. All Furness Withy's North Atlantic interests were now concentrated in Manchester Liners.

"Containerisation" is an all-inclusive operation and Manchester Liners developed into a group of inter-related companies covering not only sea carriage but also ship repair, road haulage, warehousing and engineering to enable it to provide a complete door-to-door service and control all aspects of the business.

Not only did the service have a new image; a new Manchester Liners House was opened at the end of 1969, close to the docks. Appropriately, being a shipping company office, Manchester Liners House was designed with a curved exterior to look like the front of a ship's bridge or accommodation block. The old offices in St Ann's Square had been unable for some time to cope with the increasing staff numbers and this new complex was not only able to accommodate them but also to provide offices for other tenants, including H M Customs.

Manchester Liners new headquarters, opened in 1969.

Maiden voyage of *Manchester Challenge,* loading at Felixstowe for Montreal in 1968. *(Norman Edwards Associates)*

Having pioneered the conversion to containers on the North Atlantic, Manchester Liners were then able to apply their expertise to the Mediterranean service of Prince Line where containers were introduced by the British lines in 1971.

Ever since the formation of Manchester Liners, a substantial minority shareholding had been held by Furness Withy. During 1970 Furness Withy made a bid for control and raised their holding from 42% to 56%, making Manchester Liners a subsidiary. This holding was raised to 61.6% in 1974, at which time Eurocanadian Shipholdings Ltd, operators of the Cast bulk/container service, made their bid to take over and integrate the two operations.

Royal Mail Lines Ltd and Pacific Steam Navigation Company

In 1965, Furness Withy successfully bid for the remainder of the share capital of Royal Mail Lines Ltd, which consequently became a subsidiary together with Pacific Steam Navigation Company, itself controlled by Royal Mail since 1939.

Furness Withy had long held a minority shareholding in Royal Mail Lines which had been formed in 1932 to take over the assets of the Royal Mail Steam Packet Company Ltd, RMSP Meat Transports Ltd, Nelson Steam Navigation Company Ltd and David MacIver and Company Ltd following the Kylsant Crash. The £4 million capital in Royal Mail Lines had, in 1932, been largely (£2.9 million) in the hands of the Treasury and other secured creditors who had made loans for shipbuilding under the Trade Facilities Acts. Only £1 million of shares remained with RMSP Realisation Company, the liquidation vehicle, and it was these shares which had been purchased by Lord Essendon on behalf of Furness Withy in 1937.

Pacific Steam Navigation, also previously a member of the Kylsant group of companies, remained under the control of the liquidators until 1939 when it was sold to Royal Mail Lines and thereafter became a wholly owned subsidiary, albeit operating as an independent company based in Liverpool.

With the take-over in 1965, Furness Withy added a further 39 ships to the Group fleet (Royal Mail 22, PSNC 17). Pride of place was held by the liner *Andes,* completed in 1939 and scheduled to commence her first voyage on the 100th anniversary of the granting, by Queen Victoria, of a Royal Charter to the Royal Mail Steam Packet Company. The outbreak of war frustrated these plans, she was taken up as a trooper and was not to sail on her intended service until after the war ended. Replaced on the route to South America by the three "Graces", *Andes* commenced a new role as a cruise liner in 1960. In this she proved very popular, to the extent of one lady, a regular passenger, proposed to take up full time residence on board. This was almost agreed, but the vessel was sold before the lady could sign the contract.

Both Royal Mail and Pacific Steam had rebuilt their fleets after heavy World War II losses, but by 1965 many of these were proving ill-suited to the trade, being traditional multi-deck general cargo ships. The Royal Mail service between Britain and the River Plate was suffering as a result of the diversion of trade to the Argentinian national carrier, Empresa Lineas Maritimas Argentinas (ELMA). The company's decision to replace their ageing passenger tonnage with the three "Graces", in 1959/1960, was seen in retrospect to have been a poor one as they were to be rapidly outmoded by changing travel patterns based on air transport.

The Royal Mail fleet included *Amazon, Thessaly* and *Loch Loyal*.

Whilst the Pacific Steam fleet was numerically as large as it had been since the end of war in 1945, Royal Mail was feeling the changed economic climate with national fleets taking traffic which had hitherto been handled by British and European companies. A decade earlier Royal Mail had operated a fleet of between 30 and 35 ships, now the remaining fleet of 22 vessels was to suffer continued attrition. In 1965 this was foreseen and a policy decision made not to replace the ships as they came to the end of their economic lives. By 1973 only one of the ships in the Royal Mail fleet at the time of the take-over was still in service with the Group.

Name	Built	GRT	Name	Built	GRT
Royal Mail Lines Ltd			Pacific Steam Navigation Company		
ANDES	1939	26435	SARMIENTO	1943	8346
DESEADO	1942	9630	SALAVERRY	1947	8590
DARRO	1943	9732	SANTANDER	1946	8550
DRINA	1944	9785	SALINAS	1947	8610
DURANGO	1944	9801	SALAMANCA	1948	8610
LOCH AVON	1947	8617	FLAMENCO	1950	8491
LOCH GARTH	1947	8617	KENUTA	1950	8494
EBRO	1952	7785	CUZCO	1951	8038
ESSEQUIBO	1952	7785	COTOPAXI	1954	8559
LOCH GOWAN	1954	9718	PIZARRO	1955	8564
ESCALANTE	1955	7791	POTOSI	1955	8564
EDEN	1956	7791	REINA DEL MAR	1956	21501
TUSCANY	1956	7455	CIENFUEGOS	1959	5407
ALBANY	1957	7299	ELEUTHERA	1959	5407
LOCH LOYAL	1957	11035	SOMERS ISLE	1959	5684
PICARDY	1957	7306	WILLIAM WHEELWRIGHT	1960	31320
THESSALY	1957	7299	GEORGE PEACOCK	1961	18863
YACARE	1959	1344			
YAGUARETE	1959	1344			
AMAZON	1959	20368			
ARAGON	1960	20362			
ARLANZA	1960	20362			

Houlder Brothers

The changing role of the Houlder Group in the post-war period was, to a considerable degree, the result of the skills of John Houlder. An engineer, he had served his apprenticeship with Cox and Company, the Falmouth ship repairers. A period in the office of H Clarkson and Company, the London based shipbrokers, and war service followed before he joined the family business, Houlder Brothers. In 1954 he went on to join the Furness Withy board and became the longest serving director before retiring in 1989.

His engineering training helped in the formation of Ore Carriers Ltd, and especially in the ventures into the new fields of gas tankers and offshore oil. In the carriage of gas at sea he was an early experimenter with containment systems, developing a frozen heavy oil system (although this was not in fact adopted for the Ocean Gas Transport fleet).

All the companies which went to form Furness Withy (Engineering) Ltd came from the Houlder interests. With the acquisition of Compugraphics International in 1971, the Group moved into new technology with all its potential for future growth. The Furness Withy Board had confidence in John Houlder's technical ability, as is illustrated by the Board minute relating to the ordering of the craft that was to became *Uncle John*. It is brief and to the point: "A submission by Mr J Houlder was approved".

Although the gas interests were to suffer periods of financial crisis they were, in due course, to become an integral part of the Furness Withy Group of today, whereas other areas such as insurance and the leisure industry were to be amalgamated with like interests elsewhere in the Furness Withy Group and, following changes in policy, later to be sold. For a good many years to come, Houlders Brothers' shipping fleet was to be the bulk cargo division of the Furness Withy Group.

Houlder Brothers' annual reports were always interesting as they contained reminders that the company had a number of interests which had little or no obvious connection with the main core business. One of these dated from the early days when Houlders were involved in the Australian trade. Although the Houlder shipping interests had been sold soon after the Furness Withy association commenced, ownership of the Bowen Meat Works was retained until it was sold during the Depression of the 1930's. These works, and also those at Gladstone and Hughenden, were owned by Bergl Australia Ltd, in which Houlder Brothers held a large interest. During 1917, Bergl acquired the lease of Longton Station in Queensland, a 230 mile drive south west of Townsville. When, a few years later, the Oxenhope property was added it resulted in a 1,100 square mile cattle station with a herd of 12-14,000 cattle supplying the Bowen Meat Works, as also did another cattle station of 365 square miles at Pandanus Creek. When the leases came up for renewal in 1963 the Pandanus Creek lease was surrendered but that on Longton was renewed and a programme of improvements was put in hand. By 1968, only the Longton Station and the smaller Riverside Station (of some 10 square miles) near Townsville remained. The Meat Works and the shipping office at Bowen were but memories. In London the decision was made to sell the company, now Bergl Australia (London) Ltd, and thus in due course this interesting venture into stockbreeding ended.

Avogadro, first of the gas tanker fleet.
(Skyfotos)

Ocean Gas Transport Ltd

What was to become a major interest for Furness Withy owed its birth to the Warwick Tanker joint venture between Houlder Brothers and British Petroleum, and a conversation during a train journey between John Houlder and Eric Drake of British Petroleum. The conversation turned to the disposal of gas in the Middle East oilfields, much of which was flared off and burnt.

With his technical background, Houlder was convinced that this waste gas could be saved and marketed, so on his return home experiments in the carriage and storage of liquid petroleum gas were commenced at Elstree Aerodrome. At the same time the results of Rene Boudet's experiments in France were examined. These had reached the stage where a converted railway wagon had been mounted on a barge in Trieste harbour.

Boudet was building an international gas marketing and distribution business, Gazocean, and it was agreed between him and Houlder Brothers to incorporate Ocean Gas Transport Ltd as a joint venture to build and operate liquid petroleum gas tankers for charter to Gazocean.

The first ship of the new fleet was the small *Avogadro* bought in 1964, whose primary task was to train the crews in gas handling before the larger ships entered service. In this she was eminently successful and she remained in service until sold in 1970.

Not all the ships which were built were registered in the name of Ocean Gas Transport, several having been financed with borrowed capital and these were registered, for security reasons, as owned by companies

Name	Built	Acquired	GRT		Name	Built	Acquirerd	GRT
AVOGADRO	1962	1964	855		CAVENDISH	1971	--	26802
JOULE	1964	--	2293		JOULE	1965	1973	8666
CLERK-MAXWELL	1966	--	8298		NICOLE	1967	1977	2592
HUMBOLDT	1968	--	5200		LORD KELVIN	1978	--	21374
FARADAY	1970	--	19754					

controlled by the financiers. *Clerk-Maxwell* and *Faraday* were registered in the name of Nile Steamship Company Ltd and *Joule* (ex *Havgas*) in the joint names of Morgan Grenfell and Company Ltd and Midland Montagu Leasing Ltd. For her short time under Houlder management, *Nicole* was owned by Gladstone Steamship Company Ltd, Bermuda.

Methane Tankers

The interest in, and experience with, the carriage and storage of liquid gas led to an approach from British Gas to Houlder Brothers and the creation of a joint venture to design and build *Methane Progress*. Full ownership of Methane Tanker Finance Ltd passed to British Gas in 1979 when they purchased Houlder Brothers holding.

Name	Built	GRT
METHANE PROGRESS	1964	21876

Overseas Containers Ltd

In April 1965 four leading British shipping companies announced the formation of Overseas Containers Ltd (OCL). This momentous step forward can be traced to an initiative taken by Donald Anderson, John Nicholson, Nicholas Cayzer and Errington Keville, the chairmen of P&O, Alfred Holt and Company, British and Commonwealth Shipping Company, and Furness, Withy and Company. In retrospect it is clear that this decision was possibly the most outstandingly successful taken in the post-war period, and was made by the main Furness Withy Board rather than the Shaw Savill management who were reluctant to surrender their independence and "went protesting to the altar".

The capital intensive nature of containerisation, relating not only to ships but also port facilities, containers and the associated land haulage and handling involved in this intermodal door-to-door concept led the partners to decide that a consortium was the most practicable mode of operation. They prepared a joint study and floated the new venture with an initial shareholding of 25% each. This holding was to be rearranged from time to time to reflect each partner's contribution to the consortium as trades were progressively transferred and absorbed by Overseas Containers Ltd.

Other British operators in the Australian trade soon followed suit, Blue Star Line Ltd, Port Line Ltd and Ellerman Lines Ltd establishing Associated Container Transportation Ltd.

The plans called for an investment of £45 million. Six 26,000gt containerships, each capable of carrying 1,500TEU (TEU = Twenty Foot Equivalent Unit, i.e. a 20ft container built to internationally agreed standards), were ordered early in 1967, five from German yards and the sixth (*Jervis Bay*) from Scottish based Upper Clyde Shipbuilders Ltd. Whilst construction proceeded, terminals were established in the ports to be served together with inland container depots. To gain experience trial shipments commenced with containers being carried on board the partners' general cargo ships. In 1967 two conventional cargo ships, *Delphic* and *Devon*, were transferred to Overseas Containers Ltd, from Shaw, Savill and Albion and Federal Steam Navigation Company respectively.

On 5 March 1969 the first OCL containership, *Encounter Bay*, sailed from Rotterdam, bound for Australia. As her sisters were delivered they helped build up the new service, the last of the six, *Jervis Bay*, being commissioned in May 1970. The Furness Withy contribution to the consortium consisted largely of the Shaw

Botany Bay on her maiden voyage.

155

Savill and Albion routes to Australia and appropriately the name **Jervis Bay** was allocated to the ownership of that company whilst Furness Withy themselves had **Botany Bay**.

It was intended that Tilbury would be the British port of call for the new container ships, but the port workers' unions banned the handling of the ships there and containers consequently had to be discharged at Rotterdam for forwarding to British destinations. It was to be May 1970, fourteen months after **Encounter Bay** inaugurated the service, before these problems were overcome and the first ship was able to discharge in the United Kingdom.

Name	Built	GRT	TEU
Furness, Withy & Co Ltd			
BOTANY BAY	1969	26876	1572
Shaw, Savill & Albion Co Ltd			
JERVIS BAY	1970	26876	1572

Even before the first containership entered service, plans were well advanced to extend the web of container routes, the first of these being the services from Australia to Japan and the Far East. Two ships were ordered at the end of 1968 for Australia Japan Container Line which commenced operations in September 1970. The Europe to Far East and Europe to New Zealand services followed, although containerisation of the New Zealand trade had to be postponed in 1971 due to escalating costs. The first ship for the New Zealand route, too far advanced to cancel, came into service as **Remuera** under P&O ownership; later she was renamed **Remuera Bay** after the New Zealand trade was finally containerised in 1977. Her sister, being built for Shaw Savill and Albion, was cancelled.

Through the decade prior to the compulsory purchase by the other three partners of the Furness Withy stake, Overseas Containers continued the expansion programme, with a skein of routes covering much of the globe, reaching South Africa, the Gulf and other areas except for South America.

In June 1980, following the acquisition of Furness Withy by the Tung Group, the three other partners exercised their option to buy the Furness Withy holding in Overseas Containers, and with it the two ships. In their view the competition which already existed between Overseas Containers and the Tung container interests (Orient Overseas Container Line) precluded the continued involvement of Furness Withy.

Expansion continued at Overseas Containers, and the rising fuel costs of the ships was countered by adjustment to service speeds and by a re-engining programme, which removed the fuel hungry steam turbine plants in favour of diesel alternatives. The most important subsequent development came in May 1986 when it was announced that P&O had acquired the interests of the other two partners, Ocean Transport and Trading and British and Commonwealth Shipping. The new status of OCL as a fully owned P&O company was further recognised early in 1987 when the name was changed to P&O Containers Ltd.

The Bulk Trades

Although Furness Withy had, in the early years of the 20th century, been heavily committed to bulk trades, the company acquisitions that followed resulted in near total commitment to liner services. The association with bulk trades did not however entirely disappear whilst in 1928 the appearance of **Caroni River** reintroduced tanker tonnage to the Group (the Prince Line tankers having all been sold a decade previously).

The formation, under Houlder Brothers management, of Ore Carriers Ltd and Warwick Tankers Ltd, in partnership with British Steel and British Petroleum respectively, strengthened this interest in bulk carriers and as the liner trades contracted after 1960, the list of newbuildings showed an increase both in the number and size of both dry and liquid bulk carriers.

By 1965, apart from the ships of Ore Carriers Ltd and Warwick Tanker Company Ltd, another two ore carriers and six tankers were owned. In addition there was the Group venture into bulk gas carriage with Ocean Gas Transport Company Ltd. Most of the ships in the bulk fleet, oil, dry and gas, were under long term charter rather than operating on the spot market.

The formation of the Seabridge consortium added momentum to the development of the dry bulk carrier fleet, whilst in 1969 the tanker **Abadesa** was converted in Norway to become a parcels tanker and chartered to Stolt-Nielsens Rederi A/S, Haugesund. Renamed **Stolt Abadesa**, she was joined by three other of the Furness Withy tanker fleet, **Stuart Prince**, **Tudor Prince** and **Denby Grange** which were renamed **Stolt Stuart**, **Stolt Tudor** and **Stolt Grange** respectively. In 1973 all four were sold to Stolt-Nielsens.

Seabridge Shipping Ltd

In 1968, the Furness Withy Group joined the Seabridge Consortium of British bulk carrier owners. Seabridge had been set up to bring together the fleets of member companies and employ them, with the economies of scale, in undertaking major contracts for the carriage of bulk cargo.

The consortium also included Bibby Line Ltd, Britain Steamship Company Ltd (taken over by Bibby in 1968), H Clarkson and Company Ltd, Silver Line Ltd, Bowring Steamship Company Ltd and Hunting and Son Ltd.

Furness Withy initially contributed the bulk carriers *Clydesdale* and *Orotava*. *Clydesdale* had been built for a partnership of Hadley Shipping, Houlder Line and Empire Transport, whilst *Orotava* was owned by Ore Carriers Ltd. They were renamed *Clyde Bridge* and *Orotava Bridge*.

Three further orders were placed for ships to be chartered to Seabridge, the combination (oil/bulk/ore) carrier *Furness Bridge,* bulk carrier *Orenda Bridge* and bulk/ore carrier *Winsford Bridge,* owned by Furness, Withy and Company, Ltd, Ore Carriers Ltd and Pacific Maritime Services Ltd respectively. Pacific Maritime Services was a subsidiary of the Pacific Steam Navigation Company. *Winsford Bridge* never in fact entered service either with Seabridge or under that name, because when Furness Withy withdrew from the consortium, she was still under construction. Chartered to Australian National Line she was completed and entered service as *Mount Newman*.

Name	Built	GRT	Name	Built	GRT
CLYDE BRIDGE	1967	24024	ORENDA BRIDGE	1972	69824
OROTAVA BRIDGE	1968	28880	Winsford Bridge	1973	65131
FURNESS BRIDGE	1971	91079	completed as MOUNT NEWMAN		

Furness Bridge was the first of six sisters built by Swan Hunter Shipbuilders Ltd at Haverton Hill on the Tyne, the last of which, *Liverpool Bridge,* was to gain notoriety later as Bibby Line's *Derbyshire* which went missing during heavy weather in 1980. A continuing campaign has since been conducted not only for compensation to be paid to dependents of the crew but also to have the loss blamed on design faults, rather than the weather, and for those responsible for any design weaknesses to be identified.

Although the concept behind Seabridge was sound, circumstances were to give the consortium a rough ride over the years. On several occasions their ships were committed to long term at low charter rates whilst both freight rates and costs were rising but the major factor that led to the end of the consortium was the October 1973 Yom Kippur War between Israel and her Arab neighbours. The freight market, which had been rising, relapsed into a long period of recession whilst the actions of Arab oil producers in controlling oil supplies for political reasons and then enforcing price rises led to heavy increases in bunker costs. At the time Seabridge were not only operating the members' ships, they also had a number of ships chartered-in which were increasingly failing to show a profit on their operation.

Furness Withy decided the course of wisdom was to resign from the consortium, gave the necessary three years' notice and at the beginning of 1977 withdrew. The ships concerned were either sold or retained under direct company control.

Trinidad

The 1960's were to see an upsurge of activity for the Furness Withy interests in Trinidad. In 1960 Furness Engineering (Trinidad) Ltd was formed to consolidate the ship repair interests, and a new office and showroom was planned in Port of Spain (occupied in 1963) whilst the following year Furness Withy were given the management of two ships being built by Canada as a gift to the Federal Government of the West Indies. Delivered in 1961 as *Federal Maple* and *Federal Palm* the two ships operated a regular service between the Federated islands and although the Federation was dissolved the following year, the ships continued to serve their intended route.

The tug *Maraval,* built for the Trinidad repair yard. *(R L Knight Ltd)*

When reports started to circulate that the United States Navy was planning to vacate part of the naval base at Chaguaramas and release it to the Government of Trinidad and Tobago, keen interest was taken by Furness Withy. The site to be released included two substantial deep water piers plus buildings and had previously been employed for ship repair. In 1964 a partnership was formed with Smith's Dock Company Ltd, part of the Swan Hunter Group, to lease the facility and, under Smith's Dock management, to undertake marine repairs and the construction of small craft for use in local waters. Furness Engineering (Trinidad) Ltd was absorbed into the new undertaking, Furness-Smiths Dock (Trinidad) Ltd which was formed to lease the yard and became operational in May 1966. A second joint company, Dockyard Investments Ltd, was established to order and own a tug and a floating dock to lift 11,200 tons. These were delivered in 1966, named *Maraval* and *Iere* respectively. Furness Withy also held an interest in Metalock (Trinidad) Ltd which served the needs of the ship repair facility.

The Furness Withy agency and trading interests were consolidated into a new organisation, Furness Trinidad Ltd. With the Government of Trinidad and Tobago promoting a policy of local investment, coupled with taxation legislation to discourage non-residents, shares in Furness Trinidad Ltd were accordingly made available in 1976 to enable Trinidad nationals to participate in the capital of the company. This policy was continued until, in June 1979, control passed to Trinidad interests with 49% remaining in Furness Withy hands. Thereafter Furness Trinidad Ltd ceased to be a subsidiary and became an associate company.

South American Saint Line Ltd

In 1965 Houlder Brothers purchased the South American Saint Line Ltd, Cardiff. No ships were involved, merely the name, goodwill and conference rights, also tax credits, which were a major attraction.

Dating from the formation of the Barry Shipping Company Ltd in 1926, the South American Saint Line as it was later renamed, had developed from a tramp company into a liner operation between Europe and the United Kingdom and Brazil and the River Plate. Some of the services were conference, others non-conference.

From the beginning control of the company had rested in the hands of Richard Street. Following his death in 1961, management passed through several hands until the unsettled state of shipping decided the principal shareholder, Lord Howard de Walden and Seaford, to withdraw from shipping. The ships were sold and the company placed in the hands of the liquidators until Houlder Brothers came forward with an offer to purchase. At the time H M Inspector of Taxes viewed the transaction with some disfavour as the tax credits which accrued to the new owners were of some value.

Actual ownership of South American Saint Line was vested in Ore Carriers Ltd whose bulk carrier *Joya McCance* was renamed *St Margaret* (a name twice previously carried by South American Saint Line ships). The Houlder Line *Thorpe Grange* was also renamed, recalling three previous Saint Line ships with her name *St Merriel*. In due course as part of Ore Carriers Ltd, ownership of South American Saint Line Ltd passed to the British Steel Corporation.

Stevedoring

Over the years interests had been acquired in stevedoring companies, especially in North America and the United Kingdom. These were closely linked with the liner trades operated by Group companies and included

> Tait & Pattison Ltd, Newcastle
> Bay Ridge Operating Co Inc, New York
> Bay Ridge Stevedoring Co Inc, Boston
> Hampton Roads Stevedoring Cpn, Norfolk
> Patapsco Ship Ceiling & Stevedoring Co, Baltimore
> Philadelphia Ceiling & Stevedoring Co, Philadelphia
> Economic Stevedoring Cpn of Montreal Ltd, Montreal
> Empire Stevedoring Co Ltd, Vancouver
> Clutha Stevedoring Co Ltd, Glasgow
> Holmes Stevedoring Co Ltd, Bermuda
> South American Stevedoring & Lighterage Co Ltd

A natural extension of shipowning and liner operations, ownership of stevedoring interests gave better control of that important service. However, in the United Kingdom, the Devlin Report and the decasualisation of labour that followed resulted in the cost of handling break bulk cargo increasing by some 45% in 1970.

The previous year it was recorded that Furness Withy had stevedoring interests in ten countries. At the same time there were ten stevedoring companies in the United Kingdom associated with Furness Withy.

The stevedoring industry was going through the throes of change, from a labour intensive to a capital intensive industry. Break bulk cargo was in decline, containerisation a growing trend. The British Government declared its intention to acquire the assets of the stevedoring industry and make it a nationally owned industry. With that trend towards a single employer of dock labour at each port, Furness Withy adopted a policy of disengaging from stevedoring in the British Isles. This took several years, but by 1973 the chairman could report that the divestment was virtually complete.

In North America too, the steady reduction of liner trades and in the number of Group ships calling led to the Furness Withy east coast stevedoring interests being reduced by sale and amalgamation.

The major interest to be retained, however, was in Vancouver. In 1959 the Empire Stevedoring Company Ltd had been purchased by Furness Withy and a decade later the company had opened a container terminal in Vancouver and organised a group of interests to service container ships and haul containers to their North American destinations. In the reorganisation following the Tung acquisition, Empire Stevedoring became part of the Furness Withy (Terminals) Ltd group in 1984 and, as such, was not subject to the 1990 sale to Hamburg Sud.

Ocean Monarch, entering Southampton for the last time, 5 June 1975.

Ocean Monarch (II)

In February 1970 Shaw, Savill and Albion added to their fleet the Canadian Pacific liner *Empress of England* following her withdrawal from the North Atlantic trade for which she had been launched in 1956. Renamed *Ocean Monarch*, she was to be a major element in the company attempt to capture the British based cruise market.

The purchase of this ship was to prove a financial disaster. She had been built for the cold North Atlantic route and was now to be converted into a cruise ship, for the warm tropical "Love Boat" trade. The decision to buy *Empress of England* was taken without full consideration having been given to the complexities of the project and Cammell Laird, when approached for an estimate for conversion, gave a hurried figure of £1.5 million to update and increase her passenger capacity and facilities, and remove her cargo carrying facilities in readiness for a return to service in July 1971. With labour troubles in the shipyard the anticipated three month, £1.5 million job rapidly turned into one lasting nine months and costing £4 million. It was October before she finally came into service.

In this new role *Ocean Monarch* was to give less than four years service before being withdrawn and sold to Taiwanese shipbreakers who commenced work on demolition in July 1975.

Insurance

In the nineteenth century, shipping and insurance were very close companions, many leading shipowners in ports such as London, Liverpool, Hull, Bristol and Glasgow also holding a portfolio as marine insurers. Today only Lloyd's of London survives with this tradition of individual underwriters carrying unlimited liability, but a century ago similar insurance bourses operated in other ports.

At an early stage both Furness and Houlder established insurance departments with the primary object of handling the insurance of their fleets and other interests, often integrating this with the negotiation of claims for losses made against them as carriers. It was but a short, and easy, step to take these offices into a wider market, placing business on behalf of business associates and others. The early association as brokers with the Lloyd's market was evident in the use, up to 1964, of the name "Christopher Furness" when paging any of the Furness Withy broking staff in The Room at Lloyd's.

Christopher Furness was not himself an underwriting member of Lloyd's, rather he chose the path of establishing in 1901 the Economic Marine Insurance Company Ltd (renamed Economic Insurance Company

Ltd in 1914), followed by the Whitehall Insurance Company Ltd in 1919. Houlder Brothers confined their business to broking somewhat longer, their Maltese Cross Insurance Company Ltd not being established until after World War II.

During the Depression of the inter war years and through World War II business remained at a modest level with, after 1945, Economic reinsuring a large percentage of its marine and non-marine business with other companies. On the broking side the placing of Furness Withy risks was shared between the broking department and other brokers, notably Willis, Faber and Dumas Ltd and Leslie and Godwin Ltd, with the latter companies handling the major share of the fleet insurances. At this time the most active and profitable broking office was that of Houlder Brothers.

Until 1957, both the Furness Withy controlled insurance companies and the broking department came under the same overall management. This caused problems in developing and expanding the portfolios of business as certain firms were reluctant to see their business handled by brokers and insurers controlled by their competitors who might consequently become privy to confidential information. However, both the broking and underwriting interests performed a useful task for the Group and attracted sufficient business to warrant their retention.

With increasing sophistication in the insurance market and the inevitable risk of conflict of interests between Economic Insurance Company and the broking department, it was perceived that the interests of clients and the integrity of the individual companies could be seriously prejudiced if the status quo was maintained. In 1957, therefore, the two were separated and an independent broking department established with a brief to increase efficiency, expand business and improve profitability.

During the years that followed, a number of broking firms were purchased including Sunderland based Salvus, Bain and Company Ltd in 1958. Dating from 1934 this company started operations in the offices of the Sunderland Marine Mutual Insurance Company Ltd and, in 1975, became managers of that mutual insurance company with its portfolio of tugs, fishing craft and small vessels.

With the growth of business in Trinidad, broking interests were extended to the West Indies through the purchase of Insurance Brokers (West Indies) Ltd, Port of Spain, in 1962. The West Indies broking operation later opened offices in Barbados and Guyana, with C T Bowring and Company taking a controlling interest in 1969. Ultimately Bowring took over complete ownership of the West Indies venture.

With the drive towards efficiency and profitability, the next logical step was to combine the competing offices of Furness Withy and Houlder Brothers, so late in 1963 Furness-Houlder (Insurance) Ltd was formed and commenced business with the combined assets of both broking offices in 1964. The modest scale of business to that time can be judged from the gross profits of the first year's operation, £38,000. On the formation of Furness-Houlder (Insurance) Ltd the other broking interests, Owen A Jepson and Company, Salvus, Bain and Company and Leslie Arnott and Company were transferred to become subsidiaries of the new company.

Expansion continued, both in new business, with the opening of new offices and the take-over of firms like the long established Tate, Emes and Company Ltd in 1971. Probably the most important purchase, during 1967, was that of the sound and old-established firms of M E Roberts (Insurance Brokers) Ltd and Flexible Premiums (Insurance) Company Ltd based at Stourbridge. These acquisitions provided a firm base in the Midlands upon which to develop both by marketing and by further purchases. J K Dent (Insurance) Ltd came in 1969 and B W Hunt Ltd the following year. When Kaye, Son and Company Ltd became a subsidiary company in 1972 their broking department was also absorbed. Further afield, W J Taylor and Company, Glasgow, were taken over in 1973. Within twelve years expansion took gross profits to £986,000 in 1976.

With the development of the broking business as a separate profit centre it was decided to withdraw from underwriting. In order to meet the requirements of new legislation, attain a better ratio of reserves and increase the volume of business, there was clearly a pressing need to inject new capital into Economic Insurance Company. Over the years Economic had remained an associate company until, in 1970, the purchase of sufficient shares made it a subsidiary, a step followed in 1975 by the buyout of minority holdings to attain total Furness Withy control. The following year, 1976, Economic was sold to the French L'Alsacienne Group who, later, resold to the Danish based Hafnia Group.

The Tung take-over in 1980 led to some concern at Lloyd's where the Committee were reluctant to accept foreign ownership of firms of Lloyd's brokers. This problem was overcome, although in due course, as will be mentioned later, the decision was taken to sell the broking interests.

Night of the Long Knives

"Black Friday", 13 November 1970, will long be remembered as the saddest day for many members of the Furness Withy Group staff ashore and afloat. Having endeavoured for a decade to reverse the downward trend on many services, the nettle was finally grasped by the Group and the decision taken to prune loss making areas, discontinue services where there seemed to be no prospect of returning to an acceptable level of profitability, rationalise others and streamline the organisation still further. Managers had the unpleasant task of issuing redundancy notices, a task hated by them all.

The total of twenty three ships which were to be sold cut a swathe through all the Group's fleets. At the top of the list was *Andes,* a victim of rising costs, along with the three Graces, now serving as Shaw Savill's *Akaroa, Arawa* and *Aranda.* The North Pacific route was to be terminated by the end of the year, whilst the Royal Mail services and fleet were to be severely hit with various of the Caribbean routes being transferred to Pacific Steam the following year. The full list of ships to be placed on the sale and purchase market was —

Name	Built	GRT	Name	Built	GRT
AFRICAN PRINCE	1955	3597	LOMBARDY	1958	8042
ANDES	1939	25895	MANCHESTER PORT	1966	8168
AKAROA	1959	18565	PACIFIC ENVOY	1958	9305
ARANDA	1960	18575	PACIFIC NORTHWEST	1954	9337
ARAWA	1960	18595	PACIFIC RELIANCE	1951	9337
ALBANY	1957	7299	PACIFIC STRONGHOLD	1958	9337
BLACK PRINCE	1955	3597	PICARDY	1957	7102
CHANDELEUR	1959	5224	SOMERS ISLE	1959	5515
DELPHIC	1949	10691	SOUTHERN PRINCE	1956	7731
ELEUTHERA	1959	5224	THESSALY	1957	7093
LANCASTRIAN PRINCE	1960	4735	WESTERN PRINCE	1955	7726
LOCH LOYAL	1957	10405			

These far-reaching changes placed an exceptionally heavy burden on the staff, and 1971 became a year of early retirements and redundancies, steps being taken wherever possible to minimise personal hardship.

In February 1982 *Upwey Grange* assisted the burning derelict *Aris* in the Red Sea.

Marine Losses

With the development of modern navigational aids, the number of ships lost to maritime risks was greatly reduced. Only three took place after 1960, although sadly heavy loss of life was sustained with *Royston Grange.*

Shaw Savill and Albion were to lose two ships within a short period. *Runic* was claimed as a victim by the notorious Middleton Reef, north of Lord Howe Island, on 19 February 1961. Bound from Brisbane to Auckland, *Runic* grounded during bad weather and despite efforts to refloat her, she remains there to this day. Eighteen months later *Wairangi,* on charter, grounded nearing Stockholm. Refloated with extensive bottom damage she was declared a constructive total loss and sold for breaking up.

Houlder's *Royston Grange* was in collision during fog with the tanker *Tien Chee* on 11 May 1972. Outward bound from Buenos Aires with meat and passengers for London she was still in the Plate when the casualty occurred. Tragically, fire broke out and engulfed both ships, as a result of which there were no survivors from the 73 passengers and crew on board *Royston Grange.* Subsequently the burnt out hulk was taken into Montevideo until sold and eventually towed to Spain for breaking up.

Fleet Losses — 1960 to 1991

RUNIC (Shaw, Savill & Albion Co Ltd) — 19.2.1961 ashore on Middleton Reef, 120 miles North of Lord Howe Island. Brisbane for Auckland, ballast.

WAIRANGI (Shaw, Savill & Albion Co Ltd) — 14.8.1963 ashore at Kanholmsfjarden, near Sandhamn, Stockholm Archipelago. Rio Grande for Stockholm, coffee & oranges. Refloated, broken up.

ROYSTON GRANGE (Houlder Line Ltd) — 11.5.1972 collision in fog with tanker TIEN CHEE and caught fire in Indio Channel, River Plate. Beunos Aires for London, meat. Towed in, burnt out, broken up.

Building Programme of the 1970's

Examination of the newbuilding programme of this decade reveals how clearly the role of the fleet had changed from a mere decade earlier. Traditional multi-deck general cargo ships were noteworthy by their absence, apart from six "container friendly" ships for Royal Mail and Pacific Steam service. Cellular container ships, bulk carriers, gas and oil tankers predominate, with an increasing number of orders going to shipyards outside the United Kingdom.

Oroya enters the Clyde from the Port Glasgow shipyard of Lithgows Ltd, 2 June 1977. *(J Hall (Photographers) Ltd)*

The West Coast of South America, the Pacific Steam Navigation Company's traditional area of operations, was not yet ready for containerisation, but the need to provide new tonnage to meet current demands was there. Accordingly Cammell Laird and Company (Shipbuilders and Engineers) Ltd, Birkenhead, delivered three ships in 1972/1973, *Orbita, Orduna* and *Ortega,* and these were followed by two further container friendly sisters in 1977/1978, *Oroya* and *Oropesa* from the Clyde yard of Scott Lithgow. The other general cargo ship was the sole example of the SD14, Liberty ship replacement design, to be built for the Group. Named *Derwent* when delivered by Austin and Pickersgill, she went onto the service to Brazil and the River Plate. Subsequently Metcalfe's *Dunelmia* was the only other SD14 to come into Group ownership.

Name	Built	GRT	Name	Built	GRT
ORBITA	1972	12321	OROYA	1977	14124
ORDUNA	1973	12321	OROPESA	1978	14124
ORTEGA	1973	12321	DERWENT	1979	9167

Manchester Liners steadily commissioned a series of container ships for their North Atlantic routes and also for the charter market. Apart from three smaller ships, they all came from Smith's Dock Company. With the shipyard having now delivered a total of twelve ships to Manchester Liners, the lighthearted comment was voiced by R B Stoker, chairman of Manchester Liners, that by tradition the thirteenth ship had to be delivered free of charge. Smith's Dock entered into the spirit of the matter and shortly thereafter delivered a thirteenth ship to Manchester Liners. She was not a sister of the previous deliveries however, but a 12ft fibreglass sailing dinghy suitably named as *Manchester Charity.* Manchester Liners placed her on Hollingworth Lake for the use of Manchester Liners cadets and members of the naval training corps.

In addition, smaller container ships were commissioned for the Prince Line routes to the Mediterranean.

The Chairman of Manchester Liners, R B Stoker, presents *Manchester Charity* to the Sea Cadets at Hollingsworth Lake, Manchester. *(Picture Coverage Ltd)*

Launch of *Cairnash* at Gdansk, Poland, 25 September 1976.

Name	Built	GRT	Sold	Name	Built	GRT	Sold
MANCHESTER CRUSADE	1971	12039	1982	MANCHESTER RENOWN	1974	12577	1982
FRONTIER	1972	3621	1979	MANCHESTER REWARD	1974	12577	1982
MANCHESTER VIGOUR	1973	5310	1980	MANCHESTER VANGUARD	1977	17385	1983
MANCHESTER ZEAL	1973	5310	1981	MANCHESTER VENTURE	1977	17385	1980

The mini bulk carrier and small general cargo ship fleet under the Cairn and Prince Line flags continued to be augmented. Between 1971 and 1977, eight Cairn Line ships entered service; another, the first of a four ship order with Martin Jansen in West Germany, was sold and launched as the Dutch flag *Breezand*, rather than *Cairnliner* as intended. Three of the Cairn Line mini bulk carriers, *Cairnash*, *Cairnelm* and *Cairnoak*, were products of the Gdansk shipyard, the first and only Polish built ships ever to fly a Furness Withy Group flag. Two further Prince Line ships came from Dutch yards in 1971 (one launched with a Cairn name), whilst the last two ships to carry Prince Line names were products of Swan Hunter Shipbuilders Ltd, Newcastle, in 1979.

Name	Built	GRT	Name	Built	GRT
CAIRNRANGER	1971	1598	CAIRNCARRIER	1976	1592
SAXON PRINCE	1971	1581	CAIRNASH	1977	1597
PENNINE PRINCE	1971	1599	CAIRNELM	1977	1597
CAIRNROVER	1972	1599	CAIRNOAK	1977	1597
CAIRNLEADER	1975	1592	CROWN PRINCE	1979	1479
CAIRNFREIGHTER	1975	1592	ROYAL PRINCE	1979	1479

The balance of the new commissionings were bulk carriers and oil or gas tankers. Most of the bulk carriers were destined for service with the Seabridge consortium whilst the gas tankers were destined for Gazocean operation. An order was also placed with the Daesun Shipyard in South Korea, the first Furness Withy order to Korean builders, for three 9,200 deadweight bulk carriers for charter to Furness Withy (Australia) Pty Ltd. On completion they were registered in the name of Dee Navigation Ltd. Nothing, neither the names, flag or livery, indicated that the owners were in fact Empire Transport Company Ltd, which had been renamed in 1975.

The bulk carrier *Riverina*. *(M R Dippy)*

Name	Built	GRT		Name	Built	GRT
bulk carriers				tankers		
FURNESS BRIDGE	1971	91079		HORNBY GRANGE	1979	39626
IRON BANBURY	1971	11381		ELSTREE GRANGE	1979	39626
ORENDA BRIDGE	1972	69824		gas tankers		
MOUNT NEWMAN	1973	65131		CAVENDISH	1971	26802
UPWEY GRANGE	1976	15903		FARADAY	1970	19754
LYNTON GRANGE	1976	15903		LORD KELVIN	1978	21374
ROEBUCK	1976	6802				
RIVERINA	1977	6802				
RAVENSWOOD	1977	6802				

William France, Fenwick and Company Ltd

In October 1972 management of the four ship fleet of William France, Fenwick and Company Ltd passed to Houlder Brothers.

The name William France as a shipowner is known to go back to 1765, if not earlier, from an advertisement for one of his ships sailing between London and Goole. In 1901 the present company was formed by amalgamation of the interests of William France and Company, Fenwick, Stobart and Company Ltd and H C Pelly and Company. With substantial colliery interests, the company operated a large fleet of colliers. The collieries were nationalised in 1947, and the decline in the coal trade during the subsequent decade saw the company diversify into deep sea bulk trades.

Owned in 1972 by Jessel Securities it was decided that year that William France, Fenwick and Company was now too small an entity to warrant retention by Jessel Securities, hence the transfer of management to Houlder Brothers.

The fleet of four ships were involved in a variety of trades, *Dalewood* still being in the coastal coal trade, but the other three trading further afield carrying timber, bauxite, newsprint and other bulk cargo.

Name	Built	GRT		Name	Built	GRT
CHELWOOD	1964	5440		SHERWOOD	1958	5279
DALEWOOD	1966	5390		STAR PINEWOOD	1969	19222

The four ships were purchased by Houlders in 1974, two were immediately sold, one passed to Hadley Shipping and only *Chelwood* was retained, as *Oswestry Grange*, until 1985.

Kaye, Son and Company Ltd

In 1972 Kaye, Son and Company Ltd was absorbed when the Furness Withy shareholding was increased from 45% to 100% at a cost of about £2 million. This cemented a relationship which had started nearly a century earlier when Frederick Kaye was an employee of Houlder Brothers and closely concerned with the live cattle trade from the Plate and the early refrigerated meat shipments.

Kaye left Houlder Brothers in 1893 to establish his own office in London, managing the steamers of the River Plate Fresh Meat Company, acting as London agents for Prince Line's River Plate and, later, Mediterranean services and trading in coal and insurance broking. In 1912 shipowning commenced with the steamer *Chasehill*.

In 1918 Frederick Kaye retired as Managing Director but remained Chairman until his death in 1924. His son Sydney Kaye took over as Managing Director, and, also in 1918, The Royal Mail Steam Packet Company Ltd and Furness, Withy and Company, acquired an interest in the enterprise.

Kaye's shipping interests developed further with the purchase of the Houston Line rights in the United Kingdom/River Plate trade from Cayzer, Irvine and Company. Liner trade was now added to tramp interests. It was followed in 1929 when a management contract, which lasted until 1977, was negotiated with the Jamaican banana interests whose fleet for much of the time operated under the title of Jamaica Banana Producers Steamship Company.

After Sydney Kaye died in 1941, his son Marsden Kaye remained with the company until his death in 1952 severed the active family association. With the contraction of the River Plate liner trade, which was progressively taken over by the Argentinian state owned Empresa Lineas Maritimas Argentinas (ELMA), the fleet was slowly reduced, being replaced by the London agency for ELMA. When the company was absorbed by Furness Withy in 1973, the sole remaining ship was the tanker *Kayeson* which remained in the Furness Withy fleet until she was sold in 1981. After 1973 one further ship was to hoist the Kaye flag, *Limpsfield* (later renamed *Lindfield*) from 1973 to 1977.

With the reorganisation of the Furness Withy Group into trading Divisions, Kaye lost their identity as the various functions were merged with others in the Group.

Furness Withy (Engineering) Ltd

The investments held in a small number of engineering firms which had no direct connection with the main stream shipping interests were grouped after 1976 under the appropriately named Furness Withy (Engineering) Ltd, although, as has already been mentioned, the association with the companies involved was largely of Houlder Brothers origin. They consisted of three main interests, Brooks and Walker Ltd, Fescol Ltd and Compugraphics International Ltd.

In 1938 Houlder Brothers had purchased the business of Brooks and Walker Ltd, stockists of engineering valves, tubes, fittings and pipe for a wide range of industries, from the oil and chemical trades to power and gas undertakings, building and marine applications. In due course the trade name Trent Valve was adopted for valves manufactured by the company through a subsidiary, The Trent Valve Company Ltd incorporated in 1974.

Fescol Ltd, which became a subsidiary in 1964 following a long held minority interest, was concerned with the chemical deposition of metals.

Founded in 1968, Compugraphics International Ltd became associated with Houlder Brothers who made an investment to establish the firm on a secure footing in 1971. This shareholding, of over 70% of Compugraphics capital, progressed to total ownership in 1979. The company was originally formed to provide a computer aided drafting service to civil engineers and cartographers but it was not long before the expertise of the firm was directed into the microelectronics industry, ultimately producing complete photomasks for circuit board manufacture.

The decision by Furness Withy to withdraw from non-core activities led to the end of the engineering investments when they were all sold in 1984.

Brantford

From the early days the Furness and Houlder offices had dealt with all aspects of agency work, forwarding, stevedoring and other terminal activities.

With the divisionalisation of the Group interests steadily developing, it was announced in 1971 that Brantford Holdings Ltd would be formed as the holding company to own and operate the various offices involved in the agency and forwarding sphere. At the beginning of 1972, the Furness Withy and Houlder Brothers freight agency and forwarding interests, also some port activities, began operating as Furness-Houlder (Shipping) Ltd, whilst stevedoring was placed in Furness Withy (Freighthandling) Ltd. Both companies were subsidiaries of Brantford Holdings Ltd.

The choice of the name Brantford was a pleasant reminder of the first branch office opened by Christopher Furness, at Brantford, Ontario, some ninety years earlier. It had also been used from the early days as the telegraphic address of Furness Withy.

Brantford's incorporated the existing Furness Withy and Houlder Brothers offices in London, Birmingham, Bradford, Bristol, Glasgow, Hanley, Hull, Liverpool, Manchester, Swansea and Sheffield. In addition the new operation absorbed Cairns Noble and Company Ltd and Trapp and Company in Newcastle and Middlesbrough.

At the same time, January 1972, the old established firm of Morison, Pollexfen and Blair Ltd joined the Group. With almost thirty branches throughout the United Kingdom, this company added considerably to the extent of the transportation services available to customers using air, road, rail and sea modes of carriage.

Just over two years later, in April 1974, a further merger and reorganisation took place when Furness-Houlder (Shipping) Ltd and Morison, Pollexfen and Blair Ltd were merged as Brantford International Ltd.

Chairmen

Sir Errington Keville CBE	1962-1968
John A MacConochie MBE	1968-1972
Richard, Baron Beeching	1972-1975
Sir James Steel CBE JP	1975-1979
Sir Brian Shaw	1979-1990

Six chairmen had presided over the fortunes of Furness Withy in the first seventy years. Now over a mere twenty years a further five would take office.

With the retirement of Frank Charlton in August 1962, the choice fell on Sir Errington Keville CBE. Born in 1901 he had joined Shaw Savill and Albion as a youth, being appointed a director in 1941. Membership of the Furness Withy board followed in 1950, where he became deputy chairman in 1959. In addition to serving the Group his interests ranged widely in the shipping industry and included chairmanship of the General Council of British Shipping in 1961-1962. His knighthood, in June 1962, was in recognition of his services to the industry.

Shaw Savill and Albion was also the training ground for the next chairman. John A MacConochie MBE had joined the company in 1927 and apart from service with the Ministry of War Transport between 1942

Chairmen of Furness Withy: Lord Beeching, Sir James Steel and Sir Brian Shaw.

and 1945, was to spend all his working life with the Group. Post-war service included managerial positions not only in London but also in New Zealand and Australia before his appointment as general manager of Shaw Savill Line in 1958. Becoming a Furness Withy director during 1964, he was appointed deputy chairman in May 1967 and elected chairman the following year.

The choice of the next chairman fell for the first time on someone not closely identified with the Group. This was not due to any lack of suitably qualified directors but to the desire of the Board to recruit directors with wider business experience in order to assist in developing the broader business base which was being sought for the future health and well-being of the Group. Joining the board in 1972, Lord Beeching took the chair early in 1973 when John MacConochie retired. Trained as a physicist, he had joined Imperial Chemical Industries in 1948 and helped to establish the Fibres Division (man-made fibres). Rising to be technical director and then deputy chairman of Imperial Chemical Industries, he was released from 1961 to 1965 to serve as chairman of the British Railways Board where he was responsible for an in-depth review of the railway system and the execution of many of the proposals, designed to prune the deadwood. The "Beeching Axe", taken to the railway network is still a vivid memory for many and will always be synonymous with his name. Made a life peer in 1965, Lord Beeching continued to hold many important posts both in the public and business spheres.

At Furness Withy, Lord Beeching was not only the first "outsider" in the chair but also the first part time chairman. He had an incisive mind and considered that the world was "riding for a fall". Furness Withy needed to be ready to face any period of recession, and be fit enough to survive it. The Group walked on three legs, liner and bulk trades and offshore oil. Patrick "Paddy" Naylor was appointed a director in October 1973 and undertook to prepare a strategy plan. In addition to identifying and strengthening the core business, Lord Beeching encouraged the disposal of non-essential peripherals. He also instituted a search for complementary capital intensive interests which were either non-cyclical or counter-cyclical to shipping. After careful consideration, only one business was identified that fitted this specification: illicit diamond trading. Regrettably the nature of that business precluded its further consideration.

At a meeting at the Dorchester Hotel in March 1975, the Board considered Paddy Naylor's recommendations for reorganisation. Lord Beeching envisaged that, on the adoption of these recommendations, Paddy Naylor would take up the new post of chief executive. However, the Board refused to accept the proposals, Paddy Naylor tendered his resignation and Lord Beeching, on doctor's advice and health grounds, soon afterwards resigned his chairmanship.

Although Paddy Naylor's proposals found little sympathy from his fellow directors at the meeting, reading them today leaves one wondering why as they do not appear to be revolutionary and many were, due to developing circumstances, to be adopted in the coming years. The impression is left that certain personality clashes were involved at the time.

For a second time the chairmanship went to a non-Furness Withy candidate, this time Sir James Steel CBE JP, who took up office on the retirement of Lord Beeching in 1975. Already a director of Furness Withy, he came from the Sunderland based iron and steel manufacturers, Steel Group Ltd, where he had commenced work as an apprentice in 1927. His other interests included being a director and deputy chairman of the bankers Rea Brothers Ltd, and it was in this role that he had joined the Furness Withy board in 1972.

Following the retirement of Sir James in 1979, the Group turned for its next chairman to the cadre of directors whose careers had been firmly set within the Group. The choice was Brian Shaw, who had been appointed as the Group's first managing director in 1977 and whose roots were with the Pacific Steam Navigation Company, which he had joined in 1957 after having studied law and been called to the Bar. Appointed company secretary in 1960, he moved to Royal Mail Lines the following year in a similar capacity. Following the 1965 merger he became a director of Royal Mail Lines and moved onto the main Furness Withy Group Board in 1973, having in that year also become chairman of Shaw, Savill and Albion.

Houlder Offshore Ltd

The renaming of Houlder Line Ltd as Houlder Offshore Ltd in October 1975 was an indication of the latest venture which was to take Houlders into the hostile environment of North Sea oil exploration and production and make them the premier British company in the offshore contracting field.

Bay Driller working in Morcambe Bay. *Morecambe Flame* in the distance. *(D Leech)*

Many people wondered at the oil companies venturing into this difficult area when ample supplies were still available in the Middle East, but the instability of the Gulf area posed a constant threat which became a reality with the oil embargo by Arab producers after the Arab-Israeli War in October 1973.

The first British exploration licences were issued in September 1964, and the first small North Sea offshore strike was made in the Danish Sector in September 1966, followed in December 1969 by Phillips Petroleum when *Ocean Viking* discovered the Ekofisk Field. That same month, Amoco proved the first United Kingdom strike in the Montrose Field. Others British sector strikes followed, such as the Forties, Brent and Ninian Fields and United Kingdom production of crude oil, a token amount up to 1974, reached 55 million tons in 1978.

Houlder Brothers' introduction to the offshore industry arose from the association with Gazocean. Gazocean's founder Rene Boudet had drawn attention to sub-sea diving experiments being undertaken by Comex S A at Marseilles. In due course the Houlder board became aware of the potential and formed an association with Comex in the joint British venture Comex-Houlder. The potential of the business was such that the initial investment was recovered within three years.

In 1972 it was announced that Houlder Brothers had taken a 20% stake in Kingsnorth Marine Drilling Ltd which had ordered two drilling rigs from builders in Finland. Over the years this holding was slowly increased until, in January 1980, control was achieved with a 60% shareholding. The growing fleet of Kingsnorth rigs was managed by Houlder Offshore Ltd.

Meanwhile *Oregis*, one of the old bulk ore carriers owned by Ore Carriers Ltd, was transferred to Houlder Offshore Ltd and placed in shipyard hands for conversion into the world's first specialised pipe connection vessel for operation in deep water. Whilst the long term prospects for well drilling might be questionable, there could be no doubt about the construction and maintenance requirements and, in the North Sea, the laying of pipelines from wellhead to land, their inspection and maintenance could be regarded as a long term industry.

Renamed *HTS Coupler 1*, the reconstructed ship went on trials in March 1974, but went aground at the mouth of the Tyne as she returned to port, sustaining damage that required another extended period in shipyard hands. On completion, she reverted to her original name of *Oregis* and commenced a successful career in the North Sea.

Being a converted cargo ship, there were limitations on how long *Oregis* could operate in bad weather conditions, her motion at times causing work to cease. Plans to convert a second ship, *Oremina*, were soon replaced by the idea of building a completely new vessel to perform the same services, but rather than have a conventional ship hull it would have a semi-submersible form less susceptible to the weather and waves. The summer of 1977 saw this vessel commissioned with the name *Uncle John* - after John Houlder, a nickname bestowed whilst under construction which took such a firm hold that it stuck. Another world first, *Uncle John* is a dynamically positioned semi-submersible diving support and sub-sea construction vessel. Her first job took her to the Brent Field and within a couple of years she had repaid the heavy investment made in her.

Furness Withy Chartering

The establishment of Furness Withy (Chartering) Ltd in 1971 out of the Chartering Department of Furness, Withy and Company, Ltd, during the restructuring of the Group, gave public recognition to a field of activity which had formed a basic part of the various Group companies from their early days. Those companies with origins as tramp shipping enterprises were engaged in seeking employment for their ships, whilst those employed in liner trades could be looking for suitable vessels to charter during peak periods of demand, to supplement their own fleet. Alternatively, they would place their excess tonnage on the market during quiet spells.

The various Group interests in this field were given the on-going task of not only serving Group needs but seeking business from other sources. Amongst the regular customers for the new company could be numbered a large Canadian west coast lumber company, as well as several European shipowners and charterers.

In expanding the business offices were opened in Vancouver, Melbourne, Houston and Johannesburg. Shortly after the Melbourne office opened the potential of trade in that region led to Empire Transport Company Ltd being renamed Dee Navigation Ltd and the commissioning of their three bulkers, *Roebuck*, *Ravenswood* and *Riverina* during 1976/1977, for employment under the direction of Furness Withy (Chartering) Ltd.

The first cargo handled by Furness Withy (Chartering) Ltd was woodpulp shipped on board *Veras*, which sailed from New Orleans early in 1971 bound for London. 1972 saw the commencement of the first Australian operation, a consignment of sugar making machinery loaded on the Dutch heavy lift vessel *Stella Nova* which sailed from Melbourne bound for Gove.

Since 1971 shipping has seen many changes. The company business peaked in the early 1980's, the oil crisis and excess tonnage has since influenced the market and resulted in a decline in chartering business. This has led to rationalisation and the closure of the Vancouver, Houston and Johannesburg offices. Trading patterns have changed as the industrial bases in many countries develop, whilst long term charter contracts are rarer than in the past. Whilst these have all had an influence on the business of Furness Withy (Chartering) Ltd the company has a sound base from which to adjust to future conditions.

N Z Waitangi, the first ship owned by New Zealand Line, discharging at Liverpool in May 1974. *(Robson & Baxter Ltd)*

New Zealand Line Ltd

Most of the shipping lines serving New Zealand were controlled from abroad, even the Union Steamship Company of New Zealand Ltd. With an increasing local wish to control at least some of the ships serving the important foreign trade of the country, it was decided by the New Zealand Government that it was desirable to establish a new national shipping line.

The important trade to the United Kingdom was the first to be served by the newcomer, which operated as the New Zealand Line Ltd. Shaw Savill and Albion played a major role in establishing the new venture, took a 24.92% shareholding and were appointed managers. Two Shaw Savill ships were sold to the undertaking during 1974, the refrigerated *Britannic* and *Majestic*, both dating from 1967. The initial proposal to rename them *NZ1* and *NZ2* brought public outcry, which was assuaged when the more appropriate names *NZ Waitangi* and *NZ Aorangi* were announced.

Steps were taken to order cellular container tonnage to enable the New Zealand Line to fit in with the Conference container service, the 43,704gt *New Zealand Pacific* being delivered in 1978. *NZ Aorangi* was then sold, followed by her sister two years later.

The Shipping Corporation of New Zealand, as it had now become, also undertook the development of container services from New Zealand to the Caribbean and the country's Pacific island trading partners.

However, views change and in due course the desirability of a locally owned and controlled shipping company was brought into question. It was made known that the Shipping Corporation was to be placed on the market and in 1989 its sale was finalised with ownership passing to Associated Container Transportation (Australia) Ltd.

Metcalfe Shipping Company Ltd

In 1979 the West Hartlepool based Metcalfe Shipping Company was acquired for £4.26 million. Only one ship was owned, the SD14 *Dunelmia* dating from 1977 which, the following year, was sold and renamed *New Panda*. Soon after the take-over *Deseado*, ex *Iberic*, was transferred to Metcalfe ownership until she was sold in 1981.

Metcalfe, Simpson and Company Ltd, renamed Metcalfe, Son and Company Ltd in 1915, had entered shipowning in 1903 and owned three ships between then and World War I. One, *Manchuria*, was sunk by an enemy submarine, the other two were sold by the end of the war, leaving the company without ships until 1929. In that year Metcalfe Shipping Company Ltd was established with the newly built *Dunelmia*, which remained the sole ship in the fleet until 1940. Never a large fleet, only nine ships were owned between 1929 and 1979, the last three being of the SD14 Liberty ship replacement design.

Take-over Rumours

As British shipowners reduced their commitment in the prevailing climate and looked for new investment opportunities, many became attractive to take-over operators either with a view to breaking them up and realising the capital assets or as partners for tax and other reasons. Furness Withy were not immune from this and at one stage a commentator was to write that the Group "was seen by many as a sleepy, asset rich potential target for acquisition by aggressive firms such as Slater Walker Securities".

In 1971 the Board was notified by Rea Brothers and Hambros Bank that they could speak for a combined holding of between 30% and 40% of the equity capital. In the decade that followed, with over half the capital held by only three parties, speculation was rife that a take-over was possible even though, in fact, the holdings were used to counterbalance each other.

The Board gave serious consideration to the future, intent on seeking the most beneficial path for both shareholders and staff. The merger road was an obvious one to explore and during the early 1970s various ideas were floated.

One Sunday morning the chairman, John MacConochie, received a visit from Basil Smallpeice of Cunard who wished to propose a take-over of Furness Withy by Cunard. The proposal came to nothing. Likewise one or two exploratory meetings were held with Alfred Holt and Company on a possible merger with Blue Funnel but nothing tangible resulted.

The two parties which the press watched with interest and discussed in the role of suitors were Hilmar Reksten and Keith Wickenden's European Ferries. Reksten, an Anglophile, always assumed the role of a friend and directed a flow of advice on a wide range of technical and operational matters to Furness Withy. He never broached the question of a possible take-over and the collapse of his shipping empire removed his name from the list of potential bidders. Wickenden was reported by the Sunday Telegraph as exploring a tentative bid but never took any steps along that path.

The attempt to gain control (although never amounting to a full bid for Furness Withy) which was to take much time and effort in resisting was that of Frank Narby's Eurocanadian Shipholdings in 1974, from a company considered unsuitable by the board for a variety of reasons.

The Eurocanadian Bid

Having built his fortune on the Coca-Cola concession in Egypt, Frank Narby left that country at the time King Farouk was deposed in 1952 and settled in Canada where he developed a shipping business handling bulk cargo, trading under the name of Cast and owned by Eurocanadian Shipholdings Ltd. This became a non-conference service across the North Atlantic carrying steel, copper matte and asbestos, initially with chartered ships but later developing into owning.

Onto this base cargo, Cast added a cheap container service, creaming the market and undercutting Manchester Liners and other Conference operators by loading the containers on top of the bulk cargo. This idea was not new; others had in the past employed the same methods.

In 1974 Narby proposed plans to take over Manchester Liners and integrate their operation with Cast. Eurocanadian Shipholdings commenced to buy Manchester Liners shares, although Furness Withy already held nearly 62% and about 30% was held by another investor. Eurocanadian Shipholdings announced in September 1974 that it was purchasing Manchester Liners' shares at 85p through the Stock Exchange. By paying up to £1.55 a share in the two weeks that followed Mr Narby found himself controlling 37.6%.

The matter was not simply one of who owned Manchester Liners. Other factors included the future of the large labour force employed directly and indirectly and the effect on the balance of payments should the only remaining British line operating to Canada pass to foreign control. The entire structure of the North Atlantic liner trade would also be affected as Manchester Liners were Conference members and Cast were not. A change of ownership would nullify the many operating agreements and require a complete reorganisation of services. For example Manchester Liners had working agreements with Canadian Pacific under which they operated from Liverpool and Glasgow whilst Canadian Pacific ran to Felixstowe and Rotterdam. Should Manchester Liners be integrated with Cast, the consequent competition would be to the advantage of none.

The offer to buy Manchester Liners having been rejected by the Furness Withy Board, the unsatisfactory situation then developed whereby the two parties, holding over 99% of the shares between them, were not talking to each other. Eurocanadian Shipholdings accordingly endeavoured to influence the matter by building up a substantial shareholding in Furness Withy itself.

At the end of 1975, the matter was referred to the Monopolies and Mergers Commission by the Department of Prices and Consumer Protection under the terms of the Fair Trading Act, 1973. The inquiry, chaired by J G Le Quesne, recommended that mergers between Eurocanadian and Manchester Liners, or between Eurocanadian and Furness Withy, should not be permitted and that within two years Eurocanadian should reduce their holding in Furness Withy to not more than 10%. In the meantime their voting powers would be restricted to that figure.

9. Into the Future—1980 onwards

At the end of April 1980 it was announced that the offer made by Orient Overseas (Holdings) Ltd had achieved sufficient support to become unconditional and on 30 September 1980 Furness, Withy and Company, Ltd, together with the companies owned and controlled, passed to new owners, Kenwake Ltd, a subsidiary of Orient Overseas (Holdings) which was established to conclude the purchase.

Consequent on the take-over, Professor Roland Smith, John M Clay and Henry Hildyard tendered their resignation as directors. Although Henry Hildyard was a Furness Withy man, his secondment to Overseas Containers led to his decision to remain with that company. On completion of the transfer to Kenwake Ltd, the remaining board members were joined by Chee Hwa Tung, Morley L Chao, Chen Chen Tung, Captain Mei Y Stone and John P Robertson who headed up Furness Withy (Chartering) Ltd.

Brian Shaw, appointed chairman in 1979, was constrained to comment in his statement attached to the annual report for 1979 and issued in May 1980 "Nothing will ever be quite the same again for Furness Withy". As time passed, the truth of this statement was to become clear, although factors other than the take-over were to be largely responsible.

C Y Tung

With the announcement of the sale of the Group to interests controlled by C Y Tung of Hong Kong, many had to turn to "Who's Who" to ascertain who they now worked for. Well known in the Hong Kong and Far East shipping community, but less well known in the London shipping world, C Y Tung was a shipping entrepreneur of the calibre of Furness, Houlder, Knott and others in the Group history.

Born in Shanghai in 1912, the son of a businessman, Tung Chao-Yung started work during 1929 with a Japanese firm, Kokusai Transport Company. The following year he moved to the Tientsin Navigation Company and in 1933 his ties with shipping were strengthened by his marriage to the daughter of a Shanghai shipowner.

Commencing business on his own account at Hong Kong in 1941, the entry of Japan into World War II that year delayed his plans for the future. However, in 1946 Tung was able to commence shipowning managing the Chinese Maritime Trust Ltd, buying elderly ships, many of which had served through two world wars. Amongst the first purchases in 1946 was an early British Empire Steam Navigation Company ship, *Clutha River* of 1914 which was renamed *Ling Yung* and, as such, was wrecked in 1948 whilst serving as a Chinese Nationalist troopship. The fleet grew steadily and more modern tonnage entered service until in 1956 the first ship built for the fleet, *Oriental Star*, was launched in France.

In the years that followed, Tung added to his general cargo ships a fleet of passenger ships, tankers, bulk carriers and, later, container ships. Included in the fleet was *Seawise Giant*, the largest ship yet built in the world, a tanker able to load 564,763 tons deadweight. Another was Cunard's *Queen Elizabeth*, purchased in 1970 for conversion into the floating education centre *Seawise University* as part of his involvement with education. Sadly, only days before she was to be recommissioned, a fire broke out and totally destroyed the ship.

As one facet of the enterprise (identified by the red Chinese plum blossom on the funnel) Orient Overseas Container Line was developed in the years after 1969 with the intention of creating a global container service, and into this the container interests of Furness Withy fitted well after 1980.

When he died in 1982, C Y Tung was more than a shipowner. An industrialist, banker and shipbuilder, his interests covered a wide range of activities including insurance, property and offshore drilling, as well as his personal deep interest in education.

Life as a Subsidiary

Immediate assurances were given by the new owners that Furness Withy would remain intact and continue trading with no job losses. Naturally there was unease amongst the staff, who still had the unsettling happenings of the previous decade fresh in the mind. This undertaking was, however, honoured until the Tung Group's financial collapse in 1985 after which many things changed in the rescue operation that followed.

The greatest loss to the Group occasioned by the Tung take-over was that of the interest in Overseas Containers. The other three partners viewed Orient Overseas Container Line as a major competitor. Not wishing to be both partners and competitors they invoked the clause wisely written into the consortium's articles of association and exercised their right to acquire the Furness Withy interest on terms outlined in those articles. At the time the Furness Withy interest was 15.81%, and approximately £28 million was received for it. This ended the Furness Withy and Shaw Savill and Albion interest in the liner trades to Australia and New Zealand together with the container ships *Botany Bay* and *Jervis Bay*.

Slimming Down

The years following the take-over saw shipping experiencing the worst slump in living memory, demonstrating that the sale had been well timed from the point of view of Furness Withy's shareholders. The consequences for the Furness Withy Group were clear: in 1980 they were interested as owners, managers or in manning over sixty ships, four years later this number had virtually halved.

The cause of the decline was not the Tung Group take-over but rather the sale of ships occasioned by the adverse economic conditions. One or two of the ships went for breaking up, but the majority of the vessels were sold to a variety of mainly foreign owners, many employing cheaper "third world" crews and interested in short term employment of the ships until deferred maintenance led them to the shipbreakers. Only three went to the Tung Group fleets based in Hong Kong: Manchester Liners' container ships *Manchester Venture*, *Manchester Vanguard* and *Manchester Reward*, although *Manchester Renown* and two Prince Line ships, *Royal Prince* and *Crown Prince*, passed to associated companies.

An explanation of this contraction, which would have taken place had Furness Withy retained its independence, can be drawn from the annual report for 1981. It contained a simplified table of the Group turnover and profit —

	Turnover	Profit/(loss)
Shipping	67%	(16)%
Offshore	12	99
Non-marine	11	9
Other	10	8

The bulk carrier *British Steel,* managed on behalf of British Steel Corporation.

172

Beacon Grange in the Falklands, 1982.

Shipping was not the only area to contract; in 1983 the Saxon Inn hotels were sold and the following year Furness Withy withdrew from engineering with the sale of Fescol Ltd and Brooks and Walker Ltd.

The consolidation of the Group had continued with the acquisition of Eurocanadian Shipholding's interest in Manchester Liners. The Furness Withy holding of ordinary shares in Manchester Liners consequently went up from 61.6% to 99.2% and the rest was acquired just prior to Christmas 1980, making Manchester Liners a fully-owned subsidiary.

The sale of company owned ships, and the consequent loss of jobs for the Group's sea staff, was to some degree offset by taking on the management of ships owned by Tung, Hadley Shipping and British Steel. The manning of the Hadley ships ended in 1986 but the British Steel association, which can be traced back to the Ore Carriers joint venture, continued to grow and today part of their fleet of bulk carriers is still managed by Furness Withy.

Name	Built	GRT
ABBEY	1979	64154
BRITISH STEEL	1984	90831
IRONBRIDGE	1987	90707

The Furness Withy head office in London had, since 1926, been situated in a building between Leadenhall Street and Fenchurch Street, in the heart of the shipping community. Cunard was across Leadenhall Street, Royal Mail, Blue Star and P&O further down the street. Slowly companies had been moving out, to less expensive and more convenient centres. Furness House had been occupied on a long lease and prior to expiry, whilst the lease still retained some value, the decision was taken to follow suit. The search for a new home led to Redhill and in 1987 the freehold of a new office block was purchased—the current Head Office.

Furness House, Redhill.

New Building in the 1980's

Dunedin entered service in July 1980 for the Bank and Savill Line, to run alongside Bank Line's *Willowbank* and The Shipping Corporation of New Zealand's *New Zealand Caribbean*. The Bank and Savill Line service ran in partnership with the Columbus Line of Hamburg-Sudamerikanische D G Eggert & Amsinck from Australia and New Zealand to the Caribbean and Gulf ports of the United States. *Dunedin* was sold in 1986 to be enlarged and re-enter service as *Monte Pascoal* under the Hamburg-Sud flag on the Europe to River Plate service. The Furness Withy Group retained their interest in the form of a 50% slot sharing agreement.

The following month, August 1980, the 70,000 ton deadweight bulk carrier *Pacific Wasa*, built in 1972, was acquired and renamed *Rounton Grange*. Apart from that and two oil rigs, only two new ships were to enter Furness Withy Group service during the decade, both of them specialist vessels.

First, in June 1984, came the multipurpose diving support vessel *Orelia*, taking the name of an earlier Ore Carriers ship. Houlder Offshore also commissioned the drilling rigs *Shelf Driller* and *High Seas Driller*.

Finally in April 1984, *Andes*, a 1900TEU container ship, was delivered by Hyundai Heavy Industries of South Korea. Registered as owned by Furness Withy (Shipping) Ltd she was built for the Pacific Steam Navigation service from Europe to the West Coast of South America. With eight partners—Armement Deppe, Hapag-Lloyd, Johnson Line, Nedlloyd, Marasia, CSAV, Linabol and Transnave—Pacific Steam had formed EUROSAL (EUROpe South America Line) to "containerise" the route using seven container ships, rather than the twenty conventional ships previously employed.

The container ship *Andes* transiting the Panama Canal.

The Tung Group Collapse

As mentioned earlier, the early years of the 1980's were traumatic times for all shipowners. From Europe to Japan and America, well found and long established companies were going to the wall or having to undergo drastic surgery to survive. Amongst them were names like Saleninvest, Irish Shipping, Wheelock Marden, Sanko and United States Lines. Financial institutions, who for years had considered shipping a safe investment, accumulated massive losses as owners went under and they were left virtually worthless ships on their hands, the only assets against heavy investment loans.

In 1985 the Tung Group joined the ranks of those in trouble. A number of reasons can be identified. Operating costs were high even though Far East costs were amongst the lowest; freight rates were in the doldrums due to the continued depressed state of the shipping market and, when examined, the Tung companies were seen to be operating on too high a level of financial gearing for the economic climate. Exchange rates had also moved unfavourably, against the interests of the fleet. Most of the fleet had been built using borrowed capital and the financial return from operations were insufficient to service these loans and pay interest. As creditors started to examine the empire they found a group of companies, some public and others privately owned, which took considerable time and effort to reorganise. The problems had arisen in companies privately owned by the Tung family, rather than the publicly owned arm under Orient Overseas (Holdings) Ltd, but the consequences rippled right through the group.

It became immediately apparent that Furness Withy was one of the main assets of the Tung empire. To protect the asset and prevent premature action by creditors, steps were taken by the bankers who had financed the Tung purchase of the Furness Withy Group, and to whom the Furness Withy shares were pledged as security, to place a "fence" round it whilst remedial plans were formulated. An immediate effect for Furness Withy was that in the interests of assisting the financial reconstruction of the parent company, Furness Withy were not permitted to make repayments of principal on loans when due, even though well able to do so. It would not have appeared good for some of the Tung group's creditors to be repaid normally when the rest were facing write offs under the reconstruction.

When the Tung Group rescue package was finalised, it involved a co-ordinated restructuring agreement covering both the public and private sectors of the Tung empire, supported by a credit facility from the Hong Kong and Shanghai Banking Corporation of up to US$150 million. For Furness Withy it was to mean that funds not required for normal operations were to be remitted to Hong Kong to help rescue the group, rather than being retained and re-invested. Certain sections of the business compatible with other Tung group interests were to be merged with the mainstream of the group and the remaining interests would be split into two groups, one for disposal and the other for retention.

Under Furness, Withy and Company, Ltd were grouped for retention the liner and transport interests including Empire Stevedoring in Canada and other transport subsidiaries. The Danube Navigation Company was renamed Furness Withy Investments Ltd as the holding company for the interests to be sold, covering insurance, offshore oil and gas, although later some of the gas interests were transferred to Furness Withy and Company for retention.

In 1988, it was announced that all aspects of the core container business would be integrated into Orient Overseas Container Line, including the North Atlantic interests of Dart and Manchester Liners. Manchester Liners, bereft of its shipping interests, remained as the owners of the office premises in Manchester. Henceforth agency offices in cities throughout the United Kingdom handling the container trade, and the terminal interests, replaced their Furness Withy name by signs with the red plum blossom of Orient Overseas Container Line.

After extended negotiations, the offshore interests passed to the Swedish Stena Group in 1989 to become Stena-Houlder Offshore; previous negotiation to sell to the French Forasol-Foramer Group having failed (other believed or actual bidders had included China Merchants Holdings, the Mosvold Group and Exmar). Earlier the Furness-Houlder insurance interests had been sold to the London representatives of the China Merchants Holdings, and since November 1991 have traded as Houlder Insurance Brokers Ltd.

Gazocean

The early years of the decade saw Gazocean suffer a series of setbacks with a succession of rescue packages to ensure survival. With a fleet of over thirty owned and chartered gas tankers, plummeting freight rates saw some ships on long term charter costing three times what they were able to earn. The suspension of trade in certain products between Russia and America, and the virtual closure of the American liquid petroleum gas market also contributed to Gazocean's troubles.

To raise cash in 1983 Gazocean offered, and Furness Withy accepted through Houlder Brothers, the transfer of their 50% stake in the equity of Ocean Gas Transport Ltd, the owners of six gas tankers which were on long term charter to Gazocean. Thereafter the company has remained a wholly owned Furness Withy Group subsidiary.

Matters continued to deteriorate until two years later, in 1985, losses again forced Gazocean to re-negotiate all their charters, rather than declare bankruptcy. From a sale of assets they were able to settle outstanding charter balances with eight owners, write down their capital to nil and, replacing it with a new issue, allocated 35% to the previous shareholders and 65% to the four principal creditor shipowners. At the top of this list stood Furness Withy, who received 22.8% of the new equity.

From the beginning of the Houlder Brothers partnership in Ocean Gas Transport, Furness Withy has consistently supported Gazocean in good times and bad. Since 1985, this policy has continued with Furness Withy willing to purchase further shareholdings from other partners who wished to sell. Consequently, in 1989, control of Gazocean passed to Furness Withy with the holding reaching 54%. Since the 1985 reconstruction, Gazocean have slowly moved out of troubled waters, thereby beginning financially to repay this confidence.

The gas tanker *Cavendish.* *(Skyfotos)*

Ecuadorean Gas

With the experience gained in operating gas tankers, a new opportunity was identified and development commenced in 1984 with a contract to supply liquid petroleum gas to Ecuador.

In view of the limited on-shore storage capacity, one of the large tankers was stationed at Guayaquil to accept bulk supplies purchased on the world market and shipped in. For three years *Cavendish* was employed in this role, more recently being replaced by the time chartered *Mundogas America*.

Further contracts have been undertaken based on the Guayaquil storage tanker, including at various times supplies to Peru, Chile, Salvador and Nicaragua. Distribution from Guayaquil has been undertaken by two or three smaller tankers, currently *Humboldt* and the chartered *Caribbean Venture* being employed for this role.

The Gas Tanker Fleet

Considerable change has taken place in the liquid petroleum gas fleet since 1980. Only two of the six ships owned or operated in 1980 remain, the others having been broken up or sold during or after the problems associated with Gazocean and the Tung Group financial difficulties.

The older, smaller and less economic units have gone, leaving just the larger units. The Ecuadorean venture has led to the purchase of a small capacity ship suitable for the volume of that trade and the port facilities involved, whilst time charter has been resorted to as need arises.

Name	Built	Acquired	GRT	Name	Built	Acquired	GRT
HUMBOLDT	1968	--	5200	JOULE	1965	1973	8666
CLERK-MAXWELL	1966	--	8298	LORD KELVIN	1978	--	21374
FARADAY	1970	--	19750	HUMBOLDT	1968	1987	1844
CAVENDISH	1971	--	26802	JOULE	1972	1989	2527

Offshore Oil

The oil drilling and servicing interests of Furness Withy proved to be extremely valuable as an anti-cyclical interest which enabled the Group to remain viable whilst shipping transited the doldrums. This is well illustrated in the accounts for 1982, when the Group profits were £4,987,000. Shipping lost £10,861,000 whilst the offshore interests profit of £14,688,000 enabled the Group to report an overall profit.

Houlder Offshore Ltd continued to increase their stake in Kingsnorth Marine Drilling to achieve control in 1980 and subsequently commissioned several new drilling rigs. The diving support vessel *Oregis* was sold for breaking up in 1982, being replaced by a purpose built vessel, *Orelia*, commissioned in 1984.

Whilst most of the fleet were employed in the North Sea, units were employed drilling the Morecambe Bay gas field and the two land drilling rigs spent some time on the only major British on-shore field, Wytch Farm, Dorset. The major overseas involvement commenced in 1983, a joint venture in the South China Sea undertaken by China Nanhai-Houlder Drilling Corporation using *Nanhai II* and *South Seas Driller*. When new, *Orelia* was employed in the Arabian Gulf and *HMD1*, the first land drilling rig, spent a considerable time on site in Indonesia.

The land drilling rig *HMD1* at work in Indonesia.

During the decade the oil drilling and service fleet owned, managed or manned included —

Name	Type
BAY DRILLER	Marathon Le Tourneau 116-C self-elevating slant drilling platform built 1982.
DUNDEE KINGSNORTH	semi-submersible, self-propelled drilling platform built 1975.
HIGH SEAS DRILLER	Friede & Goldman L-907 semi-submersible, self-propelled drilling platform built 1983.
HMD1	land drilling rig.
HMD2	land drilling rig.
KINGSNORTH UK	Aker H-3 semi-submersible, self-propelled drilling platform built 1976.
MORECAMBE FLAME	Marathon Le Tourneau 116-C self-elevating slant drilling platform built 1982.
NANHAI II	Aker H-3 semi-submersible, self-propelled drilling rig built 1974.
ex Pai Lung, Borgny Dolphin	
OREGIS	diving maintenance and support vessel built 1955 and converted 1974.
ex HTS Coupler 1, Oregis	
ORELIA	self-propelled multi-functional support vessel built 1984.
SHELF DRILLER	self-elevating drilling platform built 1982.
SOUTH SEAS DRILLER	Aker H-3 semi-submersible, self-propelled drilling rig built 1977.
ex Dan Queen, Moby Dick	
UNCLE JOHN	semi-submersible, self-propelled diving support, fire fighting, sub-sea construction and maintenance platform built 1977.

The semi-submersible drilling rig *High Seas Driller* being transported on the heavy lift ship *Ferncarrier*.

The Hamburg-Sud Take-over

Rumours were confirmed, in the summer of 1990, that talks were taking place between the Tung Group and the German, Bielefeld based, Rudolf A Oetker Group which controlled the Hamburg-Sudamerikanische D G Eggert and Amsinck. Negotiations were successfully completed and on 17 October ownership of Furness, Withy and Company, Ltd passed from Hong Kong to Germany, the price being $130 million. As a holding company a new concern was formed and given the name Shaw Savill (Holdings) Ltd. Sir Brian Shaw resigned as chairman, being succeeded by John Keville who, for the previous three years, had served as managing director.

In addition to Sir Brian the Tung nominees to the board also resigned, Chee Haw Tung, Roger King, Derek J Harrington, Robert H A Chase and John Hsia being superseded from Hamburg by August Oetker, Horst Schomburg and G Trulsen. They joined John Keville and Paul Edwards.

The Hamburg-Sud story dates from 1869 and the formation of the joint British-German owned Hamburg-Brasilianische D G. Hamburg-Sud itself followed two years later and was to become a major German flag operator on the route from Europe to the Plate, despite the trauma of two world wars and having to rebuild the fleet from nothing on both occasions.

Dr August Oetker had started business as a chemist in Bielefeld in 1891, a business that was to develop into a large foodstuffs producer heavily reliant on shipping for raw materials from abroad. Prior to World War II, the Oetker family had acquired an interest in Hamburg-Sud and when post-war restrictions on German shipping were lifted, they rebuilt the company. As part of the Oetker group, Hamburg-Sud returned to South America and over the years have been joined by other shipping interests, such as Deutsche Levante Linie and Deutsche Nah-Ost Linien, and have developed services to Australasia and the Far East under the title Columbus Line.

A comparison between Furness Withy and Oetker/Hamburg-Sud reveals many compatible features. The Royal Mail/Houlder services to Brazil and the River Plate matches the Hamburg-Sud route. Furness Withy were already "slot charterers" on the Hamburg-Sud container vessel *Cap Trafalgar* in this trade. Prince Line and Manchester Liners' services to the Mediterranean fit well with the Deutsche Nah-Ost Linien, whilst Pacific Steam with their West Coast of South America route extend the overall spread of the Oetker Group's Latin American trades. The gas interests again widen the overall coverage in the bulk markets.

John Errington Keville, 12th Chairman

Only twice in the history of Furness, Withy and Company Ltd, has a father and son held the post of chairman. The first time was in 1914 when Marmaduke Furness, the only son of Christopher Furness, was elected to the chair. Then in 1990, John Keville assumed the mantle which his father, Sir Errington Keville, had worn from 1962 to 1968.

John Keville has been associated with the company since 1972 when the fleet of William France, Fenwick and Company was acquired. Educated at Winchester College, John Keville served in the Royal Navy from 1952 to 1954 on board aircraft carriers and minesweepers prior to joining Houlder Brothers. Leaving them in 1957, he spent the next fifteen years with William France, Fenwick and Company Ltd.

Placed in charge of bulk operations at Houlder Brothers in 1972, with a seat on the Houlder board, John Keville was appointed a director of Furness Withy in 1977 and managing director in 1987.

Furness, Withy and Company, Today

The fleet list today with just seventeen names is a shadow of those of years past. Examination reveals a tight-knit and active group of interests with many of the old trading names retained. Some of the old companies, however, now bereft of any reason for existence, have been wound up leaving a small group centred on Furness, Withy and Company.

The container terminal interests, controlled by Furness Withy Terminals Ltd were excluded from the sale to Hamburg-Sud, and remain with the Tung group.

The liner trades are catered for by *Andes*, running to the West Coast of South America on Pacific Steam service, whilst the "slot chartered" *Cap Trafalgar*, flying the Hamburg-Sud flag, is a reminder of the Royal Mail/Houlder interests on the East Coast, operating closely with the other British lines, Blue Star and Lamport and Holt. The Mediterranean and Caribbean trades continue with chartered tonnage. The bulk trades centre around Gazocean and the other gas interests, together with bulk shipments from Australia employing chartered tonnage. In London, Furness Withy (Chartering) Ltd continues to play an important support role in broking and chartering. The management of ships for British Steel fits in well with these interests.

Down the road from the office in Redhill, the premises of Furness Travel are a reminder of the past interests in passenger travel and the leisure industry. Furness Travel remain active with three offices, their principal role being the provision of travel services to the company and other business travel, although at the same time providing full travel facilities to the public.

The Future

With the sale to Hamburg-Sud a year old, it is difficult to look into the Furness Withy second century with any clarity. However, the mutual interests with the new owners and the return to European ownership is probably better than being a remote outpost of the Tung Group in Hong Kong. The company brings several new fields of interest into the Hamburg based operation and whilst these continue to thrive and develop, they will doubtless continue to fly the Furness flag.

Shipping rationalisation is the order of today, and nowhere is it more evident than in Europe. The Oetker Group has focused its sights on the north-south trades, and in this field Hamburg-Sud, Furness Withy and the liner activities of Johnson Line of Stockholm, now named Laser Liners and purchased very recently by Oetker, are a formidable combine, certainly the largest European presence in the trade to Latin America.

British Shipping

During the first century, Furness Withy has changed its character, and continues to develop to meet the needs of the day. The early liner trades gave way, and ceased their up-market development, during the early years of the century when faced with massive competition. The company turned to tramp shipping with the support of the industrial empire which Christopher Furness had built up to ensure employment. Following the purchase of Johnston Line and then Prince Line, the nature of the Group changed, especially after the buy out of the Furness family shares in 1919 and the removal of the industrial and shipbuilding associations. Thereafter the Group developed as a major liner organisation for some forty years, the Furness Withy guise which we all knew so well.

With the changing shipping environment, Furness Withy sought new fields in containers, the offshore oil industry, oil and gas tankers and the bulk trades. In this they acted like virtually all British owners, many of whom have since decided that the future was so bleak that the best option was to cease operations. At the time when Manchester Liners were moving into containers, the competing Donaldson and Bristol City Lines were deciding that the costs were too great for companies of their size, Donaldson choosing to liquidate their interests, and the Hill family (Bristol City Line) moving into the Dart consortium which in due course was to be absorbed by Orient Overseas Container Line.

Other shipowners sought partners in diverse fields as they looked for the anti-cyclical balance: Cunard found Trafalgar House, P&O coupled with Bovis and later with Sterling, Ellerman (in two steps) joined with Cunard/ Trafalgar House before, in July 1991, taking centre stage in a massive rationalisation which involved many of the remaining British liner operators, P&O, Trafalgar House, Blue Star, Andrew Weir, Ben Line and T & J Harrison. This 1991 rationalisation centred on the dismemberment of Associated Container Transportation (ACT) with P&O taking over the Australian, Tasman and Far East trades from both Cunard Ellerman and Blue Star, together with Ellerman's South African line. ACT's transpacific route from Australasia to North America passed to total Blue Star ownership whilst Ellerman's Mediterranean, Middle East, Indian and East African trades were sold to Andrew Weir. Cunard were then left with their cruise ship operation and ownership of *Atlantic Conveyor,* on long-term bare-boat charter to Bilspedition.

Others, Ocean Transport and Trading (Holt's Blue Funnel Line) and British and Commonwealth Shipping (Clan Line and Union-Castle) chose effectively to retire from deep sea shipping. None of these changes have been painless, as witness the losses and collapse of British and Commonwealth. Furness Withy through it all have managed to live, albeit as a much changed organisation.

What Might Have Been

Looking back over the last thirty years of change there are many occasions which can be identified when different decisions might have led the Company along entirely new paths and these might have seen Furness Withy retain its independence in a different guise. Hind-sight is a wonderful thing, and a crystal ball on the table might have been a welcome management tool at some of the board meetings in the period. However, company directors do not have access to such facilities and have to make hard decisions in the light of the best information and with the greatest skill available to them. More heartache has probably been experienced by directors in the last thirty years than during the previous seventy as they tried to balance the interests of staff, shareholders, customers and others with, at times, unpalatable decisions to announce.

The decision to withdraw from the aviation field was probably the best decision in regard to that sphere, whilst the entry into the Overseas Containers consortium must be regarded as the best long term decision of the period. Other new ventures, such as off-shore, were rewarding in the short term, but huge capital was needed to remain in the big offshore league, and this market, too, became as susceptible to slumps as any other. The area which interests the writer is the many forays into the leisure industry, with cruise liners, hotels, travel agencies, and so forth. What might have happened if these had been co-ordinated and built into a single enterprise? For example, the vision of Furness Withy at the peak of the leisure field in the United Kingdom, with a spread of hotel, cruise ship, aviation and allied interests. Conversely, however, many such ventures have ended in failure, as witness the Court Line crash of 1974. Again, had a suitable "marriage partner" appeared in the 1970's, the sale to the Tung controlled interests in 1980 might never had occurred and, alongside Cunard and P&O, Furness Withy might have remained the third shipping and industrial conglomerate of the age. That could have entailed the retention of the interest in Overseas Containers (now wholly owned by P&O as P&O Containers Ltd).

But crystal gazing can only ever be a pastime. Contemplating Furness Withy's first century, we are faced with a remarkable and unique record of venture and achievement, one of which the founder and the company can justly be proud.

APPENDIX

Chronology

1853	April 23. Christopher Furness born at West Hartlepool.
1870	Christopher Furness visits Scandinavia, Franco-Prussian War.
1873	Christopher Furness admitted to partnership in Thomas Furness and Company. Office opened at Brantford, Ontario.
1878	First steamer, *Chicago*, commissioned.
1882	Christopher Furness becomes independent.
1884	Edward Withy and Company, shipbuilders, purchased.
1890	London office opened as C Furness and Company. Appointed managers of British Maritime Mortgage Trust Ltd.
1891	September 16. Furness, Withy and Company, Ltd incorporated by merging shipowing and shipbuilding interests.
1892	Chesapeake & Ohio S S Co Ltd formed.
1896	Wilson's & Furness-Leyland Line Ltd formed. Control of British Maritime Mortgage Trust Ltd achieved (renamed British Maritime Trust Ltd). Sir C Furness, Westgarth & Co Ltd formed by amalgamation.
1897	Irvine's Shipbuilding & Dry Docks Co Ltd acquired.
1898	Manchester Liners Ltd formed. Northumberland Shipbuilding Co Ltd purchased. London to New York service and ships sold by Wilson's & Furness-Leyland Line Ltd.
1900	Richardsons, Westgarth & Co Ltd formed by amalgamation.
1901	Economic Marine Insurance Co Ltd formed. Wilson's & Furness-Leyland Line Ltd sold to International Mercantile Marine.
1903	Tyne-Tees Shipping Co Ltd formed, incorporating Furness Withy's North East Coast service. Gulf Line Ltd acquired.
1906	Ships and liner service acquired from Neptune S N Co Ltd.
1907	Hessler Shipping Co Ltd acquired. Fleets of Chesapeake & Ohio S S Co Ltd and British Maritime Trust Ltd to be amalgamated into Furness, Withy & Co Ltd.
1909	Fleets of Laing S S Co Ltd and J M Wood bought. Furness Withy shipyard transferred to Irvine's Shipbuilding & Dry Docks Co.
1910	Agincourt S S Co Ltd taken over. Neptune S N Co Ltd and Norfolk & North American S N Co Ltd acquired.
1911	Formation of combine that would become Canada S S Lines Ltd. 50% share acquired in Houlder Brothers Ltd (managers of Houlder Line Ltd and Empire Transport Co Ltd).
1912	*Eavestone* completed, first British owned deep-sea motorship. White Diamond S S Co Ltd (Warren Line) purchased.
1914	50% interest taken in William Johnston & Co Ltd. Furness-Houlder Argentine Lines Ltd formed. British Empire S N Co Ltd formed. Economic Marine Insurance Co Ltd renamed Economic Insurance Co Ltd.
1915	Head office moved from West Hartlepool to Liverpool.
1916	Head office moved from Liverpool to London. Balance of William Johnston & Co Ltd acquired. Prince Line Ltd bought.
1917	Fleet of J Gardiner & Co purchased, Rio Cape Line Ltd formed. Queenstown Dry Docks, Shipbuilding & Engineering Co Ltd purchased. Irvine's Shipbuilding & Dry Docks Co Ltd sold. Furness Shipbuilding Co Ltd established.
1918	Northumberland Shipbuilding Co Ltd sold.
1919	Management buyout, severing links with Furness family, Furness Shipbuilding Co and the coal, steel and industrial interests. Ships, services and Bermuda interests of Quebec S S Co purchased. Whitehall Insurance Co Ltd formed.
1920	Trinidad Shipping & Trading Co Ltd purchased.
1921	Bermuda & West Indies S S Co Ltd formed. North Pacific route opened.
1922	Service to New York re-opened. *Dominion Miller,* the first British owned Doxford engined ship commissioned.

1928	Cairns, Noble & Co Ltd purchased.
1929	Queenstown Dry Docks, Shipbuilding & Engineering Co Ltd sold. Gulf Line Ltd wound up. Red Cross Line purchased.
1932	New York service closed.
1934	Johnston Warren Lines Ltd formed by amalgamation.
1935	Acquired control of Shaw, Savill & Albion Co Ltd and Aberdeen & Commonwealth Line Ltd.
1937	Minority holding in Royal Mail Lines Ltd acquired.
1939	Royal Mail Lines purchased Pacific S N Co.
1947	Majority interest in Bermuda hotels sold. Alexander Shipping Co Ltd purchased.
1952	Manchester Liners open service into Great Lakes.
1953	Royal Tour by Queen Elizabeth II. *Gothic* acts as Royal Yacht. Ore Carriers Ltd formed.
1954	Interest acquired in aviation through Airwork Ltd.
1957	Armorial bearings granted to Furness, Withy and Company, Ltd.
1958	Last interest in Bermuda hotels sold.
1959	Prince Line's Round-the-World service withdrawn. Houlder World Holidays formed. St Lawrence Seaway opens.
1960	Warwick Tanker Co Ltd formed.
1963	Ocean Gas Transport Ltd formed. Furness-Houlder (Insurance) Ltd formed.
1965	Overseas Containers Ltd established. Royal Mail Lines Ltd and Pacific S N Co purchased. Furness Ship Management Ltd established to integrate and rationalise.
1966	British Empire S N Co Ltd renamed Welldeck Shipping Co Ltd. Service from New York to Bermuda withdrawn.
1967	Cairn Line of Steamers Ltd acquired.
1968	Joined Seabridge Shipping Ltd. Shaw, Savill & Albion enter hotel business with White Heron Lodge, Wellington. Control of Saxon Inn Motor Hotels Ltd acquired. Manchester Liners commence first fully containerised transatlantic service with *Manchester Challenge*.
1970	November 13. "Night of the Long Knives" rationalisation. North Pacific service withdrawn. Manchester Liners Ltd becomes a subsidiary.
1971	Aviation interests (now British Air Transport (Holdings) Ltd) sold. Brantford Holdings Ltd formed to own U K agency and forwarding interests.
1972	Kaye, Son & Co Ltd and William France, Fenwick & Co Ltd acquired.
1973	Aberdeen & Commonwealth Line Ltd renamed Furness Travel Ltd.
1974	Houlder Brothers Ltd becomes a subsidiary. Houlder World Holidays sold. Morison, Pollexfen & Blair Ltd acquired. Shaw, Savill & Albion acquire minority interest in New Zealand Line Ltd.
1975	Houlder Line Ltd renamed Houlder Offshore Ltd. Empire Transport Co Ltd renamed Dee Navigation Ltd.
1976	Economic Insurance Co Ltd sold. Furness Withy (Engineering) Ltd formed to own engineering interests.
1977	Withdrew from Seabridge Shipping Ltd.
1979	Cairn Line of Steamships Ltd renamed Furness Withy (Shipping) Ltd. Metcalfe Shipping Co Ltd acquired.
1980	September 30. Group acquired by Hong Kong interests of C Y Tung through Kenwake Ltd. Interest in Overseas Containers Ltd sold. Majority of Furness Travel Ltd offices sold.
1982	Houlder Brothers acquire full ownership of Ocean Gas Transport Ltd.
1983	Saxon Inn Motor Hotels Ltd sold.
1984	Shaw, Savill & Albion hotel, travel and stevedoring interests in New Zealand sold. Furness Withy (Engineering) Ltd sold.
1987	Head office moved from London to Redhill, Surrey.
1988	Manchester Liners services integrated into Orient Overseas Container Line.
1989	Furness-Houlder (Insurance) Ltd and Houlder Offshore Ltd sold. New Zealand Line Ltd sold.
1989	Gazocean becomes a Furness Withy subsidiary.
1990	October 17. Group acquired by Rudolf A Oetker Group and Hamburg-Sudamerkanische D G Eggert & Amsinck through Shaw Savill (Holdings) Ltd.
1991	September 16. Centenary of Furness, Withy and Company, Ltd.

Chairmen of Furness, Withy and Company Ltd

Christopher, Baron Furness	1891	to 1912	Sir Errington Keville CBE	1962	to 1968
Sir Steven W Furness, Bart	1912	1914	John A MacConochie MBE	1968	1972
Marmaduke, Viscount Furness	1914	1919	Richard, Baron Beeching	1972	1975
Frederick, Baron Essendon	1919	1944	Sir James Steel CBE JP	1975	1979
Sir Ernest H Murrant KCMG	1944	1959	Sir Brian Shaw	1979	1990
Frank Charlton	1959	1962	John E Keville	1990	

Directors of Furness, Withy and Company Ltd

Christopher, Baron Furness	1891	to 1912	B Ronald Seton-Winton	1956	to 1971
Richard W Vick	1891	1919	Geoffrey N A Murrant	1956	1979
Henry Withy	1891	1908	Henry R J Hildyard	1956	1980
Captain Thomas King	1891	1895	John J Walsh OBE	1959	1961
George L Wooley	1891	1899	Alexander Wallace	1960	1961
Robert B Stoker	1891	1898	W F George Harris	1961	1969
Sir Steven W Furness, Bart	1894	1914	E Leslie Wheeler	1961	1968
Frederick, Baron Essendon	1899	1944	Cyril W Warwick	1962	1969
Robert E Burnett	1905	1945	Robert B Stoker	1963	1979
Harry C Furness	1905	1910	Peter V O Evans	1964	1974
Marmaduke, Viscount Furness	1906	1919	Harry C S Croft	1964	1977
George W Sivewright	1907	1908	John A MacConochie MBE	1964	1973
Andrew S Purdon	1907	1917	Cyril G Matthews	1965	1967
John E Furness	1907	1919	William Robert Russell	1967	1972
Walter Furness	1909	1919	John J Gawne	1967	1982
William H Beckingham	1909	1948	Robert A Henderson	1968	1971
A V Turnbull	1909	1911	Professor Roland Smith	1969	1980
Einar Furness	1910	1919	Nigel J Tatham	1970	1973
Robert J Thompson	1911	1929	W E A Robinson	1970	1971
David Cooke	1913	1919	S Wainwright	1971	1977
Ethelbert Furness	1915	1919	Sir Richard Clarke KCB OBE	1971	1972
Henry C Blackiston	1917	1935	John M Clay	1972	1980
Sydney J Forster	1919	1948	Eric B Spencer MC	1972	1976
Sir John Esplen, Bart, KBE	1919	1930	Richard, Baron Beeching	1972	1975
Robert I Dodsworth OBE	1919	1937	Sir James Steel CBE DL JP	1972	1979
Frank H Houlder	1919	1936	Patrick G Naylor	1973	1975
Walter C Warwick	1919	1962	Sir Brian Shaw	1973	1990
Norman Douglass	1919	1926	Thomas R Pulley	1976	1987
Sir Osborn G Holmden KBE	1919	1945	John E Keville	1977	**
Sir Ernest H Murrant KCMG	1924	1959	W Anthony L Roberts	1977	1984
Henry Smurthwaite	1924	1950	Sir Ralph Bateman KBE	1978	1984
William, Baron Kirkley	1930	1935	Cee Hwa Tung	1980	1990
Ian P R Napier MC	1930	1939	Morley L Cho	1980	1983
James W Nicol	1935	1945	Chee Chen Tung	1980	1987
Maurice C Houlder	1936	1954	John P Robertson	1980	1982
Kenneth Stoker	1936	1963	Captain Mei Y Stone	1980	1983
Robert Sargent	1936	1939	Richard Seymour	1982	1986
William Everall	1941	1947	Sir Paul Bryan DSO MC MP	1983	1988
William MacGillivray	1941	1959	Roger King	1983	1990
Frank Charlton	1944	1963	Ming-Hang Liang	1983	1987
Basil, Baron Sanderson of Ayot MC	1945	1965	Derek J Harrington	1983	1990
E Philip Rees CMG MC	1945	1963	David J Montier	1984	1990
Colin C Black	1947	1956	Robert H A Chase	1987	1990
John W Barron	1948	1963	John Hsia	1987	1990
Sir Errington Keville CBE	1950	1968	Michael D Revell	1987	1990
Brian, Baron Essendon	1953	1967	Paul S Edwards	1990	**
R Peyton Burnett OBE	1953	1967	August Oetker	1990	**
John M Houlder CBE	1954	1989	Horst Schomburg	1990	**
			G Trulsen	1990	**

** current directors.

Flags and Funnel Markings

Some of the many houseflags and funnel markings will be found portrayed on the end papers. The following details do not cover those in use prior to joining the Group.

The original Furness funnel of 1877 was black and was to remain so until after the death of Lord Furness in 1912, although following the formation of Manchester Liners, Sir Christopher Furness had decided to adopt their new funnel markings for the Furness Withy fleet. R B Stoker objected strongly and following a stormy interview this decision was reversed.

About 1913 the plain black funnel was relieved by a blue band carrying a white "F", reminiscent of the houseflag. As has been narrated, after World War I new funnel markings were chosen and have remained in use ever since, a black funnel with two red bands, one narrow above one wide. This was based on the Prince Line colours with the narrow, 18 inch, band added above, but no Prince of Wales feathers.

There are still those who maintain the only "true" houseflag for Furness Withy was the plain blue ensign carrying a white "F" in the centre, in use for 60 years through two world wars. However, several others have been employed.

Originally, in 1877, Thomas Furness & Co chose a blue flag carrying the firm's initials "T F & Co.". With the end of the partnership in 1882 Christopher Furness hoisted a new flag, a Union Jack defaced in the centre by a blue edged white square carrying a blue "F". About 1886 objection was raised by the naval authorities at Halifax, asserting this was unauthorised use of the national ensign. Furness responded by reverted to the earlier blue flag, this time defaced with a simple white "F". This was flown until 1946 when a burgee was introduced with, in the centre, a black ball carrying two red stripes as on the funnel and, in the upper hoist, a white "F".

In 1980 Furness Withy (Shipping) Ltd adopted a variation of the flag with the letter "F" deleted. About the same time Furness Withy (Chartering) Ltd chose another variation on the funnel colours, a black flag with the two red bands.

Although never flown at sea the Furness Withy Group has, for the last twenty years, employed as a Group ensign one with an orange field carrying, in dark blue, the Group insignia, nicknamed the "drunken fork".

The first variations from the Furness colours came in the 1890's with the appearance of ships owned by British Maritime Trust and the joint companies, Wilson's and Furness-Leyland Line and Chesapeake and Ohio Steamship Company. British Maritime Trust chose a yellow, or buff, funnel and flew a flag with the blue letters "B.M.T." on a white diamond set in a blue field. Wilson's and Furness-Leyland adopted a black topped red funnel, similar to that of Thomas Wilson, Sons and Company, and for their flag a red ground edged blue carried the white letters "W & F L". The Chesapeake and Ohio flag, a red ground on which was a white diamond with the intertwined black letters "C & O", was a reminder of the railroad partners. The black topped buff funnel carried the same black monogram on a wide white band.

When they were purchased Neptune Steam Navigation Company and Norfolk and North American Steam Shipping Company both adopted the main Furness Withy markings and flag, as did the Gulf Line, Johnston and Warren interests, the New York based ships of the Bermuda and West Indies Steamship Company and Furness Red Cross Line.

Prince Line, and their associated Rio Cape Line, continued to fly their red burgee on which were, in white, the Prince of Wales feathers. These feathers were also carried in white on a red banded black funnel. When Furness Withy adopted the two unequal red bands Prince Line added a narrow red band above their own wide red band, on which the Prince of Wales feathers continued to feature.

Two coastal companies had their own designs. The London Welsh Steamship Company had a buff funnel and a flag similar to Furness Withy, the white letters "L.W." on a blue ground. Further north Kirkcaldy, Fife and London Shipping Line had a simple black funnel coupled to an ornate flag. A red St George's Cross on a white ground had a thin blue edging to the cross. Each canton carried a blue letter, "K F S L", while a blue central shield carried a white letter "L".

Three small companies in which Furness Withy had a financial interest, and which were to become members of the Group, had their own markings. The Agincourt Steamship Company ships had a buff funnel with a blue band and flew a blue flag with a gold battleaxe. The Hessler Shipping Company's black funnel carried a flag which, on a red ground, carried a white rectangle surrounded by a white line. In the centre was a blue foul anchor. Finally the Peareth Steamship Company flag was a black "B" on a white diamond in a red ground. The same insignia was placed on the black funnel, a red band being defaced by the diamond and letter.

Manchester Liners' funnel was red with a black top and a black band. Their ships flew a white flag with a red oval in the centre on which were placed the white letters "M L". Modernised versions of the flag which changed the relative position of the letters, exhibiting them in red, removing the red oval and encircling the letters with two blue arrows signifying the two way service, were used in public relations material but never seen at sea.

The association with Houlder Brothers added a very simple and widely used flag and funnel. The flag was a white Maltese Cross on a red field; the funnel repeated this as it was black with a red band carrying the white Maltese Cross. These colours were carried not only by Houlder Line but also British Empire Steam Navigation Company, Empire Transport Company and, later, Ore Carriers Ltd.

When formed British & Argentine Steam Navigation Company used a plain black funnel and flew two pennants, each split horizontally into blue over white. Later the Houlder funnel was adopted and the blue Furness flag with the white "F" was flown above the two pennants. The joint nature of Furness-Houlder Argentine Lines was seen in the two pennants flown, above a blue one with a white "F" in the hoist and below it a red one with the white Maltese Cross in the hoist. The ships carried the Houlder funnel markings.

Houlder funnel markings were adopted for Alexander Shipping Company when they joined the Group, replacing a plain black funnel. But they retained their old flag, flown with the Houlder flag, the golden "Busy Bee" on a blue field which is believed to have been associated with their first steamer, *Beeswing*. Houlder's association with B P in Warwick Tankers was reflected in the B P shield mounted on the Maltese Cross, whilst Ocean Gas Tankers combined the Houlder and Gazocean insignia side by side or, on slim funnels, the Gazocean dolphin above the Maltese Cross.

The Cairn Line of Steamships have a long and involved funnel and flag history. From the beginning their flag had been a white pyramid on a red ground, denoting the largest cairn then known in the world, the Great Pyramid. In 1908 the purchase of the Thomson Line brought in the "Betsey Norrie", Thomson's blue and white chequered flag with origins lost in antiquity. Cairn retained the "Betsey Norrie" on the Canadian liner service, but reverted to the Cairn flag when the liner service closed and the Cairn identity was transferred to the fleet of middle-sea bulk carriers. In 1908 the Cairn funnel markings, black with a wide red band edged white and carrying a white pyramid, were merged with Thomson's red funnel with a black top, by repainting the lower black section red.

From the wreckage of Kylsant's Royal Mail crash came Shaw, Savill and Albion Company with a buff, black topped funnel. Their flag is very similar to the original colours chosen by New Zealand before the intervention of the British Government, a red St George's Cross on a white ground. The upper hoist canton is a blue ground with a red St George's Cross and four white, six pointed stars. The buff funnel also featured on the Aberdeen and Commonwealth Line ships, associated with the older Aberdeen Line flag, red over blue ground with a white, six pointed star. The Shaw Savill partnership in Crusader Shipping resulted in a buff funnel carrying a black shield on which were presented a crusader's sword and shield, symbolising an attack on the new trade from New Zealand to North America and Japan. Their black burgee also carried the same sword and shield.

When Royal Mail Lines and its subsidiary, Pacific Steam Navigation Company, joined the Group in 1965 they added, and retained, two very old liveries. Royal Mail's buff funnel accompanies a flag depicting the Royal Crown (changed in 1965 from the Tudor to St Edward's Crown) set on the centre of a red St Andrew's Cross on a white field. Pacific Steam Navigation, also with a buff funnel, have on their flag a crown centred on a blue St George's Cross with the red letters "P S N C" carried in the white cantons. The crowns date from their early origins as chartered companies and mail carriers.

When Kaye, Son and Company joined Houlder Brothers their remaining ship carried a black funnel with a white "K" inside an outline white diamond. Their square flag carried a similar white "K" inside a white outline diamond on a blue ground. Another company to join the Group, Metcalfe Shipping, carried a black funnel with a red "M" on a white band, reflected in the flag which was white, edged blue, with a red "M" in the centre.

A new colour, hiding their true origins, was seen when Dee Navigation adopted a black topped green funnel with a white band. Their flag also was green and white.

List of steamships and career summary.

Apart from the steamers owned by Houlder Brothers and Company prior to the commencement of their association with Furness, Withy and Company, the fleet lists of the various companies commence when they came under Furness Withy or Houlder Brothers management, control or majority ownership.

In the case of the early Furness Withy fleet many of the ships built as speculative ventures are identified only by a reference to a press launch report or a first entry in Lloyd's Confidential Index, being sold and deleted in the next issue. Until 1899 the Confidential Index appeared three times a year, thereafter every six months—unlike the annual nature of Lloyd's Register of Shipping—and often included ships due to be shortly commissioned.

Companies are arranged in approximate date order, in three sections (Furness, Withy and Company Ltd, Manchester Liners Ltd and Houlder Brothers and Company Ltd). Ships are listed by registered ownership (apart from non-Group finance houses in recent years, which have been ignored), rather than service. This results in many ships appearing in illogical places when nomenclature or employment are considered.

Ships are arranged according to the year built or acquired. Each entry is numbered consecutively to facilitate cross-reference when ships were transferred between companies, and the previous/next number is given in brackets after the ship's name.

In column 1 the name if carried, is shown in capitals and in lower case if it was never registered (likely if the ship was sold prior to being commissioned). Round brackets indicate the vessel was sold or transferred and not operated by the company, whilst square brackets indicate a contemplated, but not implemented, name. Names carried prior to purchase are also in lower case lettering.

The gross tonnage, in column 2, can vary over a period. The tonnage when joining the fleet has normally been used. Columns 3, 4 and 5 are the years built, acquired and sale/transfer.

If renamed on sale the new name immediately appears in the last column, number 6: if some time elapsed before renaming the year is given first in column 6. Then follow subsequent years of renaming and names, plus the date and cause of final end. In the case of missing ships the final date is that of sailing, last sighting or wireless report. Abbreviations: b.u. = broken up; TL = total loss; CTL = constructive total loss.

Index of Companies in fleet lists
(with abbreviations employed)
(This list excludes the Paraguayan Development Company and single-ship companies
managed by Houlder Brothers prior to 1899 — see pages 212/3).

Most of the fleet consisted of general cargo vessels. Other types have been identified, after their names, by the abbreviations:

bulk	bulk carrier	pass	passenger vessel (100+ berths)
bulk/oil	combined bulk carrier/tanker	p/c	passenger/cargo vessel (12-100 berths); in all cases temporary accommodation for emigrants/steerage in the cargo tween decks has been ignored.
cc	cellular container ship		
lng	liquid natural gas tanker		
lpg	liquid petroleum gas tanker		
ore	ore carrier	tank	tanker
		tug	tug

Name	GRT	Built	Acquired	Sold	Subsequent career
Thomas Furness and Company					
1. AVERILL (7)	1690	1878	--	1882	to CF
2. CHICAGO	1384	1878	--	--	8.5.1878 wrecked
3. BRANTFORD CITY (9)	2371	1880	--	1882	to CF
4. YORK CITY (12)	2325	1881	--	1882	to CF
5. BOSTON CITY (8)	2334	1882	--	1882	to CF
6. DURHAM CITY (10)	3092	1882	--	1882	to CF
Christopher Furness					
7. AVERILL (1)	1690	1878	1882	--	21.6.1883 wrecked
8. BOSTON CITY (5/78)	2334	1882	1882	1892	to FW
9. BRANTFORD CITY (3)	2371	1880	1882	--	10.8.1883 wrecked
10. DURHAM CITY (6/79)	3092	1882	1882	1892	to FW
11. NEWCASTLE CITY	2129	1882	--	--	23.12.1887 foundered
12. YORK CITY (4)	2325	1881	1882	--	22.12.1887 wrecked
13. RIPON CITY (85)	2141	1883	--	1892	to FW
14. WETHERBY (90)	2129	1883	--	1892	to FW
15. GOTHENBURG CITY (p/c)	2529	1884	--	--	27.6.1891 wrecked
16. LINCOLN CITY (p/c)	2729	1884	--	1885	CHICAGO: 1898 SALERNO: 30.6.1905 wrecked
17. STOCKHOLM CITY (86) (p/c)	2686	1884	--	1892	to FW
18. DAMARA (75) (p/c)	1779	1885	1885	1891	to FW
19. ULUNDA (130) (p/c)	1789	1885	1885	--	26.8.1890 ashore, TL, sold, repurchased 1898
20. WASHINGTON CITY	2296	1885	--	1891	1894 FRAM: 26.10.1900 wrecked
21. KATIE	2796	1880	1886	1889	DUNKELD: 25.3.1895 wrecked
22. DHU HEARTACH	149	1868	1887	1890	STARTFORTH: 1924 b.u.
23. MADURA (83)	2324	1873	1887	1889	repurchased
			1891	1892	to FW
24. SAINT LOUIS	1862	1870	1887	1888	CHEANG CHEW: 10.8.1911 wrecked
25. BALTIMORE CITY (74) (p/c)	2334	1888	--	1891	to FW
26. BARON HAMBRO	579	1861	1888	1889	1899 TARAS BOULBA: 1921 OLGA METHINITY: 1923 VERA GREELMUYDEN: 1924 NADINA: 1925 CANDILLI: 1934 ZUHAL: 21.6.1943 wrecked
27. FIRE QUEEN	1220	1864	1888	1890	FERDINAND A: 11.12.1894 wrecked
28. MEDINA ex Prince Mohamed Tewfik	286	1867	1888	1889	1904 BIRGIT: 1918 GUSTAV FISCHER: 1922 NIXE: 1925 b.u.
29. NEW BOROUGH (84)	1795	1888	--	1892	to FW
30. ORION ex Nicaragua, Orion	2297	1873	1888	1889	COLOMBO: 1906 b.u.
31. PLEIADES ex Guatemala	2297	1874	1888	1889	1891 EMILIA: prior to 13.1.1892 foundered
32. SCANDINAVIA ex Columbia, Sirius	851	1876	1888	1891	SIRIUS: 1893 b.u.
33. SULTAN ex Asia, Sultan	2525	1873	1888	--	1.3.1889 foundered
34. BLANCHE	246	1863	1889	1892	15.7.1901 wrecked
35. CARLISLE	1035	1889	--	1889	ALFONSO FIERRO: 30.3.1920 wrecked
36. CHANTICLEER	539	1853	1889	1889	23.9.1889 missing
37. MICHIGAN ex Surrey	2949	1881	1889	1889	1900 HARRY LUCKENBACH: 6.1.1918 sunk by U84
38. TRURO CITY	1006	1889	--	1890	NORMANDIE: 1913 NORLI: 1913 BISP: 20.1.1940 missing
39. TYNEDALE (381)	2217	1889	--	1891	to CFC

Name	GRT	Built	Acquired	Sold	Subsequent career
40. WITTEKIND	1047	1889	--	1891	MELITON GONZALEZ: 1916 S GINER: 1932 VERGE DE PILAR: 1936 BEGOCHU: 15.1.1942 wrecked
41. ALBOIN	1047	1889	--	1890	1905 FUKUYAMA MARU NO 6: 11.11.1917 missing
42. BUSHMILLS	2466	1890	--	1890	11.1.1911 wrecked
43. (Calcutta City)	2306	1890	--	1890	LANGOE: 1900 ACME: 1915 KJOBENHAVEN: 1919 TILTIL: 1925 ATACAMA: 1929 COLLICO: 10.5.1938 collision
44. (Calcutta City)	2303	1890	--	1890	ASHLANDS: 5.7.1900 wrecked
45. GUERNSEY	2856	1890	--	1891	1897 CIMBRIA: 1910 GURRE: 20.3.1917 sunk by U59
46. HALIFAX CITY ex Bristol	2289	1890	1890	1891	KESTOR: 1911 DEUTSCHE KAISERIN: 1914 MALTA: 1917 POLLENSA: 22.11.1919 wrecked
47. JAMES SPEIR	535	1890	1890	1891	IRMA: 1922 HEKLA: 1922 LAWRENCE: 16.2.1923 wrecked
48. MANDALAY	1915	1872	1890	1890	1893 LOUISIANA: 1906 b.u.
49. PAKEHA	4331	1890	--	1890	1909 LIZANKA: 1911 BRODERICK: 29.4.1918 sunk by UB57
50. (---)	4071	1890	--	1890	RANGATIRA: 1909 COUNT MURAVIEFF: 1911 BRODMORE: 27.2.1917 sunk by UB43
51. (---)	4050	1890	--	1890	TEKOA: 1902 HIGHLAND CORRIE: 1909 b.u.
52. TAYMOUTH CASTLE	1827	1877	1890	1892	OCAMO: 1921 b.u.
53. TYNEHEAD (382)	2258	1890	--	1891	to CFC
54. VEGA	3064	1879	1890	1890	1899 BENGUELLA: 9.1.1907 wrecked
55. (Calcutta City)	2922	1891	--	1891	DAYBREAK: 1907 LIVATHO: 9.4.1917 sunk by UB47
56. (Calcutta City)	2868	1891	--	1891	MELBRIDGE: 14.2.1907 foundered
57. CENISIO ex Centro America, Clementina	1431	1867	1891	1891	ELISA: 1895 CRUZEIRO: prior to 18.12.1895 wrecked
58. (---)	2423	1891	--	1891	CITY OF GLOUCESTER: 2.3.1906 foundered
59. (Cundall)	4637	1891	--	1891	CHANCELLOR: 1901 PALLANZA: 11.11.1915 mined and sunk
60. DUART CASTLE ex Adjutant	1839	1878	1891	1892	ORURO: 1925 b.u.
61. HISTORIAN	1830	1870	1891	1892	CIDADE DO PORTO: 19.12.1896 lost
62. (---)	4069	1891	--	1891	INCHBARRA: 1897 TELESFORA: 28.5.1917 collision
63. INCHBORVA (80)	2301	1881	1891	1892	to FW
64. INCHGARVIE (81)	2614	1882	1891	1892	to FW
65. INCHULVA (76)	2229	1881	1891	1891	to FW
66. MADRID (82) ex Aurrerra	2439	1873	1891	1892	to FW
67. OTTAWA (p/c)	1719	1891	--	--	1.11.1891 wrecked
68. STATESMAN	1865	1869	1891	1891	ALICE: 1896 TEJO: 1898 TRINIDADE: 1899 AMAZONAS: 1905 MOSSORO: 1925 b.u.
69. (Welldeck)	2907	1891	--	1891	INCHDUNE: 1898 SOLLUBE: 1907 MAR-NEGRO: 1921 ENRIQUE BALLESTEROS: 1932 NUMA: 1939 b.u.
70. ALBIANA (455)	4224	1905	--	1907	to C&O
71. CYNTHIANA (424)	3185	1905	--	1906	to BMT
72. MARIANA (456)	4204	1905	--	1907	to C&O
73. PERUVIANA (425)	3153	1905	--	1906	to BMT

Furness, Withy and Company, Ltd

Name	GRT	Built	Acquired	Sold	Subsequent career
74. BALTIMORE CITY (25) (p/c)	2334	1888	1891	--	17.7.1897 wrecked
75. DAMARA (18) (p/c)	1779	1885	1891	--	7.2.1905 wrecked
76. INCHULVA (65)	2229	1881	1891	1894	3.11.1895 wrecked
77. AUSTRALIA	2252	1870	1892	--	1893 b.u.
78. BOSTON CITY (8)	2334	1882	1892	1898	NORMAN: 1899 ARLA: 1918 ACACIA: 1923 FREJ: 1934 b.u.
79. DURHAM CITY (10)	3092	1882	1892	--	1897 b.u.
80. INCHBORVA (63)	2301	1881	1892	1892	14.2.1895 wrecked
81. INCHGARVIE (64)	2614	1882	1892	1893	1900 LEON REVEILHAC: 1900 DANTE: 1909 KENKON MARU: 9.4.1925 wrecked
82. MADRID (66) ex Aurrerra	2439	1873	1892	1894	1896 b.u.
83. MADURA (23)	2324	1873	1892	--	28.11.1895 foundered
84. NEW BOROUGH (29)	1795	1888	1892	1895	17.4.1895 ashore, TL, sold, PENSACOLA: 1906 WILHELMINA: 5.7.1916 collision
85. RIPON CITY (13)	2141	1883	1892	1897	SILVIA: 1913 PINA: 3.1917 lost (cause unknown)
86. STOCKHOLM CITY (17) (p/c)	2686	1884	1892	1898	CAROLINA P: 1901 ADELINA CORVAJA: 1902 CAROLINA P: 1906 b.u.
87. STRAITS OF BELLE ISLE ex Lord of the Isle	2484	1870	1892	1894	1895 HOKOKU MARU: 24.2.1904 blockship

At the time of incorporation business was deemed to have been carried on from 30 April 1891, hence the balance sheet included ships which were not actually transferred to the new company. These were *Gothenburg City, Washington City, Halifax City, Blanche, Taymouth Castle, Duart Castle, Ottawa* and *Cenisio*.

Interests were also held by Christopher Furness and Edward Withy and Company in 24 steamers not under their management, six of which were registered to single ship companies. In addition Furness had shareholdings in Atlantic and Eastern Steamship Company Ltd (J. Glynn and Son, managers), Liverpool, Hull Steam Shipping Company Ltd (G R Sanderson and Company, managers), Hull, and Deddington Steam Shipping Company Ltd (H Samman, manager), Hull.

Apart from these three fleets many of the other interests, in ships mainly built between 1888 and 1891, have the appearance of being deferred payment transactions, with shares held as security. It is also likely some of the ships built by other than the Withy yard were speculative orders, but it has not been possible to confirm this.

Name	Built	GRT	Name	Built	GRT
Galbraith, Pembroke & Co, London			Livingston, Conner & Co, West Hartlepool		
ETON	90	2688	GLENCAIRN	89	1136
			CARLISLE	89	1002
Hardy, Wilson & Co, West Hartlepool			GLENEDEN	90	1133
ASHLANDS	90	2303 †	GLENISLE	91	1947 †
			CITY OF WORCESTER	91	2404 ‡
Herskind & Woods, West Hartlepool					
URSA	88	2735 †	T Robinson, Sons & Co, West Hartlepool		
			JUNO	88	2430 †
John Holman & Sons, London					
GRENVILLE	88	1565	R Shadforth & Co, Sunderland		
HALDON	89	1519 †	ELMVILLE	89	1967
HAYTOR	89	1562			
LYNTON	90	1668	Steel, Young & Co, London		
BRENTTOR	90	1951	ROTHERFIELD	89	2831 ††‡§
			CAPENOR	90	2536 †§
J. Hunter, West Hartlepool			ZANZIBAR	90	2964 †§
IVY	89	1215	CHATFIELD	91	2931 ‡
			WILDCROFT	91	2958 †‡
Lindsay, Gracie & Co, Leith					
GLENBERVIE	78	1509	J Wood & Co, West Hartlepool		
			SUNSHINE	90	1589
			DAYBREAK	91	2922

† built by E Withy & Co: ‡ owned by single-ship company: § shares held by E Withy & Co.

Name	GRT	Built	Acquired	Sold	Subsequent career
88. TYNEDALE (381)	2217	1889	1892	1896	FURTOR: 29.7.1897 foundered
89. TYNEHEAD (382)	2258	1890	1892	1896	MISTOR: 5.8.1900 collision
90. WETHERBY (14)	2129	1883	1892	--	3.12.1893 wrecked
91. (London City)	4960	1893	--	1893	BEZWADA: 1912 YASUKUNI MARU: 3.11.1915 sunk by U38
92. ANTWERP CITY	3229	1894	--	1899	LILJA: 1902 ANTWERP CITY: 31.5.1911 collision
93. BAVARIAN	3030	1869	1894	1895	dismantled, 1898 b.u.
94. BULGARIAN	3118	1870	1894	--	1896 b.u.
95. CARLISLE CITY	3002	1894	--	1902	ORACABESSA: 1916 BELEM: 1932 hulked
96. HALIFAX CITY (p/c)	2141	1894	--	1900	ETRURIA: 1930 b.u.
97. ISTRIAN	2963	1867	1894	--	1895 b.u.
98. SAINT RONANS	4457	1881	1894	1899	ORION: 1.6.1899 wrecked
99. ZEBRA	551	1858	1894	--	1896 b.u.
100. ALBERT ex Visconde di Attagonia	525	1856	1895	1896	1908 GUILLAUME LE CONQUERANTE: 1908 ELSA: 1909 EOLO: 1925 b.u.
101. COVENTRY	1702	1883	1895	1895	1.10.1908 wrecked
102. EDITH	609	1864	1895	--	25.11.1895 collision, b.u.
103. (-----)	2401	1895	--	1895	HARCALO: 1899 GANECOGORTA: 1907 MAR ADRIATICO: 14.2.1917 sunk by UC21
104. OREGON (pass)	3714	1882	1895	--	1897 b.u.
105. PLATO ex Tiger	793	1857	1895	1896	1902 b.u.
106. SAINT JOHN CITY (p/c)	2153	1895	--	1900	PIEMONTE: 1928 b.u.
107. SARNIA (pass)	3728	1882	1895	--	1897 b.u.
108. SORRENTO	2208	1878	1895	1895	1895 b.u.
109. FRANCE	4281	1867	1896	--	1896 b.u.
110. GODWIT	1682	1891	1896	1897	TRYG: 1900 RAPIDO: 1916 PERRA: 27.11.1916 sunk by UB18
111. (London City) (468)	5532	1896	--	1896	to WFL
112. MANNINGHAM ex Inchmaree	1924	1880	1896	--	28.5.1896 ashore, TL, sold. 21.2.1917 sunk by UC17

Name	GRT	Built	Acquired	Sold	Subsequent career
113. MEGANTIC (469)	5532	1896	--	1896	to WFL
114. OPORTO	570	1870	1896	--	14.8.1902 collision, b.u.
115. HEATHER BELL	1253	1896	1897	1897	VERMA: 1899 SEGUNDO: 1916 C SORNI: 1929 b.u.
116. MONARCH	7296	1897	1897	1899	1927 MONARCA: 1931 b.u.
117. (Tunstall)	2463	1897	--	1897	ADMIRAL IHLEN: 1899 MENDITARRA: 1907 ISIDORO: 17.8.1915 sunk by U38
118. WHITEHALL	2068	1897	--	1897	1908 MARGARITONE: 1913 NIZZA: 1914 JAFFA: 1917 SACAVEM: 1925 FAYAL: 1927 KURBADS: 1938 b.u.
119. BARCELONA (p/c)	1802	1878	1898	--	1899 b.u.
120. (Canada) (402)	2663	1898	--	1898	to BMT
121. (-----)	7661	1898	--	1898	BENGALIA: 9.1.1905 wrecked
122. DAHOME (p/c) ex Lawang	2470	1891	1898	1911	KAISSERI: 1912 ERITREA: 1923 b.u.
123. GURLY	847	1891	1898	1898	JUNO: 1900 PORTFIRIO DIAZ: 1911 b.u.
124. HOLGUIN	842	1890	1898	1898	HEBE: 1900 BENITO JUAREZ: 1911 b.u.
125. LONDON CITY (p/c) ex Guinee, Priok	2487	1891	1898	1900	TAIHOKU MARU: 1933 b.u.
126. (Monmouth)	8001	1898	--	1898	IRISHMAN: 1902 MICHIGAN: 1926 CANDIDO: 1927 b.u.
127. RAPIDAN (452/1204)	7359	1898	1898	1902	to ET
128. SPRITE	826	1870	1898	1899	30.9.1905 foundered
129. SYLVIANA	4189	1898	--	--	1905 Japanese war prize, GOTO MARU: 8.11.1907 missing
130. ULUNDA (p/c) (19)	1789	1886	1898	1910	ELLI: 1911 b.u.
131. ALLIE	1139	1899	--	1899	CACHALOTE II: 1914 ALLIE: 5.1.1917 sunk by UB39
132. (-----)	7519	1899	--	1899	BETHANIA: 1914 PARISIAN: 1921 ESTHER DOLLAR: 1929 CHIEF SKIDEGATE: 1930 TAIHOKU MARU: end unknown
133. (-----)	8845	1898	--	1898	ULTONIA: 27.6.1917 sunk by U53
134. DALTONHALL (Sangara)	3538	1899	1900	1915	1916 AUSTRALSTREAM: 1919 GENERAL DEGOUTTE: 1921 DIMITRIOS N RALLIAS: 1936 b.u.
135. EVANGELINE (pass)	3901	1900	--	1902	TENNYSON: 1922 VALPARAISO: 1932 b.u.
136. LIZZIE	631	1900	--	1901	EIKHAUG: 1915 ANNA LEA: 27.2.1918 missing
137. LOYALIST (pass) 1902 BYRON	3909	1901	--	1903	1922 SANTIAGO: 1932 b.u.
138. (Beaumont) (414) (tank)	6060	1902	1902	1904	SEMINOLE: 1913 WABASHA; 1929 NORDSEE: 1933 b.u.
139. (-----)	9851	1902	--	1902	PANNONIA: 1922 b.u.
140. BUCCANEER	925	1890	1902	1903	1925 AGATHE: 1926 HERMAN: 1928 ALBERT: 1933 MALTA: 1936 b.u.
141. EVANGELINE (p/c) ex Clan Mackinnon	2266	1891	1902	1909	PELAGOS: 14.8.1912 ashore, b.u.
142. FLORENCE (1158)	2492	1889	1902	--	20.12.1912 wrecked
143. LONDON CITY (p/c) ex Clan Forbes	2461	1882	1902	1910	hulked: 1922 b.u.
144. LOYALIST (p/c) ex Clan Macalister	2294	1891	1902	--	27.9.1904 wrecked
145. NEW OPORTO	502	1903	--	1903	7.1.1915 wrecked
146. ST JOHN CITY (p/c) ex Clan Macnab	2265	1891	1903	1909	PONTOS: 1914 blockship: 1922 b.u.
147. DRUMBAIN	2313	1902	1904	1904	HOUTDIJK: 28.8.1914 mined & sunk
148. (Thornley)	1319	1903	--	1903	GROVEHURST: 1915 JOHANNES MAERSK: 1922 VIKING: 1953 b.u.
149. (Wearside)	1400	1903	--	1903	SIRIUS: 1907 SWANSEA BAY: 1913 MARTIN: 1923 SVOBODA: 1924 dismantled
150. ALMERIANA	1603	1905	--	1905	KEJSERINDE DAGMAR: 2.4.1944 mined & sunk
151. COLLINGWOOD	1278	1905	--	1924	JERNLAND: 1947 NAGU: 1959 b.u.
152. DURANGO	3008	1905	1905	--	26.8.1917 sunk by U53
153. FARADAY	892	1873	1905	--	1909 b.u.
154. GLORIANA	3051	1905	--	1913	REMIER: 1924 KENJO MARU: 12.6.1945 sunk by USS SKATE
155. OHIO	4006	1899	1905	1909	ZAANDYK: 22.2.1917 sunk by U21
156. RUNO	4016	1900	1905	1909	ZIJLDYK: 1928 HOFLAAN: 1932 b.u.
157. TABASCO	2987	1895	1905	--	26.1.1917 sunk by U45
158. TAMPICO	2968	1895	1905	--	19.10.1907 foundered
159. VENANGO	2938	1891	1905	1913	ROUENNAIS: 1917 WILFRED: 1927 b.u.
160. ALMERIANA ex Catania, Echuca	2861	1889	1906	--	1914 b.u.

Name	GRT	Built	Acquired	Sold	Subsequent career
161. ANNAPOLIS ex Capri, Diana	2057	1889	1906	1907	MANGORO: 1915 ISLANDIA: 1927 SAINT PARASKEVI: 1928 GUINEE FRANCAISE: 1931 AGIA PARASKEVI: 1934 b.u.
162. HALIFAX CITY ex Syracuse, John Cockerill	2464	1894	1906	1911	SYRA: 1912 TIJDITT: 1916 PARACIERS: 17.9.1917 sunk by UC64
163. QUEEN WILHELMINA	3590	1898	1906	--	8.5.1915 sunk by U9
164. RIPON	2965	1906	--	1913	FRUITHANDEL: 1916 GASCONIER: 20.8.1918 mined & sunk
165. ARABIANA (427)	3001	1907	1907	1913	TREVIER: 4.4.1918 sunk by UB23
166. BOLIVIANA (405) ex Lugano, Boliviana	4573	1900	1907	1920	ATLANTIS: 1924 LOTUS: 1925 ASMUND: 2.12.1930 ashore, CTL, b.u.
167. (Brantford)*	4232	1907	--	--	not identified
168. BRAZILIANA (Billiter Avenue)	3827	1907	1907	1914	FORFAR: 4.12.1917 sunk by UC17
169. CRAMLINGTON	1824	1907	--	--	21.10.1908 collision
170. CROXDALE (429)	1295	1906	1907	1922	1934 URANUS: 1942 HOCHMEISTER: 1945 URANUS: 1958 b.u.
171. DAGENHAM	1466	1907	--	--	8.4.1909 wrecked
172. EASINGTON	1416	1907	--	1915	24.9.1915 missing
173. GRACIANA (432)	4266	1907	1907	1908	MINISTRE BEERNAERT: 26.12.1915 sunk by UB24
174. GUARDIANA (433/1169)	6852	1907	1907	1911	to HL
175. KANAWHA (449)	3884	1893	1907	1922	GEORGETTE: 1923 b.u.
176. LUDWORTH	1301	1907	--	1923	HELENA: 1933 ATILLA: 1957 KOSAR: 1968 b.u.
177. MALINCHE (434)	1868	1906	1907	1913	29.11.1915 sunk by U33
178. NEWPORT NEWS (457)	3031	1907	1907	1913	IJZERHANDEL: 1916 SIBERIER: 5.4.1917 sunk by U86
179. NORTON (Cornwall)	4230	1907	--	1921	1923 JOHANNA: 1928 JUSTITIA: 1933 b.u.
180. POMARON (692)	1809	1907	--	1922	to JL
181. RAPIDAN (459) 1913 RAPIDAN	3760	1907	1907 1913	1907 1923	charter CLAN MACIVER: DOVENBY HALL: 1927 PANAGHIS M HADOULIS: 1933 MIREILLE: 1934 b.u.
182. RAPPAHANNOCK (450)	3884	1893	1907	--	26.10.1916 sunk by U69
183. ROANOKE (461) 1914 ROANOKE	3755	1907	1907 1914	1907 --	charter CLAN MACINNES: 12.8.1917 sunk by UB48
184. RYHOPE	1334	1907	--	1924	LYSLAND: 1960 b.u.
185. (Seaton)*	4231	1907	--	--	not identified
186. SHENANDOAH (451)	3886	1893	1907	--	14.4.1916 mined & sunk
187. THIMBLEBY	1860	1907	--	1915	BARON KELVIN: 1923 L'INVICTA: 1923 TAKASAGO MARU: 6.3.1932 wrecked
188. TUDHOE (435)	1298	1906	1907	1913	GROVEMONT: 1915 CAPITOL: 1925 VILMA: 1945 INGA L: 1954 AIRA: 1955 LISBET: 1957 b.u.
189. TUNSTALL (436) (Billiter)	3825	1907	1907 1907	1907 1915	to BMT: returned 1919 ARGOSTOLI: 1922 CARTHAGE: 1925 MARIONGA MANTACA: 1927 b.u.
190. WASHINGTON (462)	3031	1907	1907	1913	ERTSHANDEL: 1916 CHILIER: 21.6.1918 sunk by U151
191. (Welldeck)	4233	1907	--	1907	NETHERLEE: 11.2.1917 sunk by U81
192. WESTHAMPTON (437)	1860	1907	1907 1910	1909 1913	ELLI: returned AMPHION: 1915 BARON CATHCART: 1924 MARJORIE SEED: 25.12.1924 wrecked
193. WESTWOOD	1986	1907	--	--	3.10.1918 sunk by UB112
194. WHORLTON	1420	1907	--	--	12.1.1918 sunk by UB30
195. CANADIA ex Reval, Canadia, Steinhoft	2414	1898	1908	1909	MYRTOON: 1913 GYPTIS: 1919 VILLE DE NANCY: 1924 b.u.
196. CARDIFF TRADER (515) ex Broomhill	562	1878	1908	1908	to LWS
197. CASTLE EDEN	1859	1908	--	1913	BARON BLANTYRE: 3.9.1917 sunk by U89
198. CHARLESTON	1866	1908	--	--	11.12.1917 sunk by UB65
199. CUNDALL (691)	1851	1908	--	1922	to JL
200. FERNANDINA	1851	1908	--	1921	FALKENSTEIN: 1934 b.u.
201. GRANTLEY	1869	1908	--	1921	1924 KENNINGTON: 1924 BLENDA: 3.1944 sunk by aircraft
202. MARIANA (456)	4204	1905	1908	1908	GOUVERNEUR DE LANTSHEERE: 1934 b.u.
203. NORFOLK (458)	3836	1907	1908	1914	EFSTATHIOS: 27.5.1917 sunk by UC21

*It has not been possible to identify these two vessels, 167 and 185. It is likely they were completed as *Irmingard, Canterbury* or *Belle of Spain*. Other unidentified ships, from a December 1908 Fleet list, are *Valentiana* and *Numidiana* (10,000 dwt), *Emiliana* (7,250 dwt) and *Fowey* (5,250 dwt).

Name	GRT	Built	Acquired	Sold	Subsequent career
204. PORTINGLIS (689)	1867	1908	--	1922	to JL
205. RICHMOND (460)	2921	1907	1908	1914	DRONT: 1.9.1917 sunk by U28
206. ROTTERDAM (438)	4885	1907	1908	1909	SOMMELSDYK: 21.4.1910 burnt
207. THORNLEY (439)	1327	1907	1908	1927	PENELOPE: 19.5.1942 sunk by HMS TURBULENT
208. ABANA	4189	1894	1909	1913	TAMON MARU NO 15: 1916 KAIHO MARU: 11.11.1916 wrecked
209. ACARA (603)	4982	1904	1909	1911	to FSA
210. ALLEGHANY (453)	4262	1901	1909	1912	SAIGON MARU: 23.5.1929 wrecked
211. APPENINE (488)	3684	1909	--	1913	to GL
212. ASIANA	2993	1909	--	1910	ROWTOR: 1913 EFTICHIA: VERGOTTI: 1938 CALVADOS: 1940 TOURQUENNOIS: 1942 FERRARA: 1947 POLINNIA: 1958 b.u.
213. AUSTRIANA (409)	4025	1901	1909	1915	RIO VERDE: 21.2.1918 sunk by U86
214. AVALA	3751	1890	1909	1913	24.3.1918 sunk by U155
215. AXWELL	1442	1909	--	1913	13.11.1917 sunk by UB56
216. BIRMINGHAM (410)	4027	1901	1909	1915	RIO PRETO: 18.12.1922 wrecked
217. BRANTFORD (440)	4844	1909	--	1909	ANDYK: 1930 b.u.
218. CATERINO (489)	3729	1909	--	1913	to GL
219. CYNTHIANA (424)	3185	1905	1909	1914	EGRET: 28.1.1917 mined & sunk
220. FELICIANA	3109	1909	--	1909	BENBRIDGE: 1912 ITALIA: 11.5.1917 wrecked
221. HARLINGEN (644)	938	1909	--	1912	to GT
222. HOWDEN	1020	1909	--	1913	1925 ASLAUG: 25.12.1929 wrecked
223. IBEX ex Forest Brook	2689	1895	1909	1909	PATRAS: 1927 b.u.
224. INDIANA (415)	3869	1902	1909	1919	NORA SALIARI: 19.5.1924 foundered
225. LANGDALE (602)	3930	1903	1909	1911	to FSA
226. (Napoliana)	2993	1909	--	1909	ARMSTOR: 24.12.1912 missing
227. ORIANA (416/1236)	4419	1902	1909	1912	to B&A
228. (Parisiana)	3681	1909	--	1909	BENDEW: 4.4.1916 mined & sunk
229. PARISIANA (1206)	4823	1909	--	1910	to ET
230. PERSIANA (417)	4015	1902	1909	1915	RIO PARANA: 24.2.1915 sunk by U8
231. PERUVIANA (425)	3153	1905	1909	1914	JOULAN: 1922 KAMO: 9.12.1936 wrecked
232. POTOMAC (418)	3618	1902	1909	1915	1920 ROVIGNO: 5.10.1922 wrecked
233. POWHATAN (454)	4262	1900	1909	1913	SENJU MARU: 19.11.1915 sunk by U33
234. RINGWOOD	905	1889	1909	1911	NIKEA: 6.11.1914 sunk by Russian cruiser KAGUL
235. ROSSANO (491)	3729	1909	--	1913	to GL
236. ROUEN	1968	1909	--	1926	JEAN DE BETHENCOURT: 1936 JEANNE M: 2.12.1940 sunk by U37
237. SANDOWN (422) 1911 EGYPTIANA	3790	1905	1909	--	9.6.1917 sunk by U70
238. SAVANNAH (1207)	4849	1909	--	1910	to ET
239. SWALEDALE (604) ex Ile de la Reunion	3658	1897	1909	1911	to FSA
240. WENSLEYDALE (605)	3964	1903	1909	1911	to FSA
241. TOGSTON (645) (Wingate)	1057	1909	--	1913	to GT
242. WYANDOTTE (407/1239) ex Lord Roberts	4204	1900	1909	1912	to B&A
243. ADANA	3448	1897	1910	1911	MILTIADES EMBIRICOS: 1.7.1917 sunk by UC67
244. (Algeriana) (1211)	3448	1910	--	1910	to ET
245. AMANA	3412	1895	1910	--	1.12.1911 missing
246. ANAPA	3524	1896	1910	1912	TENZAN MARU: 17.5.1920 missing
247. ASAMA	4217	1897	1910	1913	ASAMA MARU: 1918 LA CHAUSSADE: 13.8.1918 sunk by UC28
248. (Graciana) (1210)	4100	1910	--	1910	to ET
249. (Waldridge)	1441	1910	--	1910	BONDICAR: 1947 CHRYSSOULA: 1947 HELLENIC CHRYSSOULA: 1954 b.u.
250. ATHENIANA (411) ex Athinaia, Atheniana	2300	1902	1911	1913	ALIDA: 1919 KARLSVIK: 1934 ALIDA GORTHON: 29.8.1940 sunk by U100
251. BACCHUS (592)	3078	1902	1911	1911	to FSA
252. CHASE SIDE (1238) ex Indradevi	5683	1900	1911	1912	to B&A
253. EAVESTONE	1781	1912	--	--	3.2.1917 sunk by U45
254. EL URUGUAYO (1237)	8361	1912	--	1912	to B&A
255. GRACIANA (464) ex Sierra Morena	3536	1903	1911	1912 / 1913 / 1924	to C&O: returned ANDREAS K: 16.3.1931 ashore, CTL, b.u.
256. LINGAN	4677	1911	--	1917	1934 b.u.
257. MESSINA (490)	4271	1911	--	1913	to GL
258. NYMEGEN ex Johanna Oelssner	894	1889	1911	1914	1915 GREYPOINT: 18.3.1917 sunk by German destroyer S20

191

Name	GRT	Built	Acquired	Sold	Subsequent career
259. (Oristano)(487)	4220	1911	--	1911	to GL
260. SALTBURN (593)	1768	1911	--	1912	to FSA
261. HOCHELAGA	4681	1912	--	1916	7.8.1930 wrecked
262. LA ROSARINA (1240)	8750	1912	--	1912	to B&A
263. SWANSEA TRADER (516) ex Crathie	480	1883	1912	1914	TANCHIN: 1927 SAN IRENEO: 1940 CASTILLO SANTACARA: 1941 PUNTA LUCERO: 1960 b.u.
264. ALGERIANA (557) ex Dettingen, Cebriana, Twickenham, Cebriana	4221	1899	1913	1915	21.9.1917 wrecked
265. CHANNEL TRADER (518)	684	1913	--	1913	to LWS
266. DIGBY (p/c) (848)	3966	1913	--	1925	to BWI
267. LLANELLY TRADER (519)	702	1913	--	1913	to LWS
268. LONDON TRADER (520)	684	1913	--	1913	to LWS
269. TEES TRADER (521)	701	1913	--	1913	to LWS
270. TUNISIANA (555) ex Balaclava	4220	1906	1913	--	23.6.1915 sunk by UB16
271. BEDALE	2107	1914	--	--	6.10.1917 sunk by U96
272. CASTLE EDEN	1949	1914	--	--	3.3.1918 sunk by U110
273. MAXTON (566) ex Start Point	3840	1912	1914	--	28.12.1917 sunk by U19
274. MOBILE	1950	1914	--	--	28.4.1915 sunk by U30
275. PENSACOLA (Tampa)	2092	1914	--	1923	CLAPTON: 1924 SAIMA: 1936 DANAPRIS: 27.4.1941 sunk by aircraft
276. SOUTH POINT (565) [Eston]	3837	1912	1914	--	27.3.1915 sunk by U53
277. VENICE (690)	1874	1914	--	1922	to JL
278. WATERLAND (763)	494	1903	1914	1920	to PL
279. WEST POINT (567) [Winton]	2413	1912	1914	--	8.10.1916 sunk by U53
280. WINGATE (688)	1911	1914	--	1922	to JL
281. ANNAPOLIS ex Lord Lonsdale	4567	1911	1915	--	19.4.1917 sunk by U61/U69
282. LEXINGTON ex Invertay	3974	1906	1915	1924	DENHAM: 1931 b.u.
283. PARISIANA (1214) ex Argentine Transport	4763	1911	1915	--	23.4.1916 sunk by U19
284. TAMAQUA ex Den of Glamis	5191	1910	1915	1922	GYOKOH MARU: 23.2.1944 wrecked
285. WYNCOTE ex Den of Ruthven	4937	1907	1915	1924	KINTYRE: 1929 POLYMNIA: 1937 SYDNEY: 1938 CORUNA: 1942 CASTILLO SIMANCAS: 1952 JARAMA: 1960 RIVADEMAR: 1962 MUNISA: 29.4.1972 ashore, CTL

(Den of Crombie (4949gt, blt 1907) also purchased but 8.11.1915 sunk by U35 prior to delivery.)

Name	GRT	Built	Acquired	Sold	Subsequent career
286. CONWAY	4003	1900	1916	--	30.4.1918 sunk by UB105
287. PETER PAN (644) ex Harlingen	938	1909	1916	1923	SIRIUS: 1923 NEWBURN: 1927 FEDDY: 5.4.1942 collision
288. POLMANTER ex Leasowe Castle, New Orleans	3515	1901	1916	1916	BAYMANTER: 11.11.1920 wrecked
289. ALLENDALE	2153	1917	--	--	25.3.1918 sunk by U101
290. BEAUMARIS	2372	1917	--	--	7.2.1918 sunk by U53
291. CRESSWELL (Guldborg)	2829	1917	--	--	5.2.1918 sunk by U46
292. EIBERGEN (594)	4767	1914	1917	1919	to FSA
293. HASLEMERE	2126	1917	--	1920	HOLMEDAL: 1935 SPIND: 23.8.1941 sunk by U564/U552
294. HELIKON	2232	1917	1917	1919	1959 b.u.
295. PROSPER	2232	1917	1917	1919	1968 b.u.
296. KEIGHLEY	2149	1917	--	1920	GRAZIELLA: 16.9.1943 sunk by aircraft
297. KELBERGEN (595)	4751	1914	1917	1919	to FSA
298. RIJSBERGEN (604) ex Swaledale, Ile de Reunion	3658	1897	1917	1919	to FSA
299. ROTA	2171	1915	1917	--	22.7.1917 sunk by UB40
300. SEDBERGH	4275	1917	--	1920	1.9.1942 wrecked
301. SIDLAW RANGE (551)	4407	1917	--	1918	to NSN
302. UBBERGEN (600)	1877	1911	1917	1919	to FSA
303. VEENBERGEN (597) ex Evesham, Albiana	4281	1905	1917	1919	to FSA
304. WAR ADMIRAL	5875	1917	--	1920	CHEF MECANICIEN MAILHOL: 1936 MALEAS: 1939 THEODOROS COUMANTAROS: 1940 KINKAI MARU: 3.10.1942 sunk by USS GREENLING
305. WAR COUNCIL	5875	1917	--	--	16.10.1918 sunk by U63

Name	GRT	Built	Acquired	Sold	Subsequent career
306. WAR HERO	5875	1917	--	1919	HATKHOLA: 1934 b.u.
307. WAR KING	9394	1917	--	1919	M S DOLLAR: 1928 CHIEF MAQUILLA: 1.12.1928 foundered
308. WAR LION	5875	1917	--	1919	JEBBA: 1933 THALIA: 16.9.1940 sunk by U99
309. WAR PILOT	5875	1917	--	1920	JEKRI: 1933 b.u.
310. WAR PRINCE	5870	1917	--	1919	COMMISSAIRE PIERRE LECOCQ: 1937 MOUNT PELION: 2.11.1942 sunk by U522
311. WAR QUEEN	5844	1917	--	1919	LIEUTENANT DE LA TOUR: 1951 CLEOPHIE IOANNA: 25.7.1952 ashore, b.u.
312. WAR SOLDIER	7446	1917	--	1919	RIPLEY CASTLE: 1932 b.u.
313. WAR SAILOR	7522	1917	--	1919	HATARANA: 18.8.1942 sunk by U214
314. WAR TIGER	5875	1917	--	1920	CAPODIMONTE: 1934 b.u.
315. WAR WOLF	5875	1917	--	1919	COMMANDANT MAGES: 1933 SAINT MALO: 12.10.1940 sunk by U101
316. HERMELIN	2232	1918	1918	1928	ST FRANCOIS RIVER: 1929 GIA LONG: 1930 DUMONT D'URVILLE: 1936 JOAN MOLLER: 1942 GYOYU MARU: 3.7.1944 sunk by USS SEAHORSE
317. FORT HAMILTON (839) (pass) ex Bermudian	5530	1904	1919	1921	to BWI
318. FORT VICTORIA (841) (pass) ex Willochra	7784	1913	1920	1921	to BWI
319. GUIANA (846)	3657	1907	1920	1922	to BWI
320. KORONA ex Monmouthshire	2874	1886	1920	1921	1924 b.u.
321. MARAVAL (703/842) ex Irrawaddy	5144	1903	1920	1921	to BWI
322. MATURA (702/843) ex Amarapoora	4556	1901	1920	1921	to BWI
323. MAYARO (702/843) ex Pegu	3896	1900	1920	1921	to BWI
324. PARIMA (847) ex Bungaree	2990	1889	920	1922	to BWI
325. (Braziliana) (764)	3496	1922	--	1922	to PL
326. CHICKAHOMINY (762/822) ex Persiana	3493	1921	1922	1924	to RCL
327. FELICIANA (687/505) 1922 LONDON MARINER 1929 IMPERIAL PRINCE	7896	1922	-- 1929	1922 1935	to GL, returned CRAFTSMAN: 9.4.1941 sunk by KORMORAN
328. PARISIANA (684/552) 1922 LONDON EXCHANGE	6640	1921	--	1925	to NSN
329. PERUVIANA (686/693)	4099	1921	1921	1923	to JL
330. TUNISIANA (765)	3482	1922	--	1922	to PL
331. ALLEGHANY (823) (Arabiana)	3489	1922	--	1923	to RCL
332. APPOMATOX (824) (Egyptiana)	3491	1922	--	1924	to RCL
333. GOWERIAN	449	1921	1922	1923	KINNAIRD HEAD: 27.12.1940 mined & sunk
334. CYNTHIANA (616) 1922 HOOSAC 1922 LONDON CORPORATION	6629	1922	-- 1928	1925 1937	to WL: returned MARIONGA J GOULANDRI: 1938 BENLOMOND: 23.11.1942 sunk by U172
335. LONDON SHIPPER 1929 BRITISH PRINCE (Australiana) (580)	7939	1923	-- 1928	1923 1935	to NNA: returned. STATESMAN: 17.5.1941 sunk by aircraft
336. LONDON IMPORTER (Indiana)	7895	1922	--	1933	HMS RELIANT: 1945 ANTHONY G: 1949 FIRDAUSA: 1963 b.u.
337. ELDON	2925	1923	--	1929	JAPIX: 1933 AMUR: not reported since 1950
338. LONDON COMMERCE 1928 ROYAL PRINCE (Nataliana)	7886	1923	--	1935	COLLEGIAN: 1948 b.u.
339. THROCKLEY	2925	1923	--	1929	MELITA: 1933 JANA: not reported since 1950
340. PACIFIC SHIPPER	6305	1924	--	--	1950 b.u.
341. PACIFIC TRADER	6327	1924	--	1937	BRAGANZA: 12.10.1944 burnt
342. PACIFIC PRESIDENT	7114	1928	--	--	2.12.1940 sunk by U43
343. PACIFIC GROVE	7114	1928	--	--	12.4.1943 sunk by U563
344. CYNTHIANA ex Silurian	6903	1924	1928	--	23.6.1928 wrecked
345. LONDON CITIZEN ex Valemore (675)	5388	1918	1928	--	1936 b.u.
346. ARIANO (502) ex War Python	5455	1918	1929	1929	FORT ARCHAMBAULT: 1951 SILVANO: 1958 b.u.
347. PACIFIC RANGER	6866	1929	--	--	12.10.1940 sunk by U59
348. MONARCH OF BERMUDA (pass) (1406)	22424	1931	--	1947	24.3.1947 fire, CTL, sold, NEW AUSTRALIA: 1958 ARKADIA: 1966 b.u.

Name	GRT	Built	Acquired	Sold	Subsequent career
349. EL URUGUAYO (1237)	8361	1911	1933	--	1937 b.u.
350. QUEEN OF BERMUDA (pass)	22575	1933	--	--	1966 b.u.
351. EL ARGENTINO (1242)	9501	1928	1934	--	26.7.1943 sunk by aircraft
352. LA ROSARINA (1240)	8345	1912	1934	--	1937 b.u.
353. FORT AMHERST (p/c)	3489	1936	--	1952	AMHERST: 1963 b.u.
354. FORT TOWNSHEND (p/c)	3489	1936	--	1952	AL AMIR SAUD: 1956 MANSOUR: 1960 ROMANTICA: 1983 b.u.
355. MANAQUI	2802	1924	1937	--	16.3.1942 sunk by U504
356. PACIFIC IMPORTER (1423) ex Samtredy	7259	1943	1947	1953	AQUITANIA: 1965 AYIA MARINA: 1969 b.u.
357. PACIFIC LIBERTY (1413) ex Samcalia	7258	1943	1947	1954	PHOEBUS: 1963 BAYHORSE: 1970 SAN GABRIEL: 1971 b.u.
358. PACIFIC NOMAD (1412) ex Samavon	7290	1943	1947	1954	NIKOLAS: 1960 STAMATIS: 3.11.1966 wrecked
359. PACIFIC RANGER (1415) ex Samdaring	7282	1944	1947	1952	SAN DIMITRIS: 1958 PRIARUGGIA: 1960 ALBARO: 1963 AIGAION: 1968 b.u.
360. PACIFIC STRONGHOLD (1430) 1954 MALAYAN PRINCE ex Tusculum Victory	7640	1945	1947	1959	WANG KNIGHT: 1959 MARINE CARRIER: 1960 ELIE V: 1964 OCEANIC WAVE: 1969 SILVER FALCON: 1970 b.u.
361. PACIFIC UNITY	9511	1948	--	1964	LAVRENTIOS: 1970 b.u.
362. OCEAN MONARCH (pass)	13654	1951	--	1967	VARNA: 1979 RIVIERA: 1979 REINA DEL MAR: 28.5.1981 burnt
363. PACIFIC FORTUNE (585)	9400	1947	1951	1965	MALAYSIA FORTUNE: 1974 b.u.
364. PACIFIC RELIANCE (1017)	9442	1951	--	1970	to RML
365. BRITISH PRINCE (836) 1957 MANDAGALA ex Stamford Victory	7681	1945	1954	1960	ORIENT TRADER: 21.7.1965 fire, CTL, b.u.
366. PACIFIC NORTHWEST (1016)	9442	1954	--	1970	to RML
367. WELSH PRINCE (834)	7381	1944	1954	1961	VERGMONT: 1971 b.u.
368. FORT AVALON (855)	3484	1949	1957	1960	AZUR MED: 1974 b.u.
369. SAGAMORE (1053) (ore)	10792	1957	--	1973	to PMS
370. EDENMORE (1051) (ore)	10792	1958	--	1973	to PMS
371. PACIFIC ENVOY 1967 LOCH RYAN 1970 PACIFIC ENVOY (1015)	9439	1958	--	1970	to RML
372. PACIFIC STRONGHOLD (1018)	9439	1958	--	1970	to RML
373. TUDOR PRINCE (tank) 1971 STOLT TUDOR	12958	1961	--	1973	1975 STOLTA: 1977 STELLA AZZURRA: 1986 AZZURRA: 1988 b.u.
374. NEWFOUNDLAND (642) 1973 CUFIC	6906	1964	--	1973	to JWL
375. NOVA SCOTIA (643) 1973 TROPIC	6906	1965	--	1973	to JWL
376. ORCOMA (1045)	10300	1966	--	1978	to PSN
377. BOTANY BAY (cc)	26876	1969	--	1980	1989 NEDLLOYD TASMAN: still afloat
378. FURNESS BRIDGE (bulk/oil)	91079	1971	--	1977	LAKE ARROWHEAD: 1982 MARCONA PATHFINDER: 1983 WORLD PATHFINDER: 1986 OCEAN SOVEREIGN: still afloat
379. RIPON GRANGE (1290) (bulk) ex Orotava, Orotava Bridge, Orotava	28880	1968	1979	1980	LEDA: 1982 UNITY: 1984 LATINI: 1986 b.u.
380. ROUNTON GRANGE (bulk) ex Pacific Wasa	40753	1972	1980	1984	CHINA MARQUIS: 1986 OCEAN PEACE: 1989 FORUM GLORY: still afloat

C Furness and Company

381. TYNEDALE (39/88)	2148	1889	1891	1892	to FW
382. TYNEHEAD (53/89)	2258	1890	1891	1892	to FW

S W Furness

383. CUNDALL	2390	1894	--	1899	OGONO: 18.8.1929 collision
384. KIRKSTALL (Lady Olivia)	1831	1895	--	1896	1908 BARON GARIOCH: 28.10.1917 sunk by UC63

R B Stoker

385. ADRIA	844	1864	1891	1891	1894 b.u.
386. SYDENHAM	2377	1891	--	1900	1907 BEATRICE: 1916 BARBRO: 14.10.1917 sunk by UC48
387. CYNTHIANA (396)	2864	1891	1892	1897	to BMT
388. MAY	1178	1890	1892	1894	5.1.1897 foundered
389. FELICIANA	2922	1891	1892	1896	1901 SERAFIN BALLESTEROS: 19.7.1928 collision
390. MANDALAY	1915	1872	1892	1892	1893 LOUISIANA: 1906 b.u.
391. DELHI	2009	1864	1893	--	1895 b.u.
392. STRAITS OF MENAI (399)	2870	1894	1896	1897	to BMT
393. STRAITS OF SUNDA	2993	1895	1896	1897	YORUBA: 17.8.1911 wrecked

Name	GRT	Built	Acquired	Sold	Subsequent career
394. LADY FURNESS (397)	3158	1895	1897	1897	to BMT
395. (Cranford)	2991	1904	--	1904	FURTOR: 1913 EMIL: 1915 AQUARIUS: 10.11.1918 collision

British Maritime Trust Ltd

Name	GRT	Built	Acquired	Sold	Subsequent career
396. CYNTHIANA (387)	2923	1891	1897	1900	SAXON KING: 1904 EGYPTIAN: 26.8.1912 wrecked
397. LADY FURNESS (394)	3158	1895	1897	--	8.11.1897 missing
398. MEDIANA	2440	1897	--	1901	1912 SIGNE: 1923 ROBERT: 1937 MYDOL: 1938 ANITA: 1939 CARTHAGE: 1954 b.u.
399. STRAITS OF MENAI (394)	2870	1894	1897	1899	1910 CHALKYDON: 14.7.1917 sunk by U155
400. (Gloriana)	3379	1898	--	1898	POLARSTJERNAN: 1915 BORGHILD: 1927 EUROS: 1934 b.u.
401. GLORIANA	2768	1898	--	1900	BETTY: 10.6.1917 sunk by U61
402. ITALIANA (120)	2663	1898	--	1900	14.9.1916 sunk by UB43
403. CEBRIANA (557)	4221	1899	--	1905	charter TWICKENHAM
				1907	1907
					to ASS
404. (Adriana)	2931	1900	--	1900	WHANGAPE: 1929 NANKING: 1934 b.u.
405. BOLIVIANA (166)	4573	1900	--	1901	charter LUGANO:
			1906	1907	returned: to FW
406. POWHATAN (454) (Austriana)	4262	1900	--	1902	to C&O
407. WYANDOTTE (242) ex Lord Roberts	4204	1900	1900	1909	to FW
408. ALLEGHANY (453)	4262	1901	--	1902	to C&O
409. AUSTRIANA (213)	4025	1901	--	1909	to FW
410. BIRMINGHAM (216) (Persiana)	4027	1901	--	1909	to FW
411. ATHENIANA (250)	2300	1902	--	1909	ATHINAIA: 1911 to FW
412. COMO	5137	1902	--	1909	GORREDYK: 1923 BENMACDHUI: 1931 b.u.
413. (Egyptiana) (481)	5140	1902	--	1902	to GL
414. (Gloriana) (138)(tank)	6060	1902	--	1902	to FW
415. INDIANA (224)	3869	1902	--	1909	to FW
416. ORIANA (227)	4419	1902	--	1909	to FW
417. PERSIANA (230)	4032	1902	--	1909	to FW
418. POTOMAC (232)	3618	1902	--	1909	to FW
419. (Gloriana)	3926	1903	--	1903	FRANK COVERDALE: 1912 ARTHUR BALFOUR: 1916 CARSTON: 1926 GOULANDRIS: 6.11.1932 foundered
420. (Gloriana)	4286	1904	--	1904	CANADA CAPE: 1915 WAIHEMO: 17.3.1918 sunk by UC37
421. (Gloriana) (554)	4240	1904	--	1904	to ASS
422. SANDOWN (237) (Egyptiana)	3790	1905	--	1909	to FW
423. (Adriana)	4169	1906	--	1906	MIDGARD: 17.6.1907 wrecked
424. CYNTHIANA (71/219)	3185	1905	1906	1909	to FW
425. PERUVIANA (73/231)	3153	1905	1906	1909	to FW
426. (Adriana) (559)	4200	1907	--	1907	to ASS
427. (ARABIANA) (165)	3001	1907	--	1907	to FW
428. BRAZILIANA (168)	3827	1907	--	1907	to FW
429. CROXDALE (170)	1283	1906	--	1907	to FW
430. (Graciana)	5520	1907	--	1907	PEI-HO: 1934 b.u.
431. (Adriana)	5420	1907	--	1907	MEINAM: 1934 b.u.
432. (GRACIANA) (173)	4270	1907	--	1907	to FW
433. GUARDIANA (174)	6852	1907	--	1907	to FW
434. MALINCHE (177)	1868	1906	--	1907	to FW
435. TUDHOE (188)	1298	1906	--	1907	to FW
436. TUNSTALL (189)	3825	1907	1907	1907	to FW
437. (WESTHAMPTON) (192)	1860	1907	--	1907	to FW
438. ROTTERDAM (206)	4859	1907	--	1908	to FW
439. (THORNLEY) (207) (Bramley)	1327	1907	--	1908	to FW
440. (Amsterdam) (217)	4844	1909	--	1909	to FW
441. ANNETTE FURNESS	1871	1907	1911	1912	GROVENESS: 1915 HOGLAND: 1916 WINNECONNE: 2.6.1918 sunk by U151
442. LADY FURNESS	1272	1906	1911	1912	GROVELEA: 1915 PHARE: 31.10.1917 sunk by UB35
443. BOWHEAD ex Z4	237	1915	1923	1926	dismantled
444. CYNTHIANA	3374	1923	--	1926	SCHWARZES MEER: 26.8.1944 scuttled, b.u.
445. PERUVIANA ex Modum	4302	1923	1923	1923	ASTRA II: 1964 b.u.

Name	GRT	Built	Acquired	Sold	Subsequent career
Chesapeake and Ohio Steamship Company Ltd					
446. APPOMATOX	2875	1893	--	1902	1910 SEYER: 13.3.1916 sunk by Russian destroyers GROMKIJ & BYSTRYJ
447. CHICKAHOMINY	2875	1893	--	1902	1910 b.u.
448. GREENBRIER	2875	1893	--	1902	2.4.1915 mined & sunk
449. KANAWHA (175)	3884	1893	--	1907	to FW
450. RAPPAHANNOCK (182)	3881	1893	--	1907	to FW
451. SHENANDOAH (186)	3886	1893	--	1907	to FW
452. RAPIDAN (127)	7359	1898	--	1898	to FW
453. ALLEGHANY (408/210)	4262	1901	1902	1909	to FW
454. POWHATAN (406/233)	4262	1901	1902	1909	to FW
455. ALBIANA (70/558)	4224	1905	1907	1907	to ASS
456. MARIANA (72/202)	4204	1905	1907	1908	to FW
457. NEWPORT NEWS (178)	3031	1907	--	1907	to FW
458. NORFOLK (203)	3836	1907	--	1908	to FW
459. RAPIDAN (181)	3760	1907	--	1907	to FW
460. RICHMOND (205)	2921	1907	--	1908	to FW
461. ROANOKE (183)	3755	1907	--	1907	to FW
462. WASHINGTON (190)	3031	1907	--	1907	to FW
463. ALBIANA ex Braemount, Corby Castle	3607	1898	1912	1913	1919 BERRIEDALE: 1921 BROCKDALE: 1924 CARDIFF: 1927 PELLEGRA: 1932 b.u.
464. GRACIANA (255) ex Sierra Morena	3536	1903	1912	1913	to FW
Wilson's and Furness-Leyland Line Ltd					
465. BOSTONIAN	4668	1888	1896	--	1913 b.u.
466. CAMBRIAN 1915 BOSTONIAN	5626	1896	--	--	10.10.1917 sunk by U53
467. GEORGIAN	5088	1890	1896	--	8.3.1917 sunk by UB47
468. IDAHO (111) 1897 LONDONIAN	5532	1896	1896	--	23-29.11.1898 foundered
469. MEGANTIC (113) 1898 ANGLIAN	5532	1896	1896	--	10.6.1917 sunk by UC75
470. ALEXANDRA (pass)	6919	1897	--	1898	MENOMINEE: 1926 b.u.
471. BOADICEA (pass)	7057	1897	--	1898	MARQUETTE: 23.10.1915 sunk by U35
472. CHICAGO 1903 ETONIAN	6408	1898	1899	--	5.3.1918 sunk by U61
473. (CLEOPATRA) (pass)	6889	1898	--	1898	MOHEGAN: 14.10.1898 wrecked
474. VICTORIA (pass)	6849	1898	--	1898	MANITOU: 1921 POLAND: 1925 NATALE: 1925 b.u.
474a WINIFREDA (pass)	6833	1898	--	1898	MESABA: 1.9.1918 sunk by UB118
Gulf Line Ltd					
475. GULF OF VENICE	3022	1883	--	1913	ANNA: 1.12.1914 fire
476. GULF OF ANCUD	2716	1890	--	1911	VOSTIZZA: 1912 MONT-AIGOUAL: 1913 GENERAL LYAUTEY: 1916 ARDECHE: 1925 b.u.
477. GULF OF BOTHNIA	3452	1891	--	1904	SCHWARZBURG: PONTA DELGADA: 14.7.1918 sunk by UC54
478. GULF OF GENOA	3448	1891	--	1903	ALTENBURG. 30.3.1909 fire, b.u.
479. GULF OF SIAM	3433	1892	--	1903	SCHAUMBURG: 1916 HORTA: 8.7.1918 sunk by UC73
480. GULF OF TARANTO	3431	1892	--	1903	MECKLENBURG: 1921 ANTOLINA PONTE: 1924 b.u.
481. RAPALLO (413)	5166	1902	1902	1909	MAARTENSDIJK: 1923 BENVRACKIE: 1927 ANI: 1933 b.u.
482. (Gulf of Carpentaria)	5804	1904	--	1904	CARPENTARIA: 1924 VEGA: 1926 MAR BLANCO: 1938 CAPO NORD: 1938 b.u.
483. SICILY ex Rhenania	1818	1881	1904	1907	LOURDES: 1907 EGEO: 31.3.1916 sunk by U39
484. TUSCANY	3001	1908	--	1914	OQUENDAO: 1920 LUCHANO: 1939 MAR TIRRENO: 1955 MUNI: 1963 b.u.
485. FELICIANA	4277	1909	--	1916	21.4.1916 sunk by U19
486. CROSSBY	3893	1907	1910	1916	BAYCROSS: 1922 TURCKHEIM: 1923 ANTONIOS D KYDONIEFS: 1935 b.u.
487. ORISTANO (259)	4220	1911	1911	1922	RYOKAI MARU: 22.8.1943 sunk by USS PLUNGER
488. APPENINE (211)	3684	1909	1913	--	4.3.1919 wrecked
489. CATERINO (218)	3729	1909	1913	1921	MARIA N ROUSSOS: 1935 SUPETAR: 12.6.1942 sunk by I-16
490. MESSINA (257)	4271	1911	1913	--	14.12.1919 foundered
491. ROSSANO (235)	3729	1909	1913	1921	POSSIDON: 8.9.1940 sunk by U47
492. BOLDWELL ex Voorburg	3118	1901	1914	1915	27.5.1917 sunk by UC20

Name	GRT	Built	Acquired	Sold	Subsequent career
493. FLORENTINO ex Gunwell, Cycle	3411	1900	1914	1914	20.11.1918 mined & sunk
494. SANTERAMO	4670	1914	--	1915	JERSEY CITY: 24.5.1917 sunk by U46
495. ORTONA (Ohio)	5524	1916	1916	--	21.6.1917 sunk by U50
496. SALERNO (658) ex Edenmore	3667	1909	1916	1921	EVELPIS: 1925 IOANNIS: 16.9.1942 sunk by U165
497. SANTERAMO (655) ex Arranmore	3045	1904	1916	1921	ANNA VASSILAKI: 1935 b.u.
498. TURINO ex Westoe Hall	4241	1914	1916	--	4.2.1917 sunk by U43
499. LUGANO	3810	1917	--	--	2.10.1917 mined & sunk
500. MODESTA	3832	1917	--	1920	25.4.1942 sunk by U108
501. RAPALLO	3811	1917	--	--	13.1.1918 sunk by U28
502. ARIANO (346) ex War Python	5155	1918	1919	1929	to FW
503. CASTELLANO ex War Spaniel	5227	1918	1919	1922	HOKKOH MARU: 28.11.1943 sunk by USS RATON
504. COMINO ex Ardgorm	4618	1918	1919	1929	DORIS: 1929 EIFEL: 1936 TUCUMAN: 17.4.1945 sunk by aircraft
505. FELICIANA (327) 1922 LONDON MARINER	7896	1922	1922	1929	to FW
506. (Oristano)	4347	1924	--	1924	SILVERFIR: 16.3.1941 sunk by GNEISENAU
507. (-----)	4354	1924	--	1924	SILVERCEDAR: 15.10.1941 sunk by U553
508. (-----)	4351	1924	--	1924	SILVERELM: 1946 GRADO: 1951 KOLONIUS: 1960 b.u.
509. PACIFIC EXPORTER (583)	6723	1928	--	1929	to N&NA
510. PACIFIC PIONEER (584)	6723	1928	--	1929	to N&NA

Hessler Shipping Company Ltd

Name	GRT	Built	Acquired	Sold	Subsequent career
511. JUPITER	2124	1901	--	1915	21.5.1917 sunk by UB40
512. LINDA FELL	3025	1906	--	1915	20.9.1915 missing
513. MYRA FELL	3024	1907	--	1915	GLODALE: 1.1.1918 wrecked
514. SALTBURN ex Norman	1840	1901	1913	1924	SCANIA: 11.9.1941 sunk by U82

London Welsh Steamship Company Ltd

Name	GRT	Built	Acquired	Sold	Subsequent career
515. CARDIFF TRADER (196) ex Broomhill	562	1878	1908	1913	LUFFMORE: 1923 b.u.
516. SWANSEA TRADER (263) ex Crathie	480	1883	1908	1912	to FW
517. WELSH TRADER ex San Miguel, Gutenberg Sea Belle	786	1891	1908	1916	WARLINGHAM: 1924 WURLAID: 1924 ERIKA: 1925 PERCY: 1931 ALBIN: 1932 LIEPAJA: 1933 b.u.
518. CHANNEL TRADER (265)	684	1913	1913	1923	GLAMORGAN COAST: 13.9.1932 wrecked
519. LLANELLY TRADER (267)	702	1913	1913	1923	YORKSHIRE COAST: 1938 SOLIN: 1963 b.u.
520. LONDON TRADER (268)	684	1913	1913	--	5.2.1915 foundered
521. TEES TRADER (269)	701	1913	1913 1916	1914 --	LADY OLIVE: returned 19.2.1917 sunk by UC18

Stocks, Turnbull and Company Ltd (Kirkcaldy, Fife and London Shipping Company)

Name	GRT	Built	Acquired	Sold	Subsequent career
522. ABBOTSHALL	421	1890	--	1911	NORMAN QUEEN: 1912 HELGOLAND: 1957 b.u.
523. KIRKCALDY	525	1903	--	1918	1935 b.u.
524. NEW ABBOTSHALL	783	1911	--	1918	DURHAM COAST: 1946 RAMARAJA: 1957 b.u.

Neptune Steam Navigation Company Ltd

Name	GRT	Built	Acquired	Sold	Subsequent career
525. CHEVIOT RANGE	3458	1903	--	1911	FEDORA: 1932 b.u.
526. PENNINE RANGE	3397	1903	--	1915	DARIUS 13.6.1917 sunk by U54
527. GRAMPIAN RANGE	3148	1905	--	1913	BERKUT: 4.8.1914 sunk by Russian coastal guns
528. NORFOLK RANGE	3054	1905	--	1913	CAMPUS: 1919 MARSHALL PLUMER: 1922 BROOKWAY: 1924 TSURUGISAN MARU: 27.10.1942 sunk by US aircraft
529. LOWTHER RANGE	3792	1906	--	--	20.4.1918 sunk by U91
530. MALVERN RANGE	3573	1906	--	1914	ZIMORODOK: 1928 ERMOUPOLIS: 21.9.1931 ashore, b.u.
531. SNOWDON RANGE	3060	1906	--	1914	WORON: 24.10.1917 sunk by UC40
532. BRANTFORD	4113	1910	--	1916	BAYFORD: 1923 PORT DE LA PALLICE: 1924 MARIA M DIACAKI: 1935 NICOLAS PATERAS: 24.6.1941 sunk by U108
533. CLEVELAND RANGE ex Forest Dale, Heathdene	3542	1898	1910	1913	GIUSEPPE G: 24.7.1918 sunk by explosion, cause unknown

Name	GRT	Built	Acquired	Sold	Subsequent career
534. CHILTERN RANGE	4220	1911	--	1914	DRAMMENSFJORD: 1924 RAISDALE: 1933 RINOS: 1937 YONG SHYANG: 1938 EISYO MARU: 5.6.1940 collision
535. COTSWOLD RANGE	4248	1912	--	1914	TRONDHJEMSFJORD: 28.7.1915 sunk by U41
536. (Hambleton Range)	3655	1913	--	1913	TANIS: 27.11.1915 sunk by U33
537. CHEVIOT RANGE	3691	1914	--	--	21.2.1918 sunk by U102
538. (Grampian Range) (1243)	4708	1914	--	1914	to BE
539. HAMBLETON RANGE	3682	1914	--	1923	SCOTSCRAIG: 1934 b.u.
540. MENDIP RANGE	4495	1914	--	1920	ARCHMEL: 1937 GRELROSA: 28.1.1941 sunk by aircraft
541. CLEVELAND RANGE ex Kirklee	3580	1897	1915	1916	CYMRIC VALE: 7.3.1923 wrecked
542. MALVERN RANGE	4524	1915	--	1922	KAMBOLE: 1937 STANTHORPE: 1938 YOLANDE BERTIN: 1941 HONDURAS: 1947 FOO HSIANG: 1953 b.u.
543. (Pentland Range)	5812	1915	--	1915	KRASNOIARSK: 1923 EASTWAY: 22.10.1926 foundered
544. SNOWDON RANGE ex Den of Kelly, Dalhanna	4662	1906	1915	--	28.3.1917 sunk by UC65
545. CAMBRIAN RANGE ex Crown	4234	1906	1916	--	9.12.1916 sunk by MÖWE
546. KERRY RANGE	5856	1916	--	1918	BLOSSOM HEATH: 1924 VOJVODA PUTNIK: 8.3.1943 sunk by U591
547. ALPINE RANGE ex Kintail	3537	1907	1917	1924	AKROPOLIS: 1929 COMTE DE FLANDRE: 1936 b.u.
548. PENTLAND RANGE ex Kincraig	3707	1901	1917	--	4.9.1918 foundered
549. GRAMPIAN RANGE (1091)	4767	1918	--	1921	to ML
550. NORFOLK RANGE	5120	1918	--	1924	SVEADROTT: 29.11.1924 ashore, b.u.
551. SIDLAW RANGE (301)	4407	1917	1918	1922	KAMIR: 1934 KYRIAKOULA: 26.2.1941 sunk by aircraft
552. LONDON EXCHANGE (328/627) ex Parisiana	6640	1921	1925	1935	to JWL
553. LONDON MERCHANT (Canadiana)	7899	1923	--	1935	POLITICIAN: 5.2.1941 wrecked

Agincourt Steamship Company Ltd

Name	GRT	Built	Acquired	Sold	Subsequent career
554. AGINCOURT (421)	4232	1904	--	--	1.3.1906 wrecked
555. BALACLAVA (270)	4220	1906	--	1913	to FW
556. CORUNNA (596)	3810	1906	--	1914	to FSA
557. DETTINGEN (403/264) ex Cebriana, Twickenham, Cebriana	4221	1899	1907	1913	to FW
558. EVESHAM (455/597) ex Albiana	4224	1905	1907	1914	to FSA
559. FLODDEN (426/598)	4226	1907	1907	1914	to FSA

Norfolk and North American Steamship Company Ltd

Name	GRT	Built	Acquired	Sold	Subsequent career
560. MONTAUK POINT	4822	1899	--	1912	1919 SNEFOND: 1920 STILLEHAVET: 1921 CARLSFELD: 1924 OMEGA: 1928 JOHNNY: 1931 b.u.
561. CROWN POINT	5218	1900	--	--	6.2.1917 sunk by U83
562. EAGLE POINT	5222	1900	--	--	28.3.1916 sunk by U70
563. NORTH POINT	5216	1900	--	1919	GENERAL LYAUTEY: 1923 b.u.
564. EAST POINT	5234	1901	--	--	9.3.1917 sunk by U48
565. SOUTH POINT (276)	3837	1912	--	1914	to FW
566. START POINT (273)	3840	1912	--	1914	to FW
567. WEST POINT (279)	3847	1912	--	1914	to FW
568. NORTHWESTERN MILLER	5046	1915	--	1927	AUGSBURG: 1941 TEIRYU MARU: 19.7.1944 sunk by USS GUARDFISH
569. SOUTHWESTERN MILLER	6514	1915	--	1927	GIESSEN: 12.3.1929 wrecked
570. CORNISH POINT ex Bland Hall	4259	1914	1916	1926	GONZEMHEIM: 1933 LISA: 1936 WALKURE: 22.12.1944 wrecked
571. (Dominion Miller) (1260)	6572	1916	--	1916	to FHAL
572. SOUTH POINT ex Albert Hall	4258	1914	1916	--	11.6.1917 sunk by UB32
573. START POINT (1090)	6540	1916	--	1921	to ML
574. ABERCORN (Mesna)	5385	1917	1917	1920	MESNA: 4.9.1924 wrecked
575. APPLEBY (Sjoa)	6041	1917	1917	1920	RINDA: 30.5.1941 sunk by U38
576. GLASTONBURY (Simla)	6041	1917	1917	1920	SIMLA: 22.9.1940 sunk by U100
577. HARTLAND POINT (673) ex Ardgorm	5131	1913	1917	1918	to JL

Name	GRT	Built	Acquired	Sold	Subsequent career
578. TENTERDEN	4127	1917	1917	1920	GRO: 7.9.1940 sunk by U47
579. DOMINION MILLER 1924 PACIFIC COMMERCE	5089	1922	--	1937	NORBRYN: 1959 b.u.
580. LONDON SHIPPER (335)	7930	1923	1923	1928	to FW
581. PACIFIC ENTERPRISE	6722	1927	--	--	9.9.1949 wrecked
582. PACIFIC RELIANCE	6717	1927	--	--	4.3.1940 sunk by U29
583. PACIFIC EXPORTER (509)	6723	1928	1929	1951	GIACOMO C: 1958 b.u.
584. PACIFIC PIONEER (510)	6723	1928	1929	--	29.7.1942 sunk by U132
585. PACIFIC FORTUNE (363)	9400	1947	--	1951	to FW
586. MAHIA (882)	7914	1917	1936	1945	to SSA
587. MAMARI (893) ex Mamilius, Zealandic	7924	1911	1936	1939	4.6.1941 wrecked
588. RARANGA (880)	7956	1916	1936	1945	to SSA
589. TAIROA (885)	7983	1920	1936	--	2.12.1939 sunk by ADMIRAL GRAF SPEE
590. WAIMANA (897) ex Herminius, Waimana	7870	1911	1936	1939	EMPIRE WAIMANA; repurchased by SSA
591. THEMISTOCLES (896) (pass)	11231	1911	1937	1945	to SSA

N V Furness Scheepvaart en Agentuur Maatschappij

Name	GRT	Built	Acquired	Sold	Subsequent career
592. ZANDBERGEN (251) ex Bacchus	3145	1902	1911	1913	GAGARA: 1918 OCTOBBRISAJIA REVOLUTSIJA: 1918 KAJAK: not reported after 1950
593. ALBERGEN (260) ex Saltburn	1777	1911	1912	--	2.4.1915 missing
594. EIBERGEN (292)	4751	1914	-- 1919	1917 --	to FW: returned 3.6.1941 sunk by U75
595. KELBERGEN (297)	4751	1914	-- 1919	1917 1951	to FW: returned PROTEUS: 1953 LUCAS TRADER: 1954 JAGRAKSHAK: 1954 LUCAS TRADER: 1959 b.u.
596. TENBERGEN (556) ex Corunna	3826	1906	1914	--	19.11.1916 wrecked
597. VEENBERGEN (558/303) ex Evesham, Albiana	4224	1905	1914 1919	1917 1920	to FW: returned VOORBURG: 1922 KARL HANS: 1933 b.u.
598. VRIJBERGEN ex Flodden	4226	1907	1914	1915	POELDIJK: 1928 SCHWARTZESEE: 1932 b.u.

Stoomvaart Maatschappij Hollandia

Name	GRT	Built	Acquired	Sold	Subsequent career
599. DRIEBERGEN	1884	1910	--	--	17.2.1917 sunk by UC66
600. UBBERGEN (302)	1870	1911	-- 1919	1917 1924	to FW: returned INGRID: 1931 MEROK: 1934 CORNELIS LENSEN: 1937 ROLFS FAULBAUMS: 1939 MAKKI F: 11.2.1944 sunk by HMS STUBBORN
601. ZEVENBERGEN	3121	1911	--	1915	VEERHAVEN: 1924 KRASNY OKTIABR: not reported since 1950

Stoomvaart Maatschappij Indische Lloyd

Name	GRT	Built	Acquired	Sold	Subsequent career
602. BEEKBERGEN (225) ex Langdale	3917	1903	1911	1916	GAASTERLAND: 22.2.1917 sunk by U21
603. GRAMSBERGEN (209) ex Acara	4995	1904	1911	1914	WAALDIJK: 1932 ACARA: 1953 b.u.
604. RIJSBERGEN (239/298) ex Swaledale, Ile de la Reunion	3662	1897	1911 1919	1917 1920	to FW: returned RIJNSBURG: 1923 b.u.
605. STEENBERGEN (240) ex Wensleydale	3935	1903	1911	1916	DRECHTERLAND: 1933 b:u:

Rotterdamsche Scheepvaart Maatschappij

Name	GRT	Built	Acquired	Sold	Subsequent career
606. VOSBERGEN ex Riddekerk, Houthandel, Dania	1437	1909	1913	1916	1923 RAMSHOLM: 18.2.1934 collision

White Diamond Steamship Company Ltd
1922 renamed **Warren Line (Liverpool) Ltd** and 1934 renamed **Johnston Warren Lines Ltd.**

Name	GRT	Built	Acquired	Sold	Subsequent career
607. MICHIGAN	4935	1887	--	1914	1916 blockship
608. SAGAMORE (p/c)	5197	1892	--	--	3.3.1917 sunk by U49
609. SACHEM (p/c)	5354	1893	--	--	1926 b.u.
610. IOWA	8370	1902	--	1913	BOHEMIA: 1917 ARTEMIS: 1941 EMPIRE BITTERN: 23.7.1944 blockship
611. BAY STATE	5064	1915	--	--	10.6.1917 sunk by U66
612. RHODE ISLAND	5655	1918	--	1926	POLAMHALL: 1928 ELENI: 25.6.1946 wrecked
613. BAY STATE (756) ex Spartan Prince, War Shark	5247	1919	1924	1928	1928 ELENI STATHATOU: 28.10.1929 wrecked
614. HOOSAC (758) ex Trojan Prince, War Perch	5226	1918	1924	1926	NEMANJA. 8.10.1942 sunk by U84

Name	GRT	Built	Acquired	Sold	Subsequent career
615. SAVANNAH (752)	5263	1918	1924	1927	NEVESINJE: 1928 COQUIMBO: 1932
ex Grecian Prince, War Hind					VALPARAISO: 1934 PRINC PAVLE: 1942
					FRANKA: 1946 KORDUN: 1959 b.u.
616. LONDON CORPORATION (334)	6629	1922	1925	1928	to FW
ex Hoosac, Cynthiana					
617. NEWFOUNDLAND (pass)	6791	1925	--	--	13.9.1943 sunk by aircraft
618. NOVA SCOTIA (pass)	6796	1926	--	--	28.11.42 sunk by U177
619. AVIEMORE (682)	4060	1920	1935	--	16.9.1939 sunk by U31
620. BEEMORE (698) (tug)	186	1929	1935	1958	MUMBLES: 1965 b.u.
621. CEEMORE (699) (tug)	186	1929	1935	1958	MURTON: 1964 b.u.
622. DEEMORE (700) (tug)	187	1930	1935	1958	MARGAM: 1965 b.u.
623. DROMORE (683)	4096	1920	1935	1955	MICTRIC: 1956 CHA: 1959 b.u
624. INCEMORE (685)	4098	1921	1935	--	16.9.1940 wrecked
625. JESSMORE (693)	4099	1921	1935	--	19.2.1941 collision
ex Peruviana					
626. KENMORE (694)	3783	1923	1935	1937	LORRAINE: 8.11.1942 scuttled
627. LONDON EXCHANGE (552)	6640	1921	1935	1938	BENRINNES: 1950 FATAKADA: 1955
ex Parisiana					MINOCHER COWASJEE: 24.1.1957 missing
628. QUERNMORE (695)	3787	1923	1935	1937	ALSACE: 24.1.1940 sunk by U44
629. JESSMORE (1373)	7061	1941	1946	1958	ANTIOPE: 1964 GLOBAL VENTURE: 1971 b.u.
ex Empire Faith					
630. OAKMORE (1379)	4700	1939	1947	--	1967 b.u.
ex Empire Kent, Levante					
631. NOVA SCOTIA (pass)	7438	1947	--	1962	FRANCIS DRAKE: 1971 b.u.
632. HEATHMORE	3825	1945	1947	1961	GRECIAN MED: 1969 IMATACA: 1972 b.u.
ex Hickory Mount					
633. NEWFOUNDLAND (pass)	7437	1948	--	1962	GEORGE ANSON: 1971 b.u.
634. SYCAMORE	3343	1950	--	1968	ELIAS L: 1973 JARA: 1975 MELTEMI: 1977
1955 WALSINGHAM					TEMI: 1979 b.u.
1957 SYCAMORE					
1965 MERCHANT PRINCE					
635. BEECHMORE	3291	1954	--	1969	MANDRAKI: 1972 NAFTILIOS: 1975
1965 ENGLISH PRINCE					MARIBER: 1977 MARI: 7.7.1978 burnt, b.u.
636. PINEMORE	3597	1955	--	1971	MALDIVE MAIL: 31.5.1975 burnt, wrecked
1965 AFRICAN PRINCE					
637. ROWANMORE	8495	1956	--	1973	ANDRIANA I: 1977 MARJORIE Y: 1979 b.u.
1958 MADULSIMA					
1960 ROWANMORE					
638. FOYLEMORE (tug)	208	1958	--	1969	FOYLEGARTH: 1983 ST BUDOC: still afloat
639. KILMORE (tug)	208	1958	--	1969	KILGARTH: 1984 AGHIOS GERASSIMOS: still afloat
640. ROSSMORE (tug)	206	1958	--	1969	ROSSGARTH: 1981 ROZI: still afloat
641. MYSTIC	6656	1959	--	1975	SEA SWALLOW: 1977 NORTH SEA: 1978
					GOLDEN RAYS: 1982 b.u.
642. CUFIC (374)	6906	1964	1973	1977	GAIETY: 1985 b.u.
1974 NEWFOUNDLAND					
1976 CUFIC					
ex Newfoundland					
643. TROPIC (375)	6906	1965	1973	1978	BOOKER VALIANT: 1980 ARAB DABBOR: 1986
1974 NOVA SCOTIA					ARAB HIND: still afloat
1976 TROPIC					
ex Nova Scotia					

George V Turnbull and Company Ltd

Name	GRT	Built	Acquired	Sold	Subsequent career
644. PETER PAN (221/287)	938	1909	1912	1916	to FW
ex Harlingen					
645. TOGSTON (241)	1057	1909	1913	1915	18.10.1917 sunk by UC47
646. WENDY	958	1913	--	1915	1935 BRIARDALE: 1937 DOVER ABBEY: 1940
					WOODSTOCK: 15.2.1941 collision

Johnston Line Ltd

Name	GRT	Built	Acquired	Sold	Subsequent career
647. FENMORE	2300	1894	--	1915	MARION DAWSON: 14.12.1917 sunk by UC21
648. VEDAMORE	6330	1895	--	--	7.2.1917 sunk by U85
649. AMORE (tug)	155	1896	--	1929	STEELOPOLIS: 1949 b.u.
650. HEATHMORE	3147	1898	--	1919	1927 GLORIA: 1933 b.u.
651. INCEMORE	3060	1898	--	--	20.8.1917 sunk by U38
652. QUERNMORE	7302	1898	--	--	31.7.1917 sunk by U82
653. GORSEMORE	3079	1899	--	--	22.9.1918 sunk by UC53
654. ROWANMORE	10320	1900	--	--	26.10.1916 sunk by U57
655. ARRANMORE (497)	3045	1904	--	1916	to GL
656. BARNESMORE	3158	1905	--	1915	WHITEHALL: 28.7.1917 sunk by U95
657. CRANMORE	3157	1905	--	1921	PELAGIA: 1933 b.u.
658. EDENMORE (496)	3667	1909	--	1916	to GL
659. BARROWMORE	3832	1911	--	--	19.2.1918 sunk by U94

Name	GRT	Built	Acquired	Sold	Subsequent career
660. FOYLEMORE	3831	1911	--	--	16.12.1917 sunk by UB55
661. JESSMORE	3911	1911	--	--	13.5.1917 sunk by U48
662. KENMORE	3919	1912	--	--	26.8.1917 sunk by U53
663. LARCHMORE	4355	1912	--	--	3.7.1915 sunk by U39
664. DROMORE	4398	1913	--	--	27.4.1917 sunk by U58
665. SWANMORE	6373	1913	--	--	25.4.1917 sunk by U43, U93 & U50
666. MAPLEMORE	4330	1916	--	1922	GIBRALTAR: 1938 MEOPHAM: 1939 ANTJE FRITZEN: 21.9.1943 sunk by TKA-15
667. PINEMORE ex Den of Ewnie	5980	1913	1916	1923	LESREAULX: 1927 CALANDPLEIN: 1935 KONSTANTINOS HADJIPATERAS: 24.10.1939 mined & sunk
668. COTTESMORE ex Swindon	4240	1917	1917	1920	AVONMEDE: 1924 HARPALION: 1931 THEOFANO: 1937 DIRPHYS: 8.6.1941 sunk by U108
669. LINMORE ex Llanover	4274	1917	1917	1920	SHANNONMEDE. 1924 HARPALYCE: 1929 LITTLETON: 1932 LEONIDAS Z CAMBANIS: 3.4.1941 sunk by U73
670. OAKMORE	4269	1917	--	1920	CLYDEMEDE: 1925 HARPAGUS: 1928 MAROUKO PATERAS: 3.11.1941 wrecked
671. SYCAMORE	6550	1917	--	--	25.8.1917 sunk by UB61
672. THISTLEMORE 1923 WHEATMORE	6506	1917	--	1928	URSULA RICKMERS: 1940 TEISIN MARU: 3.5.1944 sunk by USS FLASHER
673. HARTMORE (577) ex Hartland Point, Ardgorm	5131	1913	1918	1921	SUREWAY: 1927 JUNYO MARU: 18.9.1944 sunk by HMS TRADEWIND
674. REXMORE (1095)	6512	1918	--	1929	to ML
675. VALEMORE (345)	6629	1918	--	1928	to FW
676. BARRYMORE	6656	1919	--	1924	KUMSANG: 30.9.1942 sunk by U125
677. ERNEMORE ex Ardgay	4593	1918	1919	1922	TOHKOH MARU: 1930 TOHO MARU: 1.6.1944 sunk by USS PINTADO
678. GALTYMORE (War Sable)	4565	1919	--	1929	LISA: 1929 TAUNUS: 1937 CORDOBA: 11.9.1940 mined & sunk
679. STANMORE ex Ardgarry, (Loch-na-Torran)	4526	1914	1919	1923	KEMMEL: 1934 b.u.
680. TULLAMORE ex Ardgroom	4882	1918	1919	1922	SAIKOH MARU: 1930 SAIHO MARU: 11.11.1944 sunk by aircraft
681. WIGMORE ex Ardgrange	4543	1916	1919	1922	NANKOH MARU: 1938 NANKO MARU: 11.6.1943 lost
682. AVIEMORE (619)	4060	1920	--	1935	to JWL
683. DROMORE (623)	4096	1920	--	1935	to JWL
684. (Cedarmore) (328)	6640	1921	--	1921	to FW
685. INCEMORE (624)	4098	1921	--	1935	to JWL
686. (Jessmore) (329)	4099	1921	--	1921	to FW
687. (Rowanmore) (327)	7896	1922	--	1922	to FW
688. VEDAMORE (280) ex Wingate	1911	1914	1922	1925	ERLAND: 1939 NEEME: 22.3.1940 foundered (ice)
689. WESTMORE (204) ex Portinglis	1876	1908	1922	1923	PHYLLIS SEED: 1924 PATRIA: 1936 TRITON: 1955 b.u.
690. WIGMORE (277) ex Venice	1869	1914	1922	1926	MAI: 1931 HERLEIK: 1941 YULIN MARU: 24.2.1945 wrecked
691. WILLOWMORE (199) ex Cundall	1851	1908	1922	1923	VENTA: 1941 UNDINE: 1947 VENTA: 1955 b.u.
692. WRAYMORE (180) ex Pomaron	1809	1907	1922	1923	BIRUTA: 1954 SIGULDA: 1967 deleted from Lloyd's Register, end unknown
693. JESSMORE (329/625) ex Peruviana	4099	1921	1923	1935	to JWL
694. KENMORE (626)	3783	1923	--	1935	to JWL
695. QUERNMORE (628)	3787	1923	--	1935	to JWL
696. SYCAMORE (767)	3493	1923	--	1926	to PL
697. TRAMORE (766)	3493	1924	--	1926	to PL
698. BEEMORE (620) (tug)	186	1929	--	1935	to JWL
699. CEEMORE (621) (tug)	186	1929	--	1935	to JWL
700. DEEMORE (622) (tug)	187	1930	--	1935	to JWL

Trinidad Shipping and Trading Company Ltd

Name	GRT	Built	Acquired	Sold	Subsequent career
701. MAYARO (323) ex Pegu	3896	1900	1911	1920	to FW
702. MATURA (322) ex Amarapoora	4556	1901	1913	1920	to FW
703. MARAVAL (321) ex Irrawaddy	5144	1903	1914	1920	to FW

Name	GRT	Built	Acquired	Sold	Subsequent career
Prince Line Ltd					
704. KAFFIR PRINCE	2228	1891	--	1920	PROPONTIS: 1928 NAFE: 1933 EMMANUEL: 1933 b.u.
705. CARIB PRINCE	1975	1893	--	1920	FANI: 1924 MIHAIL ARCHANGEL: 1926 SULE: 1958 b.u.
706. CREOLE PRINCE	1988	1893	--	--	22.10.1916 collision
707. GEORGIAN PRINCE (tank)	3245	1893	--	1918	BRITISH GENERAL: 1920 EBROS: 1946 b.u.
708. ITALIAN PRINCE	3083	1893	--	--	10.11.1920 burnt
709. MEXICAN PRINCE (tank)	3028	1893	--	1918	1919 SOUTHERN ISLES: 1929 SILVA PORTO: hulked
710. TROJAN PRINCE	3196	1896	--	--	23.2.1917 sunk by U39
711. NORMAN PRINCE	3464	1900	--	1920	HYDRA: 1933 b.u.
712. SOLDIER PRINCE	3118	1901	--	--	1932 b.u.
713. EGYPTIAN PRINCE	3117	1902	--	--	12.5.1917 sunk by U38
714. MERCHANT PRINCE	3092	1902	--	1926	K LYRAS: 1936 b.u.
715. AFGHAN PRINCE	4923	1903	--	--	30.7.1918 wrecked
716. AFRICAN PRINCE	4916	1903	--	--	21.7.1917 sunk by U66
717. TUDOR PRINCE	4292	1903	--	1923	THEODOROS BULGARIS: 31.12.1930 foundered
718. WELSH PRINCE	4934	1903	--	--	13.10.1916 sunk by UB43
719. BLACK PRINCE ex Provan	3925	1903	1904	1922	GUADIARO: 1926 UDONDO: 1938 GANTE: 1938 ALBARREBA: 1948 CORUNA: 1965 b.u.
720. CORSICAN PRINCE ex Briardale	2776	1900	1907	--	7.2.1917 sunk by UB34
721. OCEAN PRINCE	5101	1907	--	--	16.12.1916 wrecked
722. ROYAL PRINCE	5547	1907	--	1924	SIC VOS NON VOBIS: 1928 BATTININ ACCAME: 1931 FORTUNATO: 1932 b.u.
723. ASIATIC PRINCE	2887	1910	--	--	30.5.1918 sunk by U63
724. EASTERN PRINCE	2885	1910	--	--	30.8.1917 sunk by U62
725. SCOTTISH PRINCE	2897	1910	--	1937	ATHINAI: 1940 PALERMO: 7.1944 sunk by aircraft
726. BURMESE PRINCE	4825	1911	--	1927	LUCILLE DE LARRINAGA: 1934 b.u.
727. CHINESE PRINCE	4834	1911	--	1925	MONVISO: 1933 b.u.
728. JAPANESE PRINCE	4876	1911	--	--	10.2.1917 sunk by UC47
729. SIAMESE PRINCE	4847	1911	--	1925	SARAGOSSA: 16.3.1932 burnt
730. BELGIAN PRINCE ex Hungarian Prince, Mohawk	4765	1901	1912	--	31.7.1917 sunk by U55
731. FRENCH PRINCE ex Bulgarian Prince, Mineola	4766	1900	1912	--	16.2.1917 sunk by MÖWE
732. HIGHLAND PRINCE ex Matteawan	3390	1901	1912	--	11.4.1918 sunk by UB50
733. PORTUGUESE PRINCE	4981	1912	--	--	1934 b.u.
734. RUSSIAN PRINCE (tank)	4158	1912	--	1918	BRITISH MARSHAL: 1929 TRITONE: 7.3.1933 stranded, b.u.
735. SERVIAN PRINCE ex Austrian Prince, Monomoy	4831	1901	1912	1923	SORRISO: 1926 b.u.
736. STUART PRINCE ex Hutton	3597	1899	1912	--	22.3.1917 sunk by U66
737. ROUMANIAN PRINCE (tank)	4147	1913	--	1929	RIVA SICULA: 20.4.1933 wrecked
738. TUSCAN PRINCE	5275	1913	--	--	15.2.1923 wrecked
739. MOORISH PRINCE	5943	1914	--	1927	ANSELMA DE LARRINAGA: 1934 b.u.
740. ROMAN PRINCE	5284	1914	--	1927	BERWICK LAW: 1932 BENLOMOND: 1935 CHRYSOPOLIS: 18.6.1936 wrecked
741. POLAR PRINCE ex Kawak, Oberon, Persia, Ingeborg, Goldenfels	3611	1895	1915	1917	18.9.1917 sunk by UB50
742. MONGOLIAN PRINCE ex Verdala	4755	1913	1917	1928	ISTOK: 1940 MAYCREST: 4.8.1944 blockship
743. SIBERIAN PRINCE (837) ex Baron Lovat	5604	1915	1917 1923	1920 1933	to PSS: returned DUNAVIS: 1939 ARLESIANA: 1942 damaged by aircraft, 1948 b.u.
744. CELTIC PRINCE	8654	1918	--	1926	SCHONFELS: 1938 BAHIA BLANCA: 9.1.1940 collision
745. GAELIC PRINCE	8634	1918	--	1926	RHEINFELS: 1939 BAHIA CASTILLO: 2.5.1940 damaged by HMS NARWHAL, b.u.
746. GOTHIC PRINCE	8600	1918	--	1927	SONNENFELS: 1939 BAHIA CAMARONES: 12.1.1945 damaged by HMS NORFOLK, BELLONA, ONSLOW, ORWELL & ONSLAUGHT, b.u.
747. KOREAN PRINCE ex Hindustan	4990	1917	1918	1934	DIAMANTIS: 5.10.1939 sunk by U35

Name	GRT	Built	Acquired	Sold	Subsequent career
748. MANCHURIAN PRINCE ex Ardgair	5119	1913	1918	1933	NAANA: 1935 LAST: 1946 SENGA: 1946 KORCULA: 1959 b.u.
749. PERSIAN PRINCE	5678	1918	--	1933	ANN STATHATOU: 1950 CADORE: 1959 b.u.
750. SLAVIC PRINCE (Gaelic Prince)	8611	1918	--	1926	RABENFELS: 1938 BAHIA LAURA: 30.8.1941 sunk by HMS TRIDENT
751. ARABIAN PRINCE	5764	1919	--	1927	ZENADA: 1933 NESTOS: 2.4.1941 wrecked
752. GRECIAN PRINCE (615) ex War Hind	5263	1918	1919	1924	to WL
753. ALGERIAN PRINCE	3089	1919	--	1936	LOUIS CHARLES SCHIAFFINO: 25.2.1941 sunk by aircraft
754. CYPRIAN PRINCE 1936 GLOUCESTER CITY	3071	1919	--	1939	1949 NAMAQUALAND: 1951 KADERBAKSH: 1961 b.u.
755. TARTAR PRINCE (838) ex War Jackdaw	5214	1918	1919 1923	1920 1933	to PSS: returned FOSTAT: 1939 STAR OF LUXOR: 10.12.1941 sunk by U130
756. SPARTAN PRINCE (613) ex War Shark	5247	1919	1919	1924	to WL
757. SYRIAN PRINCE 1936 WELSH PRINCE	3072	1919	--	1936	DEA MAZZELLA: 30.9.1943 sunk by coastal guns
758. TROJAN PRINCE (614) ex War Perch	5226	1918	1919	1924	to WL
759. EASTERN PRINCE ex Altenfels	7369	1915	1920	1926	STOLZENFELS: 20.3.1941 mined & sunk
760. (Egyptian Prince)	3300	1920	--	1920	LOUISIANA: 1927 NORD FRIESLAND: 1930 MUNSTER: 1937 CORRIENTES: 1939 MONTE MONCAYO: 1955 TAJUNA: 10.12.1957 ashore, b.u.
761. ITALIAN PRINCE (Italiana)	3478	1921	--	--	6.9.1938 burnt
762. PERSIANA (326)	3493	1921	--	1922	to FW
763. EGYPTIAN PRINCE (278) ex Waterland	494	1903	1920	1922	RAMLEH: 1930 LATEEF: 1946 RAMLEH: 1947 SHADWAN: 1986 deleted from Lloyd's Register, end unknown
764. EGYPTIAN PRINCE (325) (Braziliana)	3490	1922	1922	1946	LORRAIN: 1952 HERCULIS: 1960 b.u.
765. LANCASTRIAN PRINCE (330) ex Tunisiana	3482	1922	1922	1938	CHAMPENOIS: 18.4.1941 ashore
766. BRAZILIAN PRINCE (697) ex Tramore	3907	1924	1926	1933	VOROSHILOV: 1962 ILYICHOVSK: 1974 deleted from Lloyd's Register, end unknown
767. CASTILLIAN PRINCE (696) ex Sycamore	3908	1923	1926	1933	ENUKIDZE: 1935 GENERAL YAGODA: 1937 MICHURIN: 1946 VOROSHILOV: 1946 MICHURIN: 1969 deleted from Lloyd's Register, end unknown
768. EASTERN PRINCE (1362) (p/c)	10926	1929	--	1946	1950 EMPIRE MEDWAY 1952 b.u.
769. NORTHERN PRINCE (p/c)	10917	1929	--	--	3.4.1941 sunk by aircraft
770. SIAMESE PRINCE	6607	1929	--	--	17.2.1941 sunk by U69
771. SOUTHERN PRINCE (1426) (p/c)	10917	1929	--	1946	ANNA C: 1971 b.u.
772. WESTERN PRINCE (p/c)	10926	1929	--	--	14.12.1940 sunk by U96
773. ARABIAN PRINCE	1960	1936	--	--	1959 b.u.
774. PALESTINIAN PRINCE	1960	1936	--	1959	HAPPY MED: 1965 MIMI: 1970 b.u.
775. SYRIAN PRINCE	1988	1936	--	1959	SUNNY MED: 1969 b.u.
776. CYPRIAN PRINCE	1988	1937	--	--	6.4.1941 sunk by aircraft
777. AFRICAN PRINCE	4653	1939	--	1961	ARDMORE: 1965 KALI ELPIS: 1969 b.u.
778. LANCASTRIAN PRINCE	1914	1940	--	--	11.4.1943 sunk by U613
779. NORMAN PRINCE	1913	1940	--	--	28.5.1942 sunk by U156
780. STUART PRINCE 1951 FORT HAMILTON 1958 STUART PRINCE	1911	1940	--	1959	HALCYON MED: 24.8.1960 collision
781. TUDOR PRINCE	1913	1940	--	1957	CROCE ITALO: 1961 ORNELLA: 1964 b.u.
782. WELSH PRINCE	5148	1940	--	--	7.12.1941 mined & sunk
783. HIGHLAND PRINCE	7043	1942	--	1955	INCHSTUART: 1969 b.u.
784. CHINESE PRINCE 1950 NORDIC	9485	1943	--	--	1964 b.u.
785. ENGLISH PRINCE	7275	1943	--	1961	SIMOS: 1973 b.u.
786. SCOTTISH PRINCE	7138	1944	--	1952	VITALI: 1952 HILLCREST: 1959 SOPHIA: 1966 YANNIS: 1969 b.u.
787. MALTESE PRINCE	2361	1946	--	1963	CORONIS: 1973 b.u.
788. CYPRIAN PRINCE	2358	1949	--	1967	AGIOS DIONISIOS: 1972 IRENE'S WISH: 1973 FULMAR TRADER: 10.1.1976 fire, sank
789. CINGALESE PRINCE 1960 GALLIC 1962 CINGALESE PRINCE	8827	1950	--	1963	GLOUCESTERSHIRE: 1971 CRESCO: 1972 b.u.
790. EASTERN PRINCE 1960 BARDIC	8827	1950	--	1964	STAFFORDSHIRE: 1971 b.u.

Name	GRT	Built	Acquired	Sold	Subsequent career
791. EGYPTIAN PRINCE	3364	1951	--	1968	NIKOLAS S: 1972 b.u.
792. JAVANESE PRINCE (833)	8875	1944	1954	1961	BENLARIG: 1969 b.u.
793. BLACK PRINCE	3597	1955	--	1971	MARIA B: 20.3.1977 fire, sank
(Soldier Prince)					
794. WESTERN PRINCE	7917	1955	--	1971	MARINER: 28.3.1973 foundered
1957 ZEALANDIC					
1963 MANCHESTER TRADER					
1969 WESTERN PRINCE					
795. NORMAN PRINCE	2709	1956	--	1968	SALAMINA: 1971 DALMARIN: 1973 DODO: 1975 GEORGE S1: 1975 P DOLORES: 7.10.1975 fire, CTL
796. AFRIC	3364	1950	--	1968	GRIGORIOS: 1972 MILOS: 1975 NESTOR II: 1977 b.u.
1955 ALBEMARLE					
1957 SCOTTISH PRINCE					
797. NORTHUMBRIAN PRINCE	2709	1956	--	1968	ELEFTHEROTRIA: 1972 RODANIA: 1975 OMAR: 1983 SURAJ: 1985 KARARAI: 1985 b.u.
(Novocastrian Prince)					
798. SOUTHERN PRINCE (1021)	7917	1956	--	1970	to RML
1958 MEDIC					
1960 SOUTHERN PRINCE					
799. LANCASTRIAN PRINCE	4800	1960	--	1971	TAMARA: 1981 AMAR: 1983 AMAR I: 1983 b.u.
800. STUART PRINCE (1049) (tank)	12959	1960	--	1970	to PMS
1970 STOLT STUART					
801. CHILTERN PRINCE	1459	1970	--	1981	FRIENDSHIP: 1987 THANG LOI 02: still afloat
802. COTSWOLD PRINCE (1060)	1459	1970	--	1979	to TL
803. DERWENT (1007)	13358	1949	1970	--	1971 b.u.
ex Persic					
804. DOURO (1008)	9706	1946	1970	--	1972 b.u.
ex Hornby Grange					
805. MALVERN PRINCE	1459	1970	--	1981	VICTORY I: 1986 THANG LOI 01: still afloat
806. MENDIP PRINCE	1459	1970	--	1979	QATAR 1: 1979 RASHIDAH: still afloat
1974 CHEVIOT PRINCE					
807. CAIRNLEADER	1592	1975	--	1982	LINDEWAL: 1987 BENED: 1988 MIRFAK: 1989 FIVI: still afloat
808. CROWN PRINCE (c/c)	1479	1979	--	1985	THAI AMBER: 1989 OOCL AMBITION: still afloat
1983 MANCHESTER CROWN					
809. ROYAL PRINCE (c/c)	1479	1979	--	1985	THAI JADE: 1989 OOCL ADVANCE: still afloat
1984 CITY OF OPORTO					
1985 ROYAL PRINCE					

Rio Cape Line Ltd

Name	GRT	Built	Acquired	Sold	Subsequent career
810. GLENELG	4160	1904	1917	1922	CONSTANTINOS COUSTODONTIS: 1933 b.u.
1922 NORMAN PRINCE					
811. GLENAFFRIC	4144	1905	1917	1924	NAXOS: 1935 OGADEN: 12.8.1942 sunk by HMS PORPOISE
1922 SAXON PRINCE					
812. GLENDHU	4129	1905	1917	--	1935 b.u.
1922 STUART PRINCE					
813. GLENDEVON	4169	1907	1917	--	1936 b.u.
1922 SAILOR PRINCE					
814. GLENORCHY	4737	1909	1917	--	1.3.1920 wrecked
815. GLENSHIEL	4798	1909	1917	1935	ORION: 20.9.1948 wrecked
1922 HIGHLAND PRINCE					
816. GLENETIVE	5212	1911	1917	1935	GERMAINE: 15.12.1939 sunk by U48
1922 OCEAN PRINCE					
817. GLENSPEAN	5221	1912	1917	--	29.5.1922 collision
1922 WELSH PRINCE					
818. GLENNEVIS	5119	1917	1917	1936	PENTRIDGE HILL: 1939 BOTLEA: 30.12.1945 scuttled
1922 AFRICAN PRINCE					
819. GLENCARRON	5117	1917	1917	--	19.2.1918 sunk by U82
820. GLENLYON	4933	1917	1917	1936	ANDREAS: 1941 WAKATSU MARU: 14.12.1943 sunk by aircraft
1922 INDIAN PRINCE					
821. GLENLEE	4915	1918	--	--	9.8.1918 sunk by UB57
822. CORSICAN PRINCE (326)	3493	1921	1924	1928	JEAN ET JACQUES: 3.3.1942 sunk by MTB
ex Chickahominy, Persiana					
823. CASTILLIAN PRINCE (331)	3489	1922	1923	1946	ALSACIEN: 1959 YOLAC: 1963 b.u.
1926 SICILIAN PRINCE					
ex Alleghany					
824. SARDINIAN PRINCE (332)	3491	1922	1924	--	16.3.1941 sunk by SCHARNHORST
ex Appomatox					
825. ASIATIC PRINCE	6734	1926	--	--	16.3.1928 missing
826. CHINESE PRINCE	6734	1926	--	--	12.6.1941 sunk by U552
827. JAPANESE PRINCE	6734	1926	--	1937	WAVE: returned
1938 INDIAN PRINCE			1938	--	11.11.1943 sunk by aircraft

Name	GRT	Built	Acquired	Sold	Subsequent career
828. JAVANESE PRINCE	6734	1926	--	--	20.5.1941 sunk by U138
829. MALAYAN PRINCE	6734	1926	--	--	1953 b.u.
830. CINGALESE PRINCE	6625	1929	--	--	20.9.1941 sunk by U111
831. BRITISH PRINCE	4979	1935	1937	--	26.9.1941 sunk by aircraft
ex Sutherland					
832. SCOTTISH PRINCE	4917	1938	--	--	17.3.1942 sunk by U68
833. JAVANESE PRINCE (792)	8875	1944	--	1954	to PL
834. WELSH PRINCE (367)	7354	1944	--	1954	to FW
835. BLACK PRINCE (1390)	9904	1943	1946	1952	BEAVERLODGE: 1960 BENHIANT: 1970
1949 ZEALANDIC					VENUS: 1971 b.u.
ex Empire Regent					
836. BRITISH PRINCE (1427/365)	7681	1945	1947	1954	to FW
ex Stamford Victory					

Peareth Steamship Company Ltd

Name	GRT	Built	Acquired	Sold	Subsequent career
837. SIBERIAN PRINCE (743)	5604	1915	1920	1923	to PL
ex Baron Lovat					
838. TARTAR PRINCE (755)	5214	1918	1920	1923	to PL
ex War Jackdaw					

Bermuda and West Indies Steamship Company Ltd

Name	GRT	Built	Acquired	Sold	Subsequent career
839. FORT HAMILTON (317) (pass)	5530	1904	1921	1926	STELLA D'ITALIA: 1934 b.u.
ex Bermudian					
840. FORT ST GEORGE (pass)	7785	1912	1921	1935	CESAREA: 1938 ARNO: 10.9.1942 sunk by aircraft
ex Wandilla					
841. FORT VICTORIA (318) (pass)	7784	1913	1921	--	18.12.1921 collision
ex Willochra					
842. MARAVAL (321)	5144	1903	1921	1932	1933 b.u.
ex Irrawaddy					
843. MATURA (322)	4556	1901	1921	--	1934 hulked: 1951 b.u.
ex Amarapoora					
844. MAYARO (323)	3896	1900	1921	--	1929 b.u.
ex Pegu					
845. BERMUDIAN	237	1915	1923	1948	1959 dismantled
ex Arctic Whale					
846. GUIANA (319)	3657	1907	1922	--	1925 b.u.
847. PARIMA (324)	2990	1889	1922	--	1924 b.u.
ex Bungaree					
848. DOMINICA (p/c) (266)	3966	1913	1925	1935	BALTROVER: 1946 IONIA: 1965 IONIAN:
ex Digby, Artois, Digby					26.7.1965 capsized
849. MID-OCEAN	730	1929	--	--	16.10.1942 sunk by U160
1930 CASTLE HARBOUR					
850. BERMUDA (pass)	19086	1927	--	--	16.6.1931 & 19.11.1931 burnt, CTL. 30.4.1933
					hulk wrecked
851. NERISSA (pass)	5583	1926	1929	--	30.4.1941 sunk by U552
852. ROSALIND (p/c)	2390	1911	1929	1936	LOVCEN: 1941 COLUMBIA: 1942 BRIGADIER
ex Lady Gwendolen					GENERAL HARRY E RETHERS: 1946 WAH
					CHUNG: 1950 TERESA: 1951 b.u.
853. SILVIA (p/c)	3589	1909	1929	1935	HAITAN: 1950 b.u.
ex Orel					
854. LONGBIRD	636	1919	1930	1934	16.1.1943 collision
ex Newton Bay, Kilmuckridge					
855. FORT AVALON (368) (p/c)	3484	1949	--	1957	to FW

Cairn Line of Steamships Ltd
1977 renamed **Furness Withy (General Shipping) Ltd** and 1979 renamed **Furness Withy (Shipping) Ltd.**

Name	GRT	Built	Acquired	Sold	Subsequent career
856. CAIRNMONA	4666	1918	--	--	30.10.1939 sunk by U13
857. CAIRNVALONA	4929	1918	--	--	1952 b.u.
858. CAIRNGOWAN	5295	1919	--	1935	BRIGHTCOMET: 1936 CHI SING: 1938
(War Oriole)					YAMAHAGI MARU: 12.10.1944 sunk by aircraft
859. CAIRNDHU	5250	1919	--	1935	STRYMON: 1951 LIBERTY: 17.1.1952 wrecked
(War Camel)					
860. SCATWELL	4410	1911	1920	1928	ANTONIS G LEMOS: 24.8.1936 collision
ex Maisie					
861. CAIRNROSS	5494	1921	--	--	17.1.1940 mined & sunk
862. CAIRNTORR	5387	1922	--	--	23.10.1928 wrecked
(Alabama)					
863. CAIRNESK	5007	1926	--	1956	ZERMATT: 1959 AURORA P: 1959 b.u.
864. CAIRNGLEN	5019	1926	--	--	22.10.1940 wrecked
865. CAIRNAVON	6327	1941	1946	1961	VERGOLIVADA: 1968 b.u.
ex Empire Snow (1393)					

Name	GRT	Built	Acquired	Sold	Subsequent career
866. CAIRNGOWAN	7503	1952	--	1969	GEORGILIS: 1973 b.u.
1965 MANCHESTER ENGINEER					
1966 CAIRNGOWAN					
867. CAIRNDHU (1118)	7503	1952	--	1965	to ML
868. CAIRNFORTH (1009)	8105	1958	--	1969	to RML
1965 MANCHESTER FREIGHTER					
869. CAIRNAVON	4359	1951	1965	1965	ISTINA: 1969 JENNY MARINE: 30.10.1970 fire,
ex Schiaffino Freres, Apsara					CTL
870. CANOPIC (923)	10905	1954	1969	1973	to SSA
871. CEDRIC (921)	10902	1952	1969	1973	to SSA
872. IONIC (931)	10978	1959	1969	1973	to SSA
873. CAVENDISH (1330/1332) (lpg)	26802	1971	1983	1988	to OG
874. ANDES (cc)	32150	1984	--	--	present fleet
875. OSWESTRY GRANGE (1336)	5440	1964	1984	1985	STENJOHAN: still afloat
ex Chelwood (bulk)					

Shaw, Savill and Albion Company Ltd

Name	GRT	Built	Acquired	Sold	Subsequent career
876. IONIC (pass)	12352	1902	--	--	1937 b.u.
877. KIA ORA	6567	1907	--	1935	VERBANIA: 1940 EMPIRE TAMAR: 9.6.1944
					blockship: 1947 b.u.
878. TAINUI (1396) (pass)	9965	1908	--	1939	EMPIRE TRADER: 21.2.1943 sunk by U92
879. PAKEHA (1384)	7909	1910	--	1939	1941 EMPIRE PAKEHA:
			1946	--	repurchased: 1950 b.u.
880. RARANGA (588)	7956	1916	--	1936	to NNA: repurchased
			1945	--	1950 b.u.
881. MAHANA	8740	1917	--	--	1953 b.u.
882. MAHIA (586)	7914	1917	--	1936	to NNA: repurchased
			1945	--	1953 b.u.
883. OTIRA	7995	1919	--	--	1936 b.u.
884. MAIMOA	8011	1920	--	--	20.11.1940 sunk by PINGUIN
885. TAIROA (589)	7983	1920	--	1936	to NNA
886. MATAKANA	8048	1921	--	--	1.5.1940 wrecked
887. COPTIC	8281	1928	--	--	1965 b.u.
888. KARAMEA	8281	1928	--	--	1960 b.u.
889. TARANAKI	8286	1928	--	--	1964 b.u.
890. ZEALANDIC	8281	1928	--	--	16.1.1941 sunk by U106
891. AKAROA (pass)	15128	1914	1932	--	1954 b.u.
ex Euripides					
892. KUMARA	7926	1919	1932	1937	MARATHON: 9.3.1941 sunk by SCHARNHORST
ex Horatius, Bardic					
893. MAMARI (587)	7924	1911	1932	1936	to NNA
ex Herminius, Zealandic					
894. MATAROA (pass)	12333	1922	1932	--	1957 b.u.
ex Diogenes					
895. TAMAROA (pass)	12354	1922	1932	--	1957 b.u.
ex Sophocles					
896. THEMISTOCLES (591) (pass)	11231	1911	1932	1937	to NNA: repurchased
			1945	--	1947 b.u.
897. WAIMANA (590/1397)	7852	1911	1932	1936	to NNA: repurchased
1942 EMPIRE WAIMANA			1946	--	1952 b.u.
1946 WAIMANA					
ex Herminius, Waimana					
898. FORDSDALE	9949	1924	1933	1952	OCEAN NEPTUNE: 1954 PACIFIC TRADER:
					1956 ATLANTIC CONCORD: 1958 JUI YUNG:
					1959 b.u.
899. CERAMIC (pass)	18713	1913	1934	--	6.12.1942 sunk by U515
900. WAIPAWA	10801	1934	--	1967	ARAMIS: 1968 b.u.
901. WAIWERA	10800	1934	--	--	29.6.1942 sunk by U754
902. WAIRANGI	10796	1935	--	--	13.8.1942 sunk by torpedo boats
903. ARAWA (970) (pass)	14462	1922	1936	--	1955 b.u.
ex Esperance Bay					
904. WAIMARAMA	11092	1938	--	--	13.8.1942 sunk by aircraft
905. DOMINION MONARCH (pass)	27155	1939	--	1963	DOMINION MONARCH MARU: 1963 b.u.
906. WAIOTIRA	12823	1939	--	--	25.12.1940 sunk by U95
907. (-----)	12450	1943	--	1943	HMS CAMPANIA: 1955 b.u.
908. WAIWERA	12028	1944	--	--	29.6.1942 sunk by U754
909. WAIRANGI (1375)	13478	1942	1946	--	14.8.1963 grounded, b.u.
ex Empire Grace					
910. CUFIC (1420)	7219	1943	1947	1953	SANTA ELISABETTA: 1967 STAR: 1968 b.u.
ex Samrich					
911. TROPIC (1421)	7219	1943	1947	1952	SAN FRANCESCO: 9.6.1960 foundered
ex Samsylvan, J Whitridge Williams					

Name	GRT	Built	Acquired	Sold	Subsequent career
912. ATHENIC (p/c)	15187	1947	--	--	1969 b.u.
913. CORINTHIC (p/c)	15682	1947	--	--	1969 b.u.
914. CERAMIC (p/c)	15896	1948	--	--	1972 b.u.
915. GOTHIC (p/c)	15902	1948	--	--	1969 b.u.
916. DELPHIC	10691	1949	--	--	1971 b.u.
917. DORIC	10674	1949	--	--	1969 b.u.
918. PERSIC (1007)	13594	1949	--	1969	to RML
919. RUNIC	13587	1950	--	--	19.2.1961 wrecked
920. SUEVIC	13587	1950	--	--	1974 b.u.
921. CEDRIC (871)	11232	1952	--	1969	to CL: returned
			1973	1976	SEA CONDOR: 1977 b.u.
922. CYMRIC	11182	1953	--	--	1975 b.u.
1973 DURANGO					
923. CANOPIC (870)	11164	1954	--	1969	to CL: returned
			1973	1975	CAPETAN NICOLAS: 1985 b.u.
924. CRETIC (1057)	11151	1955	--	1976	to BH
1973 DRINA					
925. SOUTHERN CROSS (pass)	20204	1955	--	1973	CALYPSO: 1980 AZURE SEAS: still afloat
926. ARABIC	6553	1956	--	1972	LAMMA ISLAND: 1983 b.u.
1968 OROYA					
1970 PACIFIC RANGER					
1971 OROYA					
927. CARNATIC (1054)	11144	1956	--	1976	to AG
1973 DARRO					
928. AFRIC	6553	1957	--	1972	HONG KONG ISLAND: 1983 b.u.
1968 ORITA					
929. ARAMAIC	6553	1957	--	1972	LANTAO ISLAND: 1982 b.u.
1968 OROPESA					
1968 PACIFIC EXPORTER					
1970 OROPESA					
930. ALARIC	6692	1958	--	1972	IRAN NIRU: 1977 RUMI: 1979 b.u.
931. IONIC (872)	11219	1959	--	1969	to CL: returned
			1973	1978	GLENPARVA: 1979 b.u.
932. AMALRIC	7791	1960	--	1977	KYMA: 1985 MILOS V: 1985 b.u.
933. ICENIC (1058)	11239	1960	--	1977	to BH
934. ILLYRIC (1055)	11256	1960	--	1977	to AG
935. IBERIC (1062)	11248	1961	--	1979	to MS
1976 DESEADO					
936. MEGANTIC	12226	1962	--	1979	DIMITRIOS VENTOURIS: 1980 b.u.
937. NORTHERN STAR (pass)	24756	1962	--	--	1976 b.u.
938. MEDIC	12220	1963	--	1979	ODYSEFS: 1987 b.u.
939. LAURENTIC	7964	1965	--	1980	SPARTAN REEFER: 1984 b.u.
940. ROMANIC (986)	9785	1943	1965	--	1968 b.u.
ex Drina					
941. ZEALANDIC	7946	1965	--	1980	PORT LAUNAY: 1981 KHALIJ CRYSTAL: 1984 b.u.
942. RUTHENIC (987)	9801	1944	1966	1967	SUSSEX: 1967 b.u.
ex Durango					
943. BRITANNIC	12228	1967	--	1974	NZ WAITANGI: 1980 SERIFOS: still afloat
944. MAJESTIC	12227	1967	--	1974	NZ AORANGI: 1978 MYKONOS: still afloat
945. AKAROA (1257) (pass)	18565	1959	1968	1971	AKARITA: 1977 HUAL AKARITA: 1980
ex Amazon					AKARITA: 1981 b.u.
946. ARANDA (1003) (pass)	18575	1960	1968	1971	HOEGH TRAVELLER: 1977 HUAL
ex Aragon					TRAVELLER: 1980 TRAVELLER: 1981 b.u.
947. ARAWA (1004) (pass)	18595	1960	1968	1971	HOEGH TRANSIT: 1977 HUAL TROTTER:
ex Arlanza					1980 TROTTER: 1981 b.u.
948. CAIRNVENTURE	1436	1969	--	1974	SHIPMAR III: 1976 PASSAAT SANTOS: 1977
					ERIC: 1979 GHADAMES: 1986 ALEXIA: 1990
					STAR QUEEN: still afloat
949. JERVIS BAY (cc)	26876	1970	--	1980	24.1.84 wrecked
950. LANGSTONE (981)	3441	1958	1970	1974	DIMITRIOS K: 1981 b.u.
ex Saracen					
951. OCEAN MONARCH (pass)	25971	1957	1970	--	1975 b.u.
ex Empress of England					
952. CAIRNRANGER	1598	1971	--	1976	MOUNTPARK: 1982 BENEDETTO SCOTTO:
					1988 MARYLAND: 1991 SAMER: still afloat
953. SAXON PRINCE	1581	1971	--	1976	ADARA: 1986 ANDARA: 1990 PARANA STAR
1975 CAIRNTRADER					still afloat
1976 SAXON PRINCE					
(Cairntrader)					
954. CAIRNROVER	1599	1972	--	1978	GIANNIS: 1984 ANASTASSIA: 1986
					ANASTASSIA ENA: 1986 REIDA: still afloat
955. MAYFIELD	6089	1970	1973	1980	SEAFROST: still afloat
ex Olau Pil, Cap Colville					

Name	GRT	Built	Acquired	Sold	Subsequent career
956. CAIRNFREIGHTER	1592	1975	--	1982	TJONGERWAL: 1987 CENED: 1988 MEGREZ: 1989 VILARO: still afloat
957. HARDWICKE GRANGE (1199)	9234	1961	1975	1977	JACQUES: 1979 b.u.
958. OCEAN TRANSPORT (1306/1259)	8501	1962	1975	1978	to BE
959. WESTBURY (1286/1258)	8414	1960	1975	1977	to BE
960. CAIRNASH	1597	1977	--	1983	ANDREA: 1985 ST ANTON: still afloat
961. CAIRNCARRIER	1592	1976		1982	TEQUILA SUNSET: 1984 ARKLOW BRIDGE: 1990 WAVE ROSE: still afloat
962. CAIRNELM	1597	1977	--	1983	CHRISTIANE: 1985 ST CHRISTOPH: still afloat
963. CAIRNOAK	1597	1977	--	1983	LEONY: 1985 ST JAKOB: still afloat
964. DERWENT	9167	1979	--	1982	MOUNTAIN AZALEA: 1988 EVPO AGSIMONE: 1991 HANBONN CONCORD: still afloat
965. DUNEDIN (cc)	18140	1980	--	1986	MONTE PASCOAL: 1990 COLUMBUS OLIVOS: still afloat
966. CLERK-MAXWELL (1337) (lpg)	8298	1966	1984	--	1986 b.u.
967. ELSTREE GRANGE (1291) (tank)	39626	1979	1984	1984	SANTA LUCIA: 1989 SPIRIT: still afloat
968. HORNBY GRANGE (1292) (tank)	39626	1979	1984	1984	SANTA BARBARA: 1989 AFFINITY: still afloat
969. OROYA (1056)	14124	1978	1984	1986	YINKA FOLAWIYO: 1989 MERCHANT PREMIER: still afloat

Aberdeen & Commonwealth Line Ltd

Name	GRT	Built	Acquired	Sold	Subsequent career
970. ESPERANCE BAY (903) (pass)	14176	1922	1933	1936	to SSA
971. HOBSONS BAY (pass) 1936 ESPERANCE BAY	14198	1922	1933	--	1955 b.u.
972. JERVIS BAY (pass)	14164	1922	1933	--	5.11.1940 sunk by ADMIRAL SCHEER
973. LARGS BAY (pass)	14184	1921	1933	--	1957 b.u.
974. MORETON BAY (pass)	14145	1921	1933	--	1957 b.u.

Furness (Canada) Ltd

Name	GRT	Built	Acquired	Sold	Subsequent career
975. BRAZILIAN PRINCE (979) ex Outremont Park	7158	1944	1946	1954	to FML
976. ROYAL PRINCE ex Elgin Park, (Fort Simcoe)	7160	1945	1946	1949	ATLANTIC STAR: 1961 NADIR: 1972 b.u.
977. BEACON GRANGE ex Harmac Victoria, Albert Park	7157	1945	1947	1949	CONSTANTINOS: 1967 b.u.
978. ROYSTON GRANGE ex Harmac Alberni, Sapperton Park, (Fort Toulouse)	7166	1943	1947	1949	YIANNIS: 1966 b.u.

Furness (Montreal) Ltd

Name	GRT	Built	Acquired	Sold	Subsequent career
979. BRAZILIAN PRINCE (975) ex Outremont Park	7158	1944	1954	1958	FEDERAL PIONEER: 1971 b.u.

Crusader Shipping Company (jointly owned by Shaw, Savill & Albion Co Ltd, New Zealand Shipping Co Ltd, Blue Star Line Ltd and Port Line Ltd)

Name	GRT	Built	Acquired	Sold	Subsequent career
980. CRUSADER (Edith Thorden)	3461	1957	--	1972	RENTONEVERETT: 1983 b.u.
981. SARACEN (950)	3441	1958	--	1970	to SSA
982. KNIGHT TEMPLAR ex Arctic Ocean	3791	1948	1963	1968	MINDANAO SEA: 26.1.1973 burnt, b.u.

Royal Mail Lines Ltd

Name	GRT	Built	Acquired	Sold	Subsequent career
983. ANDES (pass)	26435	1939	--	--	1971 b.u.
984. DESEADO	9630	1942	--	--	1968 b.u.
985. DARRO	9732	1943	--	1967	SURREY: 1967 b.u.
986. DRINA (940)	9785	1944	--	1965	to SSA
987. DURANGO (942)	9801	1944	--	1966	to SSA
988. LOCH AVON	8617	1947	--	1967	HONGKONG OBSERVER: 1971 b.u.
989. LOCH GARTH	8617	1947	--	--	1967 b.u.
990. EBRO	7785	1952	--	1969	FORTUNE VICTORY: 1970 KALEMYO: 1978 b.u.
991. ESSEQUIBO	7785	1952	--	1968	NINGPO: 1970 KALEWA: 1979 b.u.
992. LOCH GOWAN	9718	1954	--	--	1970 b.u.
993. ESCALANTE	7791	1955	--	1970	MANES P: 2.2.70 wrecked
994. EDEN	7791	1956	--	1969	NEPTUNE GARNET: 1979 b.u.
995. TUSCANY	7455	1956	--	1970	FEDERAL HUDSON: 1973 GOLDEN KING: 1975 CHAR HSIUNG: 1980 b.u.
996. ALBANY	7299	1957	--	1971	TAIWAN: 1976 LIDO: 1979 b.u.
997. LOCH LOYAL	11035	1957	--	1971	AEGIS LOYAL: 1974 b.u.
998. PICARDY	7306	1957	--	1971	EUROPE: 1976 LIRA: 17.8.1977 fire, sank
999. THESSALY	7299	1957	--	1971	JAPAN: 1976 LIHO: 1979 b.u.
1000. YACARE	1344	1959	--	1972	still afloat
1001. YAGUARETE	1344	1959	--	1972	still afloat

Name	GRT	Built	Acquired	Sold	Subsequent career
1002. AMAZON (1257) (pass)	20368	1959	--	1966	to BE
1003. ARAGON (946) (pass)	20362	1960	--	1968	to SSA
1004. ARLANZA (947) (pass)	20362	1960	--	1968	to SSA
1005. DUQUESA (1269)	9726	1949	1968	--	1969 b.u.
1006. STOLT ABADESA (1270/1048) ex Abadesa (tank)	13398	1962	1968	1970	to PMS
1007. DERWENT (918/803) ex Persic	13350	1949	1969	1970	to PL
1008. DOURO (1191/804) ex Hornby Grange	9706	1946	1969	1970	to PL
1009. LOMBARDY (868) ex Manchester Freighter, Cairnforth	8105	1958	1969	1971	PREMIER PACIFIC: 1975 TARA SEA: 1976 GEORGIOS: 1979 MAESTRO GIORGIS: 1982 b.u.
1010. REINA DEL MAR (1037) (pass)	20750	1956	1969	1973	1975 b.u.
1011. CHANDELEUR (1038) ex Cienfuegos	5224	1959	1970	1971	EMMA M: 1974 LELA: 1981 JETPUR VICEROY: 1983 b.u.
1012. COTOPAXI (1034)	8559	1954	1970	1973	KAVO LONGOS: 1975 b.u.
1013. ELEUTHERA (1039)	5224	1959	1970	1971	MIMI M: 1974 MARIA: 1984 b.u.
1014. KENUTA (1032)	8494	1950	1970	--	1971 b.u.
1015. PACIFIC ENVOY (371) ex Loch Ryan, Pacific Envoy	9305	1958	1970	1971	AEGIS STRENGTH: 1974 b.u.
1016. PACIFIC NORTHWEST (366)	9337	1954	1970	1971	AEGIS POWER: 1974 b.u.
1017. PACIFIC RELIANCE (364)	9337	1951	1970	--	1971 b.u.
1018. PACIFIC STRONGHOLD (372)	9337	1958	1970	1971	AEGIS HONOR: 1973 b.u.
1019. PIZARRO (1035)	8564	1955	1970	1972	KAVO MALEAS: 1974 b.u.
1020. SOMERS ISLE (1040)	5515	1959	1970	1971	ELDINA: 1975 COMMENCEMENT: 1981 CARIBBEAN: 1981 MELPOL: 8.12.1981 fire, b.u.
1021. SOUTHERN PRINCE (798) ex Medic, Southern Prince	7731	1956	1970	1971	ARGOSY: 1976 ORIENT PROSPERITY: 1977 BITAS: 1978 b.u.
1022. ORBITA	12321	1972	--	1980	ANDALIEN: 1980 MORNING SUN: 1980 RUBENS: still afloat
1023. ORDUNA 1984 BEACON GRANGE	12321	1973	--	1984	MERCHANT PIONEER: still afloat
1024. ORTEGA 1980 ANDES	12321	1973	--	1982	OCEANHAVEN: 1987 KOTA AKBAR: still afloat
1025. KAYESON (1325) (tank)	28132	1961	1974	1981	AOUNALLAH: 1983 b.u.

Pacific Steam Navigation Company

Name	GRT	Built	Acquired	Sold	Subsequent career
1026. SARMIENTO	8346	1943	--	1967	MONOMARCHOS: 1970 GLADIATOR: 1971 b.u.
1027. SALAVERRY	8590	1946	--	1967	PELIAS: 12.12.1972 foundered
1028. SANTANDER	8550	1946	--	1967	NAVMACHOS: 1971 b.u.
1029. SALINAS	8610	1947	--	1968	POLYFIMOS: 1972 b.u.
1030. SALAMANCA	8610	1948	--	1967	KRONOS: 1972 b.u.
1031. FLAMENCO	8491	1950	--	1966	PACIFIC ABETO: 1982 b.u.
1032. KENUTA (1014)	8494	1950	--	1970	to RML
1033. CUZCO	8038	1951	--	1965	BENATTOW: 1977 b.u.
1034. COTOPAXI (1012)	8559	1954	--	1970	to RML
1035. PIZARRO (1019)	8564	1955	--	1970	to RML
1036. POTOSI	8564	1955	--	1972	KAVO PEIRATIS: 1976 b.u.
1037. REINA DEL MAR (1010) (pass)	21501	1956	--	1969	to RML
1038. CIENFUEGOS (1011) 1970 CHANDELEUR	5407	1959	--	1970	to RML
1039. ELEUTHERA (1013)	5407	1959	--	1970	to RML
1040. SOMERS ISLE (1020)	5684	1959	--	1970	to RML
1041. WILLIAM WHEELWRIGHT (1046) (tank)	31320	1960	-- 1976	1962 --	to PMS: returned 1976 b.u.
1042. GEORGE PEACOCK (10047) (tank)	18863	1961	--	1962	to PMS
1043. MOUNT NEWMAN (1052) (bulk) (Beacon Grange)	65131	1973	1976	1982	SOUTH VICTOR: 1987 COLITA: 1990 PAN CEDAR: 1991 IAPETOS: still afloat
1044. SAILOR PRINCE (1050) 1977 SOLDIER PRINCE ex Pennine Prince	1599	1971	1976	1979	ALFA: 1984 PHAEDRA: 1987 TRANSPORTER: 14.9.1987 fire, b.u.
1045. ORCOMA (376)	10509	1966	1978	1979	EKA DAYA SAMUDERA: 1984 b.u.

Pacific Maritime Services Ltd

Name	GRT	Built	Acquired	Sold	Subsequent career
1046. WILLIAM WHEELWRIGHT (1041) (tank)	30976	1960	1962	1976	to PSN
1047. GEORGE PEACOCK (1042) (tank)	18863	1961	1962	1969	GEORGIOS V: still afloat
1048. STOLT ABADESA (1006) (tank) ex Abadesa	13398	1962	1970	1971	STOLT TIGER: 1975 STOLT VIKING: 1983 VIKING: 1984 TRITON: 1984 NEW BRIGHTON: 1986 EMIR MAN: 1987 b.u.
1049. STOLT STUART (800) (tank) ex Stuart Prince	12668	1960	1970	1973	1976 LLAIMA: 1982 b.u.

Name	GRT	Built	Acquired	Sold	Subsequent career
1050. PENNINE PRINCE (1044)	1599	1971	--	1976	to PSN
1972 SAILOR PRINCE					
1051. EDENMORE (370) (ore)	10792	1958	1973	1975	WELCOME: 1976 DUGLASIA: 1983 b.u.
1052. MOUNT NEWMAN (1043) (bulk)	65131	1973	--	1976	to PSN
(Winsford Bridge)					
1053. SAGAMORE (369) (ore)	10792	1957	1973	1975	CAPITAN ALBERTO: 1989 TANIA: still afloat

Ardgowan Shipping Company Ltd

Name	GRT	Built	Acquired	Sold	Subsequent career
1054. DARRO (927)	11144	1956	1976	1977	LITSA K: 1979 DIMITRA: 1979 b.u.
ex Carnatic					
1055. ILLYRIC (934)	11023	1960	1977	1978	CARMILA: 1979 b.u.
1056. OROYA (969)	14124	1977	--	1984	to SSA

Blackhall Shipping Company Ltd

Name	GRT	Built	Acquired	Sold	Subsequent career
1057. DRINA (924)	10890	1955	1976	1977	UNITED VIGOUR: 1979 b.u.
ex Cretic					
1058. ICENIC (933)	11042	1960	1977	1978	AEGEAN UNITY: 1979 b.u.
1059. OROPESA	14124	1978	--	1984	MERCHANT PRINCIPAL: still afloat

Tolosa Ltd

Name	GRT	Built	Acquired	Sold	Subsequent career
1060. FIJIAN (802)	1459	1970	1979	1981	ONEHUNGA: 1983 FIJIAN: 1989 COTSWOLD
ex Cotswold Prince					PRINCE: still afloat

Metcalfe Shipping Company Ltd

Name	GRT	Built	Acquired	Sold	Subsequent career
1061. DUNELMIA	9346	1977	--	1980	NEW PANDA: 1985 TRADE FORTUNE: 1988
					TRADE FAIR: still afloat
1062. DESEADO (935)	11034	1961	1979	1981	SAN GEORGE: 1983 b.u.
ex Iberic					

Manchester Liners Ltd

Note.- in entries 1063 to 1135 the MANCHESTER prefix to ship names has been abbreviated as M.

Name	GRT	Built	Acquired	Sold	Subsequent career
1063. M ENTERPRISE	3878	1890	1898	--	14.11.1899 foundered
ex Queensmore					
1064. M TRADER	3318	1890	1898	1913	FERDINAND MELSOM: 1915 KAUPANGER:
ex Parkmore					13.12.1916 sunk by U38
1065. M CITY	7696	1898	--	--	1929 b.u.
1066. M PORT	5658	1899	--	1900	HYDASPES: 1930 b.u.
1067. M CORPORATION	5400	1899	--	--	1929 b.u.
1068. M COMMERCE	5397	1899	--	--	26.10.1914 mined & sunk
1069. M IMPORTER	4028	1899	--	1927	ALEXANDRIA: 1933 b.u.
1070. M MERCHANT	5657	1900	--	--	15.1.1903 burnt
1071. M SHIPPER	4076	1900	--	--	1930 b.u.
1072. M EXCHANGE	4091	1901	--	1925	EQUATOR: 1939 b.u.
1073. M ENGINEER	4302	1902	--	--	27.3.1916 sunk by U44
1074. M INVENTOR	4247	1902	--	--	18.1.1917 sunk by U57
1075. M MARKET	4901	1902	--	--	26.4.1903 wrecked
1076. M SPINNER	4227	1903	--	--	22.1.1918 sunk by U27
1077. M MILLER	4234	1903	--	--	5.6.1917 sunk by U66
1905 FULHAM					
1908 MANCHESTER MILLER					
1078. M MERCHANT (1127)	4152	1904	--	1920	to MOS: returned
			1930	--	1933 b.u.
1079. M PORT (1128)	4093	1904	--	1920	to MOS
1080. M MARINER (1126)	4106	1904	--	1920	to MOS
1081. M CITIZEN	4251	1912	--	--	26.4.1917 sunk by U70
1082. M CIVILIAN	4706	1913	--	1933	TASIS: 1940 EQUATEUR: 1942 BARI: 1.8.1943
					sunk by aircraft
1083. M HERO	5738	1916	--	1937	ST WINIFRED: 1939 CAPO VITA: 9.3.1941 sunk
					by HMS UTMOST
1084. M TRADER	3938	1902	1916	--	4.6.1917 sunk by U65
ex Archeboe					
1085. M COMMERCE	4144	1906	1916	--	29.7.1917 sunk by U39
ex King					
1086. M ENGINEER	4415	1905	1917	--	16.8.1917 sunk by UC16
ex Nation, Craigvar					
1087. M INVENTOR	4112	1907	1917	--	30.7.1917 sunk by U94
ex Celtic King					
1088. M BRIGADE	6021	1918	--	--	26.9.1940 sunk by U137
1089. M DIVISION	6027	1918	--	--	1953 b.u.
1090. M PRODUCER (573)	6576	1916	1921	1939	BOTWEY: 26.7.1941 sunk by U141
ex Start Point					
1091. M SPINNER (549)	4767	1918	1921	--	9.6.1944 blockship
ex Grampian Range					

Name	GRT	Built	Acquired	Sold	Subsequent career
1092. M REGIMENT	7930	1922	--	--	4.12.1939 collision
1093. M COMMERCE	5342	1925	--	1952	CORBITA: 1952 FAKIRJEE COWESJEE: 1967 b.u.
1094. M CITIZEN	5328	1925	--	--	9.7.1943 sunk by U508
1095. M EXPORTER (674) ex Rexmore	5277	1918	1929	1947	NICARAGUA: 1948 YU TUNG: 1950 RIO BAMBA: 1952 PRECILA: 1958 b.u.
1096. EL ARGENTINO (351) (half interest—1242)	9501	1928	--	1934	to FW
1097. M PORT	5469	1935	--	--	1964 b.u.
1098. M CITY	5600	1937	--	--	1964 b.u.
1099. M PROGRESS	5620	1938	--	--	1966 b.u.
1100. M MERCHANT	7264	1940	--	--	25.2.1943 sunk by U628
1101. M TRADER	5671	1941	--	--	1963 b.u.
1102. M SHIPPER	7881	1943	--	--	1969 b.u.
1103. M REGIMENT	5888	1947	--	1968	AZURE COAST II: 1971 PU GOR: 1971 b.u.
1104. M MERCHANT	7651	1951	--	1967	CLIO: 14.2.1972 burnt
1105. M PIONEER	1805	1952	--	1963	CYPRIAN MED: 1969 SAN ANTONIO: 1971 b.u.
1106. M EXPLORER	1805	1952	--	1963	C A CROSBIE: 1965 P M CROSBIE: 1968 PANAGOS L: 1971 YPERMACHOS: 1973 EMILIA: 1980 b.u.
1107. M SPINNER	7814	1952	--	1968	ESTIA: 25.11.1971 sank
1108. M PROSPECTOR ex Vigor	1400	1948	1953	1960	GEORGIOS: 1972 AGHIOS NEKTARIOS L: believed still afloat
1109. M MARINER	7850	1955	--	1968	IRA: 1975 PANDAY IRA: 1977 b.u.
1110. M VANGUARD	1662	1956	--	1963	SHELDRAKE: 1968 BAT GOLAN: 1974 WOODCHUCK: 1975 SELATAN MAJU: 1981 WIHAR I: 1985 b.u.
1111. M VENTURE	1662	1956	--	1961	PHILOMEL: 1968 BAT TIRAN: 5.8.1972 fire, b.u.
1112. M FAITH 1965 CAIRNESK 1966 MANCHESTER FAITH	4459	1959	--	1970	ILKON TAK: 1978 CHRYSEIS: 1983 b.u.
1113. M FAME 1965 CAIRNGLEN 1966 MANCHESTER FAME	4462	1959	--	1970	ILKON NIKI: 1979 EFI: 1980 PANAGIS K: 1986 b.u.
1114. M MILLER (cc) 1970 MANCHESTER QUEST	9296	1959	--	--	1976 b.u.
1115. M COMMERCE	8724	1963	--	1971	BER SEA: 1975 YANGCHUN: 7.10.1980 burnt Iran/Iraq War
1116. M CITY	8734	1964	--	1971	KOREAN WINNER: 1978 ONE WEST NO 8: 1985 b.u.
1117. M RENOWN	8742	1964	--	1971	KOREAN CHALLENGER: 1978 EDESSA: 4.2.1984 fire, CTL, b.u.
1118. M EXPORTER (867) ex Cairndhu	7506	1952	1965	1969	GEMINI EXPORTER: 1971 b.u.
1119. M PORT	8938	1966	--	1971	BIOKOVO: 1980 YDRA: 20.1.1983 fire, b.u.
1120. M PROGRESS (cc) 1971 MANCHESTER CONCEPT	8176	1967	--	1980	CHERRY BUNGA: 1985 b.u.
1121. M CHALLENGE (cc)	12039	1968	--	1978	OCEAN CONTAINER: 1989 HUNG FU: 1989 MSC SUSANNA: still afloat
1122. M COURAGE (cc)	12039	1969	--	1979	PACIFIC CONTAINER: 1989 MSC MARINA: still afloat
1123. M CONCORDE (cc)	12039	1969	--	1982	CHAR LIAN: 1984 b.u.
1124. M MERITO (cc) 1970 MANCHESTER MERIT 1972 FORTUNA (Catalina del Mar)	3414	1970	--	1975	KATHLEEN: 1987 KUDU: 1990 CEMENT TWO: still afloat
1125. M CRUSADE (cc)	12039	1971	--	1982	CHAR CHE: 1984 b.u.

Manchester Ocean Services Ltd

Name	GRT	Built	Acquired	Sold	Subsequent career
1126. M MARINER (1080)	4106	1904	1920	1925	MERCATOR: 1.12.1939 mined & sunk
1127. M MERCHANT (1078)	4152	1904	1920	1930	to ML
1128. M PORT (1079)	4093	1904	1920	1925	VOGESEN: 7.5.1940 mined & sunk

Condrons (Manchester) Ltd and **Manchester Liners (Freighting) Ltd**

Name	GRT	Built	Acquired	Sold	Subsequent career
1129. FRONTIER (cc)	3621	1972	--	1979	BOX TRADER: 1984 HARIS: 15.2.1985 fire, b.u.

Manchester Liners (Transport) Ltd

Name	GRT	Built	Acquired	Sold	Subsequent career
1130. M VIGOUR (cc) 1976 CARGO VIGOUR 1976 MANCHESTER VIGOUR	5310	1973	--	1980	VILLE D'ORIENT: 1984 BENWALID: still afloat
1131. M ZEAL (cc) 1975 CARGO ZEAL 1976 MANCHESTER ZEAL	5310	1973	--	1981	SEA HAWK: 1990 SEA LEOPARD: 1991 KURNIA SAMUDERA: still afloat

Name	GRT	Built	Acquired	Sold	Subsequent career
Manchester Liners (Intermodal) Ltd					
1132. M RENOWN (cc)	12577	1974	--	1982	RATIH: 1990 OOCL AMITY: still afloat
1975 ASIAN RENOWN					
1978 MANCHESTER RENOWN					
1133. (M Reward) (cc)	12577	1974	--	1982	R R RATNA: 1991 OOCL AWARD still afloat
1974 ASIAN REWARD					
1978 MANCHESTER REWARD					
1979 SEATRAIN NORFOLK					
1979 TFL REWARD					
1980 MANCHESTER REWARD					
Golden Cross Line Ltd					
1134. M VANGUARD (cc)	17385	1977	--	1983	ORIENTAL EXPERT: 1991 OOCL APPLAUSE:
1977 SEATRAIN TRENTON					still afloat
1979 MANCHESTER VANGUARD					
1979 KEELUNG					
1980 MANCHESTER VANGUARD					
1980 ORIENTAL VANGUARD					
1981 MANCHESTER VANGUARD					
1982 IBN MAJID					
Gough and Crosthwaite Ltd					
1135. M VENTURE (cc)	17385	1977	--	1980	ORIENTAL VENTURE: 1981 RHEIN EXPRESS: 1983
1977 SEATRAIN BENNINGTON					ORIENTAL AMBASSADOR: 1989 OOCL
1979 MANCHESTER VENTURE					ALLIANCE: still afloat
1979 MARSEILLE					
1980 MANCHESTER VENTURE					
Houlder Brothers and Company					
1898 renamed **Houlder Brothers and Company Ltd.**					
1136. HORNBY GRANGE (1159)	2356	1890	--	1899	to HL
1137. OVINGDEAN GRANGE (1161)	2413	1890	--	1899	to HL
1138. FLORENCE (1158)	2492	1889	1897	1899	to HL
1139. JOULE (lpg)	8666	1965	1973	--	1984 b.u.
ex Havgas					
1140. CLYDE BRIDGE (1335)	24024	1967	1974	1981	to SH
1977 DUNSTER GRANGE					
ex Clydesdale (bulk)					
1141. OSWESTRY GRANGE (1336) (bulk)	5440	1964	1974	1982	to SH
ex Chelwood					
1142. SHERWOOD	5279	1958	1974	1974	NISYROS ERA: believed still afloat
ex Thackeray					
Paraguayan Development Company Ltd					
1143. APA	433	1890	--	1895	CARANGOLA: 1930 b.u.
1144. ASUNCION	433	1890	--	1895	TEIXEIRINHA: 15.6.1023 wrecked
1145. PILCOMAYO	433	1890	--	1895	FIDELENSE: 1903 PILCOMAYO: 1914
					FIDELENSE: 1939 b.u.
1146. RIO PARAGUAY	433	1890	--	1895	PINTO: 5.6.1914 wrecked
Urmston Grange Steamship Company Ltd					
1147. URMSTON GRANGE (1165)	3423	1894	--	1899	to HL
Elstree Grange Steamship Company Ltd					
1148. ELSTREE GRANGE (1157)	3930	1892	1895	1899	to HL
ex Constance					
Langton Grange Steamship Company Ltd					
1149. LANGTON GRANGE (1160)	5803	1896	--	1899	to HL
Denton Grange Steamship Company Ltd					
1150. DENTON GRANGE (1156)	5838	1896	--	1899	to HL
Royston Grange Steamship Company Ltd					
1151. ROYSTON GRANGE (1163)	4213	1897	--	1899	to HL
Beacon Grange Steamship Company Ltd					
1152. BEACON GRANGE (1155)	4237	1898	--	1899	to HL
Rippingham Grange Steamship Company Ltd					
1153. RIPPINGHAM GRANGE (1162)	6827	1898	--	1899	to HL

Name	GRT	Built	Acquired	Sold	Subsequent career
Southern Cross Steamship Company Ltd					
1154. SOUTHERN CROSS (1164)	5050	1892	1899	1899	to HL

Houlder Line Ltd
1975 renamed **Houlder Offshore Ltd** and 1989 renamed **Stena Houlder Ltd.**

Name	GRT	Built	Acquired	Sold	Subsequent career
1155. BEACON GRANGE (1152)	4237	1898	1899	--	6.9.1921 wrecked
1156. DENTON GRANGE (1150)	5838	1896	1899	1900	GLENLOGAN: 31.10.1916 sunk by U21
1157. ELSTREE GRANGE (1148) ex Constance	3930	1892	1899	1919	MANU: 1926 b.u.
1158. FLORENCE (1138/142)	2492	1889	1899	1902	to FW
1159. HORNBY GRANGE (1136)	2356	1890	1899	1919	AUGUSTINA FORNER: 1927 b.u.
1160. LANGTON GRANGE (1149)	5803	1896	1899	--	5.8.1909 wrecked
1161. OVINGDEAN GRANGE (1137)	2413	1890	1899	1907	ROMAN: 1915 TAMON MARU NO 16: 7.9.1917 missing
1162. RIPPINGHAM GRANGE (1153)	6827	1898	1899	1912	LIMERICK: 28.5.1917 sunk by U86
1163. ROYSTON GRANGE (1151)	4213	1897	1899	--	1928 b.u.
1164. SOUTHERN CROSS (1154)	5050	1892	1899	--	24.12.1909 wrecked
1165. URMSTON GRANGE (1147)	3423	1894	1899	1914	blockship, Scapa Flow
1166. MALTESE CROSS	1494	1900	--	1900	CHILLAGOE: 1934 b.u.
1167. DRAYTON GRANGE	6592	1901	--	1912	TYRONE: 27.9.1913 wrecked
1168. THORPE GRANGE ex Indramayo	4188	1889	1901	--	1930 b.u.
1169. SUTHERLAND GRANGE (174) ex Guardiana	6852	1907	1911	--	1933 b.u.
1170. EL PARAGUAYO	8508	1912	--	--	1936 b.u.
1171. LA CORRENTINA	8529	1912	--	--	7.10.1914 sunk by KRONPRINZ WILHELM
1172. LYNTON GRANGE	4252	1912	--	--	1933 b.u.
1173. DENBY GRANGE	4252	1912	--	--	24.10.1918 collision
1174. OAKLANDS GRANGE	4488	1912	--	1934	NICOLAOS PIANGOS: 31.10.1941 sunk by aircraft
1175. OLDFIELD GRANGE	4653	1913	--	--	11.12.1917 sunk by U62
1176. ROUNTON GRANGE	4487	1913	--	1934	ELISE SCHULTE: 10.1.1942 wrecked
1177. HARDWICKE GRANGE	9005	1921	--	--	12.6.1942 sunk by U129
1178. UPWEY GRANGE	9130	1925	--	--	8.8.1940 sunk by U37
1179. DUNSTER GRANGE	9494	1928	--	1951	VAASA: 1958 KINYO MARU: 1963 YOKO MARU: 1974 b.u.
1180. ELSTREE GRANGE ex Abadesa	6572	1916	1928	--	3.5.1941 bombed, b.u.
1181. OVINGDEAN GRANGE ex Zapala	4895	1924	1935	1936	PEARLSTONE: 1939 CASTELBIANCO: 1941 RIO CHUBUT: 11.5.1959 wrecked
1182. ROYSTON GRANGE ex Salado, Australier, War Bison	5144	1918	1935	--	25.11.1939 sunk by U28
1183. LANGTON GRANGE ex Segura, War Pansy	5295	1919	1935	1936	NICOLAOS M EMBIRICOS: 4.11.1939 mined & sunk
1184. OSWESTRY GRANGE (1271) ex Rhodesian Prince, Argentine Transport	4684	1935	1937	--	12.2.1941 sunk by ADMIRAL HIPPER
1185. LYNTON GRANGE	5029	1937	--	--	28.12.1942 sunk by U406/U628
1186. BEACON GRANGE	10119	1938	--	--	27.4.1941 sunk by U552
1187. RIPPINGHAM GRANGE	10365	1943	--	1961	ABBEY WOOD: 1962 b.u.
1188. LANGTON GRANGE (1386) ex Empire Pennant	7043	1942	1946	--	1960 b.u.
1189. OVINGDEAN GRANGE (1368) ex Empire Buckler	7046	1942	1946	1959	SABRINA: 1961 NOEMI: 27.12.1965 ashore, CTL
1190. URMSTON GRANGE (1387) ex Empire Pibroch	7046	1942	1946	1959	ARGO GRANGE: 1960 b.u.
1191. HORNBY GRANGE (1008)	10785	1946	--	1969	to RML
1192. ELSTREE GRANGE ex Samettrick	7272	1943	1947	1960	KOPALNIA MIECHOWICE: 1972 b.u.
1193. BARTON GRANGE (1366) ex Empire Balfour	7201	1944	1949	1958	SUNLIGHT: 1967 b.u.
1194. ROYSTON GRANGE (1400) ex Fort Ash	7131	1943	1950	1952	GIUAN: 1960 CINQUETERRE: 1961 TILEMAHOS: 1965 ELICOS: 1966 b.u.
1195. OSWESTRY GRANGE	9406	1952	--	1971	DINOS METHENITIS: 1978 DINOS V: 1979 b.u.
1196. THORPE GRANGE 1971 ST MERRIEL 1972 THORPE GRANGE 1972 ST MERRIEL	8695	1954	--	1973	JOO HONG: 1975 PAN TECK: 1977 LIVA: 1979 b.u.
1197. DENBY GRANGE (tank) 1969 STOLT GRANGE	12576	1958	--	1973	STOLT PUMA: 1976 PUMA: 1976 b.u.
1198. ROYSTON GRANGE	10262	1959	--	--	11.5.1972 collision, burnt, b.u.
1199. HARDWICKE GRANGE (957)	10338	1961	--	1975	to SSA

Name	GRT	Built	Acquired	Sold	Subsequent career
1200. OREGIS (1324)	6858	1955	1973	--	1982 b.u.
1974 H.T.S. COUPLER 1					
1975 OREGIS					
1201. ORELIA	5554	1982/4			
Oswestry Grange Steamship Company Ltd					
1202. OSWESTRY GRANGE	7381	1902	--	1912	ROSCOMMON: 21.8.1917 sunk by U53
Bollington Grange Steamship Company Ltd					
1203. BOLLINGTON GRANGE (1261)	5583	1893	1915	1916	to FHAL
ex Buteshire					
Empire Transport Company Ltd					
1975 renamed **Dee Navigation Ltd.**					
1204. HAVERSHAM GRANGE (127)	7359	1898	1902	--	23.10.1906 burnt
ex Rapidan					
1205. EVERTON GRANGE	7144	1903	--	1912	MEATH: 1925 NORDICO: 1932 b.u.
1206. PARISIANA (229)	4823	1909	1910	--	13.12.1910 burnt
[Australian Transport]					
1207. EMPIRE TRANSPORT (238)	6291	1909	1910	1912	SOMMELSDIJK: 1930 ANTIOPE: 1934
ex Savannah					ATLANTIDE: 23.12.1938 wrecked
1208. BRITISH TRANSPORT	4143	1910	--	--	1933 b.u.
1209. CANADIAN TRANSPORT	4139	1910	--	--	1933 b.u.
1210. CAPE TRANSPORT (248)	4109	1910	--	1929	CHRISTOFOROS: 1932 MARGAY: 1933 b.u.
1211. INDIAN TRANSPORT (244)	4111	1910	--	1929	NAGOS: 1934 THETIS A: 14.7.1940 sunk by U52
1212. NATAL TRANSPORT	4114	1910	--	--	4.9.1915 sunk by U34
1213. AMERICAN TRANSPORT	4767	1911	--	1929	MARTHA HENDRIK FISSER: 12.2.1935 wrecked
1214. ARGENTINE TRANSPORT (283)	4763	1911	--	1915	to FW
1215. AUSTRALIAN TRANSPORT	4773	1911	--	--	23.8.1918 sunk by UC27
1216. VICTORIAN TRANSPORT	4482	1913	--	1932	EVI: 1937 ALIAKMON: 1941 missing, believed 22.11.1941 collision
1217. TASMANIAN TRANSPORT	4482	1913	--	--	1933 b.u.
1218. IMPERIAL TRANSPORT	4648	1913	--	--	11.4.1917 sunk by UC34
1219. NEW ZEALAND TRANSPORT	4481	1913	--	--	14.6.1917 sunk by UC23
1220. ROYAL TRANSPORT	4652	1913	--	1929	JOHANN WESSELS: 15.9.1941 sunk by aircraft
1221. PACIFIC TRANSPORT	4482	1913	--	--	1933 b.u.
1222. EGYPTIAN TRANSPORT	4648	1913	--	1932	HELEN MOLLER: 1933 RITA CHANDRIS: 1939 EVERIGA: 1960 deleted from Lloyd's Register, end unknown
1223. AFRICAN TRANSPORT	4482	1913	--	--	25.6.1918 sunk by UB88
1224. OCEAN TRANSPORT	4643	1913	--	--	30.1.1928 wrecked
1225. QUEENSLAND TRANSPORT	4663	1913	--	1934	MAROUSSIO LOGOTHETIS: 1940 GENERAL DUCHESNE: 1942 MAROUSSIO LOGOTHETIS: 15.5.1943 sunk by U105
1226. PANAMA TRANSPORT	4644	1914	--	--	1933 b.u.
1227. (Rhodesian Transport) (1245)	4986	1914	--	1914	to BE: returned
RHODESIAN TRANSPORT			1915	1933	ALICE MOLLER: 1946 LING YUNG: 29.10.1948 wrecked
ex Clutha River					
1228. IMPERIAL TRANSPORT (tank)	8022	1931	--	1947	MESNA: 1949 RONA: 1958 b.u.
1229. ARGENTINE TRANSPORT	7283	1944	1947	1958	ARCHANDROS: 1967 ZEPHYR: 1968 b.u.
ex Samtyne					
1230. IMPERIAL TRANSPORT (tank)	11365	1953	--	1964	ANGELIKI: 1969 b.u.
1231. ROEBUCK (bulk)	6802	1976	--	1982	SOUTH COUNTY: still afloat
1232. RAVENSWOOD (bulk)	6802	1977	--	1982	SOUTH FAITH: 1987 ST PAUL RIVER: 1988 AFRICAN GLORY: still afloat
1233. RIVERINA (bulk)	6802	1977	--	1981	FALKON: 1989 APOLLONIA FAITH: 7.11.1991 foundered
Argentine Cargo Line Ltd					
1234. LA BLANCA	6813	1906	--	--	23.11.1917 sunk by U96
1235. EL ARGENTINO	6809	1907	--	--	26.5.1916 mined & sunk
British and Argentine Steam Navigation Company Ltd					
1236. ORIANA (227)	4419	1902	1912	1913	JAVA MARU: 1932 b.u.
1237. EL URUGUAYO (254/349)	8631	1912	1912	1933	to FW
1238. EL CORDOBES (252)	5683	1899	1912	1926	PRATOMAGNO: 1932 b.u.
ex Chase Side, Indradevi					
1239. WYANDOTTE (242)	4204	1900	1912	1915	WAIMARINO: 1926 KING SING: 1929 DAISY MOLLER: 1934 b.u.
ex Lord Roberts					
1240. LA ROSARINA (262/352)	8332	1912	--	1934	to FW
1241. LA NEGRA	8312	1913	--	--	3.9.1917 sunk by UC50
1242. EL ARGENTINO (351)	9501	1928	--	1934	to FW
(half interest—1096)					

Name	GRT	Built	Acquired	Sold	Subsequent career
British Empire Steam Navigation Company Ltd					
1966 renamed **Welldeck Shipping Company Ltd** and 1983 renamed **Furness Withy (Terminals) Ltd.**					
1243. ORANGE RIVER (538)	4708	1914	--	1934	GAROUFALIA: 11.12.1939 sunk by U38
1244. BRISBANE RIVER	4989	1914	--	--	17.4.1917 sunk by U35
1245. CLUTHA RIVER (1227)	4986	1914	1914	1915	to ET
1246. DERWENT RIVER	4724	1915	--	1933	ILISSOS: 1953 b.u.
1247. SWAN RIVER (Vaal River)	4724	1915	--	--	27.9.1917 sunk by U39
1248. GAMBIA RIVER	4724	1915	--	1933	MOUNT PENTELIKON: 1934 AEAS: 7.9.1942 sunk by U165
1249. SAGAMA RIVER	4728	1915	--	1933	NITSA: 2.12.1943 sunk by I-27
1250. PENNAR RIVER	3801	1915	--	1916	GASCONIA: 16.11.1917 sunk by U63
1251. FRASER RIVER (St Lawrence River)	3805	1915	--	1921	RIVERWAY: 1927 ANZAN MARU: 3.7.1943 sunk by USS SCORPION
1252. MERSEY RIVER	700	1915	--	1916	MINIEH: 9.1.1917 sunk by MÖWE
1253. CARONI RIVER (tank)	7807	1928	--	--	20.1.1940 mined & sunk
1254. DERWENT RIVER (1370) (tank) ex Empire Coral	8602	1941	1946	1946	DERWENTFIELD: 1.9.1952 explosion, CTL, b.u.
1255. FRASER RIVER ex Samsoaring	7210	1944	1947	1952	NORTH PRINCESS: 1959 GEORGIOS A: 1960 IOANNIS K: 3.1.1968 wrecked
1256. CLUTHA RIVER (tank)	12323	1952	--	1966	ARES III: 1970 b.u.
1257. AMAZON (1002/945) (pass)	20368	1959	1966	1968	to SSA
1258. WESTBURY (959)	8414	1960	1977	1978	DIAMANDO: 1981 POLANA: 1983 b.u.
1259. OCEAN TRANSPORT (958)	8608	1962	1978	1979	ELLION HOPE: 1983 b.u.
Furness-Houlder Argentine Lines Ltd					
1260. ABADESA (571) (Dominion Miller)	6572	1916	1916	1928	ELSTREE GRANGE. 3.5.1941 bombed, b.u.
1261. CANONESA (1203) ex Bollington Grange, Buteshire	5583	1893	1916	1919	MAGICSTAR: 1929 b.u.
1262. CONDESA	8557	1916	--	--	7.7.1917 sunk by U84
1263. DUQUESA	8651	1918	--	--	18.12.1940 captured by ADMIRAL SCHEER, 18.2.1941 scuttled
1264. BARONESA	8663	1918	--	--	1947 b.u.
1265. MARQUESA	8979	1918	--	--	1949 b.u.
1266. PRINCESA	8731	1918	--	--	1949 b.u.
1267. CANONESA (War Minerva)	8286	1920	--	--	21.9.1940 sunk by U100
1268. CONDESA	10367	1944	--	--	1962 b.u.
1269. DUQUESA (1005)	11007	1949	--	1968	to RML
1270. ABADESA (1006) (tank)	13571	1962	--	1968	to RML
Renfrew Navigation Company Ltd					
1271. ARGENTINE TRANSPORT (1184) 1936 RHODESIAN PRINCE	4684	1935	--	1937	to HL
1272. KHEDIVE ISMAIL ex Atchison Victory	7677	1944	1946	1948	1964 MERCANTILE VICTORY: 23.4.1964 fire, 1966 b.u.
1273. MOHAMED ALI EL KEBIR ex United Victory	7677	1944	1946	1948	1956 CLEOPATRA: 1981 b.u.
Alexander Shipping Company Ltd					
1274. AYLESBURY ex Empire Glen	6327	1941	1945	1948	WEST WALES: 1961 PERSIAN XERXES: 1964 b.u.
1275. CHARLBURY ex Empire Clive	7115	1941	1946	1958	ISABEL ERICA: 1969 b.u.
1276. BIBURY ex Empire Ballad	6700	1942	1946	1951	STAD MAASLUIS: 1962 JAGUAR: 1966 GOLDFIELD: 1968 POSEIDON: 1969 b.u.
1277. EASTBURY ex Empire Stalwart	7066	1943	1946	1958	CONSTITUCION: 1968 b.u.
1278. HOLMBURY ex Empire Canyon	7081	1943	1946	1960	ILYASBAKSH: 1970 b.u.
1279. KINGSBURY ex Samlamu	7246	1944	1947	1960	HUTA BEDZIN: 1969 MP-ZP-GDY-6 (storage vessel): 1982 b.u.
1280. LEDBURY ex Alpha Vaal, Samdak, (John Russell Pope)	7265	1943	--	1948 1961	KOPALNIA CZELADZ: 1973 b.u.
1281. MALMESBURY (1407) ex Ocean Valley	7181	1942	1949	1955	GRANNY SUZANNE: 1958 FREE ENTERPRISE: 1959 ALEXANDROS TSAVLIRIS: 1964 NEWDENE: 1965 FREE NAVIGATOR: 1969 b.u.
1282. NEWBURY	11199	1951	--	1963	1973 b.u.
1283. QUEENSBURY	6175	1953	--	1971	SANDRA: 1973 FONG LEE: 1976 LIEN CHANG: 1978 b.u.

Name	GRT	Built	Acquired	Sold	Subsequent career
1284. SHAFTSBURY	8532	1958	--	1972	PORTLOE: 1973 ARAUCO: 1978 JAL SEA CONDOR: 3.7.1978 foundered
1285. TEWKESBURY	8532	1959	--	1972	CAMINITO: 1981 BRAZIL: 1983 b.u.
1286. WESTBURY (959)	8533	1960	--	1975	to SSA
1287. IRON BANBURY 1976 BANBURY (Banbury)	11381	1971	--	1982	LADY MARINA: 1988 ARIANE S: still afloat
1288. UPWEY GRANGE (bulk) (Aylesbury)	15903	1976	--	1982	LILY VILLAGE: 1987 PUGGI: 1990 NATALIA: 1991 RANGER: still afloat
1289. LYNTON GRANGE (bulk)	15903	1976	--	1982	NORTHERN CHERRY: 1990 CHIOS CHARM: still afloat
1290. RIPON GRANGE (1303/379) (bulk) ex Orotava, Orotava Bridge, Orotava	28880	1968	1978	1979	to FW
1291. ELSTREE GRANGE (967) (tank)	39626	1979	--	1984	to SSA
1292. HORNBY GRANGE (968) (tank)	39626	1979	--	1984	to SSA

Claremont Shipping Company Ltd

Name	GRT	Built	Acquired	Sold	Subsequent career
1293. CLAREPARK (1416) ex Samearn	7219	1943	1947	1950	ARGOLIB: 1956 AFRICAN PRINCESS: 1968 b.u.

Ore Carriers Ltd

Name	GRT	Built	Acquired	Sold	Subsequent career
1294. ORELIA (ore)	6858	1954	--	1971	ORELIA STAR: 1973 MARISUERTA: 1974 b.u.
1295. OREOSA (ore)	6856	1954	--	1971	OREOSA STAR: 1973 MARILUCK: 1975 PODGORICA: 1988 ALMADEN: 1989 b.u.
1296. OREDIAN (ore)	6859	1955	--	1971	OREDIAN STAR: 1973 MARICHANCE: 1974 b.u.
1297. OREGIS (1324) (ore)	6858	1955	--	1972	to VS
1298. OREPTON (ore)	6859	1955	--	1971	OREPTON STAR: 1973 MARITIHI: 1974 b.u.
1299. OREMINA (1323) (ore)	6858	1956	--	1972	to VS
1300. JOYA MCCANCE (1318/1322) (ore) 1966 ST MARGARET	11871	1960	-- 1969	1966 1971	to SASL: returned to VS
1301. MABEL WARWICK (ore) (1321)	11632	1960	--	1971	to VS
1302. BEAUVAL (1319/1320) (tank) 1967 JOYA MCCANCE	26535	1964	-- 1969	1967 1971	to SASL: returned to VS
1303. OROTAVA (1290) (bulk) 1969 OROTAVA BRIDGE 1974 OROTAVA 1979 RIPON GRANGE	28880	1968	--	1978	to ASC
1304. ORENDA BRIDGE (bulk) 1977 ORENDA	69824	1972	--	1978	THEODORA: 1983 SERENA: 1985 b.u.

Joint **British Empire Steam Navigation Company Ltd** and **Empire Transport Company Ltd.**
1965 joint **Houlder Line Ltd** and **Empire Transport Company Ltd.**

Name	GRT	Built	Acquired	Sold	Subsequent career
1305. SWAN RIVER	9637	1959	--	1971	PREMIER ATLANTIC: 1973 CONFIDENCE EXPRESS: 1979 BACHLONG: 1980 EASTERN CONCORD: 1983 b.u.
1306. OCEAN TRANSPORT (958)	8608	1962	--	1975	to SSA

Warwick Tanker Company Ltd

Name	GRT	Built	Acquired	Sold	Subsequent career
1307. BIDFORD PRIORY (tank)	23065	1960	--	--	1975 b.u.
1308. BRANDON PRIORY (tank)	23108	1960	--	--	1975 b.u.

Ocean Gas Transport Ltd

Name	GRT	Built	Acquired	Sold	Subsequent career
1309. AVOGADRO (lpg)	855	1962	1964	1970	CARIBGAZ: 1971 LSCO ANZAC: 1973 explosion, lost
1310. JOULE (lpg)	2293	1964	--	1970	GIAMBATTISTA VENTURI: 1983 b.u.
1311. CLERK-MAXWELL (1337) (lpg)	8298	1966	--	1983	to SH
1312. HUMBOLDT (lpg)	5200	1968	--	1984	BOLD I: 1988 EUROGAZ TWO: 1989 YUCATAN: still afloat
1313. FARADAY (lpg)	19754	1970	--	--	present fleet
1314. CAVENDISH (1330) (lpg)	26802	1971	--	1977	to M1
1315. LORD KELVIN (lpg)	21374	1978	--	1987	HELIOS: 1991 HERDIS: still afloat

Methane Tanker Finance Ltd

Name	GRT	Built	Acquired	Sold	Subsequent career
1316. METHANE PROGRESS (lng)	21876	1964	--	--	1986 b.u.

Joint **Houlder Brothers and Company Ltd** and **Alexander Shipping Company Ltd.**

Name	GRT	Built	Acquired	Sold	Subsequent career
1317. TENBURY	8252	1965	--	1973	1974 AL-BARAT: 1983 SEA EAGLE: 1984 b.u.

South American Saint Line Ltd

Name	GRT	Built	Acquired	Sold	Subsequent career
1318. ST MARGARET (1300) (ore) ex Joya McCance	11871	1960	1966	1969	to OCL
1319. JOYA MCCANCE (1302) (tank) ex Beauval	26836	1964	1967	1969	to OCL

Name	GRT	Built	Acquired	Sold	Subsequent career
Vallum Shipping Company Ltd					
1320. JOYA MCCANCE (1302) (tank)	26535	1964	1971	--	1976 b.u.
ex Beauval					
1321. MABEL WARWICK (1301) (ore)	11632	1960	1971	1975	1978 NIKOLAOS MALEFAKIS: 1980 RUBINI: 1982 engine trouble, CTL, 1983 b.u.
1322. ST MARGARET (1300) (ore)	11871	1960	1971	1975	1978 HADIOTIS: 1989 b.u.
ex Joya McCance					
1323. OREMINA (1299) (ore)	6858	1956	1972	1974	GENERALE FEDERICO: 1985 b.u.
1324. OREGIS (1297/1200) (ore)	6858	1955	1972	1973	to HL
Cairn Line of Steamships Ltd					
Late 'K' Steamship Company Ltd.					
1325. KAYESON (1025) (tank)	28132	1961	--	1974	to RML
1326. LIMPSFIELD	8219	1970	1973	1980	MARFRIO: still afloat
1976 LINDFIELD					
ex Olau Rolf, Cap Melville					
Thornhope Shipping Company Ltd					
1327. SIR JOHN HUNTER (bulk/oil)	91178	1974	--	1979	NORDIC CHALLENGER: 1981 CAST KITTIWAKE: 1983 KONA: 1988 EL CARIBE C: 1989 SAM HUNT: 1991 NAFSIKA M: still afloat
1328. SIR ALEXANDER GLEN (bulk/oil)	91178	1975	--	1980	1989 OCEAN MONARCH: 1990 OCEAN MANDARIN: still afloat
1329. GARRISON POINT (bulk)	8014	1976	--	1980	1989 JEVINGTON: still afloat
1988 ELIZABETE					
Marber One Ltd					
1330. CAVENDISH (1314/873) (lpg)	26802	1971	1977	1983	to FWS
Gladstone Company Ltd					
1331. NICOLE (lpg)	2592	1967	1977	1978	still afloat
Oceangas (Gibraltar) Ltd					
1332. CAVENDISH (873) (lpg)	26802	1971	1988	--	present fleet
Marber Two Ltd					
1333. DASHWOOD (bulk/oil)	82985	1971	1979	1981	TIFFANY: 1989 ROKKO SAN: still afloat
ex Resolute, Turcoman					
Stevinson Hardy (Tankers) Ltd					
1334. EDWARD STEVINSON (tank)	30973	1961	--	--	1981 b.u.
1335. DUNSTER GRANGE (1140) (bulk)	24024	1967	1981	1982	GULF KESTREL: 1983 FIVE FIVE STAR: 1986 b.u.
ex Clyde Bridge, Clydesdale					
1336. OSWESTRY GRANGE (1141/875) (bulk)	5440	1964	1982	1984	to FWS
ex Chelwood					
1337. CLERK-MAXWELL (1311/966) (lpg)	8298	1966	1983	1984	to SSA
Kingtown International Ltd					
1338. HUMBOLDT (lpg)	1844	1968	1987	1988	still afloat
ex Cidla					
Weststar Shipping Company Ltd					
1339. JOULE (lpg)	2527	1972	1989	--	present fleet
ex Lancashire, Leiv Eriksson					
Allied Marine Facilities Ltd					
Late William France Fenwick and Company Ltd, later Stamford Shipping Company Ltd.					
1340. STAR PINEWOOD (bulk)	19222	1969	--	1974	STAR BULFORD: 1982 STAR SUNG: 1984 SLEEPING BEAUTY: 1987 SEVEN SEAS: 1987 SEVEN S: 1987 b.u.
1341. DALEWOOD (bulk)	5390	1966	1974	1974	CYMBELINE: 1984 GREEN ROCK: 1987 ROCKY: 26.12.1988 wrecked.

Managed during World Wars

Where ships were placed under management during/after World War I and World War II the details given include name, gross tonnage, year built, period managed, managing company, also loss (if still managed—**) and purchase details if taken over by the Group. Ships are arranged in alphabetic order.

Name	GRT	Built	Managed	Mgrs.
The Shipping Controller				
1342. ALASKA	5825	1918	1918-1920	FW
1343. ASP	2350	1918	1918-1920	FW
1344. ERIKA	2666	1906	1919	FW
1345. PARIA	6086	1916	1919	FW
ex Rickmer Rickmers				
1346. PORSANGER	4363	1918	1918-1919	FW
1347. RIO NEGRO	4819	1901	1919	HB
ex Mera				
1348. SAMNANGER	4305	1918	1918-1920	FW
1349. SANTA FE	5342	1902	1919	FW
1350. SAUERLAND	10800	1918	1919	FW
(Vogtland)				
1351. TENTO	2350	1917	1918-1920	FW
1352. TREINTA-Y-TRES	4775	1906	1918-1920	HB
ex Salatis				
1353. WAR HORUS	2266	1918	1918-1919	FW
1354. WAR KARMA	2271	1918	1918-1919	FW
1355. WAR KNIGHT	7951	1917	1917- **	FW 24.3.1918 collision, mined & sunk
1356. WAR WITCH	1961	1918	1918-1920	FW
1357. WENDLAND	11446	1919	1919	FW
Minister of Shipping, Minister of War Transport and Minister of Transport				
1358. ANGLO MAERSK	7705	1930	1940- **	HB 27.10.1942 sunk by U509/U604
ex Anglo-Swede				
1359. ARTHUR HOYT SCOTT	2324	1941	1941-1943	FW
1360. BLACK OSPREY	5589	1918	1940- **	CL 17.2.1941 sunk by U96
ex War Arrow				
1360a. DRIEBERGEN	5231	1923	1940-**	FW 28.8.1940 collision
1361. COMMISSAIRE RAMEL	10061	1920	1940- **	SSA 20.9.40 sunk by ATLANTIS
1362. EASTERN PRINCE (768)	10926	1929	1946-1952	PL
1950 EMPIRE MEDWAY				
1363. EL NIL	7775	1916	1943-1949	FW
ex Tjerimai, Wadai, Marie, Marie Woermann				
1364. EMPIRE ALLENBY	9904	1945	1945-1946	PL
1365. EMPIRE ANVIL	7177	1944	1946-1947	FW
(Cape Argos)				
1366. EMPIRE BALFOUR (1193)	7201	1944	1946-1949	HB 1949 to HL
1367. EMPIRE BRIGADE	5154	1912	1940- **	CL 18.10.1940 sunk by U99
ex Elios, Hannington Court				
1368. EMPIRE BUCKLER (1189)	7046	1942	1942-1946	HB 1946 to HL
1369. EMPIRE COMMERCE	3857	1928	1940- **	FW 9.6.1940 mined & sunk
ex Christoph v Doornum, Goodleigh				
1370. EMPIRE CORAL (1254) (tank)	8602	1941	1941-1946	HB 1946 to BE
1371. EMPIRE CUTLASS	7177	1943	1946-1947	FW
(Cape Compass)				
1372. EMPIRE DEBEN	11635	1922	1945-1949	SSA
ex General San Martin, Thuringia				
1373. EMPIRE FAITH (629)	7061	1941	1943-1946	JWL 1946 to JWL
1374. EMPIRE FORTH	2471	1939	1945-1946	PL
ex Mars				
1375. EMPIRE GRACE (909)	13478	1942	1942-1946	SSA 1946 to SSA
1376. EMPIRE HALBERD	7177	1943	1943-1944	FW
(Cape Gregory)			1945-1948	FW
1377. EMPIRE HELMSDALE	2978	1934	1945-1948	JWL
ex Telde				
1378. EMPIRE HOPE	12688	1941	1941- **	SSA 12.8.1942 sunk by aircraft & submarine
1379. EMPIRE KENT (630)	4769	1939	1945-1947	JWL 1947 to JWL
1380. EMPIRE LAPWING	5358	1921	1940-1942	CL
ex Black Condor, Ala				
1381. EMPIRE MARSHAL	7836	1945	1945-1947	FW
1382. EMPIRE MIGHT	9209	1942	1944-	SSA
1383. EMPIRE NERISSA	7086	1943	1944-1949	FW
1384. EMPIRE PAKEHA (879)	8115	1910	1940-1946	SSA 1946 to SSA
ex Pakeha				
1385. EMPIRE PATROL	3334	1928	1940- **	PL 29.9.1945 burnt
ex Rodi				

Name	GRT	Built	Managed	Mgrs.
1386. EMPIRE PENNANT (1188)	7071	1942	1946-	HB 1946 to HL
1387. EMPIRE PIBROCH (1190)	7046	1942	1942-1946	HB 1946 to HL
1388. EMPIRE RAPIER	7177	1943	1943-	FW
(Cape Turner)			1946-1947	FW
1389. EMPIRE RAVEN	6100	1918	1941-1948	HL
ex Oskawa				
1390. EMPIRE REGENT (835)	9904	1943	1943-1946	PL 1946 to RCL
1391. EMPIRE SAILOR	6140	1926	1940- **	CL 21.11.1942 sunk by U518
ex Cellina				
1392. EMPIRE SHACKLETON	7068	1941	1941- **	HB 28.12.1942 sunk by U225/U123/U435
1393. EMPIRE SNOW (865)	6327	1941	1943-1946	CL 1946 to CL
1394. EMPIRE STANLEY	6942	1941	1943-	FW 17.8.1943 sunk by U197
1395. EMPIRE STARLING	6025	1919	1941- **	HB 21.11.1942 sunk by U163
ex Nockum				
1396. EMPIRE TRADER (878)	9990	1908	1940- **	SSA 21.2.1943 sunk by U92
ex Tainui				
1397. EMPIRE WAIMANA (897)	8129	1911	1940-1946	SSA 1946 to SSA
ex Waimana, Herminius, Waimana				
1398. EMPIRE WELLAND	17870	1938	1945-1946	FW ·
ex Patria				
1399. FERDINAND BOL	5704	1919	1942- **	FW 30.7.1942 collision
ex Empire Robin, Empire Oryx, West Harshaw				
(managed for Netherlands Shipping & Trading Committee)				
1400. FORT ASH (1194)	7131	1943	1946-1950	HB 1950 to HL
1401. FORT BRANDON	7131	1943	1946-1948	HB
1402. FORT ST PAUL	7137	1943	1946-1951	HB
1403. FRED W GREEN	2292	1918	1941- **	FW 31.5.1942 sunk by U506
ex Craycroft				
1404. HELVIG	2252	1937	1940-1946	PL
1405. INDIA VICTORY	7642	1944	1947-	FW
1406. NEW AUSTRALIA (349)	20256	1931	1948-1958	SSA
ex Monarch of Bermuda				
1407. OCEAN VALLEY (1281)	7714	1942	1942-1949	HB 1949 to ASC
1408. OCEAN VIRTUE	7174	1942	1942- **	PL 21.7.1943 sunk by aircraft
1409. ODDVAR II	1897	1918	1941-1946	FW
ex Bracciano, Citta di Lecce, War Wizard				
1410. PACHAUG VICTORY	7642	1944	1946-1947	FW
1411. PIETRA LIGURE	284	1912	1941-1947	FE
ex Cite de Soissons, Fredriksberg, Gudrun				
1412. SAMAVON (358)	7176	1943	1943-1947	PL 1947 to FW
(Bronson Alcott)				
1413. SAMCALIA (357)	7176	1943	1943-1947	FW 1947 to FW
(Lorrin A. Thurston)				
1414. SAMCONSTANT	7210	1944	1944-1947	FW
1415. SAMDARING (359)	7282	1944	1944-1947	PL 1947 to FW
1416. SAMEARN (1293)	7219	1943	1944-1947	HL 1947 to CS
1417. SAMLONG	7176	1943	1943- **	PL 3.8.1944 damaged by E-boat
(Elias H. Derby)				
1418. SAMPA	7219	1943	1943- **	HB 27.2.45 mined & sunk
ex William Smallwood				
1419. SAMPEP	7176	1943	1943-1948	HB
(Victor F. Lawson)				
1420. SAMRICH (910)	7176	1943	1943-1947	SSA 1947 to SSA
(William Pitt Preble)				
1421. SAMSYLVAN (911)	7176	1943	1943-1947	SSA 1947 to SSA
(J. Whitridge Williams)				
1422. SAMTAMPA	7176	1943	1943- **	HL 23.4.1947 wrecked
(Pelag Wadsworth)				
1423. SAMTREDY	7176	1943	1943-1947	PL 1947 to FW
(John Tipton) (356)				
1424. SAMTUCKY	7176	1943	1943-1948	PL
(William Blackstone)				
1425. SLESVIG	3098	1938	1943-1946	FW
1426. SOUTHERN PRINCE (771)	10917	1929	1946-1947	PL
1427. STAMFORD VICTORY (836)	7642	1945	1946-1947	FW 1947 to RCL
1428. TAOS VICTORY	7642	1945	1946-1948	FW
1429. THYRA S	1738	1936	1944-1946	PL
1430. TUSCULUM VICTORY (360)	7640	1946	1946-1947	FW 1947 to FW

Norwegian Shipping & Trade Mission (Nortraship)

Norwegian ships operated on behalf of the Minister of Shipping in 1940, prior to the establishment of the Norwegian Shipping & Trade Mission (Nortraship). Furness Withy continued to provide services to Nortraship throughout the war.

Name	GRT	Built	
1431. ALTAIR	1522	1923	18.6.1940 sunk by U32
ex Atherton			
1432. AROSA	5043	1924	
ex Wind, Elmworth			
1433. ASKELADDEN	2496	1920	
1434. ASTRA	2164	1919	
ex York Harbor			
1435. AVANCE I	1300	1912	
ex Avance			
1436. BRASK	4079	1911	15.1.1941 sunk by TORELLI
ex Bogen, Orangemead, Orangemoor			
1437. BUR	4344	1917	1.9.1942 ashore, b.u.
ex Sedbergh			
1438. ERVIKEN	6595	1921	17.10.1941 sunk by U558
1439. FAVORIT	2826	1920	16.4.1941 sunk by aircraft
ex Ionier, Fishers Island			
1440. FERNBANK	4333	1924	
1441. FJORD	4033	1914	2.12.1941 sunk by U557
ex Orla			
1442. HARDANGER	4000	1924	
1443. HELLEN	5289	1921	21.12.1941 sunk by U573
1444. INGERFEM	3978	1912	29.12.1942 sunk by U631
ex Ovre, Athamas			
1445. LEIKANGER	4003	1923	27.7.1942 sunk by U752
1446. LENDA	4005	1924	27.6.1940 sunk by U47
ex Lenfield			
1447. NOTOS	2713	1898	
ex Knut Jarl, Laura Maersk, Laura			
1448. PARA	3986	1921	
ex San Paulo			
1449. POLYANA	2267	1919	25.4.1941 sunk by U103
ex Skjoldheim, Emperor of Halifax, Canadian Signaller			
1450. RAVNANGER	3371	1919	11.11.1940 sunk by aircraft
1451. RYM	1369	1919	17.10.1941 sunk by U558
ex Mosel, Mont Rose			
1452. SAMNANGER	4276	1918	2.12.1940 sunk by U99
1453. SIREHEI	3888	1907	
ex Bratsberg			
1454. SNAR	3176	1920	
ex Grong, Fageraas			
1455. SPERO	3619	1919	
ex Pacifico, Taigi Maru			
1456. TITANIAN	4880	1924	
ex Iossifoglu			
1457. VENI	2982	1901	
ex Tonbridge			

1992 addendum

378. FURNESS BRIDGE	1992 b.u.	
925. SOUTHERN CROSS	1992 OCEAN BREEZE: still afloat	
944. MAJESTIC	1992 MYKONOS V: still afloat	
948. CAIRNVENTURE	1992 VEDIA: still afloat	
1047. GEORGE PEACKOCK	1992 b.u.	
1053. SAGAMORE	1992 b.u.	
1121. MANCHESTER CHALLENGE	1992 SWAN 1: still afloat	
1122. MANCHESTER COURAGE	1992 CITY OF LIMASSOL: 1992 b.u.	
1287. IRON BANBURY	1992 PRESIDENTE AGUIRRE CERDA: still afloat	

Name	GRT	Built	Acquired
875a. DARWIN (lpg)	43636	1977	1992
ex Gas Enterprise, Razi			

(Purchased 10 July 1992 by Furness Withy (Shipping) Ltd, intended for employment as an Ecuadorean based storage vessel).

Index of Ships

This index contains names carried during ownership or management by Furness Withy Group companies, also intended names which were never implemented.

After each name is listed the entry numbers where ships of that name appear in the fleet list, followed by numbers in italics which are page numbers where further information can be found in the text (apart from fleet list entries in the text which have not been indexed).

All ships carrying the same name during Group ownership or management are listed together and not identifed as individual vessels. Due to transfers between Group companies several entries may refer to the same ship.

General Index

Some FURNESS WITHY GROUP Flags & Funnels
(see page 183)

T. Furness & Co.
C. Furness
Furness, Withy & Co. Ltd.

Furness Withy Group

Furness Withy   Furness Withy
(Shipping) Ltd.   (Chartering) Ltd.

British Maritime Trust Ltd.

Chesapeake & Ohio S.S. Co. Ltd.

Wilson's & Furness-Leyland Line Ltd.

Manchester Liners Ltd.

London Welsh S.S. Co. Ltd.

 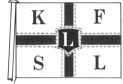

Kirkcaldy, Fife & London Shipping Co.
(Stocks, Turnbull & Co. Ltd.)

Agincourt S.S. Co. Ltd.

Hessler Shipping Co. Ltd.

Peareth S.S. Co. Ltd.

Gulf Line Ltd.

George Warren & Co. (Liverpool) Ltd.

W. Johnston & Co. Ltd.